Humanitarianism and the Greater War, 1914–24

Manchester University Press

HUMANITARIANISM
SERIES EDITOR: BERTRAND TAITHE

This series offers a new interdisciplinary reflection on one of the most important and yet understudied areas in history, politics and cultural practices: humanitarian aid and its responses to crises and conflicts. The series seeks to define afresh the boundaries and methodologies applied to the study of humanitarian relief and so-called 'humanitarian events'. The series includes monographs and carefully selected thematic edited collections which cross disciplinary boundaries and bring fresh perspectives to the historical, political and cultural understanding of the rationale and impact of humanitarian relief work.

Islamic charities and Islamic humanism in troubled times   Jonathan Benthall
Humanitarian aid, genocide and mass killings: Médecins Sans Frontières, the Rwandan experience, 1982–97   Jean-Hervé Bradol and Marc Le Pape
Calculating compassion: Humanity and relief in war, Britain 1870–1914   Rebecca Gill
Humanitarian intervention in the long nineteenth century   Alexis Heraclides and Ada Dialla
The military–humanitarian complex in Afghanistan   Eric James and Tim Jacoby
Reconstructing lives: Victims of war in the Middle East and Médecins Sans Frontières   Vanja Kovačič
Global humanitarianism and media culture   Michael Lawrence and Rachel Tavernor (eds)
Aid to Armenia: Humanitarianism and intervention from the 1890s to the present   Jo Laycock and Francesca Piana (eds)
A history of humanitarianism, 1775–1989: In the name of others   Silvia Salvatici
Donors, technical assistance and public administration in Kosovo   Mary Venner
The NGO CARE and food aid from America 1945–80: 'Showered with kindness'?   Heike Wieters
The Red Cross movement: Myths, practices and turning points   Neville Wylie, James Crossland, Melanie Oppenheimer (eds)

Humanitarianism and the Greater War, 1914–24

Edited by

Elisabeth Piller and Neville Wylie

MANCHESTER UNIVERSITY PRESS

Copyright © Manchester University Press 2023

While copyright in the volume as a whole is vested in Manchester University Press, copyright in individual chapters belongs to their respective authors, and no chapter may be reproduced wholly or in part without the express permission in writing of both author and publisher.

Published by Manchester University Press
Oxford Road, Manchester M13 9PL

www.manchesteruniversitypress.co.uk

British Library Cataloguing-in-Publication Data
A catalogue record for this book is available from the British Library

ISBN 978 1 5261 7324 9 hardback
ISBN 978 1 5261 9130 4 paperback

First published 2023
Paperback published 2025

The publisher has no responsibility for the persistence or accuracy of URLs for any external or third-party internet websites referred to in this book, and does not guarantee that any content on such websites is, or will remain, accurate or appropriate.

EU authorised representative for GPSR:
Easy Access System Europe, Mustamäe tee 50,
10621 Tallinn, Estonia
gpsr.requests@easproject.com

Typeset
by Cheshire Typesetting Ltd, Cuddington, Cheshire

*For Mathilda and for Olivia, Isabella, and Otto:
in the hope that the world they inherit and shape will be more humane,
caring, and compassionate than those that have gone before.*

Contents

List of figures	ix
Acknowledgements	xi
Notes on contributors	xii
Introduction: humanitarianism and the Greater War *Elisabeth Piller and Neville Wylie*	1

PART I: GLOBAL WAR, GLOBAL AID

1. Humanitarian aid across the ocean: Argentine contributions to the relief of Europe during the Great War
   María Inés Tato — 31

2. Sagas of swords, scrolls, and dolls: Japanese humanitarian aid to Belgium
   Hanne Deleu — 51

3. Geographies of humanitarian mobilisation: Portuguese Africa and the Great War
   Ana Paula Pires — 69

4. Philanthropy in time of war: Paul Nathan and the Hilfsverein der deutschen Juden
   Christoph Jahr — 86

PART II: THE POLITICS AND POWER OF AID

5. The neutrals at war: humanitarian competition in the Great War
   Cédric Cotter — 105

6. Neutrality and the politics of protection: the United States as a protecting power, 1914–17
   Neville Wylie — 124

7   Blockaders as humanitarians? Connecting the Allied blockade
    of Germany and postwar humanitarianism
    Phillip Dehne   147

8   Better fed than red: international famine relief, 1921–22
    Kimberly Lowe   163

PART III: THE LEGACIES AND LIMITS OF GREAT WAR-ERA RELIEF

9   Abandoning Poland: Great War humanitarianism as a history
    of failure
    Elisabeth Piller   187

10 Children and the 'hunger politics' of 1919–20: food aid to
    German children and the founding of the international Save
    the Children Movement
    Tatjana Eichert and Rebecca Gill   210

11 'The most deplorable victims'? The language of
    humanitarianism and relief to intellectuals in the era of the
    Great War
    Tomás Irish   230

12 The imperial 'guardians' of slavery: international
    humanitarianism, colonial labour policies, and the crisis of
    imperial governance under the League of Nations, 1919–26
    Christian Müller   252

Afterword
Branden Little   273

Index   285

Figures

0.1 Near East Relief, 'Hunger knows no armistice' (M. Leone Bracker), 1919 (Source: Library of Congress, Washington, DC, Prints and Photographs Division) — xvi

1.1 Poster inviting the subscription of the French Liberation Loan in 1918 (Source: Bibliothèque Municipale de Lyon, AffM0385, open licence) — 36

1.2 Advertisement of the department store A la Ciudad de Londres in Buenos Aires (Source: *Caras y Caretas* no. 892, 6 November 1915, in Hemeroteca Digital de la Biblioteca Nacional de España, open licence) — 37

3.1 Lisbon street sale to help the victims of the First World War, 1917 (Source: *Ilustração Portuguesa* no. 579, 26 March 1917, author's private collection) — 78

6.1 'Moscow January 11th 1917 Relief Division Conference', photographer unknown (Source: Missouri History Museum, David R. Francis papers N24790, Missouri Historical Society, St Louis, MO) — 138

8.1 Dr Fridtjof Nansen and Dr Reginald Farrar, Saratov, Russia, circa December 1921 / January 1922, photographer unknown (Source: Photo and Sound Archives. V-P-HIST-03534–29. International Committee of the Red Cross (ICRC), Geneva) — 176

9.1 Exhibition poster, The Polish Victims' Relief Fund. E. Verpillevy 1915; Miles & Co., Wardour St., W. (Source: Library of Congress, Washington, DC, Prints and Photographs Division) — 193

10.1 School children receiving milk from the Miss Hobhouse Hilfe, photograph preserved in Emily Hobhouse's Leipzig scrapbook (Source: Archive of Emily Hobhouse, MSS. Hobhouse, 13. Image: Bodleian Libraries, University of Oxford, https://digital.bodleian.ox.ac.uk. Creative Commons licence CC-BY-NC 4.0 © Jennifer Hobhouse Balme, 2022) — 215

11.1 Students and professors being fed in Innsbruck, June 1921, with gift from the Commonwealth Fund (Source: Hoover Institution Library & Archives, Stanford, CA, American Relief Administration European Operations, Box 857, Folder 3)   236

Acknowledgements

This collection began with a conference on Humanitarianism and the Greater War held at University College Dublin in September of 2019. We would like to thank the Irish Research Council for its generous support as well as all participants for two days of engaging discussions. Our special gratitude goes to the contributors of this volume who graciously agreed to several follow-up workshops and who rethought and reworked their papers in the midst of a pandemic. A very special thank you is due to Branden Little, who agreed to write the afterword to this volume. We are greatly appreciative of having been able to work with such a fine group of scholars.

We would also like to thank Robert Byron and Alun Richards of Manchester University Press for shepherding the collection along and to Bertrand Taithe, who was supportive of including the volume in the series on Humanitarianism: Key Debates and New Approaches from the very beginning.

Finally, we are grateful to Naomi Müller at the University of Freiburg for her valuable assistance in formatting and indexing this volume.

Elisabeth Piller and Neville Wylie

Notes on contributors

Cédric Cotter is a researcher at the International Committee of the Red Cross (ICRC) in Geneva. He is in charge of researching and writing analyses of ICRC's past actions to inform the organisation's current operations and decisions. He has authored around twenty publications related to the history of humanitarian action, the First World War, and international humanitarian law, including *(S')Aider pour survivre: Action humanitaire et neutralité suisse pendant la Première Guerre mondiale* (2017).

Phillip Dehne is Executive Dean and Professor of History at St Joseph's University in Brooklyn, New York. His book *After the Great War: Economic Warfare and the Promise of Peace in Paris 1919* (2019) describes the Paris Peace Conference through the eyes of Lord Robert Cecil, the one-time British Minister of Blockade. Dehne is also author of *On the Far Western Front: Britain's First World War in South America* (2009), along with various articles related to economic conflict during the First World War.

Hanne Deleu is a PhD student at the Department of East Asian Languages and Cultural Studies at the University of California, Santa Barbara. She holds a BA and an MA in Japanese Studies from the Catholic University of Leuven, Belgium, and an MA in Transcultural Studies from the University of Heidelberg. Her current research explores Japan's self-conscious processes of nation-building and modernisation during the early twentieth century through newly emerging gender norms and gendered practices.

Tatjana Eichert is a humanitarian analyst and policy researcher working with international humanitarian organisations. She holds a PhD in International History from the Graduate Institute of International and Development Studies in Geneva and a Master's degree in Global History from the University of Heidelberg. Her primary research fields are the history of forced migration and refugees, humanitarianism, and international organisations.

Notes on contributors

Rebecca Gill is a Reader in History at the University of Huddersfield. She works on the history of British humanitarian organisations and relief work in the late nineteenth and early twentieth centuries, with a particular interest in women's involvement. She has published widely in these areas, including a monograph on the early years of the British Red Cross and Quaker relief in war, *Calculating Compassion: Humanity and Relief in War* (2013).

Tomás Irish is Associate Professor in Modern History at Swansea University, UK. He holds a PhD from Trinity College, Dublin, and is the author of two monographs about universities in the First World War period. His work has appeared in the *Journal of Global History*, *Modern Intellectual History*, *Historical Journal*, *History of Education*, and the *European Review of History / Revue européene d'histoire*. His next monograph is called *Feeding the Mind: Humanitarianism and the Reconstruction of European Intellectual Life, 1919–1933*.

Christoph Jahr studied history, political studies, and German in Freiburg and Berlin. He received his Habilitation in 2006 and served as Lecturer and substitute professor at Humboldt University in Berlin, the University of Heidelberg and the University of Düsseldorf. He has published major monographs on desertion in the German and British armies during the First World War (1998), on the legal history of antisemitism in the nineteenth and twentieth centuries, on Paul Nathan, a German-Jewish public intellectual, political activist, and philanthropist (2018) and on the German Unification 1864–71 (2020).

Branden Little is a professor of history at Weber State University in the United States. He researches humanitarian interventions in the era of the First World War and the modern history of the US Navy and Marine Corps. He earned a PhD in history from UC Berkeley (2009), and an MA in national security affairs from the Naval Postgraduate School (2002). Little has published numerous essays and reviews.

Kimberly Lowe is Associate Professor of History at Lesley University in Cambridge, MA. She received her PhD from Yale University and has held doctoral and postdoctoral fellowships in the United States, Switzerland, and Germany. Her research interests include the history of humanitarianism, international humanitarian law, transnational social movements, and intergovernmental organisations. Her work has been published in the *Journal of Contemporary History*, *Moving the Social – Journal of Social History and the History of Social Movements*, the *Routledge History of Human Rights*, and more.

Christian Müller is Lecturer in Modern European History at the University of Aberdeen. He has held fellowships at King's College, Cambridge, St Antony's College, Oxford, and the Rothermere American Institute, Oxford and is a Fellow of the Royal Historical Society. He has published widely on European History and Europe–Asia relations, including with Matteo Salonia *Travel Writings on Asia: Curiosity, Knowledge, and Identities across the East, c. 1200 to the Present* (2022). He currently works on a co-edited volume on the Silk Roads and peripheral agency (2024) and two monographs on *German Dreams of Empire in Asia, 1820–1890* (2025) and *Gustave Moynier – the Humanitarian Imperialist*.

Elisabeth Piller is Assistant Professor of Transatlantic and North American History at Albert-Ludwigs-Universität Freiburg in Germany. She works on US and German foreign policy and transatlantic relations in the nineteenth and twentieth centuries and is the author of *Selling Weimar: German Public Diplomacy and the United States, 1918–1933* (2021) as well as articles in *Diplomatic History*, the *Journal of Contemporary History*, and the *International History Review*, among others. She is currently working on her second book, exploring US humanitarian aid and transatlantic relations in the early Cold War.

Ana Paula Pires is Assistant Professor at the University of Azores and a researcher at HTC-CFE at NOVA University of Lisbon. She was a postdoctoral student at Stanford University (2016–19) and a Remarque Fellow at the University of New York (2019). Her main topic of research is the economic and social history of the First World War, particularly its impact on Portugal and Africa. She is the author of *A Grande Guerra no Parlamento* (2018) and *Portugal e a I Guerra Mundial: A República e a Economia de Guerra* (2011), and co-editor of several books such as *Guerras del siglo XX, Experiencias y representaciones en perspectiva global* (2019) and *The Global First World War: African, East Asian, Latin American and Iberian Mediators* (2021).

María Inés Tato is a Researcher of the National Scientific and Technical Research Council (CONICET) at the Institute of Argentine and American History 'Dr. Emilio Ravignani', CONICET-UBA, Argentina, and founder and co-ordinator of the Group of Historical War Studies (GEHiGue) at that Institute. She is professor at the University of Buenos Aires, and the Master in War History – Army Faculty – National Defence University (UNDEF). She has published widely on the Falklands/Malvinas War and the First World War in Latin America and beyond.

Neville Wylie is Professor of International History at the University of Stirling. He has published widely on aspects of war, neutrality and humanitarian affairs in the twentieth century, including *Barbed Wire Diplomacy: Britain, Germany and the Politics of Prisoners of War 1939–1945* (2010) and *Britain, Switzerland and the Second World War* (2003). His most recent work includes, with Melanie Oppenheimer and James Crossland, *The Red Cross Movement: Myths, Practices and Turning Points* (2020).

Figure 0.1 Near East Relief, 'Hunger knows no armistice' (M. Leone Bracker), 1919

Introduction: humanitarianism and the Greater War

Elisabeth Piller and Neville Wylie

The First World War and its aftermath unleashed violence and suffering on a hitherto unimaginable scale. Millions of combatants and civilians were killed, wounded, imprisoned, displaced, widowed, and orphaned. Across Europe, Africa, and the Middle East, and beyond, vast numbers of men, women, and children were left in despair. In response to the myriad forms of suffering, the humanitarian field of action broadened rapidly. Key humanitarian actors like the national Red Cross societies greatly expanded their care for wounded combatants, just as the International Committee of the Red Cross (ICRC) in Geneva extended its relief work to the hundreds of thousands of prisoners of war (PoWs). Moreover, across the world people began to focus on the civilian victims of the war and postwar period. Old and new, public and private, secular and religious organisations committed themselves to alleviating food shortages in occupied Belgium, Poland, or post-Revolutionary Russia, to mitigating the complex consequences of the Armenian genocide, or to resettling the vast number of refugees. The ever more encompassing forces of destruction evoked ever more encompassing forces of humanitarianism.[1]

Scholarship on this subject has grown phenomenally. The history of humanitarianism has become a booming research field. This is no truer than for the era of the Great War, where the war's centenary gave rise to a veritable 'explosion' of scholarship on humanitarianism.[2] We have been treated to a spate of new research monographs on Great War-era humanitarianism,[3] and just in the last few years seen specific themes explored in conferences hosted in Manchester, Vienna, Milan, Minneapolis, Dublin, and Brussels.[4] These attest to the vibrancy of the field, but also the widespread appeal that the topic has engendered across different scholarly communities. As a consequence we are now considerably more conscious of the scope and nature of humanitarian engagement, the spectacular growth of humanitarian organisations like the ICRC, Near East Relief, or Save the Children, as well as the extension of humanitarian protection and concern to vulnerable groups like children or refugees.[5] Collectively these studies have established the era of the Great War as a significant moment in the evolution of modern humanitarianism, although the nature of this significance continues to be debated.[6]

Yet, despite these advances, scholarship on Great War-era humanitarianism remains surprisingly contested, episodic, and uneven. Most research has focused on national case studies and on relatively few, large-scale – and often US – organisations.[7] This is also true of the most significant and wide-ranging contribution to the field thus far: a 2014 special issue of *First World War Studies*, which centres strongly on American aid.[8] While such a focus has justification, it also runs the risk of overemphasising the impact of humanitarian non-governmental organisations (NGOs), which played an especially notable role in the United States, as well as overstating the pre-eminence of US aid. In particular, it tends to neglect more traditional, if no less crucial humanitarian actors at the time: aristocrats, churches, armies, charities, ethnic communities, and governments. In the same vein, the relative lack of comparative and transnational work has obscured connections and common themes between and among various humanitarian operations, including the role of the media, the global nature of humanitarian mobilisation, or the relationship with international politics. While there is an increasing number of monographs and edited collections that consider such themes for the nineteenth and twentieth centuries, they tend to pay relatively fleeting attention to a conflagration which is viewed in other contexts at least as the harbinger of the modern age.[9]

This collection of essays brings together economic, cultural, social, and diplomatic historians to explore the scale and meaning of humanitarianism in the era of the Great War. Conceptually, the volume rests on the idea of a geographically and temporally 'Greater War', i.e. a series of violent conflicts that were not confined to the famous European battle fronts and 1914 to 1918, but both predated and outlasted the First World War, with truly global ramifications.[10] Based on this broader understanding of the arc of violence unleashed at this time, the collection surveys the local and global dimensions of the humanitarian responses, interrogates the entanglement of humanitarian and political interests, and probes the limits of this humanitarian action and its legacies for the twentieth century. It is premised on the idea that almost nothing better demonstrates the scope and persistence of violence from about 1912 to 1923 than the humanitarian programmes devised to mitigate its consequences. The collection's overarching objective is twofold: to consider how and why humanitarian engagement can help us understand the era, and to analyse the extent to which this era shaped the development of humanitarianism, its concepts and practices, as we know them today. It convenes a diverse range of experts from various fields, positions, and countries with the aim to digest, reflect, and push forward a decade of scholarship on this topic.

A continuum of violence and compassion

A common thread to much of the new scholarship on the war is the insistence in addressing the events from a much wider temporal and geographical perspective. Historians like Robert Gerwarth, John Horne, and Erez Manela have proposed the concept of a 'Greater War' shifting the historical focus from the Western front to previously neglected theatres of war in Eastern Europe and especially Africa, Asia, and the Americas.[11] The First World War, they contend, was a 'war of empires' and its reverberations felt around the world.[12] At the same time they show how the period from 1914 to 1918 fails to capture accurately the broader dynamics of destruction. Rather they suggest the war be understood as a decade of violent upheavals that began with the Italian intervention in Libya and the Balkan Wars in 1911/12 and stretched – via revolutions, border conflicts, and civil wars – to at least 1923.[13] This broader shift aligns with a focus, inspired by social and cultural history, on the war and postwar experience of combatants and, increasingly, non-combatants.[14] New scholarships on civilians on the 'home front' as well as of interned, displaced, and occupied populations has greatly expanded traditional ideas of the war's major theatres and impact.[15] It has given us a more expansive understanding of the era of the Great War.

The study of humanitarianism is both a driver and a product of these new research perspectives. For one, it showcases a different cast of actors in the war and its aftermath. Although soldiers, generals, and governments remain of great importance, the study of humanitarianism also foregrounds the activities and experiences of philanthropic benefactors, medics, and relief workers, as well as the sick, hungry, displaced, interned, or occupied people themselves. At the same time a focus on humanitarian concerns and responses delineates the war's global impact. True, a great deal of suffering occurred on or near European battlefields but the conflict had global humanitarian ramifications. Refugee movements carried the impact of revolution, genocide, or occupation across borders, while war economies and economic warfare brought scarcity home to non-belligerent nations. A particularly notable example is the unprecedented internment of civilians and combatants around the world. The approximately nine million PoWs imprisoned during the war were confined all over Europe as well as in Africa, Asia, Australia, the Americas and the outer fringes of Siberia. In some instances, captivity was one of the defining experiences of the war: one in every three men mobilised by the Habsburg Empire was made to endure some length of captivity in enemy hands.[16] Through international law and custom, neutrals also partook in these internments, confining – as in the case of Argentina and the United States – belligerent seamen landing on their shores. Non-combatant civilian internment, too, was common during the war. Historians estimate that upwards of 900,000 civilians experienced captivity, about 800,000 in internment camps in Europe and some 50,000–100,000 in the rest of the world. In fact civilian internment visualises the reality of empires at war as it maps neatly on to imperial geographies. Citizens of the Central Powers, for example, were held not only in Great Britain or France but in Australia, Canada, and South Africa, in East Africa, Egypt, India, and the Caribbean.[17] Of course, these confinements raised different humanitarian questions, ranging from relative comforts, like receiving mail or literature, to provisions and sanitation being life-or-death decisions in Russian and Ottoman PoW camps. Tracing the Great War's suffering – and efforts to ameliorate it – will invariably take us around the world.

Humanitarian giving, too, illustrated the global reach of the 'European' war. Wartime suffering mobilised donor publics across the globe. Neutral Belgium, invaded and occupied by the German army in August of 1914, became the war's humanitarian *cause célèbre*. Belgium's fate prompted a worldwide outpouring of sympathy and charity. In the autumn of 1914 the Commission for Relief in Belgium was established as an American-Belgian endeavour, aided by Spanish, American, and Dutch diplomats, to re-victual the occupied country. Although most of its funds came from Allied governments, it also received significant amounts of worldwide charity. Americans donated food, money, and clothing; Argentinians raised subscriptions for Belgian postal workers; Norwegians knitted mittens for Belgian children; the Swiss took in Belgian orphans; the British and Dutch housed Belgian refugees; and as far away as in Japan, women organised bake sales and prepared care packages for the benefit of 'poor little Belgium'. Here, too, the imperial dimension was highly visible as donors in Canada, Australia, New Zealand, and South Africa were especially active in empire-wide collections on behalf of Belgium. Contemporaries spoke of a global case of 'Belgianitis'.[18] And although few causes were that popular, the Belgian case illustrates the worldwide scope of humanitarian responses.

Importantly, a focus on humanitarian engagement also upends the traditional chronology of the war. Foreign nationals caught unawares by the declarations of war in late July and early August 1914 were arguably the war's first victims: intimidation and expulsion began well before armies clashed in the field. Moreover, from a humanitarian perspective, the idea that the 'war' ended in November 1918 or June 1919 is nothing short of absurd. The poster that graces the cover of this collection (also Figure 0.1) announces boldly that 'hunger knows no armistice'. In many instances the true extent of devastation became visible only once the war had formally ended.[19] It took years to return home the seven million PoWs, to resettle successive refugee movements, and to nourish children back to health.[20] The armistices and peace settlements also created new devastations. Political upheavals, the collapse of empires, and the redrawing of borders, on top of the acrimonious transition from war to peace economy, resulted in mass displacement and hunger across Europe and beyond.[21] In Austria, for example, the massive loss of territory and the disruption of traditional transportation routes as well as sweeping inflation engendered a 'hunger catastrophe' among an already malnourished population.[22] And the killing did not stop in 1918 either. Revolutions, civil wars, and ethnic cleansing in the postwar years took the lives of four million people; more than British, French, and US war casualties combined. At the same time, the postwar period was also a high time of humanitarian activity. Longer-standing organisations continued their efforts, while new organisations such as Save the Children, the League of Red Cross Societies, the American Relief Administration, or the League of Nations came into being.[23] Their operations demonstrate the continuity of need just as they illustrate a postwar sense of humanitarian opportunity, a chance to finally operate unfettered by military imperatives. The postwar continuum of violence begot a continuum of compassion.

A more expansive perspective on the war is no end in itself, of course, but it helps cast doubt on the very conception of war and peace as binary opposites: were the neutrals ever truly 'at peace' from 1914 to 1918? And did not many civilians, famished or uprooted, feel the 'war' much more in 1919–20 than they had in 1915 or 1916? In this way the collection hopes to paint a holistic and diverse picture of a decade of violent conflicts and the global humanitarian crises it engendered. Within this broader framework the collection sets out to focus on three larger themes and questions:

Not an 'NGO-moment' – who are the humanitarians?

Asking about central humanitarian actors is not as banal or straightforward as it might seem. Considerable research has focused on a number of large NGOs, most of them American.[24] This is not surprising. Organisations like the American Friends Service Committee, the Jewish Joint Distribution Committee, the Near East Relief (later: Near East Foundation), or the Save the Children Fund were pioneering organisations at the time and often continue to operate today. In a world at war these NGOs seem to stand for the altruistic 'good', neither sharing the Red Cross societies' uneasy proximity to the military apparatus nor suffering the relative inadequacy of smaller or poorer charities. Despite many well-known flaws, these NGOs symbolise an impressive commitment to humanity in inhumane times. By committing

(US) wealth and influence to mitigating suffering on a large scale, they obviously helped create the humanitarian world we still inhabit.

And yet an all too exclusive focus on these organisations runs the danger of misrepresenting the nature of Great War humanitarianism and of reading post-1945 history backward. By examining humanitarian engagement in a dozen European and non-European countries, the collection showcases a range of different, if no less crucial humanitarian actors. Belligerent governments and state bureaucracies were the most important of these. Contrary to transnational histories or commonplace assumptions, belligerent governments and military authorities were the single most critical institutions administering war and postwar relief. They funded and outfitted army medical units and Red Cross societies, provisioned civilians and combatants in captivity and oversaw food supplies and resettlements. Then, as now, humanitarian aid was ultimately about gaining access to suffering groups and about the ability of creating 'humanitarian space'.[25] During the war, in particular, state and military authorities alone were in a position to grant such access, to guarantee freedom of movement and to facilitate the difficult logistics in a war zone. One might argue, of course, that belligerent governments are not humanitarian actors at all. They never intended to save strangers but primarily to save their own, and, as Elisabeth Piller shows (Chapter 9), they supported relief efforts just as long as they did not detract from waging and winning the war. Yet applying strict criteria of altruism would probably disqualify most humanitarian initiatives at the time or since. Phillip Dehne's chapter on the Supreme Economic Council (SEC) in 1919 (Chapter 7) captures this conundrum. Here the one body partly responsible for European food shortages was also in charge of Allied efforts to alleviate them. Without political and military consent, however flawed and self-serving, there would have been little humanitarian relief at all. The greatest purveyors of violence at the time were simultaneously the greatest purveyors of relief.

Neutral states and officials were another integral part of the period's humanitarian machinery. Next to peace initiatives, humanitarian relief became one of the neutrals' most important contribution to the war. A number of chapters in this collection show the range of neutral activities: they supported individual relief efforts, served as protecting powers for belligerent nations, and acted as go-betweens for belligerents, who often refused to communicate directly. Neutral Red Cross societies took on a wide range of humanitarian duties such as inspecting PoW camps. More generally neutral states and diplomats lent their connections and legitimacy to humanitarian enterprises. It is unlikely, for example, that the celebrated Commission for Relief in Belgium could have ever operated without the support of neutral diplomats in London, Brussels, and Berlin. Of course, there was no uniform humanitarian response among neutrals. As María Inés Tato explains (Chapter 1), the Argentine government remained highly cautious of humanitarian engagement, fearing for its neutrality as well as the social harmony among its large foreign-born population. Though initially hesitant, the United States came to welcome its chance at benevolent intervention in Europe, and assumed, as Neville Wylie shows (Chapter 6), extensive humanitarian duties as a protecting power. The positive US response illustrates its sense of national exceptionalism as much as its relative greater international power. In general, geographic proximity gave European neutrals less of a choice than those overseas. As Cédric Cotter demonstrates in Chapter 5, for countries like Switzerland, Sweden, Denmark, or Spain humanitarian work was also a means of survival, a way to prove the 'usefulness' of their neutrality to belligerents. It allowed traditionally neutral countries like Sweden or Switzerland to engage meaningfully in the war and to fashion for themselves a unique humanitarian identity. By foregrounding the very active but often overlooked role of smaller neutrals, the collection prompts us to see the war beyond the great powers.[26]

A host of international non-state actors complemented the work of national state and quasi-state actors. It is perhaps this group which today we most readily identify as 'humanitarian', and in part rightly so.[27] Organisations like the ICRC (a private Swiss charity) or the Commission for Relief in Belgium had the intrinsic motivation, the (volunteer) staff, the experience, and, at times, the mandate to provide effective aid. The chapters in this collection record the activities of Argentine doctors in Paris, aristocratic 'sisters of mercy' in Siberia, American foundation officers in Poland, Portuguese women volunteers in Mozambique, and Swiss clerics in Germany. In the public mind their initiatives lie at the heart of Great War humanitarianism: because of the bodies they fed, clothed, disinfected, warmed, and sheltered but also because of the example of compassion and hope they provided. Some of these humanitarians such as the Swedish nurse Elsa Brändström, known as the 'Angel of Siberia', became world-famous.

A closer look at these initiatives underlines the importance of transnational networks to the functioning of Great War-era relief. While access ultimately depended on states, lobbying for that access in the first place and effectively administering aid thereafter often depended on existing religious, social, professional, and ethnic ties. As Christoph Jahr shows (Chapter 4), aiding Jews in wartime Poland was facilitated by the global as well as local connections of Jewish organisations. In a similar vein, US diplomats, as Neville Wylie's chapter illustrates, resented the social capital that enabled Elsa Brändström and the Austrian, Hungarian, and German aristocratic nurses to tour PoW camps in Russia. Whereas the US embassy – as official protecting power – led arduous negotiations for inspection rights, high-society connections accomplished the same (and more) with much less effort. During the Great War, international, supranational, and national efforts operated – somewhat uneasily – side by side.[28]

These non-state actors also offer an immediate connection to two seriously overlooked humanitarian actors: donor publics and local 'beneficiary' populations. The war and postwar period saw an unprecedented humanitarian mobilisation. Civil societies around the world came alive with knitting circles, subscription campaigns, and fundraising bazaars. During the war, these developments were most pronounced among belligerent societies themselves. Becoming a member of the national Red Cross society, giving for wounded combatants, and feeding the urban poor became a token and test of patriotism. At a time when voluntary giving was widespread (from scrap metal to women's hair), war charity work still stood out as particularly meaningful, establishing a strong and immediate bond between home front and battle front. As several of the chapters demonstrate, women played an outsized role in this humanitarian mobilisation whether as fundraisers, nurses, or workers in orphanages and soup kitchens. Existing progressive networks, notable traditions of charity and social work, and common assumptions of acceptable female behaviour provided significant room for women's service and activism in this field. However, the fact that the great majority of women – especially local, non-elite ones – remain so little visible in historical scholarship on that era and that their activities are often seen as 'war work' rather than a purportedly more noble humanitarianism reveals the gendered blind spots we still face in studying the history of humanitarianism.[29] Still, at the time the strongly participatory nature of fundraising practices allowed home front populations, including women, children, and older people to make a direct contribution. To a lesser degree this was true also for neutral populations, to whom fundraising and humanitarian aid offered an avenue of constructive participation and 'positive neutrality' in a world event that they otherwise watched from the margins. For those with strong ethnic, cultural, or professional connections abroad, it also afforded a chance to give tangible expression to their affinity and sympathy with kin, friends, and colleagues. Very often they contributed not only directly to the care of war victims but also created the public sentiments that ultimately forced belligerents to pay heed to humanitarian imperatives.

This, finally, points to the single most neglected humanitarian actor: the beneficiaries themselves. In fact, far from being the inactive victims they are often made out to be, beneficiaries actively shaped their humanitarian narratives abroad, skilfully solicited aid, and, more often than not, made a massive contribution to the implementation of allegedly 'foreign' aid.[30] Tatjana Eichert and Rebecca Gill (Chapter 10), for example, point to the involvement of German and Austrian doctors in running an 'international' child-feeding enterprise after the war, and María Inés Tato's chapter notes how active Allied Red Cross societies were in soliciting aid for their compatriots in Argentina. What is more, beneficiaries were far from being just meekly grateful; they often questioned the motives of their benefactors or dictated the terms of relief. As Kimberly Lowe shows (Chapter 8), Russian officials hardly jumped at the chance of receiving food supplies from 'the West'. Rather, they set tight boundaries for how such aid was to be delivered. In all, 'beneficiaries' emerge not so much as passive, grateful 'recipients' but as critical partners who possessed unique expertise and exercised considerable agency.

This large cast of humanitarian actors suggests the history of humanitarianism as a particularly rich lens to study the Great War and its aftermath. It offers a window on to the very different motivations that inspired humanitarian action, encompassing the pursuit of military necessities, the search for adventure and social opportunities, the breakout of gender roles and the pursuit of prestige and security, as well as deep-seated empathy and ideological or religious conviction – and everything in between.

Entangled worlds: humanitarianism and international politics

The collection places special emphasis on investigating the connection between humanitarian engagement and international politics, broadly conceived. Great War-era humanitarianism was never a disinterested or impartial, let alone apolitical endeavour. Rather, it was informed by military and political necessities, moral convictions, racial hierarchies, and cultural affinities. It expressed and shaped the international politics of its time. Humanitarian engagement aided the mobilisation of belligerent and non-belligerent societies and served salient political and military interests the world over. To state and non-state actors 'saving strangers' became a means of implementing ideological agendas, of pursuing or protesting imperial and military ambitions, and, more generally, of accruing international prestige and influence. It was usually these considerations, not objective need, that determined when, how, and to whom humanitarian assistance was provided. As such one of the collection's key arguments is that there was never just one humanitarianism. Instead the Greater War witnessed very different and often competing humanitarianisms that were intimately tied to the era's larger questions of war and peace and the shape of the social and political order.

Humanitarianism and politics were entangled in a number of profound ways. For one, humanitarianism had an intimate connection to the social and cultural mobilisation of millions far removed from the frontlines. Fundraising brought the war home into market squares and created a tangible association to the war victims. Humanitarian narratives gave meaning to the war and frequently became part of an emerging war culture. What made humanitarian narratives so powerful, and so political, was the fact that they seemed to clearly identify, to use Makau Mutua's terms, the war's 'savages, victims and saviours'.[31] Fundraising meant identifying with the victim while also identifying the perpetrator. The reception of Belgian refugees in France or Britain, for example, cannot be divorced from tales of German atrocities. Fundraising for 'poor little Belgium' was an especially powerful way to discuss the depravity of the Germans, the heroic suffering of the Belgians, and the gallantry of the British or French.[32] In this way humanitarian narratives and practices strongly reinforced the cultural mobilisations of the Great War. Importantly this was also true further afield. In Argentina, Japan, Brazil, or the United States fundraising activities helped forge intense moral and emotional alliances. For immigrant communities, aid was among the most readily available and socially acceptable ways to express sympathy for their homeland even if, as in the case of Portuguese monarchists in Brazil, their homeland had rejected them. It was a way to construct a transnational community of fate, as Ana Paula Pires shows (Chapter 3) with regard to the 'Portuguese world'. In fact their humanitarian donations might have made immigrants and exiles feel closer to Berlin, Warsaw, or Lisbon than to their next-door neighbours in Buenos Aires, Chicago, or São Paulo. Humanitarian concern thus charts a different map of Great War alliances, one that represents what Olivier Compagnon and Pierre Purseigle have called 'geographies of belligerence'.[33] Even those not at war harboured clear sympathies which were shaped and expressed through aid. Needless to say, these different geographies, albeit constituted morally and emotionally, carried political meaning. At a moment when the international system was in flux, when nations jockeyed for independence, new borders or reparations, being identified as victim, savage, or saviour could have profound political consequences.

By the same token humanitarian ideas could as easily strain loyalties and identities as strengthen them. German military officers and officials stationed in Turkey viewed the genocide of the Armenians with profound unease and in many instances intervened to give protection to those fleeing persecution. Liberal opinion in the United Kingdom was likewise deeply wary of Russia's record on humanitarian questions, and would have looked askance at any attempt to align their values with those of the Russian Empire. Although all sides were happy to trumpet their commitment to traditional chivalric values or the more recent internationally agreed regulations, belligerent governments were loath to relinquish control of their internment policies or strike common positions with their allies on humanitarian matters. It is telling that attempts by the Entente to forge a collective policy in the face of German reprisal measures against British and French PoWs quickly ran aground and were not pursued further.[34]

Humanitarianism also impinged on international politics in more immediate ways. For one, humanitarian concern became a maker and marker of moral hierarchies. Humanitarian language was never entirely jettisoned during the war: in many instances its importance only grew. Because of their strong public resonance, humanitarian causes became key ingredients in the propaganda wars of the time. Belligerents used them extensively to win support at home and abroad: they incessantly (and often rightly) accused each other of violating the Hague and Geneva Conventions, of maltreating captive combatants and civilians, or of breaching the boundaries of civilised behaviour. Not surprisingly humanitarian rhetoric reached a climax in the lead-up to the peace treaties in 1919. As Christian Müller details (Chapter 12), the French and British employed humanitarian arguments to gain control over German colonies; the Germans, in turn, as Phillip Dehne's chapter shows, used them to contest the Allied sea blockade and expedite the return of their PoWs. As they had during the nineteenth century, humanitarian narratives enabled state and non-state actors to legitimise their (geo)political interests, and stake their claims in the new world order.

Throughout the era of the Greater War humanitarianism also helped build national visibility, prestige and influence. Humanitarian aid was an arena for strong international competition, at least partly explaining its great vitality. Like individuals or voluntary associations, nations, too, engaged in 'conspicuous compassion'. Nations vied for access to particularly prestigious war victims, hoping to bolster their own 'saviour' status in the process. For Japan Hanne Deleu illustrates (Chapter 2), aiding Belgium, an old European power, was a way to grow into its role as 'an ally' but also to affirm and publicise its own Great Power status. During the war this search for humanitarian influence was perhaps most notable in competition between neutrals, which vied for prestige and international gratitude. As the chapters of Neville Wylie and Cédric Cotter demonstrate, several neutrals – Switzerland, the Vatican, Denmark, Sweden, the United States – jostled with each other to secure the mantle of the 'humanitarian great power'.[35]

Finally humanitarian aid was a way to implement particular visions of the postwar world. As Christian Mueller's chapter explains, anti-slavery groups used traditional humanitarian language to try and recast the imperial order.[36] Tomás Irish shows (Chapter 11) how humanitarians privileged the needs of particular groups, such as intellectuals, because of their perceived importance to re-establishing a stable, peaceful, and bourgeois Europe. A similar point features in Tatjana Eichert and Rebecca Gill's chapter, where child-feeding schemes are depicted as a vision for postwar reconciliation. At the same time humanitarian aid was always a potent weapon to fight and promote competing ideologies. As Kimberly Lowe's chapter illustrates, the League of Nations hoped to use food aid to contain Bolshevism in Revolutionary Russia. The fact that the League's member governments rapidly lost interest as soon as their political aims seemed unattainable speaks to the degree to which national interests could – and invariably did – trump humanitarian need.

In all the collection attests to a range of different humanitarianisms with diverse and often rivalling aims. There were competing ideas of what precisely humanitarianism was to accomplish, who was to administer it, and why it ought to be given. For the philanthropist Emily Hobhouse (active in the early years of Save the Children), for example, aid was a radical statement of solidarity with the weak, even including the suffering enemy. For many others aid was a means to bring order and stability into the world, often synonymous with burnishing the status quo. Humanitarianism legitimated very different ideological agendas, even – and perhaps especially – when it used decidedly non-political language. It is this broad range of political implications that make the subject of aid so important for our understanding of the Great War and its aftermath.

The Greater War and the making of 'modern' humanitarianism

One question that continues to vex historians is the relation of the Great War and its aftermath to 'modern humanitarianism', frequently defined as secular and large-scale operations committed to such humanitarian principles as humanity, neutrality, impartiality, and independence.[37] How 'modern' was humanitarian engagement at the time? Looking at a broad range of humanitarian actors, the chapters in this collection recognise that the degree of professionalism and devotion to humanitarian universalism varied widely; although large-scale, fairly professional organisations like the American Relief Administration or the ICRC have come to synonymise Great War humanitarianism, a large number of humanitarian endeavours at the time were small, makeshift, and deeply partisan. In fact, as Cédric Cotter rightly points out, only the largest entities even had the wherewithal to be impartial and 'neutral'.

Historians tend to locate the roots of today's humanitarian concern in the late eighteenth and nineteenth centuries. The 1800s globalised the 'saving of strangers'. As Lynn Hunt has shown, the rise of the novel made readers identify with the suffering of (socially and geographically) distant others and created a new humanitarian sensibility.[38] The abolitionist movement championed the idea of a common humanity, and, alongside a series of violent conflicts, inspired new forms of transnational solidarity.[39] The Greek War of Independence in the 1820s, the American Civil War in the 1860s, and the Franco-Prussian War in 1870–71 all inspired considerable efforts by transnational voluntary organisations to mitigate the suffering they provoked. In the late nineteenth century, a range of natural disasters and famine in China and India as well as successive attacks on Armenians in the Ottoman Empire, sparked non-war-related humanitarian campaigns.[40] Such humanitarian concerns were the result of increasing prosperity and leisure time, the formation of bourgeois civil societies, integrating worldwide markets as well as new communication and media technologies. By the turn of the century an emerging humanitarian photography, cheaper reproduction techniques, and a sensationalist press made humanitarianism a part of an 'increasingly entertainment-oriented mass culture'.[41] By presenting emergencies as immediate and actionable, they became 'humanitarianised'.[42] Humanitarian activities were likewise frequently a product of imperial connections and imaginations. Not only did they develop in lockstep with imperial governance (and often served to legitimise it) but even seemingly anti-imperial campaigns such as anti-slavery activism tended to be deeply paternalistic and steeped in imperial thinking.[43] At the same time some of the strongest opposition to the excesses of colonialism arose from humanitarian concerns and employed the techniques pioneered by humanitarian publicity.[44] Not surprisingly perhaps, missionaries – who often embodied this ambivalence towards empire – were among the most prolific nineteenth-century humanitarians, trying to save lives as well as souls. Their missionising humanitarianism helped build imperial rule while also criticising many of its most abhorrent features, often at the same time.[45] As part of their general 'civilising mission' (European) states also undertook a range of highly selective 'humanitarian interventions', most often directed against the Ottoman Empire.[46]

Just as humanitarian concern globalised in the decades before the Great War it became increasingly anchored in institutions and legal norms. The single most famous development in this respect was the emergence of the Red Cross movement, which institutionalised the care of sick and wounded combatants. Henri Dunant's famous account of the suffering he encountered during the Italian War of Independence helped give rise to the International Committee of the Red Cross in Geneva in 1863, the Geneva Convention the following year and National Red Cross societies in Europe, the Americas, and Asia in the following decades. The Hague conventions of 1899 and 1907 were part of this effort to 'humanise' warfare, establishing boundaries for permissible behaviour. Then as now, these efforts were not without their critics, who argued that they ultimately made warfare more palatable.[47]

And yet, on the eve of the Great War, humanitarian principles and practices were still far from 'modern' in a number of important respects. For one, humanitarianism in war was severely limited and uneven. Legal protections and humanitarian access applied near exclusively to combatants, forbidding unnecessarily cruel weaponry and setting parameters for the care of sick and wounded soldiers. Civilians enjoyed far fewer protections. The Hague conferences included some provisions for the safeguarding of cultural landmarks and hospitals, outlawed the looting of undefended towns and forbade specific practices such as the use of human shields or collective punishment.[48] But besides the fact that many of these rules were violated during the war, humanitarian issues like hunger, rape, or displacement found little consideration in international law at the time. As a consequence humanitarian interventions in these fields depended on government goodwill and public whim. In fact, humanitarian responses at the time were usually grounded not in need but in pity, notions of religious charity, and/or forms of collective identification and affinity. This is not to say that there were not instances of aiding the truly 'distant other'; more often than not, Christians aided Christians (or those they hoped to Christianise) just as ethnic or professional communities aided their kin and peers abroad. What is more, for much of the nineteenth century, there existed few scientific tools to objectively measure 'need' (through calories or the BMI-index) or humanitarian technologies to help ameliorate them. Fields like social work and paediatrics notably professionalised around the turn of the century but their findings were just beginning to be implemented more broadly.[49] Finally, with the exception of Red Cross societies, mission boards, and abolitionist societies, most aid operations tended to be ad hoc, popping up when the need arose and faltering when it subsided. The humanitarian world of the Great War era bore only a faint resemblance to the permanent institutional and legal structures of humanitarian governance in place since the Second World War.

The extent to which humanitarianism became 'modern' in the era of the Great War remains debated. Perhaps the strongest proponent of the modernisation position is Keith Watenpaugh, who traces humanitarian efforts, especially the Near East Relief/Foundation, in the eastern Mediterranean and identifies it as the place where older missionary organisations were remade in a secular cast, that is, where 'modern' humanitarianism was born.[50] Protracted refugee crises called for joint efforts by the League of Nations, NGOs, and national governments and in the process produced humanitarian structures that were 'envisioned by its participants and protagonists as a permanent, transnational, institutional, neutral and secular regime for understanding and addressing the root causes of human suffering'.[51] In fact scholars of US humanitarianism have perhaps been quickest to see the Great War as a watershed in terms of 'modern' humanitarianism. Herbert Hoover's food aid operations, with their reliance on large-scale, largely state-funded, and technocratic administration, are generally – and with some justification – seen as trailblazers of modern humanitarianism.[52] Many have noted that war and postwar food relief (and issues of wartime nutrition more broadly) facilitated the adoption of scientific approaches to relief operations and prompted a move from ad-hoc emergency relief to broader preoccupations with welfare, development, and, tacitly, human rights.[53] Bruno Cabanes, in particular, has argued that the origins of a rights-based humanitarianism should be located in the aftermath of the Great War. The war saw humanitarianism become more secular and transnational and gave 'rise to a discourse that spoke less of charity and more about human rights'.[54] Alongside a 'post-war Wilsonian political moment', he argued, 'so, too, was there a "humanitarian moment" – that is, a period of several years in which important collective expectations were consolidated'.[55]

By contrast this collection remains sceptical of applying the 'modern' epithet to Great War-era humanitarianism. No doubt the war and its aftermath endowed humanitarianism with many novel attributes. It brought in a plethora of new humanitarian actors and dramatically expanded the remit of existing ones. Organisations such as the American Relief Administration operated on an unprecedented scale, while new institutions like the League of Nations found some of their earliest and most daunting tasks in addressing refugees and food crises. For the first time, large-scale managerial techniques, methods, and mentalities were applied to questions of relief in ways that were simply not present in the humanitarian actions of the previous century. The war also helped extend the image of victims of war from combatants to civilians. 'Vulnerable' subjects now included the displaced, the interned, the occupied, and the child. These groups were not accorded greater legal protection but their fate enjoyed far greater visibility. Moreover, for the first time, there were organisations that provided civilian aid on the sole basis of need, without attention to race, class, or creed. The American Relief Administration, the American Friends Service Committee, and Save the Children – alongside local doctors and social workers – spent substantial time to scientifically measure need. As Tatjana Eichert and Rebecca Gill's chapter illustrates, they charted and weighed children's bodies, allocated calories and sought to find and develop foods with just the right nutritional value.[56] New humanitarian technologies like the food parcel also became very popular.[57] Importantly, some of these organisations became permanent, ready to be deployed in another emergency.[58] Above all there was a new momentum to the humanitarian discourse as can be seen from a discussion of children's rights in 1924 or the new rights accorded to PoWs, as 'humanitarian subjects' rather than merely 'disarmed enemies', in the Geneva Convention of 1929.[59] As Phillip Dehne's chapter shows, not providing for the defeated enemy at least required some justification after the Great War era.

Yet even as we acknowledge and analyse these shifts, and even as we acknowledge the Greater War as a catalyst of humanitarian development, doubts about the essentially modern nature of Great War-era humanitarianism remain. A closer look reveals many mechanisms and attitudes reminiscent of the nineteenth century. A great majority of the chapters attest to the highly selective nature of aid. The International Committee of the Red Cross or the American Relief Administration might have focused their attention on the neediest PoW or the most seriously underweight child, but in general the war saw the survival of 'pity over need'. As Tomás Irish's chapter demonstrates, deservingness was often measured not according to the depth of distress but according to (future) service to society. Donor publics, in particular, unapologetically played national, ethnic, and religious favours. Their aid was usually an expression of sympathy. The very largest number of humanitarian organisations remained small-scale and non-permanent, and fairly large ones like the Near East Relief/Foundation or the Jewish Joint Distribution Committee focused on a single region or victim group. In fact, we ought not forget just how controversial notions of humanitarian universalism were at the time. Save the Children is feted today for saving enemy children, but its founders encountered massive opposition and – as Tatjana Eichert and Rebecca Gill's chapter shows – rapidly abandoned their daring agenda in the early 1920s. The nineteenth century also looms large through the continued importance of more traditional actors like aristocrats, missionaries, and religious functionaries.[60] For every Herbert Hoover, widely celebrated as a new type of managerial humanitarian, there was at least one 'charitable lady' like Elsa Brändström, Nora Gräfin Kinsky, or Marie of Romania. Driven by compassion, religious conviction, gendered-notions of proper female war work, and clear national affinities, these women might, in fact, just as truthfully represent Great War-era 'humanitarianism'.[61]

In all, the collection challenges the apparent clarity with which humanitarian categories can be said to have emerged at the time. The era was not so much the beginning of 'modern humanitarianism', or the end of its nineteenth-century variant, as it was a complicated transitional period with many unique accomplishments and flaws. In fact many of the chapters underline the shortcomings of humanitarianism and offer a corrective to the triumphant narrative that contemporaries themselves often read into that period. Following Johannes Paulmann's useful concept, we tend to see the Great War era more as an important 'conjuncture' in the history of humanitarianism than as a watershed moment or decisive turning point.[62]

Introduction

The collection

The collection addresses these questions in three sections. The first section focuses on global war, global aid. The contributors use humanitarian engagement as a lens to understand how the Great War and its aftermath played out globally and, to a lesser degree, locally. The chapter by María Inés Tato traces the development and impact of humanitarian mobilisation on behalf of Europe in a fragmented Argentine society. Hanne Deleu explores the humanitarian engagement of Japan, a country of otherwise limited involvement in the Great War, for Belgium and analyses how these relief efforts served the ambitions of various segments of the Japanese population. Ana Paula Pires delineates how wartime relief work helped shape the contours of the Portuguese world, emotionally and morally connecting the Portuguese mainland to its colonies in Africa and its diaspora in Latin America. The chapters demonstrate how humanitarian concern intimately linked faraway, seemingly peripheral regions of the war in Asia, Africa, and Latin America to the war's centres of gravity, how it could align home and battle fronts (through the work of women, in particular), and how it connected belligerents and neutrals around the world. In some instances the humanitarian mobilisation of non-belligerent societies proved so intense that it called into question the countries' neutrality. At the same time Christoph Jahr's chapter not only shows the global dimension and networks of Jewish aid in Eastern Europe but also assesses the impact of humanitarian operations on the ground and the difficulties of reconciling humanitarian and military necessities in occupied regions during the First World War.

The second section, on the politics and power of aid, explores the entanglement of humanitarianism and international politics after 1914. Although frequently portrayed as 'non-political' by contemporaries, humanitarian engagement was deeply embedded in Great War-era politics. Cédric Cotter illustrates that the great vitality of humanitarian endeavours during the First World War was in part fuelled by neutral powers, including Switzerland, the Scandinavian countries, and the Vatican, competing for humanitarian prestige and influence; Neville Wylie extends this line of argument by examining the United States' work as protecting power between 1914 and 1917, and casts light on the tensions it encountered in grafting humanitarian activities on to a traditionally diplomatic function. Phillip Dehne's chapter on the SEC in 1919 demonstrates how deeply embedded humanitarian aid could be in the power structures of the time: the major Allied blockade authority, responsible for considerable distress, provided also the infrastructure for food relief after the armistice. Kimberly Lowe explores the stillborn efforts of the League of Nations to engage in famine relief and shows that, while it was originally intended to thwart Russian Bolshevism, the idea of aid was abandoned as soon as that goal appeared no longer attainable. Collectively, the chapters highlight the political motivations, uses, and implications of humanitarian aid to nations, military alliances, and international organisations. Governments and individuals gave or withheld humanitarian aid to build their international influence, to strengthen their allies and subdue their enemies, and to actively shape the contours of a new world order. As these chapters show, where, how, and why humanitarian aid was given was often determined more by political considerations than objective need. As such the Greater War pioneered and consolidated some of the salient political uses of aid (including image-building and regime change) that it continues to be associated with today.

The third section interrogates the legacies and limits of the era of the Great War on the development of humanitarian ideology and practice. The chapters survey the humanitarian organisations, practices, subjects, and ethos that evolved at this time. Elisabeth Piller explores why, unlike for Belgium, no effective civilian relief was ever organised for wartime Poland, thereby highlighting the uneven impact of national interests, neutrality, and public opinion. The failure to help Polish war sufferers, she holds, should caution against following contemporary interpretations of Great War humanitarianism as a success story. Tatjana Eichert and Rebecca Gill examine the early history of the International Save the Children movement and its emergence at the intersection of contemporary social movements such as feminism and pacifism. Tomás Irish's chapter traces the efforts to save 'intellectuals' in postwar Europe, demonstrating how relief was provided in a most selective fashion and according to perceived future usefulness of the recipients. Christian Müller's chapter, finally, focuses on the League of Nations' anti-slavery humanitarianism in the 1920s, placing it in the context of the making of a new postwar order. As he shows, earlier anti-slavery networks and language helped re-establish and relegitimise European claims for continued imperial governance under moral and humanitarian terms. The chapters offer some explanations of how and why humanitarians' attention shifted towards previously neglected groups of civilian war victims, including children and intellectuals, and illustrate how the war and postwar period set the stage for humanitarian careers, bureaucracies, and structures that outlasted the twentieth century. They show, too, how longer-standing humanitarian causes and rhetoric were refashioned to serve various, not mutually exclusive, imperial, internationalist, and pacifist visions of the postwar order. As such, however, the section emphasises the inherent contradictions and limitations of humanitarianism at the time. As all chapters show, even as humanitarian operations grew and professionalised, they often remained and became deeply flawed, according assistance based on narrow criteria of ethnicity and nationality, cultural capital, media coverage or imperial ambition. While many contemporaries liked to portray their humanitarian engagement as an unblemished success, their Great War-era experience actually presaged modern-day humanitarianism in its many achievements and its many shortcomings.

Research perspectives and agendas

The chapters in this collection reflect on where the history of Great War-era humanitarianism stands in light of the research and scholarship carried out over the last decade. They also prompt us to consider some paths for future exploration. Three issues, in particular, deserve our attention.

We are in need of studies that situate humanitarianism within the era of the two world wars. Despite the enormous literature on the first and second world wars, there are few works that focus on humanitarian undertakings in both conflicts, especially based on extensive archival research.[63] This is odd, given the general agreement that the humanitarian responses to the Second World War were deeply informed by the perceived lessons of the First World War. A number of studies even treat the two world wars together, seeing them as one important 'conjuncture' in the history of humanitarianism.[64] The novel developments seen in the Great War, a common interpretation goes, were amplified in the Second World War. And yet, the connections between the two world wars are not as straightforward or teleological as might appear. The lessons people drew from Great War-era humanitarianism varied widely. While some planners judged Great War humanitarianism critically and developed post-Second World War programmes with an eye to the perceived 'failures' of the previous generation,[65] others believed the earlier operations to have been a stunning success and hence to be repeated, albeit on a grander scale.[66] These questions are integral to understanding how and why today's humanitarian world developed. In this context, the generational experience of humanitarians deserves deeper attention. Humanitarians like Elsa Brändström, Ludwik Rajchman, Herbert Hoover, Maurice Pate, Elisabeth Rotten, or Francesca Wilson – to name but a few – all applied their (different) lessons from the Great War to solving the humanitarian disaster of the Second World War.

A second issue requiring more serious attention is the experiences and interests (!) of those traditionally seen as passive beneficiaries of aid. Conversations on the history of humanitarianism have expressed frustration at how little we still know about those on the 'receiving end' of aid.[67] If humanitarian aid can open different readings on international relations, as we have suggested, it seems of paramount importance to uncover the thoughts and ambitions not only of donors and relief workers but of beneficiaries. The Great War offers a unique opportunity to do just that as historians can benefit from the meticulous record-keeping of state, including regional and municipal, bureaucracies, as well as diaries, correspondence, and other ego documents produced by highly literate populations. Studying 'beneficiary' records can help historians decentre long-told narratives and better weigh the actual significance of international as compared to local or national humanitarianism. For instance, while historians continue to be fascinated by Herbert Hoover's operations in Belgium, the national Belgian relief organisation Comité national de secours et d'alimentation (with a splendid archival collection in Brussels) has not received any major attention since the 1920s.[68] This, too, comes with a call to think more critically about how we categorise our subjects: as humanitarians, philanthropists, social workers, or 'soup kitchen ladies'. Such labels in themselves reinforce the largely artificial (and often gendered) distinction between noble international humanitarians and their trusty, if less selfless and less glamorous local 'helpers'.[69] Further problematising this distinction should produce more meaningful and nuanced histories of humanitarian encounters and will help centre (local) women, as some of the most significant, and less studied humanitarian actors in the history.

The third issue, finally, is not so much a research agenda as a call to re-examine the stories historians tell and the evidence they base them on. It is about methodological questions regarding archives, access, and the writing of humanitarian history. Acknowledging the preponderance of scholarship on (US) humanitarian NGOs, one has to recognise, too, that historians have traditionally privileged a number of highly accessible and beautifully curated archival collections.[70] These include the Rockefeller Archives, the Jewish Joint Distribution Archives, and the Hoover Institution Archives (many of which also have generous visiting fellowships) as well as the ICRC and Save the Children archives. Yet using these archives, we run the danger of replicating the success stories that humanitarian practitioners wrote into their collections and of falling prey to the exaggerated claims of 'impact' they made towards themselves and their donors. Needless to say, these repositories are also designed in a way to reaffirm preconceived notions of active donors and passive recipients. This collection thus closes with a call to look for the history of humanitarianism in different archives (such as state, company or municipal archives) and to read the available material more critically. Many of the big NGO archives boast boxes upon boxes of letters and objects of 'recipient' gratitude. Rather than taking them at face value, might we not systematically analyse the unspoken assumptions they rest on, including notions of entitlement, disappointment, or resentment? We should also focus less on the productive moments of humanitarianism, and more on those (more scarcely documented) instances when humanitarian protections failed or were not considered in the first place. Humanitarian blind spots, lives not saved, or protections not afforded, might tell us as much about humanitarianism than its stunning successes. With regard to the Great War, one history that ought to be written is that of the global 'compassion fatigue' that set in around 1916. Such a history would show the clear limits of humanitarian mobilisation and paint perhaps a more truthful image of Great War-era humanitarianism.

Notes

1 On some of these points see P. Gatrell, R. Gill, B. Little, and E. Piller, 'Discussion: Humanitarianism', in U. Daniel, P. Gatrell, O. Janz, H. Jones, J. Keene, A. Kramer, and B. Nasson (eds), *1914–1918-online. International Encyclopedia of the First World War*, November 2017, DOI: http://dx.doi.org/10.15463/ie1418.11168; the authors would like to thank Branden Little for his thoughtful comments on an earlier draft of this introduction.
2 See B. Little, 'An Explosion of New Endeavours: Global Humanitarian Responses to Industrialized Warfare in the First World War Era', *First World War Studies*, 5:1 (2014), 1–16.
3 See M. E. Cox, *Hunger in War and Peace: Women and Children in Germany, 1914–1924* (Oxford: Oxford University Press, 2019); C. Laderman, *Sharing the Burden: The Armenian Question, Humanitarian Intervention, and Anglo-American Visions of Global Order* (New York: Oxford University Press, 2019); C. Druelle, *Feeding Occupied France during World War I: Herbert Hoover and the Blockade* (London: Palgrave Macmillan, 2019); M. Tanielian, *The Charity of War: Famine, Humanitarian Aid, and World War I in the Middle East* (Stanford: Stanford University Press, 2017); C. Cotter, *(S')Aider pour survivre: Action humanitaire et neutralité suisse pendant la Première Guerre mondiale* (Geneva: Georg, 2017); J. Granick, *International Jewish Humanitarianism in the Age of the Great War* (Cambridge: Cambridge University Press, 2022); D. Rodogno, *Night on Earth: A History of Relief and Rehabilitation in the Near East, 1918–1930s* (Cambridge: Cambridge University Press, 2021); F. Kind-Kovács, *Budapest's Children: Humanitarian Relief in the Aftermath of the Great War* (Bloomington: University of Indiana Press, 2022); see also the forthcoming monograph, T. Proctor, *Saving Europe: First World War Relief and American Identity* (New York: Oxford University Press, 2023); for general context see the wide-ranging discussion in M. Hilton, E. Baughan, E. Davey, B. Everill, K. O'Sullivan, and T. Sasson, 'History and Humanitarianism: A Conversation', *Past & Present*, 241:1 (2018), e1–e38.
4 *No End to War: Cultures of Violence and Care in the Aftermath of the First World War* (Manchester, January 2019); *Post World War I Aid in*

Austria & Central Europe (Vienna, September 2019); *Humanitarianism and the Greater War* (Dublin, September 2019); *The Aftermath of the First World War: Humanitarianism in the Mediterranean* (Milan, December 2019); *Relief, Culture, and Allegiance: Humanitarianism in World War I and Its Aftermath* (Minneapolis, May 2020); *Gender, Humanitarianism and the Greater War* (Brussels, December 2021).

5 See for example J. Irwin, *Making the World Safe: The American Red Cross and a Nation's Humanitarian Awakening* (New York: Oxford University Press, 2013); K. Watenpaugh, *Bread from Stones: The Middle East and the Making of Modern Humanitarianism* (Oakland: University of California Press, 2015).

6 See the discussion below.

7 One notable exception is B. Cabanes, *The Great War and the Origins of Humanitarianism, 1918–1924* (Cambridge: Cambridge University Press, 2014), which deals with a range of national case studies; also A. Becker, *Oubliés de la Grand Guerre: Humanitaire et culture de guerre 1914–1918* (Paris: Pluriel, 1998).

8 B. Little (ed.), 'Humanitarianism in the Era of the First World War', *First World War Studies*, 5:1 (2014), 1–146.

9 See the relatively light treatment of this period in a number of collective works: J. Paulmann (ed.), *Dilemmas of Humanitarian Aid in the Twentieth Century* (Oxford: Oxford University Press, 2016); J. Paulmann (ed.), *Humanitarianism and Media: 1900 to the Present* (New York: Berghahn, 2019); F. Klose (ed.), *The Emergence of Humanitarian Intervention: Ideas and Practice from the Nineteenth Century to the Present* (Cambridge: Cambridge University Press, 2015); H. Fehrenbach and D. Rodogno (eds), *Humanitarian Photography: A History* (Cambridge: Cambridge University Press, 2015). The same is true for M. Barnett, *Empire of Humanity: A History of Humanitarianism* (Ithaca: Cornell University Press, 2011), and S. Salvatici, *A History of Humanitarianism, 1755–1989. In the Name of Others* (Manchester: Manchester University Press, 2019).

10 R. Gerwarth and E. Manela, 'The Great War as a Global War: Imperial Conflict and the Reconfiguration of World Order, 1911–1923', *Diplomatic History*, 38:4 (2014), 786–800; R. Gerwarth and J. Horne (eds), *War in Peace: Paramilitary Violence in Europe after the Great War* (Oxford: Oxford University Press, 2013); J. Winter (ed.), *The Cambridge History of the First World War: Global War*, vol. 1 (Cambridge: Cambridge University Press, 2014); J. Bürgschwentner, M. Egger, and G. Barth-Scalmani (eds), *Other Fronts, Other Wars? First World War, Series on the Eve of the Centennial* (Leiden: Brill, 2014); and D. Geppert, W. Mulligan and A. Rose (eds), *The Wars before the Great War: Conflict and International Politics before the Outbreak of the First World War* (Cambridge: Cambridge University Press, 2015).

11 See note 3; on Eastern Europe see G. P. Gross (ed.), *The Forgotten Front: The Eastern Theater of World War I, 1914–1915* (Lexington: University Press of Kentucky, 2018).

12 R. Gerwarth and E. Manela (eds), *Empires at War, 1911–1923* (Oxford: Oxford University Press, 2014).

13 Newer literature focuses on the Treaty of Lausanne as the end point of the First World War: see J. Winter, *The Day the Great War Ended, 24 July 1923. The Civilianization of War* (Oxford: Oxford University Press, 2022).
14 This shift is also visible in the rise of disability history: see, for example, M. Salvante, 'The Wounded Male Body: Masculinity and Disability in Wartime and Post-WWI Italy', *Journal of Social History*, 53:3 (2020), 644–66.
15 T. Proctor, *Civilians in a World at War, 1914–1918* (New York: New York University Press, 2010); J. Connolly, *The Experience of Occupation of the Nord, 1914–1918* (Manchester: Manchester University Press, 2018); B. J. Davis, *Homes Fires Burning: Food, Politics, and Everyday Life in World War I Berlin* (Chapel Hill: University of North Carolina Press, 2000); J. Winter and J.-L. Robert (eds), *Capital Cities at War* (Cambridge: Cambridge University Press, 1997).
16 See A. (Iris) Rachamimov, *POWs and the Great War: Captivity on the Eastern Front* (Oxford: Berg, 2002).
17 M. Stibbe, *Civilian Internment during the First World War: A European and Global History, 1914–1920* (London: Palgrave Macmillan, 2019), p. 1; for a more exhaustive list of places where civilians were interned see inter alia M. Stibbe, 'The Internment of Civilians by Belligerent States during the First World War and the Response of the International Committee of the Red Cross', *Journal of Contemporary History*, 41:1 (2006), 8; A. Bauerkämper, *Sicherheit und Humanität in den beiden Weltkriegen: Der Umgang mit zivilen Feindstaatenangehörigen im Ausnahmezustand* (Berlin: de Gruyter, 2021); M. Murphy, *Colonial Captivity during the First World War: Internment and the Fall of the German Empire, 1914–1919* (Cambridge: Cambridge University Press, 2017). More generally, R. Kowner and I. Rachamimov (eds), *Out of Line, Out of Place: A Global and Local History of World War I Internments* (Ithaca: Cornell University Press, 2022); S. Manz, P. Panayi, and M. Stibbe (eds), *Internment during the First World War: A Mass Global Phenomenon* (London: Routledge, 2018).
18 P. Purseigle, '"A Wave on to Our Shores": The Exile and Resettlement of Refugees from the Western Front, 1914–1918', *Contemporary European History*, 16:4 (2007), 441.
19 Longer-standing humanitarian crises, hidden from the public eye by occupiers and censors, came to light in the postwar period. See, for example, the case of Poland, as discussed in Chapter 9.
20 M. Housden, 'When the Baltic Sea Was a "Bridge" for Humanitarian Action: The League of Nations, the Red Cross and the Repatriation of Prisoners of War between Russia and Central Europe, 1920–22', *Journal of Baltic Studies*, 38:1 (2007), 61–83; H. Tate, 'Internment after the War's End: "Humanitarian Camps" in the POW Repatriation Process, 1918–1923', in R. Kowner and I. Rachamimov (eds), *Out of Line, Out of Place: A Global and Local History of World War I Internments* (Ithaca: Cornell University Press, 2022), pp. 269–94.
21 Hew Strachan, Mary Elisabeth Cox, and Claire Morelon are currently preparing a collection on this subject as part of their project, 'Hunger Draws the Map: Blockade and Food Shortages in Europe, 1914–1922'.

22 P. Clavin, 'The Austrian Hunger Crisis and the Genesis of International Organisation after the First World War', *International Affairs*, 90:2 (2014), 265–78.
23 See E. Baughan, *Saving the Children: Humanitarianism, Internationalism, and Empire* (Berkeley: University of California Press, 2021); Melanie Oppenheimer (ANU) is leading a team examining the history of the League of Red Cross Societies as a form of 'resilient humanitarianism', funded by the Australian Research Council.
24 See, for example, the twenty articles in the special issue on 'Don et solidarité: La philanthropie américaine durant la Grande Guerre', *The Tocqueville Review / La revue Tocqueville*, 38:2 (2017).
25 M. Acuto (ed.), *Negotiating Relief: The Politics of Humanitarian Space* (New York: Hurst, 2014).
26 J. den Hertog and S. Kruizinga (eds), *Caught in the Middle: Neutrals, Neutrality and the First World War* (Amsterdam: Amsterdam University Press, 2011); M. Abbenhuis, *The Art of Staying Neutral: The Netherlands in the First World War, 1914–1918* (Amsterdam: Amsterdam University Press, 2006).
27 David Forsythe has titled his study of the ICRC simply 'The Humanitarians', see D. P. Forsythe, *The Humanitarians: The International Committee of the Red Cross* (Cambridge: Cambridge University Press, 2005). Herbert Hoover's biographers continue to call him 'the Great Humanitarian': see G. B. Nash, '"The Great Humanitarian": Herbert Hoover, the Relief of Belgium, and the Reconstruction of Europe after World War I', *The Tocqueville Review / La revue Tocqueville*, 38:2 (2017), 55–70.
28 See H. Jones, 'International or Transnational? Humanitarian Action during the First World War', *European Review of History – Revue Européene d'historie*, 16:5 (2009), 697–713.
29 For this argument see E. Piller, 'Beyond Hoover: Rewriting the History of the Commission for Relief in Belgium (CRB) through Female Involvement', *The International History Review*, 45:1 (2022), 202–24, DOI: http://dx.doi.org/10.1080/07075332.2022.2113553; for efforts to gender the history of humanitarianism see E. Möller, J. Paulmann, and K. Stornig (eds), *Gendering Global Humanitarianism in the Twentieth Century: Practice, Politics and the Power of Representation* (Cham: Palgrave Macmillan, 2020).
30 This agency and organisation of local humanitarians and recipient populations is the subject of increasing research: see for example T. Balkelis, 'Humanitarian Crisis in German Occupied Vilnius, 1916–1917', *First World War Studies*, 13:1 (2022), 67–83; D. A. Cretu, 'Nationalizing International Relief: Romanian Responses to American Aid for Children in the Great War Era', *European Review of History / Revue européenne d'histoire*, 27:4 (2020), 527–47.
31 M. Mutua, 'Victims, and Saviors: The Metaphor of Human Rights', *Harvard International Law Journal*, 42:1 (2001), 201–45.
32 Purseigle, '"A Wave on to Our Shores"'.
33 O. Compagnon and P. Purseigle, 'Geographies of Mobilisation and Territories of Belligerence during the First World War', *Annales HSS*, 71:1 (2016), 37–64.

34 H. Jones, *Violence against Prisoners of War in the First World War: Britain, France and Germany, 1914–1920* (Cambridge: Cambridge University Press, 2011), p. 141.

35 On the Spanish case see M. Pérez de Arcos, '"Finding Out Whereabouts of Missing Persons": The European War Office, Transnational Humanitarianism and Spanish Royal Diplomacy in the First World War', *The International History Review*, 44:3 (2022), 497–523.

36 The close connection between empire and humanitarianism, also in the inter-war period, is also shown in E. Baughan, '"Every Citizen of Empire Implored to Save the Children!" Empire, Internationalism and the Save the Children Fund in Inter-War Britain', *Historical Research*, 86 (2013), 116–37; see also J. Damousi, T. Burnard, and A. Lester (eds), *Humanitarianism, Empire, and Transnationalism, 1760–1995* (Manchester: Manchester University Press, 2022); for an interesting case study, M. Tusan, '"Crimes against Humanity": Human Rights, the British Empire, and the Origins of the Response to the Armenian Genocide', *American Historical Review*, 119:1 (2014), 47–77.

37 A brief introduction to the Humanitarian Principles endorsed by the UN General Assembly is at: www.unocha.org/sites/dms/Documents/OOM-humanitarianp rinciples_eng_June12.pdf.

38 L. Hunt, *Inventing Human Rights: A History* (New York: W. W. Norton & Company, 2007); T. W. Laqueur, 'Bodies, Details, and the Humanitarian Narrative', in Lynn Hunt (ed.), *The New Cultural History* (Los Angeles: University of California Press, 1989), pp. 176–205.

39 M. Bric and W. Mulligan (eds), *A Global History of Anti-Slavery Politics in the Nineteenth Century* (Basingstoke: Palgrave Macmillan, 2013).

40 E.g. P. Balakian, *The Burning Tigris: The Armenian Genocide and America's Response* (New York: HarperCollins, 2003); R. Kevorkian, *The Armenian Genocide: A Complete History* (London: I. B. Tauris, 2011); on Indian famine, G. Brewis, '"Fill Full the Mouth of Famine": Voluntary Action in Famine Relief in India 1896–1901', *Modern Asian Studies*, 44:4 (2010), 887–918.

41 See K. Rozario, '"Delicious Horrors": Mass Culture, the Red Cross, and the Appeal of Modern American Humanitarianism', *American Quarterly*, 55:3 (2003), 419. A notable contribution is Fehrenbach and Rodogno (eds), *Humanitarian Photography*.

42 P. G. Hoffman and T. G. Weiss, *Humanitarianism, War and Politics: Solferino to Syria and Beyond* (Lanham: Rowman and Littlefield, 2017), p. 212.

43 A. Ribi Forclaz, *Humanitarian Imperialism: The Politics of Anti-Slavery Activism, 1880–1940* (Oxford: Oxford University Press), 2015; E. Baughan and B. Everill, 'Empire and Humanitarianism: A Preface', *The Journal of Imperial and Commonwealth History*, 40:5 (2012), 727–8; R. Gill, 'Networks of Concern, Boundaries of Compassion: British Relief in the South African War', *The Journal of Imperial and Commonwealth History*, 40:5 (2012), 827–44. Barnett characterises all of humanitarianism, 1800–1945, as 'imperial humanitarianism'.

44 K. Grant, 'Christian Critics of Empire: Missionaries, Lantern Lectures, and the Congo Reform Campaign in Britain', *Journal of Imperial and Commonwealth History*, 29:2 (2001), 27–58.

45 J. Paulmann, 'Humanitarianism and Empire' in N. Dalziel and J. MacKenzie (eds), *The Encyclopedia of Empire*, DOI: https://doi.org/10.1002/9781118455074.wbeoe406.

46 D. Rodogno, *Against Massacre: Humanitarian Interventions in the Ottoman Empire, 1815–1914* (Princeton: Princeton University Press, 2011); Klose (ed.), *The Emergence of Humanitarian Intervention*.

47 M. Abbenhuis, *The Hague Conferences and International Politics, 1898–1915* (London: Bloomsbury, 2018).

48 On the problems of humanitarian protection see N. Gordon and N. Perugini, *Human Shields: A History of People in the Line of Fire* (Oakland: University of California Press, 2020).

49 See, for example, the calorie experiments around 1900 in N. Cullather, 'The Foreign Policy of the Calorie', *The American Historical Review*, 112:2 (2007), 337–64, or the paediatric findings of scientists such as Clemens von Pirquet or Adalbert Czerny.

50 'Modern Humanitarianism' according to Watenpaugh is bureaucratic, professionalised, neutral, institutional, financed, and transnational: Watenpaugh, *Bread from Stones*, pp. 4–6.

51 Ibid., p. 5; see also K. Watenpaugh, 'The League of Nations' Rescue of Armenian Genocide Survivors and the Making of Modern Humanitarianism, 1920–1927', *The American Historical Review*, 115:5 (2010), 1315–39.

52 J. Irwin, 'Taming Total War: Great War Era American Humanitarianism and Its Legacies', in T. W. Zeiler, D. K. Ekbladh, and B. C. Montoya (eds), *Beyond 1917: The United States and the Global Legacies of the Great War* (Oxford: Oxford University Press, 2017), pp. 122–39; D. Maul, 'The Rise of a Humanitarian Superpower: American NGOs and International Relief, 1917–1945', in M. Bandeira Jerónimo and J. P. Monteiro (eds), *Internationalism, Imperialism and the Formation of the Contemporary World: The Pasts of the Present* (London: Palgrave, 2018), pp. 127–46.

53 On the interwar period see P. Weindling, 'From Sentiment to Science: Children's Relief Organisations and the Problem of Malnutrition in Inter-War Europe', *Disasters*, 18:3 (1994), 203–12; D. Marshall, 'Children's Rights and Children's Action in International Relief and Domestic Welfare: The Work of Herbert Hoover between 1914 and 1950', *The Journal of the History of Childhood and Youth*, 1:3 (2008), 351–88.

54 Cabanes, *The Great War and the Origins*, p. 4.

55 Ibid., p. 16.

56 See Clemens von Pirquet's NEM concept: H. Birkner, K. Freisteiner, G. Hansekowitz, and P. Panzer, *Kinderküche: Ein Kochbuch nach dem Nemsystem* (Vienna: Springer, 1927); this was part of a broader trend toward the medicalisation of warfare and relief that was also visible in Adolf Lukas Vischer's diagnosis

of 'barbed wire disease': A. L. Vischer, *Barbed Wire Disease: A Psychological Study of the Prisoner of War* (London: Bale and Danielsson, 1919).

57 S. Farré, 'Des États-Unis vers l'Europe: Colis alimentaires et secours humanitaires durant la Première Guerre mondiale et l'après-guerre (1914–1923)', *The Tocqueville Review / La revue Tocqueville*, 38:2 (2017), 161–77.

58 The League of Nations covenant (art. 25) implicitly made the creation of authorised national Red Cross societies a criterion for membership; as Jacelyn Granick notes, 'the map of international Jewish humanitarianism was forged during and after the Great War': see Granick, *International Jewish Humanitarianism*, p. 295.

59 See H. Tate, 'Le Comité international de la Croix-Rouge comme architecte du droit international: vers le Code des prisonniers de guerre (1929)', *Monde(s)*, 2:12 (2017), 203–20; N. Wylie and L. Cameron, 'The Impact of the First World War on the Law Governing the Treatment of Prisoners of War, and the Making of a Humanitarian Subject', *European Journal of International Law*, 29:4 (2018), 1327–50.

60 See I. M. Okkenhaug and K. S. Summerer (eds), *Christian Missions and Humanitarianism in The Middle East, 1850–1950* (Leiden: Brill, 2020).

61 M. Czernin, *Ich habe zu kurz gelebt: Die Geschichte der Nora Gräfin Kinsky* (Berlin: List, 2005); A. (Iris) Rachamimov, '"Female Generals" and "Siberian Angels": Aristocratic Nurses and the Austro-Hungarian POW Relief', in N. M. Wingfield and M. Bucur-Deckard (eds), *Gender and War in Twentieth-Century Eastern Europe* (Bloomington: Indiana University Press, 2006), pp. 23–46.

62 J. Paulmann, 'Conjunctures in the History of International Humanitarian Aid during the Twentieth Century', *Humanity: An International Journal of Human Rights, Humanitarianism, and Development*, 4:2 (2013), 215–38.

63 Some exceptions include Bauerkämper, *Sicherheit und Humanität in den beiden Weltkriegen*, and M. Frank and J. Reinisch (eds), *Refugees in Europe, 1919–1959: A Forty Years' Crisis?* (London: Bloomsbury Publishing, 2017); Marshall, 'Children's Rights and Children's Action'.

64 See Paulmann, 'Conjunctures'; Salvatici, *A History of Humanitarianism*; Barnett, *Empire of Humanity*.

65 B. Shepard, '"Becoming Planning Minded": The Theory and Practice of Relief 1940–1945', *Journal of Contemporary History*, 43:2 (2008), 405–19.

66 H. Hoover, 'Food for the Liberated Countries', [New York City, 8 May 1945], *Addresses upon the American Road, 1941–1945* (New York: D. Van Nostrand Company, 1946), p. 359.

67 Hilton et al. 'History and Humanitarianism, a Conversation', e16–17; For some of the strategies of getting at beneficiary voices see P. Gatrell, A. Ghoshal, K. Nowak, and A. Dowdall, 'Reckoning with Refugeedom: Refugee Voices in Modern History', *Social History*, 46:1 (2021), 70–95.

68 A. Henry, *L'oeuvre du Comité National de Secours et d'Alimentation pendant la guerre* (Brussels: Office de publicité, 1920); a short introduction to the subject in S. de Schaepdrijver, 'A Civilian War Effort: The Comité National de Secours et d'Alimentation in Occupied Belgium, 1914–1918', in *Remembering Herbert*

Hoover and the Commission for Relief in Belgium. Proceedings of the Seminar Held at the University Foundation on October 4, 2006 (Brussels: Fondation Universitaire, 2007), pp. 24–37.
69 Piller, 'Beyond Hoover'.
70 On this point see R. Dunley and J. Pugh, 'Do Archive Catalogues Make History?: Exploring Interactions between Historians and Archives', *Twentieth Century British History*, 32:4 (2021), 581–607.

Part I

Global war, Global aid

1

Humanitarian aid across the ocean: Argentine contributions to the relief of Europe during the Great War

María Inés Tato

Introduction

The Great War was a landmark moment in the development of humanitarianism. The unprecedented scale of destruction and mass violence unleashed by industrial warfare affected combatants and civilians alike and called for humanitarian aid on an equally unprecedented scale, often set into motion by national and transnational networks of solidarity. Numerous public and private initiatives sought to relieve the suffering of wounded soldiers and civilians during the conflict.[1]

Neutral Argentina participated in this global humanitarian activity through a large array of fundraising campaigns, and women as well as men volunteered as doctors, nurses, and stretcher-bearers on the European battlefields. Like other Latin American countries, Argentina had strong historical, cultural, economic, and demographic ties to Europe: it was a former colony of Spain; Britain's major commercial partner in South America; an ardent admirer of republican France; and some of its scientific and military elites had been educated in Germany; it was also home to the second largest immigrant population in the Americas, second only to the United States. The Great War profoundly affected Argentine society and triggered a high degree of social mobilisation, which, this chapter argues, can be understood through its humanitarian engagement.[2]

Argentine efforts to relieve the Old World during the Great War and those of other Latin American countries have not been systematically explored. However, they were considerable for the entire duration of the war and set important precedents for their humanitarian involvement in the Spanish Civil War and the Second World War. This chapter aims to offer a first overview of this subject. It explores Argentina's official stance towards humanitarianism and analyses the wartime humanitarian mobilisation of different social groups of Argentine society. It tackles the relief activities promoted by European residents as well as locals, and draws out moments of co-operation and tension between them; it seeks to identify the primary recipients of those humanitarian schemes as well as the donors' motivations. It also draws attention to the relatively neglected tension between formal Argentine neutrality and Argentine society's efforts to relieve suffering in war-torn Europe. The Argentine case illustrates not only the global reverberations of the war but also the transnational dimension of humanitarianism. The exchanges and interactions of different humanitarian agencies in Argentina, Europe, and the United States demonstrate an intense interconnectivity and show how the Great War blurred the boundaries between neutrality and belligerence.

The neutrality of the Argentine state

Two presidents with very different political orientations governed Argentina during the war: the conservative Victorino De la Plaza (1914–16) and Hipólito Yrigoyen (1916–22) from the Radical Civic Union party. Despite their political differences and several confrontations with the belligerents, both administrations adhered to neutrality as official foreign policy. That decision responded to a combination of factors: the absence of direct interests in the conflict; the ambition to continue trading with both sides (during a challenging time for the Argentine economy); the awareness of the country's own economic and military weakness; and the desire to preserve social harmony in light of the country's large foreign-born population. Besides, neutrality was an Argentine diplomatic tradition continued by the successive administrations since 1880, which avoided any involvement in foreign conflicts.[3]

Regarding humanitarian aid, too, the Argentine state adopted a cautious stance. In September 1914, Congress approved Law 9,501, sponsored by the National Senate president, Benito Villanueva, and Senator Adolfo Dávila. It asked the Executive to deliver $25,000 m/n[4] (US$59,000) to the Argentine Red Cross to help 'the victims and wounded of the current European war'. The money was sent through the Argentine legations in Italy and Switzerland to the International Committee of the Red Cross (ICRC) in Geneva.[5] The ICRC's Secretary-General, Paul Des Gouttes, later reported that the funds had been primarily applied to relieve the suffering of populations in occupied northern France, Belgium, and Poland, the refugees of the Upper Savoy, and those who were repatriated to France through Swiss territory. More than half of the sum had been distributed evenly among the national Red Cross societies of the (at the time) ten warring states.[6] In 1916 a remaining 5,000 F (US$849) was sent to Geneva and distributed among 'the neediest victims of the war, such as the Poles, Serbs and Belgians'.[7]

But apart from this one instance of official generosity, Argentine governments remained cautious. In February 1915, for example, the Commission for Relief in Belgium, an American-led relief organisation, asked the Argentine plenipotentiary minister in London, Vicente J. Domínguez, for his government's support for a propaganda mission to South America, to be led by Jules Destrée, an exiled Belgian politician. The objective of the mission was 'to get the people of those countries interested in the wretched victims of the war in Belgium, who increasingly depend for their upkeep on what the International Commission – under the auspices of the United States and Spain – can import and distribute there'.[8] In his answer, the Minister of Foreign Affairs, José Luis Murature, recalled the support given to the Belgian cause from many Argentine institutions, newspapers, and individuals, including the Congressional appropriation. However, given the country's precarious financial situation, he found it impossible for his government to contribute further to that humanitarian work, and 'in consequence, the moment seems inauspicious for the tour proposed by the Commission'.[9] Aware of this response, the Argentine consul in Antwerp, Augusto Belín Sarmiento, wrote to Murature explaining the serious food situation in Belgium and the transparency of the Commission's procedures. He also regretted that 'the Argentine name had not stood out yet among those that will receive the eternal gratitude of this [Belgian] tormented people'.[10]

Under Yrigoyen's term of office, requests for official aid to Belgium resurfaced – but fared no better. In February 1917 there were rumours that Argentina would join Spain in helping Belgium. Facing these unconfirmed reports, the plenipotentiary minister in Brussels, Alberto Blancas, suggested that his government offer relief to the Belgian population independently of Spain to avoid the possibility that Spain might appear 'as a protector of Belgium with Argentine products and Argentina in second place [...] otherwise, she will provide the service and others will receive the thanks and her effort will remain anonymous'.[11] After months of silence, the minister of Foreign Affairs, Honorio Pueyrredón, laconically answered that the government did not feel it opportune to address the issue.[12]

As the examples show, Argentine diplomats were clearly conscious of the political value of humanitarian action, seeing it as a useful way of enhancing the country's image and influence abroad and competing with more active neutrals such as Spain. The Argentine government, however, seems to have taken other factors into account. Financial issues clearly influenced its tacit contribution to humanitarian causes. Although the Great War was an important stimulus for some areas of the agro-exporting economy, it had no uniformly positive impact on the economy as a whole. Between 1880 and 1914 Argentina stood out as one of the main exporters of beef and grain, including especially corn and wheat, and became known as 'the granary of the world'.[13] However, in 1913, the Balkan crisis and a poor harvest had already led to a slowdown in the economy. The outbreak of the war aggravated the situation. Foreign investments and credit dried up and imports declined drastically. This affected industries dependent on overseas materials and technology. It also depressed state finances which relied heavily on import tariff revenue. As a result public spending and especially public works were delayed, and unemployment soared. Argentine trade was likewise severely affected by the belligerents' economic warfare measures, including the naval blockade, blacklists, and submarine warfare.[14] The Great War triggered a deep economic recession, the deepest in twentieth-century Argentina, which would last until 1921.[15]

Besides these economic and financial considerations, the government likely believed that aiding Belgium could undermine its official neutrality. Such a concern would certainly accord with its careful guarding of neutrality in many other instances. The two wartime administrations adopted great caution in dealing with potential conflicts with the belligerents. The British capture of a steamboat in Argentine jurisdictional waters; the allied blacklisting of German companies and their local partners; the sinking of three ships by German U-boats; and the so-called Luxburg affair (when incriminating correspondence by German diplomats became public) all illustrate that official prudence.[16] Perhaps Argentine authorities conceived humanitarian involvement in favour of Belgium, too, as a menace to the equidistance required by neutrality. They evidently preferred to abstain from humanitarian commitments that might call into question Argentina's neutrality. They also hoped to avoid provoking criticism from the country's large immigrant communities, which were often very active on behalf of their belligerent homelands.

A mobilised society

The government's neutrality in the conflict contrasted sharply with the intense involvement exhibited by Argentine society. Olivier Compagnon and Pierre Purseigle have helpfully distinguished the concept 'belligerency' (state of war) from 'belligerence' (the social experience of the conflict).[17] Following this approach, Argentine humanitarian mobilisation clearly constituted a form of belligerence. During the war years Argentine society developed an intense social and cultural activism, which was expressed in the polarisation of public opinion, passionate debates in the press, massive street demonstrations, and the enlistment of volunteers to fight in the war. But this social belligerence also gave rise to myriad humanitarian initiatives, which were not usually considered at odds with official neutrality. While the government refrained from actively encouraging humanitarian engagement, it did not restrain it either.

Information about the humanitarian mobilisation of Argentine society is fragmentary and scattered. The Argentine press – especially that of national scope – is fundamental to reconstructing Argentine contributions to aiding wartime Europe. Argentine newspapers daily reported on the countless charity activities organised throughout the country. When complemented with other primary sources (such as the records of charities, books of remembrance, and diplomatic correspondence), the press reports can illuminate Argentina's humanitarian endeavours. They provide an opportunity to examine how different actors sought to provide relief to the victims of the Great War.

In the following I will examine the initiatives of several actors, including European diaspora communities, the Argentine Red Cross, and social elites, to offer relief to the victims of the Great War.

Probably the most significant constituency involved in relief operations in Argentina were the European diaspora populations. The immigrant communities settled in the country were an essential source of humanitarian aid to Europe. Between 1857 and 1914, 4.6 million immigrants arrived in Argentina. On the eve of the Great War, the foreign-born made up 29.9 per cent of the total population of 7,885,237. This figure placed Argentina second (behind the United States) as an immigration country; and although the United States welcomed more immigrants (27 million) in absolute terms, the ratio of foreign-born to native-born was higher in the South American country.[18]

With the outbreak of the war these European communities devoted themselves to raising funds for their homelands' war effort. Long-standing social and cultural associations worked closely with special wartime committees, founded in the first weeks of the war to centralise and co-ordinate patriotic mobilisation.[19] These committees soon became active across Argentina, reaching wherever immigrant communities had settled. Women in particular spearheaded many of these charitable activities, capitalising on the prevailing gender roles associated with social care. Some of them also joined their home countries' Red Cross societies as nurses,[20] or, in the case of the British, as workers in supply depots or ammunition factories, as ambulance drivers, signallers, censors, clerks in the areas of intelligence and communications or military departments, and farmers in the Women's Land Army.[21]

These immigrant communities collected money for myriad patriotic funds, war loans, and Red Cross Societies (see Figure 1.1).

Frequently immigrant groups co-operated with 'allied' immigrant communities, as can be seen from joint initiatives (see figure 1.2).

Figure 1.1 Poster inviting the subscription of the French Liberation Loan in 1918

The funds they raised primarily assisted wounded soldiers and civilian war victims. However, some communities also apportioned some resources to help the families of local soldiers fighting on foreign battlefields and those of disabled veterans. This was particularly true of the communities from the central empires, which devoted most of the money raised to support their compatriots who found themselves put out of work as a result of the Allied blacklisting of 'enemy' firms in Argentina.[22] The Allied blockade made it difficult anyway to remit money, let alone goods, for the Central Powers across the Atlantic. The German community also used its resources to join Argentine Germanophiles in challenging the pro-Allied

Figure 1.2 Advertisement of the department store A la Ciudad de Londres in Buenos Aires, announcing two days of sales in aid of the allied Red Cross societies. The allied countries' Red Cross societies backed this solidary activity. It shows the co-operation established by the European communities and local customers' contribution to the European war effort

stance of public opinion. Their most remarkable propaganda initiative was the Spanish-language newspaper *La Unión*, which appeared for the entire duration of the war.[23] As John Horne has stated, mobilisation involved not only a response to the state's call but also a high degree of self-mobilisation within civil society.[24] From overseas, immigrant communities resorted to humanitarian work to feel close to their former compatriots, to reassert their love of and loyalty to the homeland and to make a contribution to that war effort. Even as they resided far from the battlefields, raising funds and volunteering their labour was a highly meaningful way to 'join' a larger national cause.

Immigrants had a strong presence in Argentina and their humanitarian endeavours often garnered considerable support from the wider Argentinian society. However, some of their activities also imperilled Argentina's rights as a neutral. Representatives of foreign Red Cross societies (more specifically, British, French, and Italian ones), for example, seemed to move all too freely across Argentina. The Argentine Red Cross society denounced 'the abuses that foreign Red Crosses were committing with impunity in our territory', infringing the International Red Cross Committee's General Statutes and the provisions of the Geneva Convention.[25] Their activity implied a jurisdictional conflict and an unfair competition with the neutral stance of the Argentine Red Cross, which was left wondering:

> How to admit that within a neutral country, entities invoking the name of the societies of belligerent countries can be organised and function without any knowledge or intervention by the government, or the national association that has the exclusive use of the name, emblem and badges of the Red Cross within its own territory?[26]

This issue led to repeated internal debate but ultimately prudence prevailed. One of the considerations that weighed in favour of not sanctioning belligerent Red Cross societies was the 'exceptional situation' the war had placed on their countries from a humanitarian perspective. At the same time Argentine caution was to avoid misunderstandings that could compromise Argentina's official neutrality or social harmony. Tolerance towards the belligerents' Red Cross societies could be interpreted as tacitly taking sides, allowing the Allies to collect money for the war effort and contradicting official neutrality. However, a more severe attitude, it was feared, 'could be interpreted as an obstacle to the natural expansiveness of those who, even far from the theatre of war, are linked to combatants by ties of patriotism, blood and other multiple interests'.[27] The Argentine Red Cross authorities consulted the ICRC about the attitude to adopt. The Geneva Committee recognised that the American Red Cross had raised similar concerns during the Balkan Wars. It recommended a 'certain elasticity in the application of prescriptions' but suggested the Argentine Red Cross exercise a 'certain supervision' by insisting that belligerent Red Cross societies receive official authorisation from the local society before undertaking any activities on Argentine soil. This, the ICRC hoped, would also inspire public confidence and obtain better fundraising results.[28] In its 1916 Annual Report, the Argentine Red Cross recorded with satisfaction that the abuses in the use of its name had notably decreased and that foreign entities had shown greater willingness to request its permission to raise funds.[29] However, once the war was over, some associations continued without proper authorisation, leading the Argentine government to establish exclusive rights for the Argentine Red Cross.[30] That it chose to do so after rather than during the war suggests an abiding concern to avoid compromising Argentine and Red Cross neutrality.

This is not to say that the Argentine Red Cross was completely inactive. A few days after the outbreak of the conflict, it launched a national subscription 'for the benefit of the wounded and victims of the current war, whose total amount would be remitted to the Geneva International Committee for equitable distribution according to the needs of the different nations at war'.[31] Almost all the theatres and cinemas in Buenos Aires, as well as schools and other civil associations around the country, subscribed to this campaign. However, the most significant part (73 per cent) of the 78,000 F (US$15,309) ultimately remitted to Geneva came from the Congressional appropriation mentioned above. Besides its modest fundraising efforts, the Argentine Red Cross also forwarded mail addressed to war internees in the country, such as the crew of the *Cap Trafalgar*, a German merchant-turned-war ship sunk by the British in the Atlantic in September 1914. As was customary, the Argentine government interned the survivors and took care of them until the war's end. Most of the two thousand items of correspondence the Argentine Red Cross had forwarded by early 1919 belonged to these seamen.[32]

It would be wrong to reduce Argentine humanitarianism to either the contributions of the immigrant communities or the limited actions of the national Red Cross society. On the contrary, individuals and groups of varied social backgrounds organised to relieve the war victims. They resorted to activities similar to those of immigrant communities: auctions and bazaars that sold war memorabilia and books, donated by authors or publishers; cultural and artistic shows, including theatre and musical performances, as well as conferences, film screenings, raffles, and sporting events. Some charity events were guided by an entertainment logic, intending to lure more participants and, consequently, raise more funds. Other activities – such as lectures, photography exhibitions, or films on the ravages of the war – were designed to raise awareness of the suffering provoked by the conflict and stimulate compassion and solidarity for its victims. In some cases, the organisers took advantage of the widespread curiosity about war technology to gain support for their campaigns. For instance, in 1917, the Comité Franco-Argentino held an Allied Exhibition in Buenos Aires for the benefit of different allied funds, which displayed uniforms and weapons (artillery, aeroplanes, mortars, rifles, machine guns, ammunition, gas masks) which had seen service in several battles, mainly at the Marne.[33] A small-scale replica of a trench system proved a particular attraction of the exhibition, although the plane used by Vicente Almandos Almonacid – an Argentine volunteer and ace of French aviation – also inspired the visitors' interest.[34] The Allied Exhibition sought to emphasise Allied military and technological superiority and give the public an indirect, yet tangible, connection to the real war experience.

That many of these humanitarian endeavours arose from an identification with the Allied cause is also suggested by who its main recipients were. Although the data is fragmentary, France, it seems, was the principal beneficiary of Argentine benevolence. This had much to do with Argentine perceptions of France and the engrained Francophilia of Argentine elites. At the beginning of the nineteenth century, republican and democratic France, associated with the universal principles of the 1789 Revolution, appeared as the perfect model to the leaders of the Latin American independence movements. By the middle of the century, France's image acquired a new dimension. It was no longer just the cradle of revolutions but also the mother of fine art and letters. This stimulated an exodus of Latin American intellectuals to Paris,[35] which was considered 'the Mecca of artistic pilgrimage',[36] and a place where cultural distinction and prestige might be acquired. For Latin American elites, France represented the pinnacle of sophistication and the epitome of Western progress. There was an active Latin American colony in Paris, some 4,200 strong, and mostly Brazilian and Argentine.[37] Before 1914 the social routine of the Argentine elite included frequent trips to France, especially Paris, and close contacts with the French capital's social and intellectual circles.[38]

In light of this background, as soon as the war broke out, Argentines residing in Biarritz began to raise funds for the wounded soldiers sent to convalesce in that town. Some also volunteered as nurses or stretcher-bearers, transporting the injured from the railway station to the improvised hospitals set up in hotels and casinos.[39] In early 1915 the Argentine colony launched a new fundraising campaign, encouraged by the plenipotentiary minister in France, Enrique Rodríguez Larreta, which led to the creation of a complete ambulance train (with an operating room, a sterilisation room, a hospital pharmacy, etc.),[40] twenty ambulance cars and a detachable operating room, the first of several such vehicles.[41] The wives of prominent figures of the Argentine community launched several charities, including the Work for the War Blind, founded by the wife of the landowner José Santamarina; a school for the rehabilitation of maimed soldiers, chaired by the wife of the entrepreneur Otto Bemberg; and the Society of Friends of the Artists, created by the painter Ernesto De la Cárcova's wife.[42] Mrs Josefa Dominga Balcarce – granddaughter of General José de San Martín, leader of the struggle for the independence of Argentina, Chile, and Peru – provides another example of the humanitarian contributions of the Argentine elite in France. She transformed her small palace in Brunoy into Auxiliary Hospital number 89, with a fifteen-acre rest garden, fifty beds, two operating rooms, a disinfection area, a radiology room, a laboratory, and a hydrotherapy facility.[43]

Probably the most remarkable humanitarian contribution of the Argentine community in France was the creation of the Hospital Argentino in Paris. With the support of the new plenipotentiary minister in France, Marcelo T. de Alvear, Argentine businessmen and landowners collected more than 180,000 F (US$31,228) and bought an apartment house at 14 Rue Jules Claretie, in the XVI arrondissement, near the Bois de Boulogne. The building was repurposed as a one-hundred-bed hospital,[44] with a 'large operating room; radiography, disinfection and pharmacy facilities; a dental consulting-room, etc., etc. [...] installed according to the strictest standards of hygiene, comfort and medical science'. Registered as Auxiliary Hospital Auxiliar no 108, the French military authorities classified it as 'first-class evacuation hospital for seriously injured soldiers'.[45] Unlike other foreign healthcare facilities established in France during the war, the Argentine Hospital's medical staff were drawn exclusively from Argentine doctors: Lorenzo Moss, Enrique Finochietto, Enrique Beretervide, Rafael Cisneros, and Rodolfo Quesada Pacheco.[46] Other Argentine doctors served as sanitary volunteers in France. Pedro Chutro, for example, was in charge of the Auxiliary Hospital's surgery section installed in the Lycée Buffon in Paris, where he performed more than a thousand complex surgeries.[47] The French government later recognised the labour of these Argentine doctors with the Legion of Honour.[48]

A conservative estimation of Argentine society's contribution to the French cause indicates that, by mid-1917, it had sent around 15 million F to France (US$2,602,360): a figure that placed Argentina third among American donors, behind the United States and Canada.[49]

Belgium stands out as the other main recipient of Argentine humanitarian aid. The violation of Belgian neutrality in August 1914 and subsequent German war crimes against civilians (so-called 'atrocities') became fundamental to the Allies' cultural mobilisation and the propaganda they directed at neutral audiences.[50] In this Belgian suffering both during and after the

German invasion played a major role. The events of August 1914 provoked the exodus of tens of thousands of refugees, while the harsh occupation regime, including requisitions, forced deportations, and tight rationing, placed the Belgian population in dire straits. The British naval blockade, which prevented overseas imports, aggravated the Belgian food situation.[51] The Belgian drama touched belligerent and neutral publics and generated a wave of sympathy across the globe. Whereas aid to France and other allied countries focused on supporting injured or disabled soldiers, humanitarian initiatives in Belgium were mainly directed towards relieving civilians, especially women and children.

The constant supply of allied propaganda and the harrowing accounts sent from Brussels by the Argentine writer Roberto J. Payró to the newspaper *La Nación*, the country's second most read newspaper, were vital in raising Argentine awareness about the war's violence and the need for humanitarian redress.[52] Payró himself appealed to his readers to aid the Belgian people and forwarded the appeal to other Argentine newspapers via telegram:

> The international relief congress, humanitarian and strictly neutral, asks the great Argentine newspapers to organise – as they decide more effective – subscriptions in money, clothing, and food for the victims of the war in Belgium, whom misery threatens cruelly this winter.[53]

Payró's appeal responded to the initiative of the US businessman Daniel Heineman, who convened neutral diplomats and other representatives in Brussels. Heineman was one of the central figures of the Belgian Comité National de Secours et d'Alimentation, which distributed in occupied Belgium the food aid provided by Herbert Hoover's Commission for Relief in Belgium.[54]

It is little known that there was an Argentine fundraising committee of the Commission, led by the rancher and entrepreneur Benito Villanueva. Villanueva worked alongside the Belgian banker Casimiro de Bruyn, who was the president of the Belgian War Committee, former Minister of Foreign Affairs Carlos Rodríguez Larreta, the president of the National Bank Manuel de Iriondo, the senator Adolfo Dávila, the director of *La Nación* Jorge Mitre, and representatives of cereal-exporting houses. In addition to collecting large quantities of food and clothing, the Committee received cash donations amounting to more than 1,500,000 pesos (US$627,248) which helped send several ships with wheat and corn to Belgium. In February 1915 the Commission's official branch was established in Buenos Aires, chaired by De Bruyn. It sent twenty-one ships with cereals, clothing, and canned food to Belgium.[55] The total charitable contributions sent from Argentina to the Commission reached

Table 1.1 Contributions to Belgian relief

Country	Public donations collected (US$)
US	32,109,863.69
British Empire	19,052,198.15
Argentina	200,608.77
Spain	39,455.13
Italy	34,993.66
China	20,724.13
Brazil	16,233.33

(*Source:* G. I. Gay and H. H. Fisher (eds), *Public Relations of the Commission for Relief in Belgium: Documents*, vol. 2 (Stanford: Stanford University Press, 1929), pp. 296–7.

US$200,608.77. That was far less than the donations raised in the USA or the British Empire, but far more than those raised in Spain, Italy, China, and Brazil, for instance (see Table 1.1).

There were many other initiatives for Belgium, too. In 1917 the Comité Argentino Pro Huérfanos Belgas (Argentine Committee for Belgian Orphans) was founded in Buenos Aires, presided over by the teacher Francisca Jacques, daughter of the famous French educator Amédée Jacques. Its main objective was to raise funds to build homes for the Belgian orphans. The Committee was supported by trading houses, which offered a percentage of their sales to the entity's beneficiaries on several occasions. It also encouraged Argentine children to make weekly contributions to its cause and organised cereal donations through regional committees.[56] The money collected by this Committee (100,000 F) (US$17,349, approximately $407,000 in 2023 prices) was used to buy a vast property in Uccle (Brussels) to accommodate forty-five Belgian orphan children. Inaugurated in September 1918, the Argentine Republic Home operated under the auspices of the Argentine consul Alberto Blancas, who acted as its honorary president.[57]

There are probably two main reasons why the Belgian cause found such a strong response with Argentine society. In the first place, the German violation of Belgian neutrality resonated greatly with other neutral countries because they felt themselves, potentially at least, at the whim of great-power force and aspirations. It also inspired a particular solidarity with the weak. Neutral Belgium came to symbolise the war's truly innocent suffering – a highly civilised country being crushed by overwhelming force for no apparent fault of its own. This was driven home by the civilian status and the great vulnerability of many Belgian victims, especially women and children. As such, and quite irrespective of Allied propaganda campaigns, 'poor little Belgium' had a profound effect on global opinion.

Perhaps more than any other country, it appeared uniquely deserving of international aid and sympathy.[58]

It must be noted, too, that although the populations of France and Belgium were mainly Catholic and Catholicism was the official religion of Argentina, solidarity with these countries was not inspired predominantly by religious sentiment or networks. Quite the contrary, many Catholics repudiated the French Republic for its secularism and the separation of Church and state, and Spanish religious orders were influenced by a deep hostility towards France due to historical and geopolitical factors, like the Napoleonic invasion of the Iberian peninsula and a division of Morocco considered detrimental to Spanish interests.[59] Moreover, the Argentine Church, in line with the Vatican's pacifism, limited itself to pilgrimages, masses, and prayers for peace: It did not carry out any humanitarian fundraising.[60] Importantly, while social and intellectual elites played a big role in raising donations for the Allies, there were also more modest and often anonymous contributions made by groups of very different social origins. For instance, students wove various items of clothing for allied soldiers;[61] postal employees made donations to help their Belgian colleagues who were refugees in the Netherlands;[62] and the Centre of Students of Architecture collected funds in favour of the mutilated students at the Paris School of Fine Arts.[63] There is little doubt that relief efforts were supported by a broad segment of Argentine society, whether bankers, diplomats, women's groups, or postal workers.

If we consider newspapers a reliable barometer of social mobilisation regarding the European war, the fact that most Argentine aid was directed towards the allied nations, especially France and Belgium, was significant. Clearly, this fact reflected the sympathies and affinities prevailing in Argentine society at large. This is especially clear when comparing it to Argentine aid to Italy or the United Kingdom, which remained modest in scale. Despite Italy's strong demographic links with Argentina, most contributions to its relief came from the Italian community, not Argentine society at large.[64] Likewise, the United Kingdom was the main destination of Argentine exports and the primary source of imports and investments, but it, too, received no substantial aid. The British invasions of the River Plate in 1806–7 and especially the sovereignty dispute over the Falkland/Malvinas islands since 1833 were still very much present among Argentines and contributed to anti-British sentiment.[65] Under these circumstances, admiration and compassion for Great Britain were limited.

Donations to the Central Powers were also comparatively small, even if there were a few initiatives. For instance, in 1914 the war correspondent Juan José de Soiza Reilly registered the remittance of a million marks

(US$236,407) to Germany to assist wounded German soldiers.[66] A number of Argentine doctors also volunteered for service with the German Red Cross, including Ernesto Gallardo, Urbano Fernández, and Carlos J. Torres, and the stretcher-bearer Carlos Alberto Moris.[67] Germany enjoyed the particular support of many Argentines working in law, medicine, the exact and natural sciences, and the military, that is, fields where German professional influence was particularly strong. Many Argentines in these fields had traditionally received their education in Germany and there existed myriad professional and social ties across the Atlantic.[68] However, the examples of material aid to the Central Empires were few and far between, especially when compared to pro-Allied campaigns.

How should we explain the preponderance of pro-Allied sentiment? In the first place, the focus on Western Europe reflected the mood of Argentine elites regarding civilisation models. France was conceived as a cultural and political paradigm for the Argentine Republic and, by extension, solidarity was conceded to its allies in the war. In addition Allied control of interoceanic communications (news agencies and telegraphic services) from the early days of the war meant that information reaching Argentina was filtered and mediated to suit an Allied agenda. In terms of wartime sympathies, this played an important role.[69] Besides, the demographic superiority of 'allied' communities (51 per cent of the foreign population over 6 per cent from the Central Powers) also explains the limited appeal of the Central Empires' cause among the Argentine public.[70]

Conclusions

Some conclusions can be drawn from the brief examination of Argentina's humanitarian actions during the war. In the first place, official neutrality, that is, non-belligerency, coexisted with passionate social belligerence, which cut across different social groups. That simultaneity reveals that diplomatic neutrality must not be equated with social indifference or impartiality regarding the war. Humanitarian contributions were often an expression of solidarity towards one or another warring faction. Still, they did not usually alter the widespread conviction that neutrality remained the foreign policy best suited to Argentine interests – at least until 1917.[71] While the Argentine executive remained aloof from the humanitarian campaigns, many diplomats serving in Europe showed a strong commitment to philanthropic activities aimed at the war victims. The Argentine ministers in France (first Enrique Rodríguez Larreta, then Marcelo T. de Alvear) and in Belgium (Alberto Blancas) played a crucial role in developing relevant charities to help allied soldiers and civilians.

The Argentine diplomatic body's dedication to humanitarian endeavours in their countries of service contrasted with the distance adopted officially by Argentina's government.

In the second place, humanitarian aid was not solely, perhaps not even primarily, concerned with objectively measured need. Rather it was a form of material co-operation based on close identification with a belligerent cause and intended to aid its war effort. While the Allies received the majority of humanitarian donations, the Central Powers enjoyed considerably less support. By contrast, as the fundraising efforts of the Argentine Red Cross showed, the campaigns focused on providing neutral relief registered only narrow outcomes. Great War humanitarianism was fuelled – to some degree at least – by the desire to take sides and express sympathies. As such the Great War witnessed considerable tensions not only between an international sphere of neutral humanitarian aid and the nationalism of the states at war, as Heather Jones has shown.[72] In neutral Argentina a biased humanitarianism prevailed on an impartial, neutral, nonpartisan relief. In this way Argentine humanitarian aid connected this neutral country with warring Europe, showing a decentred and interconnected geography of the Great War that defies traditional categorisations.

Notes

The research for this chapter was developed in the context of the Project UBACYT 20020190100007BA 'Argentina y los conflictos bélicos del siglo XX: una aproximación desde la historia social y cultural de la guerra', financed by the University of Buenos Aires (UBA), led by the author, and based in the Ravignani Institute – UBA/National Scientific and Technical Research Council – Argentina (CONICET), and a fellowship granted by the Hoover Institution – Stanford University for a research stay.

1. B. Little, 'An Explosion of New Endeavours: Global Humanitarian Responses to Industrialized Warfare in the First World War Era', *First World War Studies*, 5:1 (2014), 1–16.
2. M. I. Tato, *La trinchera austral: La sociedad argentina ante la Primera Guerra Mundial* (Rosario: Prohistoria, 2017).
3. J. A. Lanús, *Aquel apogeo: Política internacional argentina, 1910–1939* (Buenos Aires: Emecé, 2001), pp. 43–4, pp. 51–2.
4. Pesos moneda nacional, the Argentine currency at the time ('Ley n° 9501 acordando $25000 a la Cruz Roja Argentina con destino al socorro de las víctimas y heridos de la guerra europea', AH0066/1, 24, 33, Archivo del Ministerio de Relaciones Exteriores y Culto (AMREC), Primera Guerra Mundial, Buenos Aires, Argentina). This equated to $1.7 million in 2023 prices.

5 'Ley n° 9501', AH0066/1, 3, AMREC.
6 Ordinary General Meeting, 15 May 1915, *Libro de Actas del Consejo Directivo del 22/07/1912 al 20/12/1921*, Archivo de la Cruz Roja Argentina (henceforth ACRA, LACD), 135–6, Buenos Aires, Argentina. The author thanks the authorities of the Argentine Red Cross and especially Mrs Helena Capozzoli for granting access to these materials.
7 Ordinary Session, 31 July 1916, ACRA, LACD, 179.
8 'Otros auxilios para belgas víctimas de la guerra', 6, AH0066/3, AMREC.
9 'Otros auxilios para belgas víctimas de la guerra', 9, AH0066/3, AMREC.
10 'Otros auxilios para belgas víctimas de la guerra', 14, AH0066/3, AMREC.
11 'Sobre ayuda a Bélgica', 1, AH0067/2, AMREC.
12 'Sobre ayuda a Bélgica', 4, AH0067/2, AMREC.
13 A. Rayes, 'Los destinos europeos de las exportaciones argentinas durante la *gran expansión*', *REMS-Revista de Estudios Marítimos y Sociales*, 5/6 (November 2012/13), 119–27.
14 R. Weinmann, *Argentina en la Primera Guerra Mundial: neutralidad, transición política y continuismo económico* (Buenos Aires: Biblos – Fundación Simón Rodríguez, 1994), pp. 41–54; P. Gerchunoff and L. Llach, *El ciclo de la ilusión y el desencanto: Un siglo de políticas económicas argentinas* (Buenos Aires: Ariel, 2005), pp. 68–74.
15 Gerchunoff and Llach, *El ciclo de la ilusión*, pp. 69–70.
16 Lanús, *Aquel apogeo*, pp. 65–72.
17 O. Compagnon and P. Purseigle, 'Geographies of Mobilisation and Territories of Belligerence during the First World War', *Annales HSS* (English Edition), 71:1 (2016), 49.
18 F. Devoto, *Historia de la inmigración en la Argentina* (Buenos Aires: Sudamericana, 2003), p. 247; *Tercer Censo Nacional levantado el 1° de junio de 1914* (Buenos Aires: Talleres Gráficos L. J. Rosso & Cía., 1916), vol. II, pp. 395–96; 'U.S. Immigrant Population and Share over Time, 1850-Present', Migration Policy Institute, accessed 19 August 2019, www.migrationpolicy.org/programs/data-hub/charts/immigrant-population-over-time.
19 On the European communities' responses to the war see María Inés Tato, 'Identities in Tension: Immigrant Communities in Argentina and the Challenge of the Great War', *National Identities*, 24:1 (2020), 1–16, 5, https://doi.org/10.1080/14608944.2020.1745767.
20 'Cruces Rojas', *Caras y Caretas* (21 December 1918).
21 A. L. Holder, *Activities of the British Community in Argentina during the Great War 1914–1919* (Buenos Aires: The Buenos Aires Herald, 1920), pp. 249–51.
22 V. Kramer, 'Solidaridad étnica en tiempos de guerra: la Casa de Trabajo alemana en Rosario, 1916–17', in O. Compagnon, C. Foulard, G. Martin, and M. I. Tato (eds), *La Gran Guerra en América Latina: Una historia conectada* (Mexico: CEMCA – IHEAL/CREDA, 2018), pp. 429–44; G. W. Zimmerli, 'La Cruz Roja Alemana', *Germania*, 11:1 (November 1915).
23 M. I. Tato, 'Fighting for a Lost Cause? The Germanophile Newspaper *La Unión* in Neutral Argentina, 1914–1918', *War in History*, 25:4 (2018), 473;

La Unión, similarly to most national newspapers, published between 25,000 and 50,000 copies per day, although exact circulation numbers vary according to sources.

24 J. Horne, 'Introduction: Mobilising for "Total War", 1914–1918', in J. Horne (ed.), *State, Society and Mobilisation in Europe during the First World War* (Cambridge: Cambridge University Press, 1997), pp. 5–7.
25 Extraordinary Session, 5 November 1915, 156–7, ACRA, LACD.
26 Extraordinary Session, 5 November 1915, 167, ACRA, LACD.
27 Ordinary General Meeting, 4 June 1917, 200, ACRA, LACD.
28 Ordinary General Meeting, 4 June 1917, 201–2, ACRA, LACD.
29 Ordinary General Meeting, 4 June 1917, 198, ACRA, LACD.
30 Ordinary Session, 16 May 1919, 269, ACRA, LACD.
31 Ordinary Session, 7 September 1914, 98, ACRA, LACD.
32 Ordinary General Meeting, 29 May 1920, 429, ARC, LACD.
33 The Comité Franco-Argentino was founded in Buenos Aires in 1917, chaired by the landowner Carlos Madariaga. Among others, it counted on the support of the former foreign ministers Luis María Drago and Manuel Augusto Montes de Oca, the French writer Paul Groussac, The French Chamber of Commerce, and the French Patriotic Committee.
34 Comité Franco-Argentino, *Exposición Aliada Guerra y Arte* (Buenos Aires: Comité Franco-Argentino, 1917); 'La Guerra', *La Prensa* (8 June 1917).
35 D. Rolland, *La crise du modèle français: Marianne et l'Amérique latine. Culture, politique et identité* (Rennes: Presses Universitaires de Rennes, 2000).
36 B. Colombi, 'Camino a la meca: Escritores hispanoamericanos en París (1900–1920)', in J. Meyers (ed.), *Historia de los intelectuales en América Latina*, vol. 1 (Buenos Aires: Katz Ediciones, 2009), p. 544.
37 In the 1920s Argentines formed the major colony: see J. Streckert, 'Latin Americans in Paris, 1870–1940: A Statistical Analysis', *Jahrbuch für Geschichte Lateinamerikas / Anuario de Historia de América Latina*, 49:1 (2012), 193–4.
38 L. Losada, *La alta sociedad en la Buenos Aires de la Belle Époque* (Buenos Aires: Siglo Veintiuno Editora Iberoamericana, 2008), pp. 151–66.
39 J. J. de Soiza Reilly, 'Panoramas de la guerra. Francia: Los hospitales de sangre', *La Nación*, 29 October 1914.
40 A. Sux, *Los voluntarios de la libertad: Contribución de los latino-americanos a la causa de los Aliados* (Paris: Ediciones Literarias, 1918), pp. 43–5.
41 J. de París, 'Ambulancias argentinas en la Cruz Roja Francesa', *Caras y Caretas* (9 July 1915).
42 Sux, *Los voluntarios de la libertad*, pp. 48–9.
43 H. C. Gotta, J. Buroni, A. Buzzi, A. Sahores, A. Moreno, and M. Sanguina Caballero, *Apoyo de sanidad de los argentinos a los franceses en la Primera Guerra* (Buenos Aires: Editorial Alfredo Buzzi, 2017), p. 76.
44 Gotta et al., *Apoyo de sanidad*, p. 106.
45 Sux, *Los voluntarios de la libertad*, pp. 43–7.
46 Gotta et al., *Apoyo de sanidad*, p. 106.

47 Ibid., p. 90.
48 Ibid., p. 90, p. 124, p. 140.
49 This equates to $61 million in 2023 prices. Sux, *Los voluntarios de la libertad*, pp. 49–50.
50 J. Horne and A. Kramer, *1914: Les atrocités allemandes. La vérité sur les crimes de guerre en France et en Belgique* (Paris: Tallandier, 2011), pp. 28–9; A. Rasmussen, 'Mobilising Minds', in J. Winter (ed.), *The Cambridge History of the First World War*, vol. 3 (Cambridge: Cambridge University Press, 2014), pp. 399–400.
51 For an overview of the invasion and occupation of Belgium see S. de Schaepdrijver, *La Belgique et la Première Guerre mondiale* (Brussels: Peter Lang, 2006).
52 On Payró's war chronicles see M. I. Tato, 'Trapped in Occupied Brussels: Roberto J. Payró's War Experience, 1914–1915', in F. Rash and C. Declercq (eds), *The Great War in Belgium and the Netherlands: Beyond Flanders Fields* (London: Palgrave Macmillan, 2018), pp. 143–61; *La Nación* had a daily circulation of 110,000–120,000 copies.
53 R. J. Payró, 'Destrucción: La guerra vista desde Bruselas (Diario de un testigo)', article dated 9. October 1914 and published *in La Nación* (12 April 1915), in R. J. Payró, *Corresponsal de guerra: Cartas, diarios, relatos (1907–1922)* (Buenos Aires: Biblos, 2009), p. 883.
54 On the Commission and Herbert Hoover's role see G. Nash, *The Life of Herbert Hoover: The Humanitarian, 1914–1917* (New York: W. W. Norton, 1988), and *The Life of Herbert Hoover: Master of Emergencies, 1917–1918* (New York: W. W. Norton, 1996). For a critical assessment of this institution see E. Piller, 'American War Relief, Cultural Mobilization, and the Myth of Impartial Humanitarianism, 1914–17', *The Journal of the Gilded Age and Progressive Era*, 17:4 (2018), 619–35.
55 'Acción de los belgas', in A. Gerchunoff and A. Bilis (eds), *El álbum de la victoria* (Buenos Aires: E. Danon, 1920), unnumbered page; 'Subsidio de $100.000 votado por el Senado argentino a favor de los desvalidos belgas', 1915, AH/0066/2, 4, 12, AMREC. 8.1 per cent of the relief supplies (most of them purchased) came from Argentina behind the US's 60.2 per cent and Canada's 19.4 per cent (G. I. Gay and H. H. Fisher, *Public Relations of the Commission for Relief in Belgium: Documents* (Stanford: Stanford University Press, 1929), vol. 2, p. 474.
56 'La guerra', *La Prensa*, 14 April 1917; 6 May 1917; 21 November 1917; 14 December 1917.
57 'Informe de la Legación argentina en Bélgica sobre inauguración del asilo de huérfanos con fondos enviados por el comité belga instalado en esta capital', 1919, AH/0067/17, 1–6, AMREC.
58 M. Abbenhuis and I. Tames, *Global War, Global Catastrophe: Neutrals, Belligerents and the Transformation of the First World War* (London: Bloomsbury, 2022), pp. 28–42.
59 Tato, *La trinchera austral*, p. 104.
60 Ibid., pp. 114–15.
61 'La caridad y la guerra', *Caras y Caretas* (1 January 1915).

62 'Subsidio de los empleados de Correo y Telégrafos para sus colegas belgas refugiados en Holanda', 1915, AH/0066/4, AMREC.
63 'La guerra', *La Prensa*, 12 October 1917.
64 On the Italian community's contribution to its homeland's war effort see M. I. Tato, 'Italianitá d'oltremare: La comunità italiana di Buenos Aires e la guerra', in A. Scartabellati, M. Ermacora, and F. Ratti (eds), *Fronti interni: Esperienze di guerra lontano dalla guerra* (Naples: Edizione Scientifiche Italiane, 2014), pp. 213–26.
65 This last issue was particularly exploited by German propaganda during the war. M. I. Tato, 'La cuestión Malvinas y las batallas por la neutralidad argentina durante la Gran Guerra', in M. I. Tato and L. Esteban Dalla Fontana (eds), *La cuestión Malvinas en la Argentina del siglo XX: Una historia social y cultural* (Rosario: Prohistoria Ediciones, 2020), pp. 17–38.
66 J. J. de Soiza Reilly, '*Fray Mocho* en la guerra: En Alemania', article dated in Berlin 16 December 1914 and published in *Fray Mocho* 143 (22 January 1915).
67 Ibid.
68 Rolland, *La crise du modèle français*, p. 143.
69 Tato, *La trinchera austral*, pp. 39–41.
70 *Tercer Censo Nacional*, pp. 395–6.
71 In 1917 German submarine warfare, the entry of the United States into the war and the so-called 'Luxburg affair' eroded that certainty and led to the polarisation of public opinion between neutralists and promoters of severing relationships with Germany: see Tato, *La trinchera austral*, pp. 119–40.
72 H. Jones, 'International or Transnational? Humanitarian Action during the First World War', *European Review of History / Revue Européenne d'Histoire*, 16:5 (2009), 699–701.

2

Sagas of swords, scrolls, and dolls: Japanese humanitarian aid to Belgium

Hanne Deleu

Introduction

> To the brave Russian and Belgian soldiers: let this package of Japanese tea, which carries the devotion of the Japanese people, serve as a way to quench the thirst from your daily victories, and let it multiply your courage as we pray that you do not abandon the beautiful reward that is victory.

This encouraging message was imprinted in French on ten thousand bags of Japanese green tea to be donated to Belgian soldiers in 1914.[1] It is just one example of the many donations Japan made to Belgium during the First World War, which included not just substantial funds and many small, often hand-made, tokens of sympathy but also thousands of old Japanese manuscripts and scrolls, a decorated vase for the Belgian royal family, and even a sword for King Albert I.

While Japan's military contribution to the Great War remained rather limited, the nation continued to aid Belgium – which the Japanese press continuously presented as a small and young nation inhabited by an infinitely heroic and brave population – until 1926. A diverse pool of actors, ranging from Japanese officials to women's organisations to large corporations, encouraged, organised, and financially supported these humanitarian campaigns. During the Great War Japan came alive with collections for a faraway country few Japanese had previously had any connection to – but why?

This chapter will explore the Japanese humanitarian activities for Belgium during and after the Great War, paying special attention to the plethora of motivations and objectives that propelled the country's charitable activities. While scholars have shown that Japan's political and economic involvement in Great War-era Europe was part of the nation's quest for international acknowledgement, they have so far neglected its various humanitarian efforts.[2] This neglect is perhaps most perplexing with regard to the humanitarian campaigns for Belgium, which were not only among the period's largest but also reached furthest into Japanese civil society.

Because these aid campaigns benefited a country that had previously played little role in Japanese debates or imaginations, the Belgian case brings the motivations behind Japanese aid into especially bold relief. The chapter not only focuses on official contributors but includes the efforts of those who at first sight would not be considered diplomatic brokers: Japanese women, journalists, and businessmen. It identifies the main motivations that drove contributors to sacrifice time and money to help people living on the other side of the world. In this way the chapter reveals the truly global reverberations of events on the Western front, explores significant shifts in Japanese society, and provides some historical answers to the perennial question of why societies and individuals save strangers at all.

Based on extensive analysis of two national high-circulation newspapers, the *Asahi shinbun* (est. 1879) and the *Yomiuri shinbun* (est. 1874), the chapter shows that three major motives inspired donation campaigns for the Belgian population and the royal family. First, part of the Japanese population was driven by a sense of emotional connection and responsivity. This sentimental investment in the Belgian cause and empathetic reaction to its perils reflected a range of reasons, including Japanese experiences after the First Sino-Japanese War (1894–95) and the Russo-Japanese War (1904–5) and an emotional response to wartime images and news reporting, as well as a general sense of compassion. Secondly, the act of fundraising for an international ally such as Belgium provided an opportunity for individuals, organisations, and companies to embody, rehearse, and perform patriotism. For Japan, Belgium became a sort of model nation, both through its prominent position in the political and industrial world order, as well as through its patriotic defiance of foreign interference. Japanese girls and women in particular were encouraged to show their patriotism by practising domestic skills, such as handicrafts, and their involvement was a practical expression and performance of new gendered expectations towards women. For Japanese corporations, too, donations to the Belgian population and royal family became a way to prove their loyalty not so much to the Belgian as to the *Japanese* cause. It is not without a certain irony that participating in international humanitarian efforts affirmed and communicated national belonging and patriotic sentiment. Finally, humanitarian aid intended to present Japan as a reliable and civilised ally. It was rooted in a desire to prove that Japan was a sophisticated global power worthy of standing equally at the side of its allies in the larger international political and economic theatre.

These three sets of motivations – sympathy, patriotism, and search for international recognition – must be understood as ideal types, of course to be sure. In reality, Japanese wartime charity was multifaceted, often serving a variety of overlapping purposes at the same time. As such, the

Japanese case exemplifies how humanitarian aid is never a purely political, economic, military, or even humanitarian activity. Nor is it the sole domain of state representatives, governments, or public institutions. Instead, Japanese humanitarian aid to Belgium was born from the labour, investment, and interests of various participants. As such, it is a powerful reflection of the global dimensions of the Great War as well as a unique window into how Japanese civil society engaged locally with and made sense of that conflict.

Compassion and emotional connectivity

Looking at various motivations behind Japanese aid to Belgium one needs to look first at the mediation of Belgian suffering and the emotional responses and acts of compassion it elicited. From 1914 onward the Belgian fate resonated strongly with the Japanese people, with humanitarian aid serving as the most immediate reflection of that concern. At first glance the Japanese concern for Belgium might appear startling, given the relatively fleeting interactions between the two societies before the war.[3] The spontaneous compassion and sympathy that many Japanese seem to have felt towards Belgium were the product of two important developments.

The first were the emotive images and writings created by the Japanese media. In the decades prior to the war lower production costs, increased advertisement revenues, and greater literacy had resulted in the expansion and rising popularisation of print media in Japan, especially newspapers and magazines. Beginning with the German invasion in August 1914 and continuing during the war years, Japanese media reported on Belgium with great frequency and often substantial depth.[4] Throughout they highlighted the brutal nature of the German army's advance, the extent of destruction and the desperate plight of the population. The cruelty of Belgium's wartime reality was often described in vivid and lugubrious detail. 'No one can dispute,' wrote the *Yomiuri shinbun* in representative fashion in January 1915,

> that the most miserable of them all are the Belgian people, whose country is being overrun by the soldiers and horses of other countries, who have no home, no food to eat, and no time to think of the greying elderly freezing in the cold. Even if one's wife or daughter is crying of starvation with a baby at their breast, they cannot be saved. Little girls weep tears of blood with no way to protect themselves, infants wander the streets without a guardian, and those who take the slightest opportunity to seek refuge in other countries do not know whether their husbands or fathers are alive or dead.[5]

Dramatic titles such as 'How the People of Belgium Are Suffering from the Tyranny of the German Army: An Unprecedented Tragedy'[6] or 'A Feast of Torture: Belgian Tears, German Inhumanity'[7] illustrate how these media drew the reader's attention and harnessed the sentimental quality of sensational reporting.

The harrowing images conjured up by these writings were strongly reinforced by visual representations of Belgian suffering. Previous scholarship has identified the propagandist and emotive value of visual media, especially with regard to inspiring compassion, and this was certainly true in the Japanese case.[8] Alongside pictures published in newspapers and magazines, theatre plays, magic lantern shows, newsreels, and exhibitions visually presented the deprivation of the Belgian population and managed to invoke strong emotional responses among spectators across Japan. Lantern slideshows seem to have been of particular importance for Japan's humanitarian mobilisation and were used by Belgian officials and Japanese organisations alike. In 1915 the Belgian Consul General in Yokohama, Charles Basten, gave a lecture at Waseda University about the tragedies taking place in Belgium, using magic lantern slides to illustrate Belgians' ordeal, and, as the *Yomiuri shinbun* surmised, 'to raise sympathy from the university students'.[9] Later, in February 1917, the *Asahi shinbun* organised its own magic lantern show in an Osaka youth centre, with the projections being accompanied by a translated testimony written by the Belgian Consul General in Kobe.[10] Two months later, a magic lantern slideshow presenting scenes from destroyed Belgian landscapes, pictures of Belgian refugees, and the royal family were shown at a school in Tokyo. Two thousand people, including parents and their children, paid to witness these tragic images, and the proceeds were donated to aid the Belgian victims. According to the newspaper reporting on the event, the projections had 'moved the visitors deeply'.[11] Lantern slideshows were complemented by other visual representations. In May 1918, the translated version of the Russian writer Leonid Andreyev's theatre piece 'The Sorrows of Belgium' was performed by a Japanese theatre group.[12] Portraying Belgium as the main character who provides shelter and solace to a mad girl – meant to represent the tormented Belgian population – the story honoured Belgian wartime patriotism and confronted the audience with the misery of war.[13] Newsreels, screened in movie theatres and occasionally accompanied by live narration, also featured images of the ongoing war. With titles such as 'We Should Have Sympathy for Belgium: The German Army's Tyranny'[14] and 'Belgium Leuven's Misery After the War',[15] these media actively put a spotlight on humanitarian disasters. Photo exhibitions of the war in Belgium also confronted the Japanese public with the terror experienced by the small nation.[16] Not all of these presentations directly asked for donations, but they did raise awareness of the humanitarian costs of war and arguably shrank the emotional, and for a while geographical, distance between Belgium and Japan. Importantly, theatre plays, lectures, magic lantern shows, and newsreels all targeted different audiences, reaching beyond those who would normally buy or read newspapers or wartime magazines. Writings and visualisations of that sort helped carry the news on the sorrows of Belgians into different strata of Japanese society and presented Belgian distress as immediate and actionable.

Although media coverage played a significant role in eliciting responses to Belgian distress in Japan (as elsewhere), the strong resonance rested also on historical experiences particular to Japan. True, Japanese civilians had never experienced modern warfare on a similar scale at home, but they did understand its devastating consequences. Already two decades earlier, the First Sino-Japanese War had highlighted the need for welfare support of veterans and their dependents.[17] At the time, nurses tended to war victims and noblewomen raised funds for bereaved families.[18] Ten years later, during and after the Russo-Japanese War, myriad private organisations continued to deal with its humanitarian fallout by offering their services to veteran families, orphans, or widows.[19] These recent experiences ensured that newspaper articles titled 'Relief for Belgian Children'[20] or 'Grand Opera Benefit for Belgian Orphans'[21] resonated more strongly with the Japanese public and were often immediately comprehensible and meaningful to them. While one can partly attribute Japanese aid to political or nationalist aspirations (see below), ignoring its sentimental motivations would yield a skewed and incomplete picture. More so perhaps than diplomats or industrialists, private donors established an emotional connection to the Belgian cause that drove and bolstered fundraising campaigns.

Embodying and performing patriotism through charity

Yet it would be wrong to attribute Japanese aid only to an often spontaneous sense of sympathy and compassion. In fact, aid was not only inspired by emotional responses but also and increasingly became a stage for the performance of patriotic sentiments. Successively after 1914, aiding Belgium became a public demonstration of a donor's dedication to the Japanese nation's domestic convictions and international ambitions. This not only applied to wealthy philanthropists or state representatives but was also evident in Japanese civil society more generally. For women's organisations as well as companies, humanitarian acts became a public platform to ascertain and act out their patriotism.

This patriotic dimension of aid is especially notable with regard to Japanese girls and women. By contributing to the international war effort, humanitarian aid provided them an opportunity to exert their national citizenship. As scholars have shown, many women's organisations, such as the Canadian Six Nations Women's Patriotic League or the American Young Women's Christian Association, provided relief not solely for their own soldiers and their dependants but also for the Belgian population. International wartime charity allowed women to cultivate and perform their patriotism, while also enhancing the international perception of their nation.[22] Similar mechanisms were at play in Japan. From the first, women played a paramount role in aiding Belgium. In January 1915 the Japanese Ladies' Solidarity organisation for Belgium was founded in Tokyo. Headed by two famous female educators, Fusako Yamawaki and Umeko Tsuda, the organisation was supported by many wealthy noblewomen. Early on the organisation located itself in a wider global movement. 'In order to sympathise with the poor Belgian people,' the association proclaimed, 'our society of women, like those in Europe and the United States, has organised a Belgian sympathy association.'[23] Eventually, by selling hand-sewn dolls made by female students, nationwide fundraising calls, and financial support from the Imperial Household, the organisation managed to collect over ¥50,000, for which the Belgian Queen herself expressed gratitude.[24] These activities were but a small part of wider female involvement. Several girls' schools, for example, agreed to teach their students about the ongoing war and asked them to put aside some of the money which they earned by 'doing handicrafts or other things they felt confident about'.[25] Japanese Red Cross Society nurses also organised several charity events, including a charity night at the Imperial Theatre[26] and a collection of money for bandages for the Belgian army.[27] In a similar vein the wives of both foreign and Japanese diplomats and female members of the Imperial Household ran and attended charitable events for members of the upper class, including bazaars and benefit concerts. So completely did the *Yomiuri shinbun* identify Belgian fundraising as a female endeavour that it confined most of its reporting on these events to the newspaper's 'women's section'.[28] Looking at this female mobilisation it becomes clear that humanitarian aid was a prominent means of expressing wartime patriotism to a global audience. The Japanese Ladies' Solidarity organisation for Belgium, for example, explained its wide-ranging fundraising campaign with its determination 'to live up to our name as a first-class country'.[29]

In the Japanese context, charity as an expression of patriotism was linked to new social expectations towards women, which crystallised in the 'good wife, wise mother' concept that had emerged in the mid-Meiji period. According to this new gendered ideal, caring for children, older people, or the sick unburdened the state, and thus became an act of selfless patriotism.

Japanese women became the fosters of the state, nursing the nation through their devotion to those the state did not succeed in helping.[30] The patriotic wartime mobilisation of women or girls through charity had already been visible during the Russo-Japanese War. In 1904, female students had prepared care packages for Japanese soldiers abroad and donated the money they raised by selling handmade goods at a school bazaar.[31] A Catholic girls' school in Tokyo organised a Christmas market and donated the proceedings to the Army Ministry.[32] Fulfilling one's patriotic duties through charity, and using the opportunity to further develop domestic skills such as needlework, was also supported by women's associations which sought to educate women on their roles and duties in society.[33] Accordingly, selling tea at a charity bazaar for Belgian children was seen as the perfect occasion to teach young girls the virtues and skills needed to prepare tea, as befitting of a loyal daughter, good wife, wise mother, and patriotic citizen.[34] In 1917 the Japanese government in a study on female wartime contributions in Europe itself affirmed the benefits of practical and educative charity, such as handicrafts, by women's groups.[35]

Yet charitable acts not only offered a stage for the performance of Japanese patriotism, they also, by reflecting on the courageous acts of defiance committed by the Belgian population, taught the Japanese public what ideal patriotism looked like. By celebrating Belgian women's courage, for example, they were to educate Japanese women on the patriotic value of personal sacrifice, frequently expressed through a selfless desire to protect one's nation and children. For example, the article 'Women and Children also Pick Up Their Swords: Awaking Belgium' described the valour of Belgian women and how protecting their families always remained their priority.[36] Another sensational depiction of Belgian women defending their country can be found in a picture in the *Yomiuri shinbun*, showing female soldiers carrying large rifles at their sides.[37] In 1918 an article titled 'Belgian Women during Wartimes Do Not Play to the Tune of the Enemy' recounted how a Belgian woman, prompted by a German soldier to play the piano, had brazenly played the national anthem.[38] Following a similar line of dramatic reporting, the wartime magazine *The Truthful Accounts of the European War* published a number of anecdotes from a young Belgian nurse under the title 'The True Accounts of a Brave Belgian Nurse'.[39] The courage of Belgian soldiers and the royal family was also addressed in multiple publications, often headed by captivating titles such as 'The Praiseworthy Belgian Army',[40] 'Belgians Mocking the German Army',[41] or the slightly more cinematic: 'The Belgian King Boards a Balloon to Reconnoitre the Enemy's Position'.[42] This tendency to celebrate Belgian patriotism and bravery was also apparent in the 1918 monograph *Belgium's Righteous War* – a publication in which Japanese state representatives projected Japanese national values on to the Belgian population and its acts of patriotic intrepidness.[43] These and other publications presented Belgium and its population as a patriotic model and aiding them became a means of rehearsing and performing Japanese patriotism through charitable sacrifices.[44]

In all this, popular print media, such as newspapers and magazines, played a profound role. Not only did they craft humanitarian narratives and disseminate information on charity events but they also helped reinforce their patriotic framing. For example, newspapers regularly printed donor rolls that made public and celebrated individual generosity and (financial) sacrifice. They often expressed particular appreciation for the smallest yet most selfless donations, such as the 50 sen (one sen is one hundredth of one yen) donated by a seventy-four-year-old man who sympathised with the misfortune of Belgians after having lost his own house in a fire.[45] Such reporting certainly elicited additional giving; even more importantly perhaps, it made sure that patriotic giving (or lack thereof) became public knowledge and hence could be rewarded (or sanctioned). Individual donors could be publicly recognised for demonstrating their loyalty to Japan's suffering ally and, effectively, to Japan itself.

In some instances, newspaper companies went one step further and initiated their own fundraising endeavours, no doubt hoping to use this display of patriotic humanitarianism to acquire symbolic capital and boost circulation. Such was the case with *Asahi shinbun*. From February 1915 on it published a series of forty-seven announcements titled 'Sympathy Money for Belgium', launching a three-month-long fundraising campaign. The initial editorial explained how Belgium was being violated by German troops and called for 'Sympathy Money' to be sent to the newspaper.[46] The following months also illustrate the important nexus between Japanese giving and appropriate expressions of Belgian gratitude. Just four days after the beginning of the campaign, the *Asahi shinbun* published a letter in which the Belgian minister to Japan, Georges Della Faille, expressed his gratitude for the fundraising drive to the company in the name of his king, his government, and all Belgians.[47] On 15 May, another letter of gratitude was published together with an announcement that nearly ¥30,000 had been collected.[48] Later that year Della Faille reached out yet again with 'An Appeal to the Righteous Spirit of the Japanese to Support the Belgian People'. Newspaper fundraising thus opened a Belgian-Japanese dialogue and gave Belgians, in particular, a platform to reach out to the Japanese public.[49]

More curious and symbolic than the 'Sympathy Money' Campaign – but presumably driven by similar motivations – was the sixteenth-century sword which the newspaper company presented to the Belgian King Albert I in January 1915, affectionately calling him 'our Albert'. A written message accompanying the gift lauded Belgium's unparalleled courage and exalted its endeavour to exterminate injustice and protect humanity, even with its own fate at stake.[50] The journey of the sword from Japan to Belgium was covered heavily and *Asahi shinbun*'s overseas correspondent handed over the sword with great pathos. 'As a foreigner', he claimed to be deeply honoured to be allowed to unsheathe and present the weapon in front of a king on whose life a bounty had been placed by the enemy. He considered himself, as he made clear, a representative not only of the *Asahi shinbun* but also of the Japanese people. King Albert responded with gratitude and praised Japan as an industrially and military developed nation.[51] The *Asahi shinbun* responded to the king's message of appreciation by sponsoring a magic lantern event on suffering of the Belgian people.[52] The *Asahi shinbun* as a company had clearly come to recognise the value of associating itself with a patriotic cause like Belgium.

Judging from these examples, Japanese aid to Belgium acquired patriotic value in two ways. Firstly, Belgian citizens and their acts of defiance provided a template for what it meant to be patriotic and allowed the Japanese public to reflect on different ways in which they themselves could live up to their civic duties. At the same time, acts of transnational compassion, especially to heroic Belgium, helped to underline Japanese virtues and to publicly demonstrate and perform (gendered) notions of Japanese patriotism.

A political goodwill campaign

Finally, it must be acknowledged that Japanese humanitarian mobilisation, as spontaneous and heartfelt as it often was, was embedded in larger political agendas, most notably Japan's search for international recognition and equal standing. Japan's military involvement in the Great War, small though it was compared to that of its fellow Allied Powers, has been described less as an act of moral commitment to its allies than an imperial expansionist quest to gain a strong foothold in Asia. It has also been regarded as a strategic goodwill campaign, intent on gaining international recognition for Japan as a global power.[53] In fact, despite the revisions of the unequal treaties, established in the nineteenth century by mostly North American and Western European nations, the country had struggled to be accepted as a modernised and civilised state deserving of equal treatment. While extraterritoriality and unfair tariffs had been lifted domestically, Japanese citizens continued to face discrimination abroad. The California Alien Land Bill in 1913 is one example of the biased treatment of Japanese citizens by Western powers.[54] Racial inequality also surfaced in political discussions on international alliances. For example, the Anglo-Japanese Alliance had been renewed in 1911 chiefly to limit Japan's naval range and restrict the influx of Japanese immigrants in British territories.[55]

At the time Japan did not only want to be accepted as an equal, it also desired to be acknowledged as the leading power in East Asia. These sentiments would later lead Japan to push for the Racial Equality Clause in the League of Nations, but the rejection of the clause only highlighted the limits of Japan's global authority.[56] Still, Japan's methods of inspiring goodwill were not entirely exhausted. In the era of the Great War, humanitarian campaigns were a primary means to establish itself as a modern and benevolent nation. While presented as an act of selfless compassion, humanitarian aid also became a political tool, whether through its diplomatic implications or politically beneficial yields; and Japan was no exception.[57]

Several examples may illustrate the political dimension to Japanese aid. The 1915–16 mission of the Japanese Red Cross Society (JRCS) to Europe was one prominent effort of trying to achieve a positive reception of Japan's modernisation. Three groups of around twenty carefully selected JRCS nurses and doctors were sent on relief missions to the United Kingdom, France, and Russia. As members of the global Red Cross movement, these 'medical ambassadors' seemed particularly suited to represent the sophistication of Japan's medical science and advanced humanitarian organisation.[58] The organisation's president explicitly acknowledged that the mission would reflect both on the reputation of the JRCS and on 'the prestige of the Japanese empire'.[59] At Netley Royal Victoria Military Hospital (near Southampton in the United Kingdom) Japanese nurses and doctors cared for roughly 2,500 patients, effectively demonstrating the JRCS's ability to operate according to Western concepts of humanitarian values and practical standards.[60] Similar political hopes inspired the humane treatment of European prisoners of war held in Japan. Tales of friendships and co-operation between the prisoners and Japanese guards dominated future narrations of these events.[61] One newspaper editorial even claimed that Japan's treatment of PoWs should serve as an example to the rest of the world.[62] During the Great War humane treatment and humanitarian activities became means to prove and illustrate Japan's degree of development and civilisation.

Yet neither charitable efforts nor their political intentions were limited to (quasi-)state entities like the JRCS. Rather, the Great War continued pre-Meiji-era traditions of non-state interventionist approaches to welfare. Social relief in Japan had typically relied on local mutual aid and the mobilisation of social elites whose generosity was expected to limit the state's financial responsibility for the sick and poor.[63] Keeping this in mind, it is often hard to draw a clear line between private and public actors. This was apparent in the humanitarian efforts for Belgium. Private actors, such as the industrialist Shibusawa Eiichi or the aristocrat Satsuma Jirōhachi, acted as representatives of the Japanese state and assumed the financial burden of the government's international goodwill and humanitarian campaigns. One example is the Economic Association for the Sick and Wounded Soldiers of the Allied Nations established by Shibusawa in 1917. The organisation's board included affluent industrialists, like the board chairman of the Tokyo Stock Exchange, the president of the Mitsubishi family-owned shipping company Nihon Yusen Kaisha, and the chairman of the Kirin Beer Company. The association was supported by Prime Minister Terauchi Masatake's cabinet and profiled itself as a private and public organisation, even as its activities barely included non-elites. Although the association ultimately fell short of its ambitious fundraising goal, it illustrates the blurring of boundaries between public and private in Japanese relief campaigns.[64] Companies involved did not only intend to commit an act of sympathy and patriotism; they also wished to help Japan and themselves claim a place in a new postwar world order.[65]

Japan's humanitarian politicking might be said to have reached its high-point in 1921 with Crown Prince Hirohito's European tour and Japan's subsequent donations to the Central University Library of Leuven. From April until July of 1921 Hirohito traversed the war-ravaged lands of Western Europe, expressing his sympathy and grief to his European allies. The journey was no ordinary sightseeing trip but was to prepare him for his role as the future Emperor of Japan.[66] Although the journey's official chronicles denied that the tour had any political intentions, it did stress that the visit was to correct 'flattering misconceptions' about Japan. These mostly concerned European stereotypes that cast the nation as ancient and 'oriental' rather than one 'of modern industrialism, enterprise, and progress'. To counter these fallacies, the royal envoy was to show that the Japanese enjoyed a similar level of sophistication and civilisation – and humanitarian aid turned out to be the perfect means to this end.[67] During his visit to Belgium in June the Crown Prince offered 5,000 F to the mayor of Brussels to relieve the suffering of the capital's poor.[68] On top of a visit to Liège and Ypres, he also visited the ruins of the library of the Catholic University of Leuven, whose destruction (including 300,000 manuscripts) by German invaders had become a touchpoint of international sympathy for Belgium and a much-cited symbol of German 'barbarism'. It was at this site of savage destruction – where 'German Culture Ends', as an on-site banner informed – that the representation of Japanese culture began.

Two months after Hirohito's return, a Japanese national committee of L'Oeuvre Internationale de Louvain was founded to join the international project of reconstructing the library. By 1926 the committee had donated a collection of over 13,682 Japanese books and scrolls purchased from

700,000 F collected in Japan. Additional donations included a tea set used for tea ceremonies, a decorated vase, a box with materials used for calligraphy, and bookshelves.[69] Importantly, these would all be housed in a new Japanese room at the library, which was meant to showcase 'the civilization of Japan and the far Orient', as the Japanese ambassador to Belgium, Mineichirō Adachi, noted. Wealthy families and modern research institutes were the main contributors, such as the Mitsui industrialist family, the Bank of Japan, the Ministry of the Imperial Household, universities, and scientific organisations. The committee itself included major representatives of Japanese philanthropy such as the businessman Eiichi Shibusawa and Prince Saionji. The manuscripts dating from before the Meiji Revolution covered a wide range of topics representing Japan's more traditional culture, such as arts, science, medicine, and religion. However, the collection of more recent works, including Japanese translations of foreign publications, was to represent a modernised Japan that had caught up with Western expectations of civilisation. Irrespective of the books' contents, the donations carried high symbolic value for Japan. As the reconstruction of Leuven's library was often likened to the reconstruction of civilisation itself, Japan symbolically took its place among other civilised great power donors.

Overall the donation proved a good investment. It was well received in Belgium and resulted in another round of appreciations and representations. A Belgian honorary doctorate for ambassador Adachi was immediately reciprocated by the announcement that the aristocrat Jirōhachi Satsuma would fund a seminar called the Satsuma Chair at the Catholic University of Leuven, covering Japanese topics. The quasi-official nature of this private act of philanthropy is underlined by the fact that the seminar's contents were to be approved annually by the Japanese embassy.[70] This train of events, lasting into the mid-1920s, illustrate an almost seamless transition from humanitarian relief to cultural reconstruction and diplomacy in the postwar years. Part of what made that transition so smooth, it is fair to assume, was that both wartime aid and postwar gifts were elements of a wider political campaign to showcase Japan's high level of civilisation and its adoption of Western values and standards.

Conclusion

At first glance Japan's humanitarian involvement in the First World War appears puzzling. The country deliberately limited its military participation, minimising its practical contributions to the Allied victory in November 1918. At the same time, Japan supported its allies through humanitarian aid. Belgium, as a global representative for the suffering of the valiant yet helpless, became a subject of compassion which hinged on the aspirations and motivations of a diverse group of actors.

Visual and print media informed Japanese society on the plight of Belgium and tapped into audiences' emotional responsivity, which was clearly heightened by recent war experiences. Japanese mass media depicted Belgians as victims of unspeakable acts of inhumanity, whilst also repeatedly painting them as patriotic martyrs. These contradictory representations of Belgium expose the versatile use of international charity for Japan: the suffering of Belgians affirmed the necessity for Japanese to mobilise themselves and make sacrifices for allies while also presenting extreme examples of patriotic self-sacrifices. Drawing on traditions of civil welfare and new gendered norms, affluent and female citizens, in particular, were expected to present their loyalty to Japan through acts of compassion. It was this diverse group of donors, ranging from industrial magnates to schoolgirls, who carried the weight of demonstrating Japan's progress to the world.

The question remains whether their humanitarian support for Belgium actually helped stakeholders achieve their goals. There is at least some evidence to that effect. Domestically, the mobilisation of women through charity anchored their role as patriotic caretakers of the nation. In 1919 the JRCS and the Patriotic Ladies' Associations announced that they wanted to continue to 'contribute to the preservation of the state' through relief work and handicrafts, following the British example.[71] Civil participation of women and girls through philanthropy continued to play an important role in the interwar period, and co-operation with the government allowed for (minor) improvements in women's public rights as citizens. Women's organisations gradually became absorbed by the state until finally, in the Second World War, the boundaries between most public and private organisations dissolved.[72]

On an official level the Japanese Red Cross Society joined the League of Red Cross Societies, founded in 1919, where its membership played a decisive role in the establishment of the organisation. According to the JRCS's representative, Japan's inclusion would be essential in maintaining 'the international standing of Japan as a world power'.[73] Nevertheless, when the League of Nations rejected the Racial Equality Clause in 1919 – largely due to British dominions trying to prevent Asian immigration – it denied Japanese citizens the right to be treated as equals. One contemporary Japanese commentator even attributed this failure to the fact that the Japanese delegates had been raised by uneducated traditional wet nurses, internalising the notion that Japan was still unmodern.[74] In this instance Japan's performance of modernity through humanitarian aid fell clearly short of the desired effect, thereby sharply illustrating the limits of humanitarian politics. In 1933, Japan withdrew from the League of Nations and continued its imperialist agenda, blaming its departure on Japan's unequal treatment.[75]

In the case of Belgium, however, Japan's compassion did not go unrewarded. In 1921, the Japanese legation was upgraded to an embassy and Mineichirō Adachi, a strong supporter of wartime Belgium, was appointed to ambassadorial rank. A direct product of wartime support, this elevation of diplomatic status paved the way for a more equal representation of Japan in Belgium.[76] The Satsuma Chair also continues at the Catholic University of Leuven to this day and the 1926 collection of scrolls and books miraculously survived the second time the library was destroyed during the Second World War. In 2015 the two countries celebrated their 150-year-old friendship, although Japanese aid was, tellingly perhaps, not mentioned.[77]

Belgium was attributed many different roles by Japanese donors. To some Belgium represented a 'small nation' that had roused significant interest, investment, and support from global powers, a treatment many Japanese industrial and political actors desired for their own country. To others Belgium became a textbook example for patriotism, and allowed them to display similar sentiments through charity. And lest we forget the horrifying inhumanity of war, to many the suffering of Belgians became a source of emotional familiarity and transnational solidarity. While one can speculate on what specific incentives drove particular individuals or groups, the Japanese case does clearly highlight the intersectional character of humanitarian aid, stressing how one action or one person could be encouraged by multiple motivations, and how trying to disentangle these different motivations can do injustice to the complexity of people's lived realities. After all, who is to say whether the schoolgirls aiding Belgium were primarily concerned with living up to their obligations as young women, wanted to contribute to Japan's global ascendency, were instead moved by compassion, or simply followed their teacher's instructions? Perhaps tea producers or newspaper companies did use charity as a way to market their businesses or promote Japan's international image rather than trying to console their bereaved Belgian allies in what they considered the most compassionate and culturally meaningful way: by offering quenching green tea and legendary swords.

Notes

1 Fifteen thousand bags, produced by the Central Association for Tea Industry in Tokyo, carried the same message in Russian for Russian troops. 'Ro Hakugun ni Nihoncha', *Asahi shinbun*, 4 October 1914, p. 5.
2 Previous literature on Japan's activities in the war focuses mainly on its military or political participation, as well as the economic gains it obtained by its industries

profiting from the paralysis of Europe's industrial production. For more information on these perspectives refer to F. R. Dickinson, *World War One and the Triumph of a New Japan, 1919–1930* (New York: Cambridge University Press, 2013); T. Minohara, T. Hon, and E. Dawley (eds), *The Decade of the Great War: Japan and the Wider World in the 1910's* (Leiden: Brill, 2014); G. Xu, *Asia and the Great War: A Shared History* (Oxford: Oxford University Press, 2017).

3 Official ties between the two nations started only in 1866 with the signing of the Treaty of Amity, Commerce and Navigation. D. De Ruyver, 'The First Treaty Between Belgium and Japan (1866)', in W. F. Vande Walle and D. De Cooman (eds), *Japan & Belgium: An Itinerary of Mutual Inspiration* (Tielt: Lannoo, 2016), pp. 21–2.
4 J. L. Huffman, *Creating a Public: People and Press in Meiji Japan* (Honolulu: University of Hawai'i Press, 1997).
5 'Berugī dōjōkai katsudō kaishi', *Yomiuri shinbun*, 28 January 1915, p. 5.
6 This article also features a picture of Belgian refugees. 'Berugī kokumin wa ikani konkushitsutsu aru ka', *Asahi shinbun*, 2 December 1915, p. 3.
7 'Gochisō no kōmon: Berugījin no namida', *Yomiuri shinbun*, 4 April 1917, p. 5.
8 One striking example is the use of sensational imageries by the Red Cross in the early twentieth century in order to raise sympathy for its humanitarian actions. K. Rozario, '"Delicious Horrors": Mass Culture, the Red Cross, and the Appeal of Modern American Humanitarianism', *American Quarterly*, 55 (2003), pp. 417–55.
9 'Wadai no Berugī sanjō gentō', *Yomiuri shinbun*, 15 February 1915, p. 5.
10 'Hakkoku sanjō kōenkai', *Asahi shinbun*, 28 February 1915, p. 2.
11 'Hongō shōgakkō no Berugī gentōkai', *Yomiuri shinbun*, 27 April 1917, p. 4.
12 'Yūrakuza: Berugī no hiai', *Asahi shinbun*, 3 May 1918, 7; 'Berugī no hiai', *Yomiuri shinbun*, 7 May 1918, p. 6.
13 M. L. Arnold, 'War Plays Today', *The Advocate of Peace*, 78:3 (March 1916), pp. 69–74.
14 As published in a programme leaflet of the Tōkyō Shinkyōkyoku Kabukiza on 28 February 1915. This leaflet belongs to the Ritsumeikan Daigaku Kokusai Heiwa Myūjiamu's Hatano Uichirō collection.
15 The leaflet of this live narrated newsreel belongs to the Ritsumeikan Daigaku Kokusai Heiwa Myūjiamu's Hatano Uichirō collection.
16 'Tada hitotsu no shinbunshi', *Yomiuri shinbun*, 20 January 1917, p. 5; J. Schmidt, 'Not a Secondary Experience: The First World War in Japanese Mass Media, Ministerial Bureaucracy Publications, Elementary Schools, and Department Stores', in A. P. Pires, J. Schmidt, and M. I. Tato (eds), *The Global First World War African, East Asian, Latin American and Iberian Mediators* (London: Routledge, 2021), p. 151.
17 D. W. Kinzley, 'Changing Views of Poverty and Social Welfare in the Nineteenth Century', *Journal of Asian History*, 22:1 (1988), 20.
18 S. H. Nolte and S. A. Hastings, 'The Meiji State's Policy Toward Women, 1890–1910', in Gail Lee Bernstein (ed.), *Recreating Japanese Women* (Berkeley: University of California Press, 1991), pp. 161–2.

19 One example is the wartime day care centres, called *hokanjo*, which took care of the children of families whose fathers served or had died in the Russo-Japanese War. K. S. Uno, *Passages to Modernity: Motherhood, Childhood, and Social Reform in Early Twentieth Century Japan* (Honolulu: University of Hawai'i Press, 1999), pp. 76–7.
20 'Berugī jidō kyūzai', *Yomiuri shinbun*, 10 April 1917, p. 4.
21 'Berugī koji no tame', *Yomiuri shinbun*, 13 February 1916, p. 5.
22 More on this matter and other ways in which women committed to acts of patriotism at the home front can be found in P. Grant, *Philanthropy and Voluntary Action in the First World War: Mobilising Charity* (Abingdon: Routledge, 2014); S. R. Grayzel, 'Mothers, Marraines, and Prostitutes: Morale and Morality in First World War France', *The International History Review*, 19:1 (1997), 66–82; I. Sharp and M. Stibbe, *Aftermaths of War: Women's Movements and Female Activists, 1918–1923* (Leiden: Brill, 2011).
23 'Berugī dōjōkai katsudō kaishi', *Yomiuri shinbun*, 28 January 1915, p. 5.
24 'Go man en o Berugī kōshi e', *Yomiuri shinbun*, 13 July 1915, p. 4.
25 'Zenkoku joshikō yori Berugī e kifu', *Yomiuri shinbun*, 8 March 1915, p. 3.
26 'Shirofutagi jizenkōgyō', *Asahi shinbun*, 14 April 1916, p. 6.
27 'Kaku hidenka yori hōtai kizō: Isamashiki Berugīgun e', *Yomiuri shinbun*, 11 October 1914, p. 5.
28 'Ongaku jizenshi', *Asahi shinbun*, 9 April 1918, p. 7; 'Dōjō jizenichi', *Asahi shinbun*, 18 May 1916, p. 5.
29 'Berugī dōjōkai katsudō kaishi', p. 5.
30 S. Garon, 'Women's Groups and the Japanese State: Contending Approaches to Political Integration, 1890–1945', *Journal of Japanese Studies*, 19:1 (1993), 5–41.
31 'Jogakkō ga kōnai ni juppeibako ya jizenbako', *Yomiuri shinbun*, 12 December 1904, p. 3.
32 'Kurisutokyō jogakkō no jizenkai', *Yomiuri shinbun*, 31 October 1894, p. 3.
33 The Aikoku Fujinkai, meaning Patriotic Ladies' Association, is one of the most well-known organisations that cultivated patriotic acts through relief work and teaching practical skills such as needlework. More can be found in K. Morita, 'Activities of the Japanese Patriotic Ladies' Association', in M. Mikuta (ed.), *Women, Activism and Social Change: Stretching Boundaries* (London: Routledge, 2005), pp. 49–70.
34 'Berugī jidō kyūzai no kyōiku bazā', *Yomiuri shinbun*, 24 June 1917, p. 4.
35 Rinji Gunji Chōsa Iinkai, *Ōshūsen to Kōsen Kakkoku Fujin* (Tokyo: Senryūdō, 1917), pp. 20–3.
36 'Onna ya kodomo mo tsurugi o motte: Okiteru Berugī', *Yomiuri shinbun*, 18 August 1918, p. 5.
37 'Jū o motte okiteru Berugī no jogun', *Yomiuri shinbun*, 11 September 1914, p. 5.
38 'Senji no Berugī fujin teki ni kokka o danzu', *Yomiuri shinbun*, 16 June 1918, p. 4.
39 'Yūkannaru Berugī kangofu no jitsuwa', *Ōshū Sensō Jikki*, 37 (1915), pp. 57–61.

40 'Tanshōsubeki Hakugun', *Asahi shinbun*, 30 October 1914, p. 2.
41 G. Roche, 'Dokugun o kurōsuru Berugījin', *Ōshū Sensō Jikki*, 45 (1915), pp. 117–19.
42 'Hakkokuō kikyū ni norite tekijinchi o teisatsusu', *Asahi shinbun*, 5 October 1914, p. 5.
43 C. Buffin, *Hakkoku no Gisen*, trans. Machida Shirō (Tokyo: Teimi Shuppansha, 1918).
44 F. Kurosawa, 'Japanese Perceptions of Belgium in the Meiji and Taisho Periods', in W. F. Vande Walle and D. De Cooman (eds), *Japan & Belgium: An Itinerary of Mutual Inspiration* (Tielt: Lannoo, 2016), pp. 187–214.
45 'Shizu no onna no dōjōkin gojū sen o Berugīmin e', *Yomiuri shinbun*, 21 February 1915, p. 5.
46 'Hakkoku dōjō gikin boshū', *Asahi shinbun*, 10 February 1915, p. 3.
47 'Hakkoku kōshi no kanshajō', *Asahi shinbun*, 14 February 1915, p. 8.
48 'Hakkoku dōjō gikin', *Asahi shinbun*, 15 May 1915, p. 3.
49 'Berugī kokumin no sanjō nit suki Nihon kokumin no gishin ni utau', *Jiji shinpō*, 8 October 1915.
50 'Tachi kenjōki (5) Berugī kōtei (5) Sojinkan', *Asahi shinbun*, 24 April 1915, p. 6.
51 'Tachi kenjōki (17) ekken (ue) Sojinkan', *Asahi shinbun*, 10 May 1915, p. 6; 'Tachi kenjōki (18) ekken (shita) Sojinkan', *Asahi shinbun*, 11 May 1915, p. 6.
52 'Hakkoku sanjō no gentō', *Asahi shinbun*, 1 March 1915, p. 5.
53 Dickinson, *World War One and the Triumph of a New Japan*, pp. 20–2.
54 Xu, *Asia and the Great War*, pp. 188–91.
55 At the same time, while this quest for racial equality could be perceived as an outcry made by Japan in order to gain global acceptance of non-Caucasian nationalities, the Japanese delegates were not inspired by compassion for all other nationalities. Japan still maintained discriminatory double standards for other Asian nationalities, even referring to them as their 'second-rate' Asian neighbours. Minohara et al., *The Decade of the Great War*, p. 24.
56 For more on the racial equality clause refer to N. Shimazu, *Japan, Race and Equality: The Racial Equality Proposal of 1919* (London: Routledge, 1998).
57 M. N. Barnett, *Empire of Humanity: A History of Humanitarianism* (Ithaca: Cornell University Press, 2011), p. 33.
58 H. Tomida and G. Daniels, 'Medical Ambassadors: Japanese Red Cross Nurses in Great Britain, 1915–1916', *Seijō Daigaku Hijōkin*, 4:1 (2009), 107–11.
59 Y. Makita, 'The Alchemy of Humanitarianism: The First World War, the Japanese Red Cross and the Creation of an International Public Health Order', *First World War Studies*, 5:1 (2014), 121–2.
60 B. C. Hacker and M. Vining, *A Companion to Women's Military History* (Leiden: Brill, 2012), pp. 204–5.
61 Despite stories of the excellent treatment of First World War PoWs, the reality of camp life was not as rosy as depicted in remembrances of that period. M. Murphy, 'Brücken, Beethoven und Baumkuchen: German and Austro-Hungarian Prisoners of War and the Japanese Home Front', in J. Bürgschwentner,

M. Egger, and G. Barth-Scalmani (eds), *Other Fronts, Other Wars? First World War Studies on the Eve of the Centennial* (Leiden: Brill, 2014), pp. 132–5.
62 'Horyo no taigū: Wagakuni wa mohan', *Asahi shinbun*, 12 October 1914, p. 3.
63 The history of modern Japanese welfare can be found in S. Garon, *Molding Japanese Minds: The State in Everyday Life* (Princeton: Princeton University Press, 1997), pp. 25–59.
64 In the end, the organisation managed to rake together only ¥1,818,554.472, hardly two-thirds of the originally planned amount. Belgium received ¥363,000. T. Izao, 'Daiichiji Sekaitaisen to Minshū Ishiki: Futatsu no Kanmin Gassaku Bokinundō o Megutte', *Nihonshi Kenkyūkai*, 535 (March 2007), 112.
65 Izao, 'Daiichiji Sekaisen', 106.
66 The tour started on 3 March and lasted until 3 September. Detailed accounts of the tour can be found in Y. Futara and S. Sawada, *The Crown Prince's European Tour* (Osaka: The Osaka Mainichi Publishing Co., 1926).
67 Ibid., pp. 7–10.
68 'Het Bezoek van Kroonprins Hirohito aan België', *De Telegraaf*, 13 June 1921.
69 'Une Donation d'Exception', Université Catholique de Louvain, accessed 3 October 2021, https://uclouvain.be/fr/bibliotheques/respat/une-donation-d-exception.html.
70 An additional ¥60,000 was collected to prepare and ship the collection. W. F. Vande Walle, *Orientalia: Oosterse Studies en Bibliotheken te Leuven en Louvain-la-Neuve* (Leuven: Leuven University Press, 2001), pp. 65–75.
71 'Aikoku Fujinkai wa nani o shiteiruka', *Asahi shinbun*, 24 May 1919, p. 5.
72 Garon, *Molding Japanese Minds*, pp. 140–5.
73 Makita, 'The Alchemy of Humanitarianism', 123.
74 'Wagakuni no katei de yatou mukyōiku no uba wa hoka', *Yomiuri shinbun*, 16 September 1919, p. 4.
75 Shimazu, *Japan, Race and Equality*, p. 179.
76 Kurosawa, 'Japanese Perceptions', pp. 234–5.
77 '150 Years of Friendship between Japan and Belgium', Embassy of Japan in Belgium, accessed 3 October 2021, www.be.emb-japan.go.jp/150jb/en/index.html.

3

Geographies of humanitarian mobilisation: Portuguese Africa and the Great War

Ana Paula Pires

Introduction

Portugal's African empire may have been geographically distant from the Portuguese mainland, but it was inseparable from the country's national identity. It was ever present in the life of the Portuguese based on an image of heroism and a myth of the historical mission of the Portuguese nation to colonise other peoples. The idea of a 'Portuguese world' resonated powerfully among its elites and the wider public alike. Portugal saw itself as a Western European as much as an imperial power and the symbiosis between metropolis and colonies was integral to nationalist discourses over the nineteenth century. Writings such as those by the nineteenth-century historian and politician Oliveira Martins famously strengthened nationalist narratives about an indissoluble Portuguese overseas colonial world.[1] But what happened to these imperial and intra-imperial imaginations and connections during the Great War? How were these links maintained, affirmed, or challenged – and how can a focus on humanitarian relief help us understand cross-empire elaborations?

The Portuguese Republic had not yet completed its fourth year when on 28 June 1914 the heir to the Austro-Hungarian throne, Franz Ferdinand, and his wife, the Duchess of Hohenberg, were assassinated in Sarajevo. The Portuguese army was ill-prepared and in the midst of a reorganisation. As such, it was more honed towards internal defence than any sort of intervention in Europe or the African colonies. None the less, Portugal was forced to engage in military confrontations long before it formally joined the war in March 1916. The Portuguese Empire in Africa bordered on German colonies, leading to repeated border infringements and armed clashes. Over the course of the war some eight thousand Portuguese soldiers lost their lives violently, the vast majority of them in Africa. The Republican government came to see the conflict as an opportunity to pursue one of the main ambitions of the Portuguese October revolution of 1910: to end a period of decadence and decline and to reclaim the country's international role as a great colonial power, recognised by France and Great Britain.

This chapter will analyse one central aspect of the Portuguese world, namely the humanitarian mobilisation in and for Africa between 1914 and 1918, focusing on Angola and Mozambique, two Portuguese colonies that were directly affected by military operations. It will reveal the impact both of industrialised killing and of humanitarian altruism at the start of the twentieth century, and disclose the efforts made by individuals and institutions to mediate suffering in the periphery of a networked and globalised world; by doing so it will focus on intra-imperial relations, an uncommon topic in the history of humanitarianism. Humanitarianism, as I hope to demonstrate, showed the transatlantic and inter-imperial dimension of Portugal's involvement in the war and how emotions associated with suffering, caused by conflict or political change and instability, played a significant role in the shaping of global 'affective communities'. I follow Emma Hutchison's definition of an 'affective community', by considering trauma not only as an individual but as a collective experience, highlighting how emotions can be mobilised for common and political ends, including humanitarian projects, and, as this chapter will show, such emotions could not only generate cross-state humanitarian actions but were, also, responsible for intra-imperial mobilisation.[2]

Over the past twenty-five years historical accounts of the Great War have undergone significant shifts. There has been a decisive 'turn' to the study of society and culture, which has also opened the field to transnational and comparative study of European empires in Africa.[3] At the same time the crisis of confidence that afflicted global humanitarianism by the end of the 1990s prompted institutions and individuals to reflect on the nature, value, and consequences of relief work, and consider anew the historical roots of their endeavours. Oddly, Portuguese historians have been slow to respond to this trend. So far as the history of Portuguese Africa is concerned, studies of humanitarianism have remained almost solely concerned with efforts to end slavery in the early nineteenth century.[4] The only study to analyse humanitarian relief in Mozambique during the Great War approaches the subject from a medical perspective and disregards similar efforts in Angola, or the other colonial possessions.[5]

To address this gap this chapter seeks to reconstruct humanitarian mobilisation in and for the Portuguese colonial empire in Africa between 1914 and 1918. In doing so it acknowledges a different perception on how intra-imperial relations were built. Based on Portuguese and African newspapers and research carried out in the Portuguese Red Cross Archives in Lisbon, it will analyse the home-front humanitarian structures which sustained the mobilisation of aid in the Portuguese colonial empire during the war years.

The chapter is in two sections. The first explores geographies of humanitarian mobilisation and discusses the ways in which Portugal's African colonies participated in activities to mitigate the horrors of modern warfare. The intercontinental telegraph not only propelled the integration of global markets but also led to an intense circulation of news, concepts, and practices. It helped create a sense of global suffering upon which notions of international humanitarian action developed. This, in turn, helped shape the understanding of peace and war for wider publics, including the Portuguese living in Angola and Mozambique. The second section on transnational relations analyses how humanitarian mobilisation provided a moment of unity for the Lusophone community. The chapter pays attention to the significant array of initiatives that originated in Portugal's capital, Lisbon, where the political regime strove to modernise and convert a Catholic nation into a secular and patriotic society. At the same time it will look into the Portuguese living in Brazil and the United States of America who self-mobilised in response to fighting in Europe and Africa and its human costs. The chapter concludes with some remarks about the motivation to assist war victims which is not only a product of individual sentiment but also a function of social and collective behaviour, advancing a reflection on the historical conjunction of humanitarianism and imperialism.

The Great War gave way to a world that was unrecognisable to those who held power in 1914. It opened a period characterised by mass death and landscapes of destruction on an industrial scale.[6] Spaces like the Portuguese colonies of Angola and Mozambique are invariably overlooked on account of the marginal impact they had on the outcome of the military struggle. And yet these allegedly 'peripheral' regions were not spared from the consequences of the conflict. The war altered their structures, the rhythm and routines, and transformed both private and public life.[7] The experiences of these colonies reveal the importance of humanitarian relief activities to combat the suffering created by modern warfare. Moreover they demonstrate the role and importance of social mobilisation in colonial spaces. To truly understand Portuguese involvement in the Great War, it is necessary to look at individuals and the web of associations, brought together in a common cause, that sustained the empire-wide relief effort, intertwining the local, national, and international levels.

Portugal and the Great War

Despite its dehumanising features, the Great War and its horrors also had the effect of mobilising support, of intensifying collective emotions and of building on what Ute Frevert calls a 'moral economy of feelings and attitudes'.[8] Portugal's experience of the Great War reflected this common trend just as it was unique in some respects; a latecomer to the conflict, the state entered the war only in March 1916. In the meantime, between 1914 and March 1916 Portuguese political life played out against the increasingly pressing question of whether to enter the conflict. The nature of the debate was determined by national and international factors, both of them related to questions of empire.

The first aspect that shaped Portuguese responses was the recent founding of the Republic. It was only in October 1910 that Portugal, one of Europe's oldest and longest lasting global empires, had become one of only three republics in Europe. According to republican propaganda, a single and indivisible empire was indispensable to Portugal and its defence had to be assured at all costs. This conviction rested, from the start, on the much wider and complex question of ensuring that Portugal's political change at home would revitalise the empire and – this was the second aspect guiding Portuguese considerations – would ensure a more satisfactory relationship with its main ally and most dangerous adversary, Great Britain. In fact in the wake of Franz Ferdinand's assassination the geo-strategic position of Portugal's territories in Africa was vulnerable, its hold on these territories rather weak and its overall economic and financial state alarmingly poor. This forced the Portuguese government to approach international events with great caution. At the same time the Anglo-Portuguese Treaty of 1373, the world's longest-surviving defensive diplomatic alliance, compelled the Portuguese government (a minority cabinet) to act in co-ordination with the British monarchy just as it considered British support a key factor in helping the young Republic achieve international recognition.

These circumstances explain Portugal's cautious and ambivalent response to the Great War. On 1 August 1914 the Portuguese Minister of Foreign Affairs, Freire de Andrade, requested the Portuguese Minister to London, Teixeira Gomes, to clarify with the British Foreign Office the position Portugal should take towards the conflict. On the following day Gomes informed the Portuguese Minister of Foreign Affairs that Under-Secretary of State Sir Eyre Crowe understood that Portugal should remain neutral, but without making any formal declaration to that effect. This was a clear violation of the resolutions of the Second Hague Conference of 1907, which had explicitly stated that, in any situation of war, a state must declare its neutrality or belligerence. However, on 21 August 1914 Prime Minister Bernardino Machado issued a decree that led to the organisation and dispatch of two mixed deployments (mountain artillery, cavalry, infantry, and machine-gunners) to Angola and Mozambique, Portugal's most important African colonies. In the legislation's preamble, the government recognised the essential nature of 'duly supplying some of the southern border posts in the province of Angola and in the North of Mozambique'[9] in order to prevent a possible German invasion. At this point 1,525 men were sent to Angola and 1,477 to Mozambique. While these initial numbers sound small, they amounted to a tenth of the manpower available to the Portuguese army at the time. What is more, these numbers quickly escalated and between 1914 and 1918 Portugal sent 39,000 men (more than its entire 1914 army) to fight in Africa.

Portugal's ambiguous position since the outbreak of hostilities, that is, that it was then neither belligerent nor neutral while being closely tied to Great Britain, was also manifest in the fact that the expeditions were officially organised by the Ministry of the Colonies and not the Ministry of War. By the same token the measures adopted by Portugal, with British approval, were presented as merely pre-emptive in nature, and aimed at colonial defence. In fact, Portugal was generally eager not to offend or alarm Germany. In a circular sent to his colleagues in government and the Portuguese ministers in London and Madrid, Freire de Andrade expressed himself opposed to the mere thought of Portugal's intervention on the Western Front, and denounced what he considered to be the use of 'language which is sometimes offensive and even insulting to Germans and Germany's leaders by part of the press [...] especially since it might be construed that the government approves of it, consenting to it without the least reproach'.[10] These tactics seem to have been quite successful. At the time, the stationing of Portuguese troops in Africa did not result in a declaration of war by Germany or its allies.

But the war also posed internal political questions. In 1914 republican politics had reached an impasse with no political party trusting the other. Portugal was divided about an intervention in the war. This division reflected a broader political fissure between more radical republicans on the one hand and monarchists, Catholics, and more moderate republicans on the other. They were generally divided not over whether to support the Western allies but how precisely to go about it. There was a great deal of opposition – except for the most radical wing of the republicans – to sending an expeditionary force to the Western Front. In addition to this initial lack of clarity, and the polarisation of the Portuguese society over involvement in the war, the making of a war culture proved challenging in a largely rural, and often illiterate country.

Geographies of humanitarian mobilisation

It is in this larger context that we must understand efforts to provide aid and relief assistance to troops deployed to Africa. Although most members of the colonial and metropolitan population were sceptical about the need to send troops to Africa and were not generally attracted to empire – more Portuguese immigrated to Brazil every year than had settled in Portugal's African colonies – the military expedition sparked an immediate humanitarian mobilisation. Following Prime Minister Machado's declaration of 21 August, the Portuguese Red Cross received 'declarations from civil doctors and qualified nurses [...] in order to enlist in that patriotic service [in Africa]'.[11] Already a week earlier the Portuguese Red Cross had advertised in the press for 'all qualified male and female nurses, who do not have hospital commitments and wish to be part of the staff at a unit for the wounded that would eventually be set up in Lisbon, to please present their diplomas to the Red Cross office'.[12] A few days later the Lisbon newspapers were swift to publish a circular received from the International Committee of the Red Cross that stated that all 'resources should be firstly dedicated to sanitation services for national troops'.[13] In addition to initiating a subscription campaign across the country, the President of the Portuguese Red Cross Society, Domingos Tasso de Figueiredo, also asked the President of the municipal Council of Lisbon to donate an ambulance to the Society for deployment in Angola[14] and retired military personnel immediately volunteered for the Portuguese Red Cross medical mission destined for southern Angola. These efforts were, of course, connected to the growing movement that sought to humanise the conflict in order to render it compatible with 'civilisation'.[15] Individually it also reflected the fact that humanitarian action was seen as a form of civic diplomacy and as a means of expressing solidarity in a common cause. Above all, however, it showed the importance for Portuguese elites, including the national leaders of the Red Cross society, of preserving the world's fourth largest empire.[16] Africa might have been a peripheral theatre in the Great War but, given the imperial and political interests of Portuguese elites and their limited means to pursue them, it seemed an excellent battlefield – one on which to win a significant political victory.

The emerging humanitarian mobilisation was also visible in the colonies themselves. In October 1914 a branch of the Portuguese Red Cross was founded in Lourenço Marques (present-day Maputo, Mozambique) and local venues and businesses soon lent themselves to its cause. The Varietá theatre, for example, hosted an event 'in honour of the expeditionary forces, with part of the revenues from the spectacle reverting in favour of the victims of war and the Delegation of the Red Cross in this Province'.[17] Lourenço Marques also saw the emergence of a Female Aid Commission for Portuguese Soldiers which set about collecting donations to assist troops on campaign in eastern Africa.[18] Another commission of mixed-race persons from the regions of Manica and Sofala 'took the initiative to monthly, and throughout the duration of the war, collect from their compatriots, the amounts that they are able to bestow, destined for a support fund for the Portuguese Red Cross delegation in Lourenço Marques'.[19] That said, racial prejudice and segregation remained widespread during the war and the groups selected as recipients of aid were primarily white soldiers.[20] Although mainland republicans had a vested interest in this humanitarian mobilisation, such activities show that it also emerged spontaneously and from below.

As would soon become all too obvious, such humanitarian assistance was desperately needed. The colony's military garrison was small and badly prepared. Most of its members (old and new) had little or no formal military training, and the troops dispatched from Portugal arrived in a poor physical state. For the most part, these men proved incapable of withstanding the rigours of the tropical climate. Many arrived ill, victims of the terrible hygiene conditions which characterised the journey. Under these circumstances, the humanitarian committees provided much needed medical supplies just as they expressed popular support for the Portuguese troops.

The need was even more pressing in Angola, where actual fighting broke out as early as August 1914. German colonial troops crossed the border to attack Portuguese garrisons in southern Angola and northern Mozambique soon after the conflict in Europe began. In December 1914 a German foray into southern Angola, ostensibly to secure supplies, escalated, leading to the destruction of the fort at Naulila, a local Portuguese stronghold.[21] By and large the humanitarian mobilisation mirrored that in Lourenço Marques. In the capital, Luanda, there was popular backing for a national subscription campaign raised by the Lisbon newspaper *O Século* with donations going to those injured in the war.[22] By the end of 1914 the Luanda-based Grémio Pátria Integral association had raised 238$69 escudos for the Portuguese war wounded.[23]

The Portuguese Red Cross was responsible for almost the entire clinical and nursing services for the military units deployed in the south of Angola. Volunteers soon arrived from Lisbon and, despite transport difficulties, made it to Lubango, where the flag of the Convention of Geneva was unfurled over a hospital building that contained two wards for whites and one for blacks. These Red Cross initiatives received broad support from the population of the colonies and mainland alike. In late 1914 the owners of the Hotel Paris in Benguela launched a Volunteer Battalion of Benguela and showed films to raise funds for the Red Cross. On the founding of the Red Cross branch in Lubango, the musicians Viegas, Marrecas Ferreira, and Tamagnini Barbosa donated the proceeds of a *fado* song (a form of Portuguese singing characterised by mournful tunes and lyrics), entitled the Expeditionary *Fado*, to the Portuguese military. The company Cinematográfica Ervedosa & Co also staged a performance, with the revenues, totalling 19$43 escudos, going to the same cause.[24] In Angola the Red Cross branch enlisted several female volunteers from the colony for their medical teams: reflecting a trend seen in Britain and France since the late nineteenth century that perceived women as important members of the 'civilizing mission of the colonial enterprise'.[25] Importantly, this was not an autonomous committee but a colonial institution operating under the auspices of the Portuguese Red Cross Society.[26] Present in all these initiatives was the mistaken assumption that the war would be short. Even the Red Cross declared that the military operations in southern Angola would be 'terminated during the month of August or in early September', and consequently saw no need to request the government to rent a property for a private Red Cross hospital.[27] In reality it would take until the autumn of 1915 before the lost territory was again secured, at which point Allied forces had also conquered Southwest Africa.

What makes these humanitarian activities so significant is that they ran directly counter to what was otherwise a pronounced scepticism about sending troops to the colonies. In the main there was a consensus to dispatch troops to Africa only among the political elite. For the most part, the colonial and metropolitan population doubted the necessity of this action and heatedly debated the topic in the press. These doubts were clearly articulated in the colonies affected. The Lourenço Marques newspaper *O Africano* expressed its bewilderment at the situation in December 1914: 'Since we have not yet understood the undoubtedly powerful reasons which led the government to send both to Angola and this province the military expeditions. [...] Six or eight thousand armed and equipped men came to the colonies, and to what end? To defend our colonial sovereignty, isn't that what we are told? Well, where exactly is that defence?'[28] Despite this lack of consensus Portuguese Africa willingly participated in humanitarian relief activities to support Europe's fight in the war. *O Africano* itself provides an excellent example. Although frustrated by certain decisions made in Lisbon, it lost no time in launching a public subscription campaign in aid of soldiers taken prisoner by German forces in Angola.[29] As such examples suggest, relief work could be a common denominator, a joint national endeavour which transcended political disagreements and geographical distances.

One particularly notable feature of this humanitarian mobilisation, both in the mainland and in the colonies, was the prominent involvement of women. When war broke out in the summer of 1914 the writer Ana de Castro Osório believed the conflict would represent a major opportunity for republican women to show their capabilities and initiative. She founded the Feminine Commission for the Motherland (Comissão Pró-Pátria) to mobilise women for voluntary service, whether that meant making clothing or gathering donations for the soldiers and victims of the war. However, the main objective of this intellectual group was to achieve political and social reform, first and foremost the right to female suffrage. This political agenda points to one major motivation behind humanitarian assistance, as the Commission simultaneously used its humanitarian work to promote a distinct female identity and prove the value of women – and their deservingness of political influence – to the Portuguese nation.[30] Women were also heavily involved in the colonies. In Angola, the wife of the colony's governor played a key role in organising humanitarian support. She founded a delegation of the Portuguese Women's Crusade with the goal of undertaking 'the great altruistic idea of aiding the men who are fighting and their families'.[31] Through female and elite networks the Crusade managed not only to ensure the participation of the majority of associations, centres, clubs, and newspapers of Luanda but also to enlist the support of more distant locations. For instance the inhabitants in Amboim, some 250 kilometres from the capital, began raising funds for Portuguese war victims.

It is also interesting how this humanitarian mobilisation made major use of, indeed was made possible by, sport and other popular forms of entertainment. As noted above, film screenings and *fado* songs were some of the popular means of attracting public funds and support. Another fundraising initiative involved a showjumping competition organised by the Portuguese Riding Society (the Red Cross would later honour the Riding Society with its First-Class Cross). Ticket sales from the inauguration of Lisbon's velodrome in late 1914 also benefited the troops mobilised for combat in Angola.[32] It was these popular measures that allowed humanitarian concerns to reach and to resonate with a large and diverse part of society, both in Portugal and the colonies, especially as that society was, as mentioned above, often rural, illiterate, and not yet at war. It is also worth highlighting the participation of children in this fundraising: students in the Casa Pia Orphanage of Lisbon were requested by the Red Cross to put on a performance of gymnastics in the Zoological Garden, while students from across the country produced 1,292 pieces of clothing for the Portuguese soldiers then deployed in southern Angola.[33] In Lourenço Marques a festival of sport was held with proceeds going to the Portuguese and British Red Cross societies and the Female Commission for Aid to the Portuguese Soldier. Such events reached deep into society, brought together otherwise distant social groups and created a sense of social responsibility and national solidarity. Accordingly the festival of sport was described by the *O Africano* newspaper as being less 'a festival of charity' and more 'complying with a duty'. In fact the paper drew a clear distinction between the duties of the state and the duties of civil society, not least in humanitarian terms. 'The state',

Figure 3.1 Lisbon street sale to help the victims of the First World War, 1917

it wrote, 'cannot overcome all of the lack of comforts nor above all is it an entity that may dispense caring, the essential moral support. [...] The state complies with its duties, handing out cartridges and marching orders; the nation complies with its duties by providing to those who stand up on its behalf the manifestation of its pride, the extent of its care.'[34]

So how does this humanitarian mobilisation relate to wartime politics? Portugal's intervention in the Great War aimed at restoring for the country its sense of national dignity. This was considered vital not just for foreign policy but also for domestic politics. The Republic's international prestige loomed large in official thinking, as it would help consolidate the regime's standing at home. This hinged, of course, on success in waging war on the African front, as Portugal's colonial heritage was considered by all Portuguese as a sacred endowment to the country that stretched back to the Golden Age of Discoveries. Portugal's military record failed to live up to these expectations: Portuguese forces took years to recover the ground they had lost to German colonial forces in the opening months of the war. From a political perspective, however, the republicans' objectives were ultimately realised. The Entente's victory ensured that Portugal would be spared the danger of seeing its colonies used as bargaining chips in a Great Power peace settlement. Instead, it left the war with its colonial possessions and colonial mission intact. More importantly perhaps, the war, and humanitarian engagement in particular, helped forge a greater sense of imperial unity. By providing a sense of solidarity and proximity between mainland Portugal and its far-flung empire, and sparking a remarkable social mobilisation across the Portuguese world, humanitarian aid ended up playing a significant role in helping to safeguard the integrity of the Portuguese empire.

Transnational relations: aid and the Portuguese world

These observations also hold true for larger parts of the Portuguese world. The picture we have painted for Portugal's most important African colonies was replicated in part or whole across Portugal's other colonial possessions. Throughout the war Portugal drew on donations from São Tomé and Principe, from Guinea Bissau (where the inhabitants of Farim staged their own collection),[35] from Macao (where the Commission led by the wife of the governor gathered 'four thousand pieces of clothing, coats and bandages'),[36] and from Cape Verde, the archipelago where, courtesy of the initiative of the resident British community, a concert was held at the Mindelo Municipal Council.[37] Efforts to ameliorate Portuguese suffering were truly global in nature and demonstrate the existence of communities of care among the different parts of the empire, even as the deployment of troops was controversial; they therefore illustrate the development of a culture of humanitarianism across the empire, as well as the existence of the Portuguese nation as a unified moral community.

Portugal's entrance into the war in Europe in March 1916 provided a particular moment of unity for the Lusophone community at large; the Portuguese in Brazil and in the United States self-mobilised to support fighting in Africa and in Flanders, gathering funds for the children and widows of the soldiers killed. Perhaps the most astounding example of this sense of belonging was displayed by the deposed king Manuel II. Although married to a German and forced to live in exile in England since the founding of the Republic in 1910, Manuel heartily supported Portugal's alignment with the Entente from 1916 onwards. He volunteered for service in the British Red Cross, and his mother Amélie, French by birth, visited France soon after the outbreak of the conflict to get a first-hand impression of the destruction. The former queen of Portugal immediately lent her support to several local charities and hospitals in Britain, and the royal family became deeply involved in fundraising for Portuguese soldiers, fighting in Europe and in Africa. Their actions demonstrate that humanitarianism needs to be analysed beyond the framework of domestic politics, and must be seen as a way to overcome traumatic and violent experiences, such as those lived by the Portuguese royal family.[38] Humanitarian mobilisations were capable, indeed, of creating an affective community since 'traumatized individuals often turn to a wider community in an attempt to both better understand and gain recognition for what they have gone through'.[39] In Benguela it was the royal household's former photographer José Pedro Passaporte, living in Angola since the overthrow of the monarchy, who took the initiative to found a Red Cross branch, a colonial institution under the auspices of the Portuguese Red Cross Society.

Similar mechanisms were at play in Brazil. Already in 1915, the Portuguese Republican Centre of São Paulo opened a delegation of the Portuguese Red Cross. A significant proportion of the Portuguese expatriate community in Brazil during the war were monarchists, but their humanitarian mobilisation served to strengthen their bonds with Republican Portugal and temporarily regain their 'loss of confidence in established social structures and forms of community'.[40] Though politically divided, the community nevertheless created a joint Great Commission for the Nation (Grande Comissão Pró-Pátria) to co-ordinate donations from the Portuguese community in Brazil. It set out to be 'an autonomous work, without subjection to other, already founded works destined to alleviate or relieve one of the greatest misfortunes caused by the war'.[41] Its most emblematic project was the assistance it provided for war orphans, an Institute established in Coimbra to apply 'the clothing, education and instruction of these orphans according to the criteria appropriate to their social conditions and in order for the salutary influence of the education that they received to be exercised in keeping with the social class they come from'.[42] The Great Commission also liaised with the Portuguese Committee to the Secours aux Militaires et Civils prisoniers de Guerre, headquartered in Lausanne, Switzerland. It assembled resources necessary to provide three diverse packages a month to the 163 Portuguese prisoners of war in German hands.[43] In its own words, the Commission aimed to be 'a militant army of altruism and labour, and not of death and destruction; those who do not have to get soaked in blood; those who are also essential to victory, to whom the mission of reparation is entrusted'.[44]

These transnational connections, which were also representations of people-to-people internationalism, once again, were especially evident in female networks. The prime movers in the initiative were the wife of the Republic's President, and the wives and daughters of government ministers who described their goals as 'a patriotic and humanitarian institution, set up to provide material and moral assistance to those in need on account of the state of war with Germany'.[45] Very clearly, these republican women saw this as a unique opportunity to demonstrate women's public service. It was, paradoxically, this republican women's 'crusade' that the Brazilian Great Commission for the Nation sought closer ties to. Soon after its founding the Commission established a sub-commission to communicate and co-ordinate with the Portuguese Women's Crusade. As this example shows, a common transnational concern and the mechanisms of women's mobilisation, in particular, could temporarily set aside political differences in favour of a common project.

These measures contributed to the consolidation of a global affective community stretching between South America, Africa, and Europe, dedicated to alleviating Portuguese suffering. Emotions should, therefore, be seen as influential and particularly revealing to mobilise a community beyond the immediate boundaries of the nation-state, affirming a collective sense of identity, as shown in the case of the Portuguese community living in Brazil. This sense of belonging determined the ways in which the Portuguese diaspora was able to reconfigure its collective identity and feel and experience the conflict, developing what the historian Filipe Ribeiro de Meneses considers 'a common response to the experience of a world at war',[46] stretching across the Atlantic. As a result, wartime aid illuminated emotional attachments worldwide.

Conclusions

Despite the mass death and destruction unleashed in the summer of 1914, the Great War gave rise to a humanitarian moment that forged connections between disparate actors and ultimately spread to every corner of the globe. The Lusophone world played its part in these transformations, and spawned a network of humanitarian relationships that connected Lisbon with Lourenço Marques, Cape Verde, Hong Kong, and Rio de Janeiro. This transnational humanitarian mobilisation for Portuguese war victims not only offers a more comprehensive picture of the shape and scope of the Portuguese world but it also highlights the truly global dimension of the First World War, even beyond the actual fighting.

The research findings through an overlooked case study of intra-imperial connections are relevant for the history of cross-state humanitarianism not just in Portuguese Africa but also for the Commonwealth engagement in the two world wars or the experience of the German Empire in the First World War once humanitarianism linked all key belligerents in several ways.

Paying attention to the humanitarian mobilisation of the Portuguese world also throws light on a cast of less traditional and non-state actors. It was sustained by hundreds of volunteers operating in sometimes small but well-organised structures, such as the Feminine Commission for the Motherland, the Portuguese Women's Crusade, the Female Commission for Aid of the Portuguese Soldier and the Great Commission for the Nation. Women were especially active participants, using their skills to collect money and nurse those in need; at the same time their humanitarian organisation aided their struggle for greater political rights and social independence. The war also contributed greatly to the imperial growth and importance of the Portuguese Red Cross. At the time of the Armistice the Portuguese Red Cross operated forty-three branches, across the mainland, in its archipelagos, and in Portugal's African colonies. It trained staff, created infrastructures, and handled hundreds of volunteers across the home front, Flanders, Angola, and Mozambique. It relied heavily on donations raised across the Lusophone world, and by 8 April 1919, the public subscription for war victims it had opened four years earlier reached a total of 1,056,562$25 escudos (US$525,000: approximately $9.1 million in 2023 prices). The global reach of these organisations allows us to trace the involvement of Portuguese civil society in the Great War.

Importantly, humanitarian organisations continued to play a prominent role in Portuguese society. Portugal's wartime casualties were modest in comparison with the slaughter wrought on other societies: a mere eight thousand killed and thirteen thousand wounded. As these losses were insufficiently large to create a sense of a 'lost generation', the Republic found it difficult to generate a consensus on the war's meaning. After the return of peace, those Portuguese who had participated in the war acquired a multiplicity of new identities: veterans, mutilated, gassed, crippled. The last were the most visible victims of the conflict, the men who brought home the horrors of war. Humanitarian organisations, namely the Red Cross, responded to this 'brutalisation of violence' by providing aid, especially medical care, to these soldiers whether they returned home from Flanders, Angola, or Mozambique. All in all, exploring humanitarian engagement reveals a different dimension of Portuguese society in the era of the Great War, one that goes beyond political strive and dissent.

Notes

1 V. Alexandre, 'Questão nacional e questão colonial em Oliveira Martins', *Análise Social*, 135:1 (1996), 184; see also A. P. Pires, 'The First World War in Mozambique: Public Discourses and Representations of Identity', *National Identities*, 24:1 (2020), 55–68.
2 E. Hutchison, *Affective Communities in World Politics* (Cambridge: Cambridge University Press, 2016), pp. 40–50.
3 J. Horne, 'End of a Paradigm? The Cultural History of the Great War', *Past & Present*, 242:1 (2019), 179.
4 M. Bandeira Jerónimo, *Livros Brancos, Almas Negas: A 'missão civilizadora' do colonialismu português c. 1870–1930* (Lisbon: ICS, 2010).
5 H. da Silva, 'A Cruz Vermelha Portuguesa em Moçambique na Primeira Guerra Mundial. Esboço Histórico', *Revista CEPIHS*, 6 (2016), 415–41.
6 Horne, 'End of a Paradigm?', 159.
7 S. Goebel and D. Keene, 'Towards a Metropolitan History of Total War: An Introduction', in S. Goebel and D. Keene (eds), *Cities into Battlefields: Metropolitan Scenarios, Experiences and Commemorations of Total War* (Farnham: Ashgate, 2011), p. 11.
8 U. Frevert, 'Wartime Emotions: Honor, Shame, and the Ecstasy of Sacrifice', in U. Daniel, P. Gatrell, O. Janz, H. Jones, J. Keene, A. Kramer, and B. Nasson (eds), *1914–1918-online. International Encyclopedia of the First World War*, 8 January 2017, DOI: http://dx.doi.org/10.15463/ie1418.10409; https://encyclopedia.1914-1918-online.net/article/wartime_emotions_honour_shame_and_the_ecstasy_of_sacrifice?version=1.0; U. Frevert, *Emotions in History – Lost and Found* (Budapest: Central European University Press, 2011), pp. 178–9.
9 *Ordem do Exército*, no. 19, 1st series, 21 August 1914.
10 *Portugal na Primeira Guerra Mundial (1914–1918): As negociações diplomáticas até à declaração de Guerra*, vol 1 (Lisbon: Ministério dos Negócios Estrangeiros, 1997), p. 26.
11 Circular (to all municipalities not already members of the Red Cross), 26 October 1914, Portuguese Red Cross Historical Archive (AHCVP), *Participação em catástrofes internacionais – Documentos Manuscritos 1893–1935*.
12 *Diário de Notícias*, 15 August 1914.
13 Letter, Copiador no. 2, 1914, AHCVP, *Sociedade Portuguesa da Cruz Vermelha*.
14 Domingos Tasso de Figueiredo (Portuguese Red Cross President) to Henrique de Vilhena (President of the Municipal Council of Lisbon), 7 January

1915, AHCVP, *Sociedade Portuguesa da Cruz Vermelha*, Copiador no. 1, January–March 1915.
15 M. Schulz, 'Dilemmas of "Geneva" Humanitarian Internationalism: The International Committee of the Red Cross and Red Cross Movement, 1863–1918', in J. Paulmann (ed.), *Dilemmas of Humanitarian Aid in the Twentieth Century* (Oxford: Oxford University Press, 2016), pp. 36–7.
16 A. P. Pires and R. Nunes, 'Portuguese Humanitarian Efforts during the First World War', in A. P. Pires, M. I. Tato, and J. Schmidt (eds), *The Global First World War: African, East Asian, Latin American and Iberian Mediators* (London and New York: Routledge, 2021), pp. 206–27.
17 'No "varietá"', *O Africano*, 17 October 1914, p. 1.
18 Comissão Feminina de Auxílio ao Soldado Português, 'Obra Patriótica: Comissão Feminina de auxílio ao soldado português', *O Africano*, 27 May 1916, p. 1.
19 'Carta da Beira', *O Africano*, 31 May 1916, p. 1.
20 A. P. Duarte, A. P. Pires, and B. C. Reis, '"The Other Portuguese Flanders": Strategic Ambition and Operational Disaster in the Portuguese Great War in Mozambique', in A. Samson, A. P. Pires, and D. Gilfoyle (eds), *There Came a Time … Essays on the Great War in Africa* (Richmond: TSL Publications, 2018), p. 161.
21 M. F. Rollo, A. P. Pires, and F. R. de Meneses, 'Portugal', in U. Daniel, P. Gatrell, O. Janz, H. Jones, J. Keene, A. Kramer, and B. Nasson (eds), *1914–1918 Online. International Encyclopedia of the First World War*, 30 August 2017, DOI: http://dx.doi.org/10.15463/ie1418.11152, https://encyclopedia.1914-1918-online.net/article/portugal.
22 'Para os feridos da guerra', *A Província*, 22 October 1914, p. 1.
23 Santos Ferreira to Miguel do Sacramento Monteiro (President of the Grémio Pátria Integral), 18 December 1914, AHCVP, *Sociedade Portuguesa da Cruz Vermelha*, Copiador no. 3, 1914.
24 *Relatório e Contas da Formação Sanitária da Cruz Vermelha em serviço junto da coluna de operações no Sul de Angola* (Lisbon: Tipografia de Adolfo de Mendonça, 1916), p. 11.
25 A. S. Fell, 'Nursing the Other: The Representation of Colonial Troops in French and British First World War Nursing Memoirs', in S. Das (ed.), *Race, Empire and First World War Writing* (Cambridge: Cambridge University Press, 2011), p. 158.
26 A similar example had been practised by the British during the Boer War: see R. Gill, 'Networks of Concern, Boundaries of Compassion: British Relief in the South African War', *The Journal of Imperial and Commonwealth History*, 40:5 (2012), 835.
27 Portuguese Red Cross to Máximo Brou (Delegate of the Red Cross on the medical mission in Southern Angola), 21 July 1915, AHCVP, *Sociedade Portuguesa da Cruz Vermelha*, Copiador no. 3, July–December 1915.
28 'Sempre neutros! Portugal e a Alemanha', *O Africano*, 30 December 1914.
29 'Para os heróis de Naulila', *O Africano*, 18 September 1915, p. 1.

30 M. Barnett, *Empire of Humanity: A History of Humanitarianism* (Ithaca: Cornell University Press 2011), p. 35.
31 'Portugal na Guerra e a cooperação de Angola', *A Província* (30 July 1916), p. 2.
32 'A União aprova o programa inaugural', *A Capital*, 24 November 1914, p. 2.
33 Letter, Red Cross President to the Secretary General of the Ministry of Public Instruction, 9 July 1915, AHCVP, *Sociedade Portuguesa da Cruz Vermelha*, Copiador no. 3, July–December 1915.
34 'Festa Sportiva', *O Africano*, 2 June 1917, p. 1.
35 Red Cross Secretary General to the Governor of Guine Province, 6 October 1917, AHCVP, *Sociedade Portuguesa da Cruz Vermelha*, Correspondência Geral, September–December 1917.
36 Santos Ferreira (Red Cross Secretary General) to Berta de Castro e Maia, 20 April 1915, AHCVP, *Sociedade Portuguesa da Cruz Vermelha*, Copiador no. 2, April–June 1915.
37 General Correspondence, AHCVP, *Sociedade Portuguesa da Cruz Vermelha*.
38 Manuel was the younger son of King Carlos. On 1 February 1908 the King and his elder son, Luís Filipe, were assassinated by anarchists in the streets of Lisbon while riding an open carriage. Only Queen Amélie and her other son Manuel survived. Manuel then unexpectedly, at the age of eighteen, ascended to the Portuguese throne.
39 Hutchison, *Affective Communities*, p. 35.
40 Ibid., p. 47.
41 *Grande Comissão Portuguesa Pró-Pátria relatório apresentado à grande assembleia dos subscritores em 16 de Março de 1918* (Rio de Janeiro: Tipografia do Jornal do Comércio de Rodrigues & C.ª, 1918), p. 119.
42 *Grande Comissão Portuguesa Pró-Pátria relatório apresentado à grande assembleia dos subscritores em 16 de Março de 1918*, pp. 8–9.
43 AHCVP, *I Guerra Mundial: Comissão Portuguesa dos prisioneiros de Guerra / Agência Internacional de Prisioneiros de Guerra CICU, Livros Correspondência. Subscrições. Participação das delegações Pietás (1914–1920)*, 1 vol.
44 *Grande Comissão Portuguesa Pró-Pátria relatório apresentado à grande assembleia dos subscritores em 16 de Março de 1918*, p. 87.
45 *Estatutos da Cruzada das Mulheres Portuguesas* (Lisbon: Imprensa Nacional, 1916).
46 F. R. de Meneses, 'Introduction: The Lusophone World at War, 1914–1918 and Beyond', *e-Journal of Portuguese History*, 15:1 (2017), 1–2.

4

Philanthropy in time of war: Paul Nathan and the Hilfsverein der deutschen Juden

Christoph Jahr

Introduction

When James Simon, the chairman of the Relief Organisation of German Jews (Hilfsverein der deutschen Juden / Hilfsverein) looked back in 1926 on a quarter of a century of his association's activity, he depicted the Great War as almost a happy time, in which transatlantic co-operation in particular had worked better than ever before. 'In Germany as well as abroad, we found understanding for our goals and willing support everywhere,' Simon wrote, adding that it was especially the US-American co-religionists who had made it possible to 'set up a comprehensive relief organisation'. On the other hand, 'the political decline and impoverishment after the war forced us [...] to limit our activities'.[1] Simon's reflections highlighted not only the particularly close connection that existed between the German and US Jewish relief organisations during the Great War but also the diverging developments faced by Jewish communities on both sides of the Atlantic.

In current research on Jewish humanitarianism the Anglo-American perspective predominates not least because the state of research on German and Austro-Hungarian Jewish aid organisations remains unsatisfactory.[2] This chapter will introduce a German-Jewish perspective on Great War Jewish humanitarianism by focusing on the Hilfsverein. For pragmatic reasons it will concentrate on the activities of Paul Nathan (1857–1927),[3] the de facto leader of the Hilfsverein and the central actor in the field of non-Zionist philanthropy in prewar Germany. The chapter examines the obstacles faced by the Hilfsverein in general, and Nathan in particular, in trying to organise humanitarian aid in Eastern Europe. It will discuss these points by first sketching Jewish ideas of charity and international philanthropic networks prior to 1914; it will then analyse German-Jewish humanitarian aid campaigns, internal Jewish frictions, and the larger political questions during the Great War. Thirdly, the chapter will touch upon the international context with a focus on the US.

Jewish humanitarian traditions in Europe

When writing the history of humanitarianism during the era of the Great War, a look at the Jewish communities of Europe is of particular interest. Because of their diasporic situation and their status as a traditionally marginalised and often persecuted group, Jewish communities were not only extremely vulnerable to the effects of unrest, material hardship, and persecution in times of war but were also especially dependent on the support of their respective home states, that is, the states they were citizens of, for their aid organisations. At the same time all Jewish communities, to varying degrees, had their loyalty to their respective homelands called into question. Practising transnational solidarity and promoting humanitarian aid in favour of a population group in an 'enemy state' was therefore particularly delicate, because it always ran the danger of fostering antisemitism at home. Suggesting an aid campaign in favour of persecuted Jews in an allied state was scarcely less problematic, as this could be understood as an unsolicited interference in an ally's internal affairs. This problem affected the Jewish communities both in the Central Powers and in the Entente with regard to the threatened Jews in the war zones of Russian Poland and the Baltic states, in Austrian Galicia, and the Balkans (especially in Romania) as well as in the Ottoman Empire, most notably in Palestine.

In Jewish tradition caring for the weak always played an important role.[4] The term Zedakah (literally 'righteousness' or 'justice') came into use only in the post-biblical period through the Talmud and Rabbinic literature and is used almost exclusively for 'charity'. It is seen as a religious obligation for the donor and an entitlement for the beneficiary. As the attitude towards the poor hardened in the course of the nineteenth century, the traditional religious forms of charity were often seen as outdated or even socially harmful and hence assumed new forms. Once largely direct and indiscriminate, it became increasingly secularised and impersonal and was delegated to special agencies and trained professionals. From the early nineteenth century onwards local, national, and international Jewish philanthropic ventures emerged, which initially focused on the traditional support for the Old *Yishuv*, the tiny Jewish settlement in Ottoman Palestine that depended heavily on donations from Jewish communities abroad. However, Jewish efforts to present their humanitarian initiatives as a universal enterprise were systematically delegitimised by anti-Semites who saw it as evidence of the 'Jewish conspiracy' to dominate the world.

These suspicions only grew stronger when Jewish philanthropic organisations began acting on a global scale and combining charity with defending Jewish rights abroad, as happened from the mid-1800s. The Damascus affair of 1840, a case of antisemitic blood-libel, saw European Jews operate as global actors on the diplomatic stage for the first time.[5] The case of Edgar Mortara, a child torn from his Jewish parents and forcibly baptised in the Papal State in 1858, marked the birth of the Board of Delegates of American Israelites (1859) and, even more importantly, the French Alliance Israélite Universelle (AIU) in 1860. Simultaneously, the London Board of Deputies (established in 1760) extended the scope of its international activities, while the London-based Anglo-Jewish Association (AJA) (1871) and the Israelite Alliance in Vienna (Israelitische Allianz zu Wien, 1872) were both founded to follow the example of the AIU.

Over the course of the second half of the nineteenth century the scope of Jewish humanitarian enterprises extended to the realms of education and economic development. A network of kindergartens, orphanages, and elementary and secondary schools developed. The AIU in particular was very successful in these activities and saw itself engaged in a civilising mission to promote French language and culture along with French commercial and political interests. Some Jewish humanitarian organisations also concluded that the most effective and sustainable way to help Jewish communities in distress was in fact to facilitate migration – mostly to the Americas, but also to Palestine.[6]

The Hilfsverein der deutschen Juden in Berlin reflected this wider development, although it was founded only in 1901, some four decades after the AIU and three decades after its sister organisations in Britain and Austria.[7] Its dominating figure was Paul Nathan, who was born in 1857 into a wealthy Jewish bourgeois family in Berlin connected to the highest circles of Prussian society.[8] Nathan was a protégé of the great liberal politicians and publishers Eduard Lasker and Ludwig Bamberger. For more than twenty years he served as managing editor of Theodor Barth's influential Berlin liberal weekly *The Nation* (*Die Nation*). However, Nathan's career as a party politician never took off. As Nathan once remarked, it was 'the impossibility of creating anything fruitful [in Germany], that pushes me to the Middle East'[9] – and into international humanitarian aid, one may add. In 1901 he helped found the Hilfsverein, one of the most influential German-Jewish associations of its time, which soon swelled to some thirty thousand members. Nathan embodied the modern professional manager and built up a dense and widespread network. Until his death in Berlin in 1927 Nathan was 'widely regarded as the leader of non-Zionist German Jewry'.[10]

The Hilfsverein's first major humanitarian aid campaign focused on the immediate relief for the victims of the 1903 pogrom in Kishnev, Russian Empire (today Chişinău, Moldova). The Kishinev incident, considered by many scholars to be a 'turning point in Jewish history',[11] saw forty-nine Jews killed, hundreds of Jewish women raped, and fifteen hundred Jewish homes damaged. It also brought the word *pogrom* into the global lexicon and spurred widespread Jewish migration. In the aftermath of Russia's defeat by Japan in 1905 and the civil unrest that followed, the Hilfsverein became active for the second time; many aid campaigns followed. Its humanitarianism was, however, as patronising as it was benevolent. In a letter to his alter ego in London, Lucien Wolf, Nathan complained in June 1905 that the 'non-Jewish Russians are incapable, but the Jewish Russians are unfortunately not much more capable. [...] [I]f the Russians do not act with the necessary determination and prudence, *we* in the West have to do it in their place.'[12] His paternalistic view of the 'Eastern Jews' ('Ostjuden') was typical of most 'Western Jews' at the time. Humanitarian aid went hand in hand with a sense of superiority that saw the recipients of aid not as equals but as subordinates in need of guidance.

In addition to direct emergency aid for impoverished Jewish communities in Eastern Europe, the Balkans, and the Ottoman Empire, promoting education also played a prominent role. The AIU was particularly present in the Levant and North Africa, the Vienna Alliance in the eastern provinces of the Habsburg monarchy and the AJA in Russia.[13] Co-operating as well as competing with its older sister organisations, the Hilfsverein built up a dense network of educational institutions. It administered up to fifty schools and similar educational institutions with some 6,500 pupils.[14] The main focus was on Palestine with over three thousand pupils in twenty-eight institutions, fourteen of them in Jerusalem alone. The beacon of the Hilfsverein's 'educational humanitarianism', however, was the Technische Hochschule in Haifa, today known as Technion – Israel Institute of Technology – and one of the world's leading research universities.[15] An additional field of activity was the fight against antisemitism and the malicious myths it rested on. Nathan himself published numerous educational brochures and newspaper articles on the subject. He also campaigned in favour of Jewish victims of 'ritual murder' – the best-known case being that of the Ukrainian Mendel Beilis.[16] In the decade before the Great War the Hilfsverein had thus taken its place in the comparatively vast and sophisticated network of Jewish humanitarian organisations in Europe.

German-Jewish humanitarian aid: from the Balkan Wars to the postwar period, 1912–24

The Hilfsverein's first wartime mission began one and a half years before the assassinations in Sarajevo pushed Europe into the abyss. Although the Balkan Wars of 1912–13 did not result in a war between the major European powers, they were in many ways 'the beginning of the First World War',[17] not least because they were fought with excessive violence from all sides, anticipating what was shortly to follow. In early 1913 Nathan and

Bernhard Kahn,[18] the Hilfsverein's General Secretary, accompanied by Elkan Adler from the AJA, inspected the war zone in Bulgaria and northern Greece, visited endangered Jewish communities, and collected data on them. Nathan was even granted audiences with King Georg V of Greece, and with the Czar and the Czarina of Bulgaria. Although these meetings achieved little in practical terms, Nathan recognised their symbolic and prospective political value: 'the presence of our commission', he wrote, 'as representatives of Western European associations, was a powerful means of protecting the Jewish population from attack. [...] The authorities and the non-Jewish population have realised that the representatives of the state attach importance to a good relationship with the Jews, and this effect will continue after our departure.'[19] It may be disputed how deeply rooted in reality Nathan's self-assured judgement was. It is, however, significant that he ascribed to his humanitarian mission aspects that are usually associated with state-centred foreign policy. This is not entirely surprising as the Hilfsverein had also performed governmental tasks in the years before 1914 in controlling Jewish emigration from Eastern Europe overseas. In fact, Hilfsverein officials controlled the border crossing, the transit through Germany and the journey across the Atlantic.[20] This proximity to the state would give the Hilfsverein an elevated position in the first years of the Great War.

The Hilfsverein's humanitarian activities began immediately in August 1914, and focused on Germany itself, where enemy nationals were stranded by the outbreak of fighting.[21] Official policy towards enemy aliens was improvised and inconsistent during the early weeks of the war, but it is fair to say that national, class, and racial biases played an important role. Civilians from the Russian Empire were particularly singled out for victimisation, as they were considered more dangerous and 'undesirable' than their French and British counterparts, and consequently attracted more attention from the authorities and the public.

Although the majority of Russian nationals in Germany were non-Jewish, Reich Chancellor Theobald von Bethmann Hollweg assigned the Hilfsverein as the central agency for organising support and repatriating those civilians deemed 'harmless'. Bernhard Kahn, who oversaw the return of twenty thousand Russian subjects via Denmark and the Netherlands, nevertheless faced serious opposition. In his unpublished postwar memoirs he reflected laconically that 'it was not very easy to persuade the German military authorities to permit [...] relief work of a German group on behalf of the enemies'.[22] Despite these difficulties Kahn succeeded in clearing the 'Russian Camp' ('Russenlager') Ruhleben near Berlin where the Russian civilians had been interned. His success enabled the German authorities to convert Ruhleben into the central internment camp for the British male civilians who were arrested on 6 November 1914, among them a considerable number of Jews. They received humanitarian aid, kosher food in particular, from Berlin's Jewish community.[23]

In the long run, however, the repatriation of the Russian civilians from Germany proved to be a relative sideshow for Jewish humanitarianism. Continuing their prewar relief work, it was obvious to all Jewish communities in Europe and the United States that their co-religionists in Eastern Europe and the Ottoman Empire were in particular need of help. This became all the more urgent as the Eastern Front ran right through the main Jewish settlement areas. Approximately half of the world's Jews lived in Russian Poland and the infamous 'pale of settlement' of the Empire's Western Provinces. By March 1915 $457,000 had been collected throughout Europe and in the United States to be used almost exclusively for the Eastern Front.[24] As will be shown, this state of affairs elevated the position of US actors who were able to serve as neutral mediators when co-operation between European organisations broke down. But it also gave particular prominence to German Jewish organisations. Because this area of Eastern Europe was soon to be occupied by the Central Powers, any distribution of aid required the support or at least acquiescence of German authorities and made organisations like the Hilfsverein crucial to providing relief on the ground. It clearly helped that, since Eastern Europe, and the Russian Empire in particular, had been the Hilfsverein's principal field of activity before the war, it could rely on a well-developed network of local agents who could help administer relief and evaluate the material needs of the civilian population.[25]

Behind the scenes, however, various political conflicts raged in Germany. The first was the long-standing struggle between Zionist and non-Zionist organisations on who could rightfully claim to speak for the German Jews. Humanitarian aid for Eastern Europe soon became one of the major battlefields of this struggle.[26] Before 1914, the 'assimilationists' dominating the Hilfsverein had the upper hand in representing 'Jewish interests' in foreign policy. As early as 1902, however, Max Bodenheimer, one of the leading German Zionists, had tried – unsuccessfully – to convince the Foreign Office that Zionism could be an asset to German foreign policy as it promised to orient Jews living in the Russian Empire towards Germany.[27] Not surprisingly, Bodenheimer immediately seized the opportunity offered by the war to garner support for his moderate brand of Zionism.[28] In a memorandum entitled 'Concurrence of German and Jewish Interests in the World War', dated 4 August 1914, he tried to convince the German Foreign Office of the total congruence of Zionism to Germany's war aims in the east. He argued that Germany should establish an 'East European Federation' in which 'all ethnic groups were to enjoy national autonomy', including the

Jews. To support this claim, the Committee for the liberation of Russian Jews (Komitee für die Befreiung der russischen Juden) was brought into being on 17 August 1914. To counter these Zionist ambitions, Nathan founded the Interconfessional Committee for the Alleviation of Suffering in the occupied Eastern territories (Interkonfessionelles Komitee zur Linderung der Not in den besetzten Ostgebieten) in September 1914, but Bodenheimer's cause continued to attract support. In October 1914 he was invited by Erich Ludendorff to the German headquarters in the East (Ober Ost), where he was received 'with great affability'. But he soon realised that he could not trust Ludendorff since 'we were for him only insignificant pawns on the chess board of the war'. Although the Commander-in-Chief of the Eastern Army, Paul von Hindenburg, went so far as to express 'a benevolent interest in the endeavours' of Bodenheimer's committee and offered 'to further its aims', the practical result of Bodenheimer's initiative was close to nil.[29]

It is clear that both sides looked to humanitarian aid to further their political interests. The Zionists never saw humanitarian aid as an end in itself but rather as a point of departure for their broader agenda. But while Bodenheimer criticised Nathan for his alleged refusal 'to consider the question of the East European Jews from any other than the humanitarian point of view',[30] the Hilfsverein's insistence on the non-political nature of relief was itself a political move, trying to curb the wider ambitions of the Zionists by limiting them to purely humanitarian aid. Despite their conflicting interests, both sides eventually co-ordinated their efforts, which consisted primarily of ensuring that people were supplied with food and shelter. Particularly urgent was the need to care for the hundreds of thousands of refugees.[31] The Hilfsverein, which dominated the humanitarian aid on the Eastern Front in the years 1914 and 1915, covered the area of the Oberbefehlshaber Ost (in the shape of the Jüdisches Hilfskomitee für Polen und Litauen), while Bodenheimer's Committee for the East covered the area south of Ober Ost, i.e. the so called Generalgouvernement Warschau (which comprised only a part of Russian Poland). A third player, the Free Association for the interests of Orthodox Jewry (Freie Vereinigung für die Interessen des orthodoxen Judentums) was also involved. Thus all three varieties of German Jewry (the secular and highly assimilated, the Zionist, and the Orthodox) were active in the field of humanitarianism. It was only in February 1918 that the three finally joined forces under the umbrella of the Union of Jewish organisations for the Protection of the Rights of the Jews in the East (Vereinigung jüdischer Organisationen Deutschlands zur Wahrung der Rechte der Juden des Ostens). This move 'effectively ended the boycott of Zionism by the German Jewish organisations'[32] just as it indicated that the leading role of the Hilfsverein had passed.

Yet there was also a second set of contentious issues at the time, one regarding German identity, patriotism, and the compatibility of national and transnational solidarities. The fact that the Hilfsverein lost ground in the struggle for influence over Germany's foreign policy during the war was unexpected, in so far as the Hilfsverein wholeheartedly supported the German war effort. It, too, lionised the German army as the liberator of the Jews and other oppressed minorities. Nathan insisted that the German and Austria-Hungarian empires were 'fighting not only for their own political, economic and cultural existence but also to free the entire world from Moscovite and British paternalism'.[33] Notwithstanding such demonstrative Jewish support for the war effort, antisemitism soon grew and the German authorities continued to show latent hostility towards Jewish organisations. In early November 1915 the Hilfsverein, joined by the Grand Lodge of the Independent Order of B'nai B'rith (Großloge für den Unabhängigen Orden B'nai B'rith)[34] and the Aid Committee for the Distressed East European Jews (Hilfskomitees für die notleidenden osteuropäischen Juden) initiated a fundraising drive called an 'Appeal for the needy in the occupied parts of Russia'. The Berlin Police Department, however, ordered the title to be changed to 'Appeal for the suffering *Jews* [emphasis added] in the occupied parts of Russia'. Apparently, it was not sufficient for German authorities that the Jewish nature of the relief was clear from the three institutions in charge; it was to be marked additionally, hardly with friendly intentions.[35] In this way Jewish humanitarian aid was forcibly 'Judaised' and in a certain sense de-Germanised.

This aspect became increasingly apparent the longer the war dragged on. By organising philanthropy in times of war Nathan, wittingly or not, became deeply implicated in German occupation policy and war aims. By April 1916, according to a report by the Hilfsverein, almost 1.8 million Jews were living under German occupation. This number rose to as many as three million as the German and Austro-Hungarian armies advanced further east. By providing aid to this group, the Hilfsverein clearly helped stabilise the German occupation regime, pacifying a suffering and discontent population and quieting international criticism of Germany's wartime actions. But by aiding war victims and supporting the German war effort to attain greater visibility, the Hilfsverein also increasingly found itself complicit in initiatives that ran directly counter to its long-held beliefs and humanitarian positions. In fact, it was not the Jews alone who hoped for humanitarian aid. In March 1915 Nathan complained to Theodor Wolff about the 'hatred of the Poles against the Jews', who also tried to prevent 'the Jewish population from being supported as well as they are'.[36] In 1916 it became increasingly obvious that German foreign policy now privileged (Christian-)Polish interests over Jewish in the Generalgouvernement

Warschau. Even worse, Jews were clearly overrepresented amongst the forced labourers recruited by the German authorities.[37] Erich Ludendorff, the de facto dictator in the Ober Ost occupation area, saw the Jews as a disruptive obstacle to his plans to establish a German 'Musterprotektorat' ('model protectorate').[38] This became apparent with shocking brutality when he summoned the leadership of the Hilfsverein – James Simon, Paul Nathan, Franz Oppenheimer and Bernhard Kahn – to his headquarters in Kovno (today Kaunas, Lithuania) in February 1916, and announced his plan to push ahead with the mass emigration of Russian Jews in order to get rid of 'superfluous eaters'. 'The Jewish representatives were rather stunned by Ludendorff's ideas,' Kahn recalled, 'but nobody dared to speak up. I finally got up and spoke against Ludendorff's plan.' Ludendorff reacted with icy silence, but did not pursue his plans to turn the Hilfsverein into an instrument of forced migration – which was exactly what happened to the Hilfsverein after 1933.[39] The full force of the destructive energy inherent in Ludendorff's increasingly hostile attitude towards the German-Jewish organisations was revealed when Kahn reported on his experiences to the board of the Hilfsverein after his return. Kahn's assessment that war hero Ludendorff was 'politically very reactionary' was acknowledged by Moritz Sobernheim with an indignant: 'It is a shame to say such a thing. You are not a German!' 'And so what' was Kahn's laconic reply.[40] The Hilfsverein's humanitarian involvement was not only marred by long-standing intra-Jewish struggles but it also raised difficult questions about German patriotism, belonging, and the shrinking space for transnational solidarity in an increasingly total war.

The rise of American-Jewish humanitarianism in the era of the Great War

The open and covert political power struggles that unfolded in the field of humanitarian aid between the various Jewish groups in Germany were increasingly overlaid and reconfigured by the American Jewish Joint Distribution Committee (JOINT). The JOINT gained enormous influence over the course of the war as it had a near-monopoly on all funds raised by the two-million-strong Jewish community in the United States: the largest and wealthiest in a neutral country. Paul Nathan had closely co-operated with Jacob H. Schiff, a leader of the American Jewish Committee, for a decade before the war broke out. Nevertheless, the American Jewish associations, although deeply engaged financially, lacked experience in operating large-scale international philanthropy for civilians. Remote from the European theatres of war, they were heavily dependent on the aid network of German and Austro-Hungarian Jews, not least because the British blockade made it impossible for American relief supplies to be transferred directly to Eastern Europe. The German and Austro-Hungarian aid organisations, in turn, relied heavily on American money, the more so as the war dragged on. Ninety per cent of the 77 million marks raised by the Hilfsverein for humanitarian aid in Eastern Europe between 1914 and 1921 came from donors outside Germany; the vast majority from the US. The alliance between the Hilfsverein and the JOINT was critical for humanitarian aid in Eastern Europe.[41] While the JOINT raised money and resources, the Hilfsverein organised the distribution of the relief aid in the war zone. The money transfer was handled through Max M. Warburg's Hamburg-based bank, which had reliable family and business ties with Jacob Schiff's Loeb & Co. in New York. Additionally, Felix M. Warburg, Max's elder brother, was one of the JOINT's leading figures. He secured the US State Department's swift support, ensuring that US money was forwarded to the aid committees on the Eastern front. This was a clear indication of the 'special connections leading American humanitarian organisations often enjoyed with the US government'[42] – a practice quite different from that experienced by the Hilfsverein with the German government.

Despite the initially close co-operation, the JOINT increasingly limited the influence of German organisations. This was partly out of a concern for the dispute between German assimilationists and their Zionist antagonists.[43] Tired of the cabal that occupied German Jewry, the JOINT successfully confined the influence of the German aid associations and insisted on renaming the Jewish Aid-Committee for Poland and Lithuania into Jewish Aid-Committee for Poland and Lithuania *for the Administration of American funds* (emphasis added). By 1916 the JOINT had developed considerable expertise, networks, and experience, independent from European organisations. That year it produced a memorandum entitled 'The Jews in the Eastern War Zone', documenting the plight of Eastern European Jewry.[44] The fact that an American Jewish organisation was capable of compiling such an astounding amount of data showed the extent to which US Jews had emancipated themselves from their European brethren, not only in raising funds but also in organising humanitarian aid around the globe. This enabled the JOINT to assume some of the tasks of the German-Jewish aid organisations. The transatlantic balance of power, at least as far as the Jewish communities were concerned, had shifted and the German squabblers had been disempowered by 'Uncle Sam'. Emphasising the Americanness of its aid was an astute move that clearly served the interests of the JOINT vis-à-vis its German partners. The US government, too, had no reservations in labelling Jewish funds 'American' as it cast the United States in a positive light and opened many doors for exercising influence in various fields, not least the economy.⁴⁵ In all, these developments gave American Jewish organisations a much more prominent role in Eastern Europe.

The marginalisation of the Hilfsverein continued and accelerated after American entry into the war in April 1917. In June 1917 the American Jewish Relief Committee, which collected funds for the JOINT, announced that 'American money' should henceforth be distributed by US citizens and not 'through the Committee in Germany, headed by James Simon and Paul Nathan'. The JOINT succeeded in establishing a reliable transfer option via the Netherlands.⁴⁶ It was also active in Russia, where one to two million Jews were forced from their homes as the Central Powers advanced eastward. Unable to build up a network of its own, the JOINT relied on the Central Jewish Committee for the Relief of Sufferers of War (Evrejskij komitet pomošči žertvam vojny), which used the pre-existing networks of its affiliated organisations to distribute money. These aid campaigns ran successfully until they were disrupted by the Russian Revolution of March 1917 and more or less halted after the Bolshevik takeover of power.

At the same time the equation of Jewry and Bolshevism and the subsequent rise of antisemitism made the situation even more uncomfortable for the Jews in the shatter-zone of the Russian Empire. According to contemporary Russian reports, between January and July 1919 alone, some 26,000 people were killed during pogroms in Ukraine.⁴⁷ At the same time, the antisemitic stereotype of 'Jewish supremacy' became ever more bizarre. The American Relief Administration, for example, headed by the Quaker Herbert Hoover, was frequently accused of favouring Jewish over Christian needy.⁴⁸ While the American public and government were hostile to the Soviet Union, the American Jewish Joint Agricultural Corporation (Agro-Joint) was founded in July 1924 to organise the resettlement of urban Soviet Jews to farming colonies in the Crimea and the Ukraine. By 1937 over a hundred thousand Jews had been resettled on one million acres of land at a cost of $16 million.⁴⁹ However questionable many aspects of this co-operation with Stalin's totalitarian regime may have been, the sheer fact that American-Jewish humanitarian aid continued on a great scale after the end of the Russian Civil War marks a stark contrast to the work of the German Hilfsverein.

In fact the Hilfsverein – hampered by political unrest and economic deprivation at home – was no longer able to provide substantial humanitarian aid abroad after 1918 and was largely forced to restrict itself to domestic projects.⁵⁰ Two final attempts by Nathan to regain the international initiative came to nothing. In September 1925, he held talks with the Soviet Foreign Minister Georgy Chicherin over aid measures for Soviet Jews. The following year, he drafted a large-scale resettlement plan to ease population pressure in western Russia by resettling impoverished Jewish families. Neither project led to any practical result.[51] Nathan's close friend and first biographer, Ernst Feder, noted a few months after his death in March 1927 that his 'assumption that the Americans needed us for the Russian things' was an 'illusion';[52] so too was his appreciation of the Soviet organisations whose aim was to orient the Jews towards new professions. It is hard to disagree with Feder's judgement: Nathan had by this stage lost touch with reality. In the process, he had somehow 'missed' the astounding rise of US philanthropy.

Conclusion

The years 1912 to 1924 were a period of monumental expansion of Jewish humanitarianism as well as equally monumental shifts within it, most notably the rise of US philanthropy. When Bernhard Kahn, who had served as the Hilfsverein's General Secretary for a decade, became the new director of the JOINT in Europe in the spring of 1921, the Hilfsverein's chairman James Simon frankly admitted that in serving the JOINT Kahn could 'fulfill greater tasks than he could within the framework of German Jewry'.[53] While Nathan's and the Hilfsverein's activities after 1918 were essentially restricted to Germany, Kahn became a 'global player', embodying the shift of influence, resources, and power of Jewish philanthropic organisations from Europe to the US. The 'Americanisation' of the philanthropic relief work in Europe was a legacy of the war whose lasting consequences became apparent in the inter-war years.

In reflecting on Nathan's activities and the Hilfsverein's humanitarian aid work, it is clear that the terrain they traversed was a hard-fought political field, in which different actors struggled for resources and power. Nathan – and with him the Hilfsverein – not only had to fight to gain the support of the German government and military authorities for his aid projects. As a result of the war he also lost ground to his Zionist opponents and US Jewish organisations. Humanitarian aid in times of war is often considered one of the few rays of hope in dark times. Aid workers operating in the war zone deserve our full admiration for their altruism and often life-threatening commitment to 'saving strangers'. But if one considers the political conditions under which this aid was provided, it is difficult to avoid the conclusion that the delivery of wartime humanitarian aid is in part – and often unavoidably so – a component of national war efforts. The experience of the Hilfsverein during the Great War exemplifies the thin line between co-operation and complicity that aid organisations continue to grapple with to this day.

Notes

1 Hilfsverein der deutschen Juden (ed.), *Festschrift anläßlich der Feier des 25jährigen Bestehens des Hilfsvereins der Deutschen Juden, gegründet am 28ten Mai 1901* (Berlin: Buchdruckerei Marx & Co., 1926), p. 4; On Simon: O. Matthes, *James Simon: Mäzen im Wilhelminischen Zeitalter* (Berlin: Bostelmann & Siebenhaar, 2000); E. Feder, 'James Simon: Industrialist, Art Collector, Philanthropist', *The Leo Baeck Institute Year Book*, 10:1 (1965), 3–23; R. Michael, 'Simon, James', in F. Skolnik (ed.), *Encyclopaedia Judaica*, 2nd ed., vol. 18 (Detroit: Macmillan Reference USA, 2007), pp. 611–2. I wish to thank the editors for their fruitful comments.

2 On the dearth of research on German organisations see F. M. Schuster, *Zwischen allen Fronten: Osteuropäische Juden während des Ersten Weltkrieges (1914–1919)* (Cologne: Böhlau, 2004), p. 55. By contrast the state of research has improved significantly for the Jewish aid organisations in the US. This may explain why the recent, thoroughly researched account by J. Granick, *International Jewish Humanitarianism in the Age of the Great War* (Cambridge: Cambridge University Press, 2021) tacitly equates *international* Jewish humanitarianism with *American* Jewish humanitarianism, as do other contributions on this topic.

3 For more on Nathan see C. Jahr, *Paul Nathan: Publizist, Politiker und Philanthrop, 1857–1927* (Göttingen: Wallstein, 2018). Unfortunately, there is no up-to-date account of the Hilfsverein's widespread humanitarian activities.

4 For the following see 'Charity (Tzedakah): Charity Throughout Jewish History', Jewish Virtual Library, accessed 31 May 2022, www.jewishvirtuallibrary.org/charity-throughout-jewish-history.

5 For the following see L. M. Leff, *Sacred Bonds of Solidarity: The Rise of Jewish Internationalism in Nineteenth-Century France* (Stanford: Stanford University Press, 2006); D. J. Penslar, 'The Origins of Modern Jewish Philanthropy', in W. Ilchman, S. Katz, and E. Queen II (eds), *Philanthropy in the World's Traditions* (Bloomington: Indiana University Press, 1998), pp. 197–214; C. Fink, *Defending the Rights of Others: The Great Powers, the Jews, and International Minority Protection, 1878–1938* (Cambridge: Cambridge University Press, 2004).

6 See T. Brinkmann, 'The Road from Damascus: Transnational Jewish Philanthropic organisations and the Jewish Mass Migration from Eastern Europe, 1840–1914', in D. Rodogno, B. Struck, and J. Vogel (eds), *Shaping the Transnational Sphere: Experts, Networks and Issues from the 1840s to the 1930s* (New York: Berghahn Books, 2015), pp. 152–72. In this context, important early organisations are the Hebrew Immigrant Aid Society (1884), the Baron de Hirsch Fund (1891), or the Jewish Colonization Association (ICA, 1901).

7 Brief overview: W. F. Ze'ev, 'Hilfsverein der deutschen Juden', in F. Skolnik (ed.), *Encyclopaedia Judaica*, 2nd ed., vol. 9 (Detroit: Macmillan Reference USA, 2007), pp. 106–7.

8   On Nathan see E. Feder, *Paul Nathan: Politik und Humanität. Ein Lebensbild* (Berlin: Deutsche Verlags-Gesellschaft für Politik und Geschichte, 1929); E. Feder, 'Paul Nathan, the Man and His Work', *Leo Baeck-Institute Year Book*, 3:1 (1958), 60–80; Jahr, *Paul Nathan*. Nathan's great-uncle was the private banker to Prussia's King and Germany's first Emperor, Wilhelm I.

9   A. Wiener, 'Paul Nathan – Darstellung und Deutung: Zum 100. Geburtstage am 25. April 1957', *AJR Information, issued by the Association of Jewish Refugees in Great Britain*, 12:4 (1957), 6 (my translation).

10 B. Barkow, *Alfred Wiener and the Making of the Holocaust Library* (London: Vallentine Mitchell, 1997), p. 7.

11 See S. J. Zipperstein, *Pogrom: Kishinev and the Tilt of History* (New York: Liveright Publishing Corporation, 2018); M. Noam Penkower, 'The Kishinev Pogrom of 1903: A Turning Point in Jewish History', *Modern Judaism: A Journal of Jewish Ideas and Experience*, 24:3 (2004), 187–225.

12 Nathan to Wolf, 16 June 1905, YIVO Institute for Jewish Research New York, RG 348 Folder 40, 3117 (my translation and emphasis); see E. Bar-Chen, 'Two Communities with a Sense of Mission: The "Alliance Israélite Universelle" and the "Hilfsverein der deutschen Juden"', in M. Brenner, V. Caron, and U. R. Kaufmann (eds), *Jewish Emancipation Reconsidered: The French and German Models* (Tübingen: Mohr Siebeck, 2003), pp. 111–21.

13 See Z. Szajkowski, 'Conflicts in the Alliance Israélite Universelle and the Founding of the Anglo-Jewish Association, the Vienna Allianz and the Hilfsverein', *Jewish Social Studies*, 19:1/2 (1957), 29–50.

14 For the following see E. Burkard, 'Überwindung von Armut durch Bildung: Das Schul- und Bildungswerk des Hilfsvereins der Deutschen Juden, 1901–1937/1938' (PhD dissertation, University of Siegen, 2016), http://dokumentix.ub.uni-siegen.de/opus/volltexte/2016/1012/; C. Jahr, 'Wohlfahrt und Weltpolitik: Die Tätigkeit des Hilfsvereins der deutschen Juden in Palästina, 1901–1920', in Institut für jüdische Geschichte Österreichs (ed.), *'Zedaka' (hebr. Gerechtigkeit): Jüdische Wohlfahrt und Armenfürsorge bis 1938* (St Pölten: Institut für jüdische Geschichte Österreichs, 2020), pp. 56–63.

15 For a short overview see Y. Dori, 'Technion, Israel Institute of Technology', in M. Berenbaum and F. Skolnik (eds), *Encyclopaedia Judaica*, 2nd ed., vol. 19 (Detroit: Macmillan Reference USA, 2007), pp. 571–2.

16 Beilis was the victim of a blood libel charge in Kyiv in 1911. He was legally acquitted partly due to an international support campaign, in which Paul Nathan, Lucien Wolf, and Lord Nathaniel Rothschild played a leading role: see 'Menahem Mendel Beilis', Jewish Virtual Library, accessed 29 September 2021, www.jewishvirtuallibrary.org/menahem-mendel-beilis; Jahr, *Paul Nathan*, pp. 117–19.

17 R. C. Hall, 'Balkan Wars 1912–1913', in U. Daniel, P. Gatrell, O. Janz, H. Jones, J. Keene, A. Kramer, and B. Nasson (eds), *1914–1918-online. International Encyclopedia of the First World War*, 8 October 2014, DOI: http://dx.doi.org/10.15463/ie1418.10409, https://encyclopedia.1914-1918-online.net/article/balkan_wars_1912-1913.

18 On Kahn see C. Jacobowsky, 'Bernhard Kahn', *Nordisk judaistik / Scandinavian Jewish Studies*, 3:1 (1979), 21–31. A comprehensive biography, however, is still lacking.
19 P. Nathan, E. Adler, and B. Kahn, *Bericht über das Balkanhilfswerk, erstattet von dem nach dem Balkan entsandten Delegierten*, Union des Associations Israélites (Brussels and Berlin: July 1913), p. 35; confidential typescript, Leo Baeck-Institute New York (LBINY), DR 46.1 U5 (my translation); see Jahr, *Paul Nathan*, pp. 180–1.
20 See T. Brinkmann, 'From Oswiecim to Ellis Island: Jewish and Other Transmigrants and the Evolution of Border Controls Along Germany's Eastern Border, 1885–1914', in A. Małek and D. Praszałowicz (eds), *Between the Old and the New World: Studies in the History of Overseas Migrations* (Frankfurt am Main: Peter Lang, 2012), pp. 109–23.
21 For the following see C. Jahr and J. Thiel, 'Adding Colour to the Silhouettes: The Internment and Treatment of Foreign Civilians in Germany during the First World War', in S. Manz, P. Panayi, and M. Stibbe (eds), *Internment during the First World War: A Mass Global Phenomenon* (London: Routledge, 2018), pp. 44–45; Hilfsverein der deutschen Juden (ed.), *Festschrift*, pp. 17–18; most recently R. Müller, *'Feindliche Ausländer' im Deutschen Reich während des Ersten Weltkrieges* (Göttingen: Vandenhoeck & Ruprecht, 2021), pp. 270–83.
22 B. Kahn, Memoirs 1914–1921: 'Beginning of World War I: Relief activities for the victims of the War', LBINY, ME 344a, p. 15.
23 On Ruhleben see M. Stibbe, *British Civilian Internees in Germany: The Ruhleben Camp, 1914–18* (Manchester: Manchester University Press, 2008); C. Jahr, 'Zivilisten als Kriegsgefangene: Die Internierung von "Feindstaaten-Ausländern" in Deutschland während des Ersten Weltkrieges am Beispiel des "Engländerlagers" Ruhleben', in R. Overmans (ed.), *In der Hand des Feindes: Kriegsgefangenschaft von der Antike bis zum Zweiten Weltkrieg* (Cologne: Böhlau, 1999), pp. 297–321; N. Durbach, 'Keeping Kosher in the Camp: Feeding Interned British Jews during the First World War', *Immigrants & Minorities*, 38:1–2 (2020), 1–26.
24 This equates to approximately $13 million in 2023 prices. G. Motta, *The Great War against Eastern European Jewry, 1914–1920* (Newcastle upon Tyne: Cambridge Scholars Publishing, 2017), p. 41.
25 Schuster, *Zwischen allen Fronten*, pp. 285–7.
26 Since the first Zionist Congress in Basel in 1897, this political movement, founded by Theodor Herzl, was particularly anchored in German-speaking Central Europe. The headquarters of the Zionist Organisation (today the World Zionist Organisation, Tel Aviv) was first in Vienna, then in Berlin, before it was moved to neutral Copenhagen in 1916. The dispute between assimilationist and Zionist Jews in other European countries as well as in the US was admittedly even more fierce than in Germany; see H. Lavski, *Before Catastrophe: The Distinctive Path of German Zionism* (Detroit: Wayne State University Press, 1996), pp. 91–2.
27 J. Ticker, 'Max I. Bodenheimer: Advocate of Pro-German Zionism at the Beginning of World War I', *Jewish Social Studies*, 43:1 (1981), 13.

28 Ticker, 'Max I. Bodenheimer', 15–18; Z. Szajkowski, 'Jewish Relief in Eastern Europe 1914–1917', *Leo Baeck Institute Year Book*, 10:1 (1965), 24–56.
29 M. Bodenheimer, *Prelude to Israel*, ed. H. H. Bodenheimer, trans. I. Cohen (New York: T. Yoseloff Publ., 1963), p. 248, p. 251; the Committee later changed its name to a less compromising Komitee für den Osten (Committee for the East).
30 Bodenheimer, *Prelude to Israel*, p. 238.
31 Hilfsverein der deutschen Juden (ed.), *Festschrift*, pp. 15–16.
32 See Lavski, *Before Catastrophe*, p. 39.
33 P. Nathan, *Die Enttäuschungen unserer Gegner: August, September, Oktober. Eine Vierteljahresabrechnung* (Stuttgart: Deutsche Verlags-Anstalt, 1914), pp. 34–5 (my translation). Of course this did not apply only to German Jews: the majority of French, British, and Austro-Hungarian Jews also supported the war policies of their respective home countries; see M. Rozenblit, 'The European Jewish World 1914–1919: What Changed?', in M. L. Rozenblit and J. Karp (eds), *World War I and the Jews: Conflict and Transformation in Europe, the Middle East, and America* (New York and Oxford: Berghahn, 2017), pp. 35–7.
34 See A. Reinke, 'Between Ethnic Solidarity and National Allegiance – The German Order of the B'nai B'rith', *Jahrbuch des Simon-Dubnow-Instituts / Simon Dubnow Institute Yearbook*, 1 (2002), pp. 321–42.
35 See Jahr, *Paul Nathan*, p. 151.
36 Ibid., p. 151 (my translation).
37 See A. Stempin, *Das vergessene Generalgouvernement: Die Deutsche Besatzungspolitik in Kongresspolen 1914–1918* (Paderborn: Ferdinand Schöningh, 2019), pp. 418–95, pp. 463–70 in particular; J. Thiel and C. Westerhoff, 'Forced Labour', in U. Daniel, P. Gatrell, O. Janz, H. Jones, J. Keene, A. Kramer, and B. Nasson (eds), *1914–1918 online. International Encyclopedia of the First World War*, October 2014, DOI: http://dx.doi.org/10.15463/ie1418.10409, https://encyclopedia.1914-1918-online.net/article/forced_labour.
38 V. G. Liulevicius, *War Land on the Eastern Front: Culture, National Identity, and German Occupation in World War I* (Cambridge: Cambridge University Press, 2000); J. Matthäus, 'German Judenpolitik in Lithuania during the First World War', *The Leo Baeck Institute Year Book*, 43:1 (1998), 155–74.
39 In 1933 the Hilfsverein had to change its name to Hilfsverein der Juden in Deutschland (Relief Organisation of Jews in Germany), and in 1939 it was forcibly merged with the Reichsvereinigung der Juden in Deutschland (Reich Association of Jews in Germany). Instead of helping Eastern European Jews emigrate overseas, it now had to organise the emigration of German Jews from their homeland. For context see D. Jünger, *Jahre der Ungewissheit: Emigrationspläne deutscher Juden 1933–1938* (Göttingen: Vandenhoeck & Ruprecht, 2016).
40 B. Kahn, Memoirs 1914–1921: 'Beginning of World War I: Relief activities for the victims of the War', LBINY, ME 344, pp. 41–5.
41 For the following see C. Tessaris, 'The War Relief Work of the American Jewish Joint Distribution Committee in Poland and Lithuania, 1915–18', *East*

European Jewish Affairs, 40:2 (2010), 127–44; Motta, *Great War*, pp. 42–8; Schuster, *Zwischen allen Fronten*, pp. 342–4.
42 Granick, *International Jewish Humanitarianism*, p. 57; p. 41.
43 Szajkowski, 'Jewish Relief'; Jahr, *Paul Nathan*, pp. 153–5; In the long run, however, the Zionists gained the upper hand: see N. Wiener Cohen, *The Americanization of Zionism, 1897–1948* (Hanover, MA, and London: Brandeis University Press, 2003).
44 In January 1916 Elkan Adler and Philip Henry had visited Russia on behalf of the JOINT: see Motta, *Great War*, pp. 48–9; Granick, *International Jewish Humanitarianism*, p. 3.
45 Granick, *International Jewish Humanitarianism*, p. 68.
46 Ibid., pp. 46–64; Motta, *Great War*, pp. 48–51.
47 O. Budnitskii, *Russian Jews between the Reds and the Whites, 1917–1920* (Philadelphia: University of Pennsylvania Press, 2012), p. 102; on the pogroms during the civil war, pp. 216–74.
48 Ibid., pp. 296–333; Bruno Cabanes, *The Great War and the Origins of Humanitarianism, 1918–1924* (Cambridge: Cambridge University Press, 2014), p. 237.
49 Equating to $281million in 2023 prices. See A. L. Kagedan, 'American Jews and the Soviet Experiment: The Agro-Joint Project, 1924–1937', *Jewish Social Studies*, 43:2 (1981), 153–64.
50 To facilitate their aid twelve rival Jewish philanthropic associations (among them the Hilfsverein and its Zionist antagonists) finally joined forces under the umbrella of the Arbeiterfürsorgeamt der jüdischen Organisationen Deutschlands, led by Bernhard Kahn; see Jahr, *Paul Nathan*, pp. 161–4.
51 Paul Nathan, *Das Problem der Ostjuden: Vergangenheit – Zukunft* (Berlin: Philo-Verlag, 1926).
52 Feder Diary, 21 July 1927, S. 85, LBINY, AR 7040, Diaries I; Jahr, *Paul Nathan*, pp. 218–22.
53 Quoted in Jahr, *Paul Nathan*, p. 104.

Part II

The politics and power of aid

5

The neutrals at war: humanitarian competition in the Great War

Cédric Cotter

Introduction

In recent years historians have become increasingly interested in the position and role of neutral states during the Great War.[1] Research has explored political, social, cultural, and economic aspects that expose how the neutrals were involved in and affected by the conflict.[2] A growing literature has also begun to highlight the importance of neutrals' humanitarian activities, exploring the phenomenon from a transnational perspective.[3] Still, the neutrals' contribution to the humanitarian effort during the war warrants further attention. As a discussion published in the online *International Encyclopedia of the First World War* notes, there is still much historians can learn from studying the national background of humanitarian actors, the role of neutrals, and the 'moral capital' of humanitarianism.[4] The chapter attempts to answer this call, reviewing the humanitarian initiatives, the motivations, and above all the salient competition of a number of neutral actors during the Great War.

By 1914 only a handful of countries had explicitly sought to integrate humanitarian action into their foreign and internal policies. The Vatican had traditionally dispensed charity, but Switzerland's conversion to 'humanitarianism' had been a gradual one. Berne had only reluctantly agreed to convene the conference in 1864 that gave rise to the Geneva Convention of that year. Thereafter, however, the Swiss authorities quickly grasped the political value of associating themselves with humanitarian issues,[5] particularly after the 'successful' internment of the 87,000 men of the French Armée de l'Est, under General Bourbaki, which sought sanctuary in Switzerland in February of 1871.[6] But beyond Switzerland and the Vatican few neutral countries had established credible 'humanitarian' credentials before 1914. For most the Great War provided their first significant opportunity to expand into this area.

Regardless of these previous experiences in the humanitarian field, the onset of war in 1914 saw what one commentator has dubbed 'an explosion of new endeavors'.⁷ In neutral countries literally hundreds of state initiatives sprung up, as well as myriad semi-private and private, secular and religiously inspired organisations. Humanitarian responses ranged from large-scale Red Cross national societies to tiny bureaux set up by a handful of wealthy individuals. These disparate agencies sought to protect and assist sick and wounded soldiers, prisoners of war, civilian internees, displaced people, or children. The abundance of charities reflected the breadth of suffering caused by the war. But while humanitarian needs were seemingly limitless, these various entities often found themselves competing for the same causes.

What was the nature of these neutral initiatives and how did they coordinate and cross-fertilise their practices and knowledge? How and why did neutral countries and organisations engage in humanitarian competition and what did they seek to gain from their endeavours? To answer these questions, this chapter draws on archival material and secondary literature to explore two specific case studies: the competition between Switzerland (or Swiss entities) and the Vatican, and the rivalry between Scandinavian countries, largely exercised through their respective national Red Cross societies, and, in part at least, arbitrated by the International Committee of the Red Cross (ICRC). The chapter will conclude by highlighting the common features and characteristics of these competitive interactions.

A fight for prestige: Switzerland, the ICRC, and the Vatican

Let us first turn to Switzerland, the ICRC, and the Vatican. Before looking more closely at their interaction and rivalry it should be noted that the fates and activities of Switzerland and the ICRC were closely connected during the Great War. Both entities worked together and the ICRC constituted a major diplomatic asset for the Swiss authorities. The ICRC president, Gustave Ador, was a member of the parliament until 1917, when he was elected to the political executive, the Federal Council, after which point he was responsible for directing both the ICRC and the foreign policy of the Swiss Confederation.⁸

The genesis of the rivalry between the Vatican and the Swiss ICRC, discussed further below, has its roots in the creation of the Red Cross Movement and the first Geneva Convention of 1864. While the Catholic Church had traditionally been prominent in ministering to the needs of war victims, modern humanitarianism and the Red Cross movement were more inspired by traditions of philanthropy and evangelism. The Vatican disapproved of the Red Cross's 'secular' approach to humanitarianism and its explicit privileging of material over spiritual relief. It was sceptical of the ICRC's leadership, its 'sectarian spirit', and its alleged links to the freemasons.[9] Even though the First World War and its secular and national aspects deeply affected the way humanitarian aid was conceived and provided, these views continued to shape the Vatican's dealings with the ICRC after 1914.[10]

At the outbreak of the conflict both the Vatican and the ICRC immediately embraced humanitarian activities, leading them to co-operate as well as compete with each other. One of their earliest and most lasting humanitarian commitments during the war was to secure information about interned soldiers. Hundreds of thousands of families were desperate for news and information about their husbands, fathers, and sons sent to the front. Many felt powerless and sought the assistance of local clergy to help find news about their loved ones' whereabouts. Pope Benedict XV responded by opening a tracing service, which by 1918 had handled over seven hundred thousand inquiries. It was particularly effective in connecting Italian families with their loved ones detained in Austria-Hungary.[11] Local bureaux were also set up at the local level; for instance in Rheine (Germany) by Bishop Schulte and in Fribourg (Switzerland), where Bishop Bovet established the Mission Catholique Suisse. The Vatican also arranged for the production and distribution of relief parcels.[12] Beyond the Vatican the war gave a boost to the development of organisations inspired by the Catholic faith.[13]

The role played by the Catholic Church complemented the efforts carried out by other actors such as the ICRC and its International Agency for Prisoners of War as well as numerous national Red Cross societies. Collaboration between the ICRC and the Vatican covered a number of areas. The Mission Catholique Suisse benefited from the technical and diplomatic support of both the Vatican and the Swiss Confederation, illustrating the convergence of their mutual interests and goals.[14] Prisoners of war frequently failed to distinguish between visiting ICRC delegates and representatives of the Mission Catholique Suisse: they were, after all, all Swiss citizens inspecting prisoners of war camps.[15] What mattered was not their origin or ideological motivation but rather their ability to improve the prisoners' lot and conditions of internment. Even though all these actors wanted to have a prominent role in tracing displaced people and visiting detention sites, the need and suffering were so large that they usually managed to collaborate without stepping on each other's toes.

The ICRC, the Vatican and Swiss federal authorities also innovated in such areas as the repatriation and neutral internment of wounded and sick prisoners of war.[16] The earliest actions aimed at repatriating civilians stranded in enemy territory at the outbreak of the war, but attention quickly shifted to other categories of war victims. On 12 November

1914, Gustave Ador, president of the ICRC and a National Councillor of Switzerland, urged Arthur Hoffmann, Federal councillor in charge of foreign affairs, to offer Swiss assistance in repatriating prisoners of war whose wounds made them incapable of bearing arms and whose continued detention was of no value to either side.[17] According to Ador, the initiative represented a tangible act of neutrality that would resonate well with public opinion in the belligerent countries and generate gratitude for Switzerland.[18] In January 1915 the Confederation was ready to support this initiative with the Swiss Red Cross.[19] On 2 and 3 March the first trains left Lyon and Constance for Switzerland.[20] Ultimately, even though only a limited number – 2,650 in March 1915, 2,343 German soldiers and 8,668 French soldiers by November 1916 – of badly wounded or sick soldiers benefited from the initiative, it was a true humanitarian success in that it demonstrated how, by working through neutral intermediaries, the belligerents could reach agreements that met the humanitarian needs of their citizens. Encouraged by this precedent, new proposals were put forward over the following months, most notably the idea of interning select sick and wounded soldiers in Switzerland, where they could better recover than in belligerent internment camps.[21]

The Vatican, too, was becoming increasingly interested in this area of activity from late 1914, in obvious competition with the Confederation. Having failed to negotiate a Christmas truce, the Pope had suggested a PoW repatriation, very similar to a Swiss initiative, to the belligerent governments on 31 December 1914.[22] In the spring of 1915, without prior consultations with neutral governments, the Pope came forward with a proposal to intern certain categories of wounded and sick soldiers in neutral countries – where they would enjoy much greater comforts – and sent a representative to negotiate with the Swiss government.[23] In May, the Swiss Federal Council accepted the Pope's proposal, but insisted that the project was presented as a complement to the Swiss initiative.[24] After six months of hard negotiations, the first cohort of two hundred prisoners, all suffering from tuberculosis, arrived on 26 January 1916 in Switzerland, where they were distributed to hotels and sanatoria across the country.[25] By the time the war came to an end, some 67,000 soldiers had benefited from internment in Switzerland.

While both direct repatriations and neutral internment were being implemented and proving their value, pressure mounted to augment the arrangements and extend their remit to other categories of prisoners. In April 1916 growing awareness of the psychological impact of long-term captivity prompted the Vatican to suggest offering neutral internment to prisoners who had been detained for more than eighteen months.[26] In September 1916 the Swiss discussed with the French Red Cross the possibility of including prisoners who had three children and more.[27] Despite the reluctance of a very cautious Arthur Hoffmann, the Swiss government agreed to a pilot project with a small group of prisoners falling within these new categories in January 1917.[28] It would take another year to achieve definitive agreement on further operations. The so-called Berne Agreement of March and April 1918 widened the categories of internees who could be repatriated to their country of origin: prisoners older than forty-five years of age, those aged forty with more than three children, and those who had been in captivity for over eighteen months.[29] The agreements could have led to the repatriation of more than a hundred thousand soldiers; but the Armistice intervened before the agreement could come fully into force.

As these examples show, the Vatican and the Swiss occupied the same humanitarian ground and found themselves promoting complementary humanitarian activities. They shared similar objectives and were prepared to collaborate to achieve them. The Swiss Federal Council discussed the Pope's proposals and was ready to implement them. But at the same time, they also competed for the prestige, visibility, and political benefits that were believed to flow from these initiatives. The Vatican's moral aims were not necessarily aligned with secular but faith-inspired activities carried out from the 'Protestant Rome': during the war, neutral states were heavily criticised by belligerents, who neither understood nor approved of their position. Moreover, as large parts of their economies were often directly controlled by the belligerents, neutrals faced grave difficulties in ensuring the supply of food and raw materials. Both countries were therefore anxious to have their neutrality acknowledged and respected by the belligerents, not least to overcome their isolation and secure their interests in the shifting international environment. Humanitarian activities helped strengthen their moral authority, generate a sense of gratitude and obligation among the belligerents, and burnished their standing as neutrals. For example, Switzerland explicitly pointed to its humanitarian services when negotiating a food supply agreement with the United States in 1917.[30]

It is not surprising, then, that, although in their bilateral communications and public utterances the two sides frequently spoke of their common mission and mutual respect, neither party was averse to using humanitarian activities for self-promotion, or even belittling the other's contribution. For instance, following the ICRC's appeal against the use of chemical weapons in February 1918, the Pope expressed himself happy to be '*assisted* [emphasis added] by people and institutions generously oriented towards the same goal'.[31] In a similar vein, when the repatriation issue was first raised in early 1915, Gustave Ador was adamant that the prestige in launching the programme should accrue to Switzerland and encouraged Swiss newspapers to emphasise the initiative's Swiss origins.[32] In a letter to the Swiss Red Cross president Ador insisted that 'the public should know these things to avoid others benefiting from an initiative that we have the right to claim. [...] It would be deplorable if, being at the origin of these initiatives, either through the president of the Confederation, or through us [the ICRC], Switzerland would not play an important role in this humanitarian task.'[33] These words were obviously directed at the Vatican, and over the following years Ador frequently reiterated such sentiments. In January 1916 he informed the president of the French Red Cross that the idea to intern soldiers had originated with the ICRC,[34] and, in December of that year, he claimed the Vatican had occupied only an 'unofficial' role in the talks over repatriating fathers with large families.[35]

Both Berne and Geneva clearly viewed the Vatican as a rival; and the feeling was mutual. But it is also clear that this rivalry had limits, and did not prevent them collaborating in humanitarian tasks that benefited tens of thousands of prisoners of war. In many respects the strengths of the two parties were complementary. The Vatican possessed immense moral authority, while the Swiss had the wherewithal to transform ideas into concrete action.

The Scandinavian competition

Humanitarian competition was also apparent among the northern neutrals. For the Scandinavian powers the Great War was in many respects a transformative moment in their historical development. As Lina Sturfelt notes, 'the war gave the Nordic countries new roles in the international arena as civilised role models and "humanitarian great powers", propagating the idea of benevolent Nordic neutrality'.[36] Denmark first became a central point for tracing activities on the Eastern front.[37] On 3 October 1914 the ICRC asked the Danish Red Cross to set up an agency, similar to that operating in Geneva, to focus on Russia, Austria-Hungary, Serbia, and Germany.[38] The Danish replied positively and, with the support of the royal ministry of the interior, 160 people started to work in dedicated offices, with a similar number of volunteers working from home.[39] Despite some early hesitation on the part of the belligerents – the German and Russian Red Cross societies initially wanted to exchange prisoner lists directly or through Swedish channels[40] – and the difficulty in getting accurate and timely lists of prisoners from the Russians,[41] by the end of the war the Copenhagen agency had assembled some 3.5 million index cards on individuals.[42] The agency received 251,000 letters for tracing requests in 1915, 429,000 in 1916, and more than five hundred thousand in 1917.[43]

Like the Dutch, the Danes also sent ambulances, funded from state and private sources, to operate behind the front lines in Belgium, Estonia, France, Russia, and Serbia.[44] And like the ICRC and the protecting powers, the Danish Red Cross sent delegates to inspect internment camps in Russia, Germany, and the Ottoman Empire.[45] In 1916 Denmark had thirty-six delegates operating abroad,[46] and consciously modelled its inspection reports on those written by ICRC delegates.[47] Aristocratic 'nurses' coming from the country of the internees occasionally accompanied them.[48] The Danish Red Cross also sent parcels to prisoners of war, for instance those prepared by wealthy women participating in the 'Dana programme'.[49] In addition to standard relief items such as food and clothing, the Danish Red Cross worked with the YMCA and the Oeuvre Universitaire Suisse to send spiritual relief.[50] A special section was set up in 1915, partly funded by the government, which sent more than four hundred thousand books to places of internment in Germany, Austria-Hungary, France, Great Britain, Russia, and Switzerland.[51] To facilitate the work of the delegates and the distribution of relief, the Danish Red Cross eventually established offices in Petrograd, Moscow, Kiev, Vienna, Berlin, and Paris.[52] These offices in turn inspired the ICRC and prefigured its future use of permanent delegations in the field.

The Swedes were just as – if not more – involved in humanitarian activities as their Danish neighbours. The Swedish Red Cross founded a committee for prisoners of war in June 1915 and was active in many countries on the Eastern front. For instance, by the end of 1917, it had sent 41 trains (1,016 coaches) of relief to Russia,[53] and in 1917, 115 trains departed from China, Tientsin, and Vladivostok.[54] Like the Danes the Swedes established offices in Russia for the distribution of relief.[55] The number of prisoners to benefit from the intervention of the Swedish Red Cross was impressive: by June 1918 it was calculated that Swedish assistance had reached 1,258,700 Russians and 83,900 Romanians in Germany; 853,000 Russians and 40,000 Romanians in Austria-Hungary; 1,732,764 Austro-Hungarians, 172,675 Germans, 47,685 Ottomans and 145 Bulgarians in Russia.[56] Led by Elsa Brändström, daughter of the Swedish ambassador in Russia, nurses visited prisoners of war camps and took care of the sick and wounded.[57] They worked in parallel with the 'aristocratic' nurses who were allowed into Russia from Germany and Austria-Hungary.[58] In total they provided material and medical care to more than seven hundred prisoners across Russia, including Siberia and Turkestan.[59] The presence of neutral female nurses was unique during the First World War.[60] In other words, like belligerent countries, both Sweden and Denmark quickly set up massive assistance operations, partly through their Red Cross society. It is important to note that, in terms of size, scale, and geographical scope, the Scandinavian operations dwarfed those organised by the ICRC. Scandinavian countries also organised or hosted initiatives similar to those arranged in Switzerland; between 1915 and 1918 some 63,463 wounded prisoners were repatriated through Sweden from 1915 onward,[61] and, until 1918, 63,463 prisoners benefited from repatriation.[62]

These programmes were often transnational in origin as well as in implementation. For example the exchange of prisoners was widely acknowledged as a Swiss initiative (with the support of the Vatican),[63] but in August 1916 the ICRC asked the Red Cross societies of Denmark, Sweden, Norway, and the Netherlands whether they could arrange the internment on their soil of men who had been prisoners for more than eighteen months.[64] While Sweden had to decline – its hospitals, hotels, and sanatoria were already fully occupied[65] – Denmark welcomed Russian, Austrian, and German wounded and sick who were treated like prisoners of war.[66] To organise these initiatives and improve internment conditions a significant number of international conferences were held. Three conferences took place in Stockholm between December 1915 and December 1916, gathering Germany, Austria-Hungary, Russia, and Sweden. Germany and Great Britain met in The Hague in July 1917. The following month, Stockholm hosted another conference between Russia, Germany, and Austria-Hungary; and Germany, Austria-Hungary, Romania, Russia, the Ottoman Empire, Sweden, and Denmark met yet again in October and November 1917 in Copenhagen. In November 1917 Christiania (Oslo) also welcomed Germany, Austria-Hungary, Russia, and Norway. A month later the same protagonists, minus Norway, met in Petrograd.[67]

Beyond this impressive level of transnational collaboration, Scandinavian states' and organisations' involvement triggered a real competition in which the ICRC also played a specific role. On the one side, the ICRC arguably stoked this competition by choosing the Danish Red Cross to set up its tracing agency. On the other, it used its position within the Red Cross and Red Crescent movement to moderate the effects of this competition. Bent Blüdnikow's research has exposed the depth of rivalry between the Scandinavian governments and Red Cross societies in administering aid to prisoners of war.[68] When the ICRC decided that a tracing agency for the Eastern front was necessary, Sweden lamented that Copenhagen was chosen.[69] The Swedish Red Cross reacted with its own uncoordinated initiatives. To supplant the Danish, it unsuccessfully proposed to the Russians to take care of information related to German and Austro-Hungarian prisoners.[70] In 1915 it created a commission for Russian and German prisoners.[71] The Danish Red Cross objected and henceforth regularly complained to the ICRC, criticising both the Swedish Red Cross[72] and other Swiss private charities that did not always share information on the whereabouts of soldiers.[73] The ICRC reminded the Swedish that they were not responsible for tracing activities.[74] It also reassured the Danes: 'you can see that we keep you in the first position, confirming the mandate we have given you. [...] You retain our complete trust and you remain the sole owners of the official mandate we have conferred to you.'[75] A few months later the ICRC acknowledged that 'charitable competition' was a reality it had to deal with.[76]

The organisation of international conferences by the Swedish government followed a similar pattern. In November 1915 Prince Karl (head of the Swedish Red Cross) informed the ICRC that he was organising a conference gathering Russian, Austro-Hungarian, German, and Swedish Red Cross societies.[77] The ICRC complained to the Swedish that, as an internationally recognised body, it should at least have been informed in advance.[78] In 1917 the ICRC and Switzerland tried to expand the categories of prisoners eligible for repatriation. Edouard Odier, member of the committee *and* Swiss minister in Russia – just one of many examples of the close alignment of ICRC and Swiss interests – was instructed to promote the idea in Russia and Scandinavian countries.[79] To improve the co-ordination the ICRC sent diplomatic missions to Berlin, Copenhagen, and Stockholm.[80] Inspired by the ICRC's proposal, the Austrian, Russian, and Swedish Red Cross societies gathered in Stockholm in August to find new solutions for exchanges of prisoners on the Eastern front. Yet again the ICRC was informed of the conference only once it had started, and the Danish Red Cross was not even invited.[81] As a consequence, the ICRC claimed the paternity of the proposals and suggested that exchanges of prisoners should be direct, thereby bypassing Sweden.[82] Only in late 1917 did relations slightly improve when the Danish, Swedish and Norwegian Red Cross created a 'northern committee' of Red Cross societies,[83] ensuring closer co-operation on repatriation operations and between delegates in the field.[84]

While Danish–Swedish competition will be considered below, why did Geneva favour the Danish Red Cross over the Swedes? The sources are silent on this matter, but some hypotheses can be made. First, personal affinities likely played a part in the ICRC's choice. The Genevan organisation decided to mandate a national society with which it had cordial relations. The 'obedient' behaviour of the Danish Red Cross might have been preferred to the free and individualistic initiatives of the Swedish Red Cross. The ICRC might have considered the Swedish attitude a threat, for both its leadership over the Red Cross movement and Swiss political interests. Favouring the Danes sidelined a direct competitor for the ICRC and Switzerland's humanitarian reputation. The Swiss were clearly eager to establish their humanitarian primacy not only vis-à-vis the Vatican. Throughout they were happy to trumpet the fact that they 'did what neither Holland, Sweden nor America do; we watch over what remains from international conventions, from signed treaties and given words'.[85] At the pragmatic level the strong anti-Russian sentiment in Sweden might also have helped convince the ICRC that Denmark could better guarantee a neutral and efficient action towards Russia.[86] Both practical and geographical reasons might have worked in Copenhagen's favour as a location for a tracing agency.

The reasons behind the humanitarian commitment

As has been shown, humanitarian competition between neutrals was ubiquitous, and at times petty. But why did neutral countries and organisations even compete in the first place? What did they hope to gain from their humanitarian activities? Although some hints have been offered above, a brief look, country by country, followed by more general reflections, might help better understand this competition.

In Switzerland, humanitarian aid proved to be a useful tool for both foreign policy and internal cohesion. Swiss authorities were quick to use the rhetoric of humanitarianism to justify Switzerland's neutrality and highlight the value. They also hoped the internment of wounded soldiers would help guarantee their food supply.[87] Despite voicing their criticism of Switzerland, the belligerents largely acknowledged their debt to Swiss agencies and considered Swiss humanitarianism to be a mitigating circumstance to its neutrality.[88] Often overlooked is the crucial role humanitarianism played *within* Switzerland. Humanitarian action was an important pillar of Switzerland's 'culture of neutrality'.[89] Helping war victims gave real meaning to Swiss neutrality, provided a common goal around which the population could mobilise, and helped buttress Switzerland's social and national cohesion, especially at a time when French- and German-speaking citizens often had diverging views on the war, forcing the authorities to find a good balance between sympathies. Moreover humanitarian endeavours became a major way for women to help safeguard Switzerland (with men carrying out military duties), regardless of their social status. Several private committees were inspired and directed by wealthy women. At the ICRC Marguerite Cramer played a prominent role in managing the International Agency for Prisoners of War, then became the first woman ever to visit several European capitals as a 'delegate' of the ICRC and the first woman to join the committee in 1918.[90]

In practice, of course, many private Swiss organisations and individuals conducted their affairs with little reference to Switzerland's policy of neutrality. Helping specific groups was a meaningful, yet still sufficiently 'neutral' way to express sympathy and preference for one belligerent and support the war effort of one side.[91] However, practical considerations should not be ignored either. Most charitable organisations were simply too small to operate even-handedly. Only the biggest organisations, such as the Swiss authorities, the ICRC, and the Swiss Red Cross, had the wherewithal to provide impartial aid. Moreover a closer look suggests that the idea of a 'humanitarian trench'[92] dividing the Swiss population in French-speaking and German-speaking people is problematic. Charities working in favour of the victims in Entente countries could be found in the German-speaking cantons, and not just in the *Suisse romande*.[93] While diasporas obviously helped their country of origin, such aid also reflected prewar connections. For example several committees in favour of the Belgians were created by individuals who either had strong ties with the country or felt that Belgium was an innocent victim of the conflict.

Importantly, despite the often-partisan nature of humanitarian commitments, the official narrative around humanitarian action remained very inclusive. Irrespective of the particular heterogeneity of the Swiss population – in terms of geography, social background, religion, language, and, of course, attitudes towards the belligerents – Switzerland was presented as a country that united around a humanitarian goal. Through humanitarian action, even if it benefited but one side, all Swiss citizens were united in the pursuit of a common goal. The authorities, the ICRC, and the media developed an inclusive narrative of humanitarian commitment that encompassed the whole population, regardless of its actual commitment. The First World War completed the construction of the Swiss humanitarian mission and made it part of its national identity.[94]

The Vatican embraced humanitarian activities in order to recover its former moral authority and overcome its diplomatic isolation.[95] The humanitarian initiatives co-sponsored by the Pope were a way to garner gratitude from the beneficiaries, their families, and their governments and ultimately to attain a better international position and recognition.[96] To some extent these objectives could be compared with those of Spain,[97] and were similar to those of Switzerland. This explains the intense collaboration, as well as the equally intense frictions, between those countries, as they were trying to achieve the same political goals.

The Danish government clearly understood the importance of humanitarian aid for its foreign policy, especially towards Germany and Russia. As other neutral states were involved in these activities, it was necessary to follow this trend anyway.[98] This is why, like most other countries, the Danish government expanded its control over its national Red Cross society. Sweden had a similar experience, with state and private humanitarian initiatives that provided the country with 'a certain independence of action and enhanced, and perhaps even changed, the national self-image', if perhaps not to the same extent as Switzerland.[99]

Overall, common trends and patterns are discernible. Most European neutral states, including those not analysed here, shared the same challenges and aims. Because of their geographic, economic, moral, or humanitarian role(s), neutral countries were clearly more than mere peripheral actors in the war. Their war was a time of troubled peace. The belligerents were highly ambiguous in their attitude towards them. On one hand, they were frequently critical of the neutrals, and often accused them of implicitly siding with their enemies. On the other hand, they appealed to the neutral gallery in justifying their ideology and actions. Belligerents and, more importantly, their populations also directly benefited from the humanitarian commitment of the neutrals. And yet the First World War ultimately damaged the reputation of neutral states. Many either entered the war (Italy, the USA, most of the countries of Latin America) or ended the war disappointed with their status (the Netherlands, Spain, Norway, etc.).[100] Switzerland, Denmark, and Sweden are perhaps the three notable exceptions to this general trend. In this environment humanitarian aid was one of the few acceptable – and constructive – aspects of neutrality, if not the only one. For this reason almost all neutral powers tried to engage in humanitarian activities and include them in their diplomatic toolkit. Competition was a natural result of this development.

Humanitarianism also, however, played an important role in the so-called spiritual or emotional mobilisation of neutral publics. By deeply engaging with the war's suffering, neutral populations had an experience that was, in some respects, similar to that of a belligerent home front. True, their experience of war was indirect. There was no 'real front' generating death, destruction, and suffering.[101] And in many neutral countries like Denmark, Spain, the Netherlands, and, as María Inés Tato demonstrates in Chapter 1 above, Argentina as well, the populations struggled with their status for just that reason. Humanitarian engagement constituted a way to understand, see, and experience the horrors of warfare, mobilise the population, and strengthen social cohesion. Humanitarian action eventually gave sense to neutrality, and probably endowed neutral publics with a feeling of moral superiority.[102]

Despite the seemingly endless nature of humanitarian needs, these common objectives triggered competition between all these actors, forcing them to highlight their differences and uniqueness and to promote themselves vis-à-vis their rivals. It illustrates the entanglement of humanitarian action and both international and internal politics.

Conclusion

This leads us to a few concluding remarks. First, the humanitarian competition went far beyond neutral states and the First World War. Belligerent countries, especially the United States after 1917, were eager to use humanitarian aid for political and ideological purposes and amplified this phenomenon.[103] As Neville Wylie shows in Chapter 6 below, these traits were already latent in American behaviour as a protecting power before 1917. But whereas for small and medium powers the humanitarian rhetoric was an argument for their survival, the Americans could adopt a more proactive, not to say ideological and imperialist, attitude. In 1917, after years of cordial relations with the ICRC, the American Red Cross changed its set-up, governance, and objectives. The relations with the Genevan organisation deteriorated as both vied for leadership in the Red Cross movement.[104] This rivalry continued in the aftermath of the war and was intensified by the creation of a new League of Red Cross Societies established by victorious countries in 1919. Competition between the League and the ICRC became one of the hallmarks of the interwar years.[105]

Humanitarian competition did not prevent collaboration, co-ordination, and mutual support. As has been shown, many private, semi-private, or state organisations worked together on the Western front, to the benefit of thousands of prisoners of war and civilian internees and refugees. Switzerland and the Vatican succeeded in convincing the belligerents to accept innovative humanitarian measures for their prisoners of war. These inspired similar initiatives on the Eastern front. The ICRC, national Red Cross societies, and protective powers – the United States, Spain, Switzerland, Denmark, the Netherlands – exchanged camp reports and observations.[106] The most prominent organisations installed liaison offices and warehouses in Geneva and other Swiss cities, with Switzerland acting as an important nerve centre of humanitarian aid in Europe. The transfers and circulations of ideas, people, information, and goods show that humanitarian action at that time was already a transnational phenomenon.

However, if it was transnational in its realisation, humanitarian action remained governed by national interests. The grand, universal ideas of compassion and charity first and foremost served the political objectives of states. The governments' stranglehold of their respective national Red Cross societies is an eloquent example. This was obvious in belligerent countries,[107] but also in neutral states, where governments strengthened the close antebellum relations with their national Red Cross society and worked to align their activities with the foreign political interests of the state. Even the 'international' ICRC remained very close to the Swiss government and always sought to act in a way that enhanced the interests and the reputation of its host country.[108] If humanitarian action was already a genuinely transnational practice, it remained governed by national and political considerations. The examples of humanitarian competition analysed above constitute a perfect illustration.

Notes

1 The opinions expressed in this article are those of the author and do not necessarily reflect the ICRC's point of view.
2 A. Clavien and C. Hauser, 'Les états neutres et la neutralité pendant la Grande Guerre: une histoire pas si marginale', *Relations internationales*, 159 (2014), 3–6.
3 For examples see below.
4 P. Gatrell, R. Gill, B. Little, and E. Piller, 'Discussion: Humanitarianism', in U. Daniel, P. Gatrell, O. Janz, H. Jones, J. Keene, A. Kramer, and B. Nasson (eds), *1914–1918-online. International Encyclopedia of the First World War*, 9 November 2017, DOI: http://dx.doi.org/10.15463/ie1418.11168, https://encyclopedia.1914-1918-online.net/article/discussion_humanitariani sm?version=1.0.
5 I. Herrmann, *L'humanitaire en questions: Réflexions autour de l'histoire du Comité international de la Croix-Rouge* (Paris: Cerf, 2018); I. Herrmann, 'From Polemical Topics to Magnetic Concepts: Humanitarianism and Anti-Semitism in Switzerland', *Journal of Political ideologies*, 15:1 (2010), 51–68; I. Herrmann, 'La Suisse entre peur de l'autre et devoir humanitaire', in M. Viegnes (ed.), *La peur et ses miroirs* (Paris: Editions Imago, 2009), pp. 109–21.
6 H. de Weck, 'Armée Bourbaki', 26 January 2016, www.hls-dhs-dss.ch/textes/f/F26892.php; François Bugnion, 'L'arrivée des "Bourbaki" aux Verrières, L'internement de la Première Armée française en Suisse le 1er février 1871', *Revue Internationale de la Croix-Rouge*, 4:818 (1996), 191–203.
7 See B. Little, 'An Explosion of New Endeavors: Global Humanitarian Responses to Industrialized Warfare in the First World War Era', *First World War Studies*, 5:1 (2014), 1–16.
8 C. Cotter, '"Notre grande force consiste dans notre indépendance absolue de tout pouvoir politique." Les liens troubles entre le CICR et la Confédération pendant la Première Guerre mondiale', in V. Lathion and R. Durand (eds), *Action humanitaire et quête de la paix: Le prix Nobel de la paix décerné au CICR pendant la Grande Guerre* (Geneva: Georg, 2019), pp. 230–47.
9 D. Debons, 'Le CICR, le Vatican et l'oeuvre de renseignements sur les prisonniers de guerre: rivalité ou collaboration dans le dévouement?', *Relations internationales*, 138 (2009), 41–2.
10 M. O. Draenert, 'Kriegschirurgie und Kriegsorthopädie in der Schweiz zur Zeit des Ersten Weltkrieges' (PhD dissertation, University of Heidelberg, 2011), pp. 51–2; A. Fleury, 'Le Saint-Siège et les négociations de 1917', *Guerres mondiales et conflits contemporains*, 170 (1993), 18; V. Harouel, *Genève – Paris,*

1863–1918, *Le droit humanitaire en construction* (Geneva: Société Henry Dunant, Comité international de la Croix-Rouge, Croix-Rouge française, 2003), p. 704; F. Latour, 'L'action du Saint-Siège en faveur des prisonniers de guerre pendant la Première Guerre mondiale', *Guerres mondiales et conflits contemporains*, 253 (2014), 55–6.

11 Latour, 'L'action du Saint-Siège', 44, 55–6.
12 J. Pollard, 'Pope Benedict XV', in U. Daniel, P. Gatrell, O. Janz, H. Jones, J. Keene, A. Kramer, and B. Nasson (eds), *1914–1918-online. International Encyclopedia of the First World War*, 2 May 2019, DOI: http://dx.doi.org/10.15463/ie1418.11363, https://encyclopedia.1914-1918-online.net/article/pope_benedict_xv?version=1.0.
13 See P. J. Houlihan, 'Renovating Christian Charity: Global Catholicism, the Save the Children Fund, and Humanitarianism during the First World War', *Past & Present*, 250:1 (2021), 203–41.
14 F. Yerly, 'Grande guerre et diplomatie humanitaire: La mission catholique Suisse en faveur des prisonniers de guerre (1914–1918)', *Vingtième Siècle, Revue d'histoire*, 58 (1998), 17–18.
15 A. Becker, *Oubliés de la Grande Guerre: Humanitaire et culture de guerre* (Paris: Hachette Littératures, 2003), p. 193.
16 Among the many publications of the past ten years: T. Bürgisser, 'Internees (Switzerland)', in U. Daniel, P. Gatrell, O. Janz, H. Jones, J. Keene, A. Kramer, and B. Nasson (eds), *1914–1918-online. International Encyclopedia of the First World War*, 29 September 2015, DOI: http://dx.doi.org/10.15463/ie1418.10735, http://encyclopedia.1914-1918-online.net/article/internees_switzerland; M. Walle, 'Les prisonniers français internés en Suisse 1916–1919', in C. Vuilleumier (ed.), *La Suisse et la guerre de 1914–1918: Actes du colloque tenu du 10 au 12 septembre 2014 au Château de Penthes* (Geneva: Editions Slatkine, 2015), pp. 151–73; A. Huber, *Fremdsein im Krieg: Die Schweiz als Ausgangs- und Zielort von Migration, 1914–1918* (Zurich: Chronos Verlag, 2018); A. Huber, 'Des "hôtes de guerre bienvenus" ou des "étrangers indésirables"? L'internement de prisonniers de guerre malades ou blessés en Suisse de 1916 à 1919', in Lathion (ed.), *Action humanitaire et quête de la paix*, pp. 270–84; S. Barton, *Internment in Switzerland during the First World War* (London: Bloomsbury, 2019).
17 Gustave Ador to Arthur Hoffmann, 12 November 1914, in Commission nationale pour la publication de documents diplomatiques suisses (ed.), *Documents diplomatiques suisses*, vol. 6 (Berne: Bentelli, 1981), no. 72; Harouel, *Le droit humanitaire en construction*, 703; D. Palmieri (ed.), *Les Procès-Verbaux de l'Agence internationale des Prisonniers de Guerre (AIPG). Edités et annotés par Daniel Palmieri (Minutes of the AIPG)*, 11 November 1914, www.icrc.org/fre/assets/files/publications/icrc-001-4220.pdf.
18 ICRC to the Swiss Red Cross, 29 December 1914, ICRC archives (ACICR) C G1 A 42-02.
19 Swiss political department to the Swiss legation in Paris, 9 January 1915, *Documents diplomatiques suisses*, vol. 6, no. 86.

20 *Minutes of the AIPG*, 1–2 March 1915.
21 Draenert, *Kriegschirurgie*, p. 50; S. Wolf, *Guarded Neutrality: Diplomacy and Internment in the Netherlands during the First World War* (Leiden: Brill, 2013), p. 148.
22 Latour, 'L'action du Saint-Siège', 45–6.
23 Ibid., 47–8.
24 Minutes of Meeting of the Swiss Federal Council from 7 May 1915, 26 July 1916, *Documents diplomatiques suisses*, vol. 6, no. 120.
25 Walle, 'Les prisonniers de guerre', p. 58.
26 Latour, 'L'action du Saint-Siège', 50–1.
27 Swiss political department to the French embassy in Berne, 5 September 1916, *Documents diplomatiques suisses*, vol. 6, no. 211.
28 *Minutes of the AIPG*, 11–16 December 1916; Minutes of Meeting of the Swiss Federal Council, 26 January 1917, *Documents diplomatiques suisses*, vol. 6, no. 257.
29 C. Cotter, 'The 1918 Bern Agreements: Repatriating Prisoners in a Total War', *Humanitarian Law & Policy Blog*, 29 March 2018, https://blogs.icrc.org/law-and-policy/2018/03/29/1918-bern-agreements-repatriating-prisoners-of-war/.
30 C. Cotter (S')*Aider pour survivre: Action humanitaire et neutralité suisse pendant la Première Guerre mondiale* (Geneva: Georg Editeur, 2017), pp. 368–76.
31 Cardinal Gaspari to the ICRC, 24 February 1918, ACICR A CS 8.
32 Minutes of the AIPG, 7 January 1915.
33 ICRC to Colonel Bohny, 7 January 1915, ACICR C G1 A 42–02.
34 Gustave Ador to Marquis de Vogüe, 14 January 1916, ACICR C G1 A 43–02.01.
35 *Nouvelles de l'Agence internationale des Prisonniers de guerre*, 16 December 1916.
36 L. Sturfelt, 'Humanitarianism (Sweden)', in U. Daniel, P. Gatrell, O. Janz, H. Jones, J. Keene, A. Kramer, and B. Nasson (eds), *1914–1918-online. International Encyclopedia of the First World War*, 22 January 2018, DOI: http://dx.doi.org/10.15463/ie1418.11214, https://encyclopedia.1914–1918-online.net/article/humanitarianism_sweden.
37 Cotter (S')*Aider pour survivre*, pp. 423–9.
38 ICRC to the Danish Red Cross, 3 October 1914, Danish national archives (Rigsarkivet), 10001 Dansk Røde Kors, 1876–1982 Korrespondance, Korrespondance 1910–1916, vol. 11.
39 Document sans titre et non daté décrivant les activités de la Croix-Rouge danoise, ACICR C G1 C 01–04.09.
40 ICRC to the Danish Red Cross, 23 November 1914, Rigsarkivet, 10001 Dansk Røde Kors, 1876–1982 Korrespondance, Korrespondance 1910–1916, vol. 11; Russian Red Cross to the Danish Red Cross, 21 October / 3 November 1914; Russian Red Cross to the Danish Red Cross, 5/18 December 1914, Rigsarkivet, 10001 Dansk Røde Kors, 1876–1982 Korrespondance, Korrespondance 1910–1916, vol. 11.

41 Rapport de Marguerite Cramer et Victor Van Berchem sur leur mission en Allemagne, ACICR C G1 A 16–09.
42 Minutes of the AIPG, 32; B. Blüdnikow, 'Denmark during the First World War', *Journal of Contemporary History*, 24:4 (1989), 688.
43 Minutes of the AIPG; Blüdnikow, 'Denmark during the First World War'.
44 Minutes of the AIPG; Blüdnikow, 'Denmark during the First World War'; N. A. Sørensen, 'Humanitarianism (Denmark)', in U. Daniel, P. Gatrell, O. Janz, H. Jones, J. Keene, A. Kramer, and B. Nasson (eds), *1914–1918-online. International Encyclopedia of the First World War*, 19 November 2018, DOI: http://dx.doi.org/10.15463/ie1418.11309, https://encyclopedia.1914-1918-on line.net/article/humanitarianism_denmark.
45 Document sans titre et non daté revenant sur les activités de la Croix-Rouge danoise, ACICR C G1 C 01–04.09.
46 Blüdnikow, 'Denmark during the First World War', p. 689.
47 Danish Red Cross to the ICRC, 15 September 1915, ACICR C G1 A 22–03.
48 Pro Memoria, 20 May 1916, Rigsarkivet, 10001a Dansk Røde Kors Krigsfangeafdelingen København, 1916–1917 Korrespondance med og ang. kontoret i Petrograd, vol. 157.
49 Blüdnikow, 'Denmark during the First World War', pp. 687–8.
50 Rigsarkivet, 10001a Dansk Røde Kors Bogkontor, København, 1917–1919 Korrespondance med forskellige personer, bd. 122 et Rigsarkivet, 10001a Dansk Røde Kors Paris-kontoret, 1918–1920 Korrespondance, Section Boulogne 1919–1920, vol. 32–3.
51 La Croix-Rouge danoise. Section pour livres destinés aux prisonniers de guerre, Rigsarkivet, 10001a Dansk Røde Kors Paris-kontoret, 1918–1920 Korrespondance, Section Boulogne 1919–1920, vol. 32–3.
52 Russian Red Cross to the Danish Red Cross, Petrograd office, 22 October 1916, Rigsarkivet, 10001a Dansk Røde Kors Krigsfangeafdelingen København, 1916–1917 Korrespondance med og ang. kontoret i Petrograd, vol. 157; Danish Red Cross, Berlin Office, to the Hilfs-Ausschuss für Gefangenenseelsorge, 21 August 1918, Rigsarkivet, 10001a Dansk Røde Kors Berlin-kontoret, 1917–1919 Kopier af udgåede breve, vol. 51.
53 Rapport fait en mai 1918 sur l'activité du comité de secours aux prisonniers de guerre de la Croix Rouge Suédoise pendant la période Juin 1915 – avril 1918, ACICR C G1 C 01–04.10; Minutes of the AIPG, 11 May 1918.
54 Rapport fait en mai 1918 sur l'activité du comité de secours aux prisonniers de guerre de la Croix Rouge Suédoise pendant la période Juin 1915 – avril 1918, ACICR C G1 C 01–04.10; Minutes of the AIPG, 11 May 1918.
55 ICRC to Edouard Odier, 1 May 1917, ACICR C G1 A 15–33.
56 Minutes of the AIPG, 20 July 1918.
57 A. (Iris) Rachamimov, *POWs and the Great War: Captivity on the Eastern Front* (New York and Oxford: Berg, 2002), p. 172.
58 G. H. Davis, 'National Red Cross Societies and Prisoners of War in Russia, 1914–18', *Journal of Contemporary History*, 28:1 (1993), 40.

59 L. Radauer, 'Brändström, Elsa', in U. Daniel, P. Gatrell, O. Janz, H. Jones, J. Keene, A. Kramer, and B. Nasson (eds), *1914–1918-online. International Encyclopedia of the First World War* 8 October 2014, DOI: http://dx.doi.org/10.15463/ie1418.11309, http://encyclopedia.1914-1918-online.net/article/brandstrom_elsa.
60 Rachamimov, *POWs and the Great War*, p. 163.
61 *Nouvelles de l'AIPG*, 6 July 1918.
62 Sturfelt, 'Humanitarianism (Sweden)'; *Nouvelles de l'AIPG*, 6 July 1918.
63 *Neue Zürcher Zeitung*, 17 October 1916, ACICR C G1 A 42–02; Prince Charles to the ICRC, 12 May 1917, ACICR C G1 A 16–10.04.
64 ICRC to various Red Cross societies, 23 August 1916, ACICR C G1 A 43–06.01 ACICR C G1 A 43–08 ACICR C G1 A 43–09 ACICR C G1 A 43–10.
65 Swedish Red Cross to the ICRC, 15 September 1916, ACICR C G1 A 43–10.
66 Danish Red Cross to the ICRC, 23 September 1916, ACICR C G1 A 43–08; Rapport d'Edmond Boissier et Marguerite Cramer sur leur mission à Copenhague, ACICR C G1 A 16–10.03.
67 Tableau des principales conventions et conférences internationales relatives aux prisonniers de guerre, ACICR C G1 A 09–01.
68 Blüdnikow, 'Denmark during the First World War', 691–2.
69 Ibid.
70 Unknown author to the ICRC, 10–23 May 1915, ACICR C G1 A 15–33.
71 Procès-verbaux de l'AIPG, 13 July 1915.
72 Danish Red Cross to the ICRC, 10 July 1915, 11 November 1915, 26 November 1915 and 10 January 1916, ACICR C G1 A 15–16.
73 Danish Red Cross to the ICRC, 16 November 1916, ACICR C G1 A 15–16.
74 ICRC to the Danish Red Cross, 14 July 1915, ACICR C G1 A 40–17.
75 ICRC to the Danish Red Cross, 1 December 1915, ACICR C G1 A 15–16. All translations are those of the author.
76 ICRC to the Danish Red Cross, 21 November 1916.
77 Hungarian Red Cross to the ICRC, 13 November 1915, ACICR C G1 A 09–05.
78 ICRC to the Swedish Red Cross, 27 November 1915, Swedish Red Cross to the ICRC, 20 November 1915, ACICR C G1 A 09–05.
79 ICRC to Edouard Odier, 1 May 1917, ACICR C G1 A 15–33.
80 ACICR C G1 A 16–10.01.
81 Prince Charles to the Austrian Minister of War, 14 August 1917, ACICR C G1 A 42–02; Swedish Red Cross to the ICRC, 21 August 1917, ACICR C G1 A 09–09.
82 ICRC to Prince Charles, 22 August 1917, ACICR C G1 A 42–02.
83 See various documents in ACICR C G1 A 09–16.
84 Schlussprotokoll, 28 December 1917, Rigsarkivet, 10001a Dansk Røde Kors Berlin-kontoret, 1917–1919 Kopier af udgåede breve, vol. 50.
85 E. Doumergue, 'Monographies d'Oeuvres', *Foi et Vie*, 11 (16 June 1916), 225.
86 M. Kuldkepp, 'Sweden's Historical Mission and World War I', *Scandinavian Journal of History*, 39:1 (2014), 126–46.

87 Au sujet des prisonniers blessés en Allemagne, Lyon, 23 February 1915, ACICR C G1 A 43–02.01.
88 Cotter, (S')Aider pour survivre, chapter 5.
89 For a definition of this concept and an analysis of its various components, ibid., p. 253.
90 Ibid., pp. 328–32.
91 Ibid., pp. 297–301.
92 'fossé humanitaire', based on the 'fossé moral', or 'Graben' in German.
93 Cotter, (S')Aider pour survivre, p. 300.
94 Ibid., chapter 4.
95 Yerly, 'Grande guerre et diplomatie humanitaire', 17; Yerly, 'Catholicisme et Grande Guerre: la voie humanitaire', in J.-C. Favez, H. U. Jost, and F. Python (eds), *Les Relations internationales et la Suisse: Actes du colloque du 3e cycle romand d'histoire moderne et contemporaine* (Lausanne: Editions Antipodes, 1998), p. 184.
96 F. Latour, *La Papauté et les problèmes de la paix pendant la Première Guerre mondiale* (Paris and Montreal: L'Harmattan, 1996), p. 297.
97 Cotter, (S')Aider pour survivre, p. 440.
98 Blüdnikow, 'Denmark during the First World War', 684.
99 Sturfelt, 'Humanitarianism (Sweden)'.
100 M. Brolsma, 'Making Sense of the War (The Netherlands)', in Daniel, P. Gatrell, O. Janz, H. Jones, J. Keene, A. Kramer, and B. Nasson (eds), *1914–1918-online. International Encyclopedia of the First World War*, 27 July 2017, DOI: http://dx.doi.org/10.15463/ie1418.11125, https://encyclopedia.1914-1918-online.net/article/making_sense_of_the_war_the_netherlands.
101 Cotter, (S')Aider pour survivre, pp. 254–5.
102 Ibid., pp. 452–7.
103 J. F. Irwin, *Making the World Safe: The American Red Cross and a Nation's Humanitarian Awakening* (New York: Oxford University Press, 2013).
104 Cotter, (S')Aider pour survivre, pp. 488–99.
105 I. Herrmann, 'Décrypter la concurrence humanitaire: Le conflit entre Croix-Rouge(s) après 1918', *Relations internationales*, 151:3 (2012), 91–102.
106 Cotter, (S')Aider pour survivre, pp. 468–9.
107 J. F. Hutchinson, *Champions of Charity, War and the Rise of the Red Cross* (Boulder and Oxford: Westview Press, 1996); H. Jones, 'International or Transnational? Humanitarian Action during the First World War', *European Review of History / Revue européenne d'histoire*, 16:5 (2009), 697–713.
108 Cotter, (S')Aider pour survivre, pp. 211–37; Cotter, 'Notre grande force', pp. 230–47.

6

Neutrality and the politics of protection: the United States as a protecting power, 1914–17

Neville Wylie

Introduction

One of the curious features of the history of humanitarianism during the era of the Great War is that the institution that arguably 'benefited' most from the unprecedented wave of suffering was not a humanitarian organisation at all but a political one. Protecting powers – neutral states entrusted with protecting belligerent interests in the territory of their enemies – based their work in 1914 on a loose set of customary practices. Their assumption of humanitarian responsibilities over the following years was hesitant and largely haphazard. Yet by the time the war entered its final stages, belligerents had granted neutral diplomats 'definite, explicit, comprehensive and mandatory' rights to oversee the treatment of prisoners of war and civilian internees.[1] This development was confirmed after the war when officially designated protecting powers – and not non-governmental humanitarian agencies – were identified as the principal 'organs of control' in the Prisoner of War convention of July 1929. Attempts to fashion a similar code for civilians, though ultimately unsuccessful, also envisaged a similar status for protecting powers.[2]

The elevation of protecting powers in humanitarian affairs is particularly noteworthy given that their record between 1914 and 1918 is largely one of failure. As Verena Moritz observes, when compared with the dogged efforts of the flourishing voluntary, non-governmental sector, the work of protecting powers looks ponderous and lethargic.[3] Neutral diplomats 'did not apparently always show the appropriate interest' in their tasks. 'Spanish diplomats in Germany and Austria-Hungary, who were meant to take care of soldiers of the Tsarist army, hardly found any fault with [their] conditions', despite Russian prisoners being routinely subjected to abuse and ill-treatment. American diplomats, she contends, were 'similarly reserved'.[4] Belligerent governments ultimately chose to resolve humanitarian disputes through face-to-face, or 'proximity', meetings, rather than working through the diplomatic channels of their protecting power. It was precisely because

American diplomats in Berlin had been so frustrated in carrying out their protecting power duties that on entering the war Washington insisted on strengthening the hand of protecting powers in its agreement with Germany on prisoners of war in the autumn of 1918.[5]

Protecting powers are also intriguing subjects for investigation for the problem they pose to our standard categories. Historians distinguish two processes at work behind humanitarian interventions during the war. One, evident in the work of national Red Cross societies and medical services, was based on a sense of patriotism, duty, honour, and sacrifice and a desire to support the *national* war effort. The other, embodied in the work of the International Committee of the Red Cross (ICRC), the Young Men's Christian Association (YMCA), and arguably the Vatican as well, aimed at sustaining a neutral international humanitarian sphere in which aid was dispensed impartially to all those in need, irrespective of nationality.[6] Protecting powers fit comfortably in neither category. Though members of quintessentially state-based organisations, neutral diplomats were called upon to put national interests and professional assumptions aside and operate in a sphere of activity where universalist values took precedence over national ambitions, and non-state actors were the principal protagonists and norm entrepreneurs.

This chapter draws on the experience of the United States government between 1914 and 1917 to consider the role of protecting powers as humanitarian agents. Washington was the conflict's pre-eminent protecting power, representing all eight major belligerent governments. It was a natural choice for Berlin and London, having acted in this capacity during the Franco-Prussian and Boer Wars, and protected Japanese interests in St Petersburg during the recent Russo-Japanese War. Traditional accounts of humanitarianism during the Great War not only accord the US a major role but also depict its work as a story of success. By contrast, as this chapter shows, American experience as a protecting power is distinctly chequered. Though US diplomats were certainly more successful than their Spanish counterparts, who shouldered several prominent mandates during the war, they nevertheless struggled to leverage American prestige or diplomatic assets to the full. By assuming responsibility for inspecting civilian and military internment camps in early 1915, American embassies became quasi-humanitarian agencies. But the mantle of 'humanitarian actor' never sat comfortably with American diplomats who were professionally and culturally unsuited to promoting the kind of universalist values espoused by other actors operating in this space. The tension between serving the *political* interests of their government and furthering the *humanitarian* interests of those they were mandated to represent was ultimately unresolved.

Before addressing these issues it is important to understand the position occupied by protecting powers by 1914. The institution traced its roots back to the convention whereby Christian states offered protection to their co-religionists abroad. The practice was manifest in European relations with the Muslim world from the mid-fifteenth century, but its scope broadened dramatically over the course of the nineteenth century, as European overseas commercial activities intensified and confidence in European cultural superiority encouraged states to impose their values on 'uncivilised' societies abroad. By the mid-nineteenth century protecting powers began to be used in times of war, supervising the return of diplomats, protecting embassy premises, and providing assistance to enemy nationals caught on the wrong side of the battle lines. Although these services were predominantly diplomatic in nature, as the century progressed, 'humanitarianism' began to feature in protecting power discourse. This was prompted by the declining use of prisoner exchange cartels in preference for mass internment, the rise of nation-states, and introduction of universal male conscription.[7] During the Franco-Prussian War Swiss and American diplomats appealed to both international law *and* the precepts of humanity in trying to dissuade the French authorities from interning or expelling German civilians from French territory. The conflicts that pockmarked the century's end also saw neutral diplomats transmit lists of prisoners of war and visit sites of detention.[8]

Although the Hague conventions of 1899 and 1907 and the Geneva Convention of 1906 did not accord specific responsibilities to protecting powers, their silence on an institution which had figured so prominently in recent conflicts suggests that recourse to protecting powers was considered part of the customary practice of 'civilised' states. This reflected broader assumptions, prevalent from the middle years of the century, about the role of neutral states in promoting peace and limiting the spread of war.[9] In holding belligerents to 'civilised' standards, sufficient to permit the swift return of peace once the conflict had run its course, protecting powers acted implicitly on behalf of the *whole* community of nations, not just their mandating power. It was France's departure from expected conduct in 1870, and the implications this had for the nature of international relations, that prompted the US ambassador – supported by his colleagues in the *corps diplomatique* in Paris – to take up the cause of his German protégés, not their plight per se.[10] At the same time the Fourth Hague Convention of 1907 signalled a definitive end to the practice of ransoming prisoners for personal gain, and shifted accountability for prisoners from the individual who captured them to the government the latter served.[11] With responsibility for prisoners' care, treatment, and upkeep now firmly in the hands of state authorities, it was a natural step for governments to look to state-based institutions to support them in their duties. States might not have agreed on a clear set of responsibilities for protecting powers, but it was clear that sovereign entities, and not just the nascent non-governmental sector, were poised to assume responsibilities when major war returned to the continent in 1914.

Humanitarian diplomacy

From the outset the US government sought to embed the protecting power remit within the regular conduct of diplomacy rather than acknowledge it as a discrete and novel area of activity. Its ambassadors were merely invited to include humanitarian subjects in their routine communications with foreign governments. At no time in the summer of 1914 did Washington seriously contemplate refusing the provision of 'good offices' from warring governments in Europe. This remained the default position throughout the war, despite the burgeoning number of protecting power mandates and the burden this placed on US missions abroad. For the State Department, the principal motivation for extending the offer of 'good offices' lay in repeating the success of 1904–5, when American protection of Japanese interests had paved the way to President Roosevelt's brokering of Russo-Japanese peace talks and his subsequent award of the Nobel Peace prize. Offering 'good offices' met the twin objectives of burnishing America's credentials as the world's foremost neutral power while strengthening its hand to shape the outcome of a conflict in which it was not directly engaged. It was, as Secretary of State W. J. Bryan put it on 5 August 1914, not only an 'international duty' but one which conveniently afforded the opportunity to 'exert [American] influence for peace'.[12]

The problem with this position was that its success depended on an early end to the war, or a willingness, on Washington's part, to invest in a diplomatic strategy capable of adapting to changing circumstances in Europe. Neither of these proved to be the case. The instructions circulated to US missions in Europe in mid-August 1914 were tightly drawn. They stressed the *unofficial* and *limited* nature of American 'good offices' and gave ambassadors no licence to take the initiative or promote humanitarian values more broadly.[13] Events in Europe quickly exposed the limits of this approach. At a practical level, the emotions unleashed over the summer of 1914 ensured that even routine functions proved challenging. Before the American *Chargé d'affaires* could secure the German embassy in St Petersburg, a mob ransacked the building, killing a doorman, and destroying everything of value inside. His lacklustre performance drew stern criticism in Berlin, where the embassy acquired a reputation for indolence which it never lost.[14]

In the Ottoman Empire local authorities repeatedly broke US diplomatic seals to enter consular premises and remove archives. More significantly, the hardening of attitudes towards 'enemy aliens' and minority populations of 'suspect' loyalty led to the imposition of increasingly draconian restrictions, and transformed what should, in theory, have been simple 'actuarial' consular functions into critical humanitarian services.[15] American diplomats were likewise called upon to broker agreements for the repatriation of older people, the infirm, or civilians of non-military age or negotiate improvements in their conditions.

The failure of either side to secure a decisive military victory before the winter should have led to a reassessment of Washington's position as a protecting power. Not only did it dash American hopes of securing a quick diplomatic 'win' at the peace talks but it forced US missions to offer 'good offices' at a hitherto unimaginable scale. By Christmas 1914 the Paris embassy had dispensed over five thousand separate payments to destitute 'enemy' nationals; US consular staff in Moscow claimed to process payments in excess of the entire payroll of the US army at that date.[16] And yet Washington's actions from early 1915 tended in the opposite direction. The State Department failed to grasp how the embassies' custodial duties upended traditional priorities. The challenge essentially boiled down to managing the belligerents' expectations without rebounding on America's own interests. Technical developments certainly helped. The adoption of the typewriter in the early years of the century – the US legation in Vienna was an early convert in 1901 – allowed embassies to transmit 'authentic' copies of foreign communications; but the danger of confusing the messenger for the message nevertheless remained.[17] As the ambassador Frederic Penfield noted in early 1916, the 'almost daily communication of some desire of one or other of the enemy Governments' led to the authorities throughout the Dual Monarchy regarding him as 'three-quarters enemy'.[18] Not surprisingly, he, and his ambassadorial colleagues, never tired in counselling Washington against accepting new mandates as the war progressed.[19]

The core problem for Washington lay in the scope and form of the services rendered to foreign governments. For State Department officials US embassies were 'protecting powers' in name only; the 'protection' they provided ultimately depended on the whim of the local authorities. US diplomats were expressly prohibited from associating themselves with the content of foreign communications and were discouraged from venturing opinions on wider humanitarian matters. The conundrum this posed was encapsulated in an exchange in June 1916 between Penfield's counsellor in Vienna, Ulysses Grant-Smith, and the US consul in Fiume, over whether the embassy should protest against Austria's taking of civilian hostages. Grant-Smith faithfully towed the Department's line. 'We must all of us, disabuse our minds of the idea that we are "representing" in any degree, any country but the United States of America.' America's functions were 'altogether those of a friend exercising his good offices between persons who have quarrelled and between there can be no direct communication. The only possible way for us to accomplish anything in these matters is through personal appeals to the authorities in question, and our endeavours can be successful only in the same measure as our relations are cordial with them.' As for protecting foreign nationals from deportation, imprisonment, or worse, Grant-Smith's views were clear: 'The Austro-Hungarian authorities can shoot each and every alien enemy within her borders and the US authorities would have no rights under law or treaty to protest'.[20]

It was only in Turkey that Washington was prepared to allow its staff to depart from a position of strict impartiality and actively intervene in the conflict. Though never rationalised as such, the latitude accorded reflected the long tradition of European intervention in protecting foreign interests – Christian sites and communities – in the Ottoman lands. Nowhere else did the administration agree to such robust communiqués, or so consciously frame its actions in terms of upholding the customary laws, norms, and practices of the 'international community'.[21] This reached its apogee in late 1916, when, at London's behest, the Department drew on its *own* authority in urging the Ottoman authorities to improve the conditions of detention for Entente prisoners. Washington justified the intervention on the grounds that it had rendered Turkey similar services – in investigating complaints regarding the ill-treatment of Turkish prisoners in Russia – but it also, tellingly, claimed to be acting in accordance with 'the higher interests of humanity'.[22]

There was, nevertheless, a pervasive reluctance in the Department to reinforce its protecting power operations. It was perfectly content to leave the Constantinople embassy in the hands of a *Chargé d'affaires* from February to late October 1916, despite acknowledging that the embassy's effectiveness hinged on having an ambassador in post, rather than a minister. The ambassador's absence effectively shut the embassy out of the corridors of power for nine months; for much of this time responsibility for advancing foreign interests in the Empire rested with the Dutch minister and a delegation from the ICRC.[23] Even elsewhere, US diplomats felt constrained by the Department's restrictions. The insistence, for example, that ambassadors follow protocol and channel all dealings through the ministry of foreign affairs, though of little consequence in 1914, was increasingly debilitating from 1915, as civilian ministries ceded control to the military, and responsibility for prison camps passed to provincial military authorities and interior ministries. The impact was felt particularly acutely by David R. Francis, who arrived in St Petersburg in early 1916 with strict instructions to confine his contacts to the foreign ministry, despite the fact that the ministry had little influence over Russian detention policies.[24]

Washington was also reluctant to acknowledge the extent to which US prestige was invested in the fulfilment of its protecting power work and to provide its ambassadors with the wherewithal to make a success of their mission. In the summer of 1916 it flatly refused to consider allowing invalided Austro-Hungarian prisoners to convalesce in the US, despite the much-trumpeted support lavished on Vienna's enemies in Belgium, Poland, and Serbia.[25] Moreover, Washington failed to appreciate that, in the absence of official sanction, its ambassadors would find their own way to 'play' the protecting power card. Penfield's counterpart in Berlin, James Gerard, personally intervened to help the YMCA secure access to Russian camps. He also arranged for the transfer of an American Red Cross ambulance team to Russia to attend to the needs of German PoWs. Both initiatives were expressly designed to counteract criticism of America's lacklustre protection of German interests in Russia, which by late 1915 had become so vociferous that Gerard's staff feared Berlin might transfer the protecting power mandate to Sweden.[26]

In Berlin at least, Gerard's efforts were taken as tangible evidence of American good faith. Attempts to leverage value from America's broad protecting power network were likewise welcomed. In early 1915 the ambassador George Marye appealed to his British counterpart to help improve conditions for Central Power prisoners in Russia, on the grounds that news of their harsh treatment might embarrass liberal opinion in the UK.[27] The exercise was repeated the following spring, when reports of typhus outbreaks in Siberian camps prompted the US embassy in Vienna to co-ordinate an approach to the Russian and British authorities.[28] Neither initiative led to any substantive result, and, in the main, American efforts to capitalise on its position and triangulate diplomatic manoeuvres were sporadic and largely ineffectual.[29] But not all American initiatives were either benevolent or necessarily prudent. David Francis arrived in St Petersburg in early 1916 intent on restoring American credibility and drawing a line under the ineffectual mission of his predecessor. By all accounts he was temperamentally unsuited to humanitarian work, which he saw as an impediment to efforts to further US commercial interests. His staff took the view that 'having assumed responsibility under the instructions of the Department for the care of German interests in Russia, the Embassy must be left entirely free to do so'.[30] This included the right to decide on which communications to pass to the Russian authorities. Francis's cavalier behaviour left him open to the charge of violating US neutrality, and, while it may have endeared him to his Russian hosts, it effectively abrogated responsibility for acting as a go-between, and left the Tsar's government in the dark over

German intentions.[31] How this benefited either party, let alone the prisoners, must be questioned. In Berlin and Vienna American diplomats tried as best they could to moderate the tone of any official communications forwarded to Francis, but, as late as September 1916, Francis freely admitted withholding correspondence from the Russians if he believed 'no good could result therefrom – only increased human suffering'.[32]

Protecting powers as humanitarian agents

The Department's August 1914 circular made it abundantly clear that American 'good offices' were to be confined to diplomatic services. The last thing Bryan intended was for his diplomats to assume responsibility for alleviating the suffering caused by the war. This included dabbling in the area of military captivity, notwithstanding the fact that American diplomats had visited Japanese prisoners detained in Russia during the Russo-Japanese War a decade earlier. Throughout the summer and autumn of 1914 the Department carefully monitored the conduct of its staff to avoid any obvious 'mission creep'. Thus, in mid-September it censured *Chargé d'affaires* Charles Wilson for lodging protests with the Russian authorities over the condition of prisoners he had seen passing through Moscow en route to camps further to the east.[33] Given the pressures facing US embassies in Europe, it is perhaps unsurprising that Bryan's efforts failed in their principal object. Barely a month after admonishing Wilson's interventions in St Petersburg, a series of events, set in motion by Walter Hines Page, the US ambassador in London, forced Washington to change its tune and effectively transformed protecting powers into humanitarian agencies.

The precise details of Page's actions need not concern us. Tiring of lurid stories about the ill-treatment of British prisoners, Page dispatched one of his staff to Germany to investigate camp conditions in person.[34] Predictably, the visit prompted calls in Berlin for Germany to be afforded the same privilege.[35] The Department's belated attempt to call a halt to the initiative merely created confusion and had to be abandoned shortly thereafter. Washington was also unable to prevent Berlin insisting that visiting US diplomats interviewed prisoners' representatives and interceded on their behalf with the camp or official authorities. Spawned from what was, in the Department's eyes, a 'diplomatic blunder', the resulting 'three-point treaty', concluded in March 1915, committed both sides to exchange camp regulations and permit neutral diplomats to inspect PoW camps and mediate disputes between the prisoners and the detaining authorities.[36] The 'treaty' transformed protecting powers into active participants in PoW affairs. It became the centrepiece of Anglo-German PoW relations and was applied, in various degrees, to other theatres. In due course it provided the template for the supervisory arrangements included in the belligerents' wartime agreements regulating PoW affairs in the final years of the war.

It is important to note that neither Page nor Gerard was moved to action by the sight of emaciated, maltreated prisoners. True, the crowded and unsanitary conditions facing prisoners in Russia and elsewhere alarmed neutral observers, but, by this date, US diplomats were still intuitively inclined to side with their hosts and accept official pronouncements at face value.[37] Lapses in treatment were put down to the challenge of accommodating prisoners in such unprecedented numbers, and not to collective or individual malice and indifference. The inspiration behind the system of regular camp inspections instead sprang from Page's desire to 'straighten out the almost hopeless tangles and lies about prisoners' and his belief that the greatest threat to prisoners' wellbeing came from the propensity of their own governments to assume the worst of their enemies and resort to reprisals at the slightest provocation. Formal, periodic, camp inspection would, Page hoped, resolve incipient difficulties in the management of PoW camps, and over time convince the warring factions that their adversaries could be trusted to treat prisoners humanely.

Recent research has shown that these assumptions were ultimately faulty. Historians have questioned the extent to which traditional, liberal, law-based norms survived into the war, and have instead emphasised the violent, arbitrary nature of detention regimes and the way attitudes became radicalised over the course of the conflict.[38] It was not just the increasing penchant for reprisals that threatened prisoners' wellbeing, as the belligerents' readiness to abandon basic humanitarian standards in pursuit of political, military, or economic advantages. The most flagrant abuses occurred in PoW labour companies stationed behind the front lines, which were first instituted in September 1915 with Germany's use of Russian prisoners but was widespread in most armies by the following summer and remained so for the remainder of the war, despite repeated attempts to negotiate an end to the practice.[39] None of the belligerents was prepared to admit neutral diplomats into areas of active military operations.

Even away from the battlefields, however, the nature, purpose, intensity, and ultimately success of camp visits varied widely. The inspection regime reached its fullest form in Western Europe where America possessed a dense network of consular offices and delegates were formally allowed to 'inspect' the camps and comment on prisoners' physical and mental state, their living conditions and nutritional intake. American diplomats, and their Spanish counterparts, increasingly struggled, however, to overcome the objections of local authorities, or to dissuade the belligerents from temporarily suspending elements of the inspection regime as a reprisal for alleged infringements by their adversaries. The intensity of oversight also varied widely. In Turkey American embassy and consular officials were barred from conducting any camp visits whatsoever, while in Russia delegates were grudgingly allowed to visit, but not formally inspect, sites of detention. In early 1916 the US consul general in Moscow estimated that he would require about fifty men to replicate the kind of regime operated in Western Europe, yet it was not until early 1917 that the number of staff at his disposal reached double figures. Between April 1915 and February 1917 the Americans visited just seventy-seven camps across Russia; only twenty-one of these received repeat visits. Despite Page's and Gerard's best intentions, therefore, the involvement of representatives of sovereign powers in camp visits proved insufficient in itself to convince belligerent governments to live up to the spirit, far less the letter, of The Hague regulations.

How did individual diplomats view their new 'humanitarian' responsibilities? The answer inevitably depended on the character and beliefs of those involved. Hoffman Philip, who was left as *Chargé d'affaires* in Constantinople for nine months in 1916, appears to have been inspired by the same universalist spirit that motivated delegates of the ICRC. Reflecting on his experience after the war, he wrote:

> What interested me the most, and what also brought with it the most satisfaction, was my work in connection with the relief of wounded and other prisoners of war [...]. Little as this was, for I was hampered in every way possible by Turkish (and German) officials, yet I know that something was accomplished, and the gratitude displayed by certain unknown British and French heroes in Turkish hospitals from time to time has left a life-long impression upon me. The stoic courage with which these prisoners of war bore the shocking neglect and hardships to which most of them were subjected was what should be recorded.[40]

It was perhaps natural for Philip to empathise with his Western protégés, held captive by an enemy whose cultural practices were so alien to a man born into an east-coast family and educated at the University of Cambridge.[41] The conditions US officials encountered in PoW camps and work detachments in Siberia and the trans-Caspian region likewise frequently left them shocked. The physical and mental toll led some diplomats and camp inspectors to the brink of exhaustion and forced many to take extended periods of sick leave. Only one of the six diplomatic staff assigned to Penfield's embassy in Vienna was fit for duty by early 1917.[42] Most camp inspectors lasted in post barely six months. Even those diplomats like James Gerard, whose direct contact with prisoners was slight, were moved by what they saw and heard. The only time Gerard admitted to losing his temper was when he confronted a German official with the news that Germany's two million prisoners, systematically 'insulted and underfed and beaten and forced to work as slaves', would return home 'with such a hatred of all things German that it would not be safe for Germans to travel [abroad]'.[43] The apparent spontaneity of Gerard's outburst suggests he was not speaking for the prisoners alone.

Yet while the outlooks of US diplomats were clearly affected by humanitarian sentiments, such universalist impulses coexisted alongside attitudes that reflected narrower, political considerations. The impartiality projected by US diplomats was not so much a reflection of their humanitarian idealism as a function of the political position espoused by the US government. Officials on both sides of the conflict were not above questioning the integrity and political biases of 'hyphenated-Americans'. When this occurred, US ambassadors tended to emphasise the 'Americanness' of their staff; their 'Puritan New England ancestry' and 'best American stock'.[44] The embassy in St Petersburg went one better in 1916 and vetoed anyone bearing a German surname from service in Russia. But diplomats' impartiality also reflected wider shifts in neutral opinion in the US. The torpedoing of the *Lusitania* in May 1915 sapped the enthusiasm of some temporary camp inspectors and led to some testy encounters with those they were employed to protect. Such strains were particularly evident after Washington terminated its mandate for German interests in early February 1917, leaving staff in Russia in the incongruous position of having to administer to the needs of Germany's ally, Austria-Hungary. So many embassy assistants unilaterally downed tools and headed home at this point that ambassador Francis was effectively left with little choice other than to hand over responsibility for Austro-Hungarian interests to his Swedish counterpart, even though Vienna did not formally sever relations with the US until April.

For the most part, however, the outlook of US embassy staff was influenced less by the need to accommodate different, and potentially divergent, visions of neutrality, and more by a tendency to view humanitarian problems through a political lens and to limit the search for solutions to diplomatic means. This lay at the root of Page's and Gerard's instigation of camp inspections in early 1915, and the propensity for US diplomats to situate 'humanitarian services' within a broader strategy of political and diplomatic engagement. The position was exemplified by John Brinckerhoff Jackson, a foreign service official of twenty-six years' standing, who headed the Berlin embassy's British bureau from early 1915. For Jackson the whole point of the camp inspections was to provide him with the wherewithal to mediate between the two conflicting parties and defuse incipient tensions. Having spent the first twelve years of his diplomatic career in Berlin, Jackson enjoyed good connections in the German ministries. By mid-1915 he was reputedly on 'such good terms with the military authorities that a word from [him would] ensure an immediate improvement' in camp conditions.[45] To complement his German contacts, Jackson wrote weekly private letters to the British Foreign Office mandarin Horace Rumbold, in which he attempted to set out the situation as he saw it. Mindful that extracts from American reports were likely to appear in periodic Parliamentary White Papers, Jackson also insisted that camp inspection reports excluded any material likely to excite public anxiety or resentment in the UK. Although his 'pro-German proclivities' occasionally rankled – Rumbold thought some of his letters 'might have been written from the Prussian War Office' – the British were genuinely grateful for Jackson's efforts and acknowledged that his motives were 'wholeheartedly devoted to the interests of [British] POWs in Germany'.[46]

The wisdom of Jackson's approach to camps inspections appeared to be borne out in the experience of the US staff in Russia in early 1916. A robust report on the inept handling of a typhus outbreak at Stretensk PoW camp in the winter of 1915–16 so infuriated the Russian authorities that they not only demanded the author, camp inspector William Warfield, leave the country forthwith, but started ignoring the embassy's requests for travel permits.[47] Desperate to rebuild relations, ambassador David Francis bent to Russian pressure. He acquiesced to Warfield's departure and agreed to disband the American Red Cross ambulance team, sent over by Gerard, on the grounds that their earlier assignment in Germany made them politically 'suspect' in Russian eyes. Francis's First Secretary, the foreign service official Fred Dearing, meanwhile overhauled the embassy's administration of enemy interests to focus on relief, rather than reporting, and went out of his way to cast doubt on any accounts, from whatever source, that painted the Russian authorities in a bad light. Nevertheless, notwithstanding these efforts at ingratiation, it was not until October 1916, nine months after Warfield's diplomatic 'faux pas', that the Russians allowed the embassy to resume regular camp visits.

While Jackson's artful drafting of camp inspection reports might seem justified to professional diplomats like Fred Dearing – men 'sent to lie abroad for the good of their country' – it was not an outlook uniformly shared by all those involved in the exercise of America's 'good offices'. Camp 'inspectors' such as Warfield were typically engaged directly by the embassy itself, rather than through the State Department, and on criteria that reflected the needs of the particular context. In Germany camp visits were initially co-ordinated by the assistant naval attaché, Dr Karl Ohnesorg, former assistant surgeon in the US navy. It was Ohnesorg who persuaded the embassy to turn to physicians when the scale of camp visits exhausted the available manpower in the embassy. Physicians had the advantage of being older than regular embassy attachés, they possessed the necessary expertise to evaluate the camps' food and hygiene conditions, and the status to talk on near-equal terms with camp commandants.[48] It was not long before such independently minded men baulked at subjecting their reports to Jackson's editorial pen. Tensions reached a peak in the summer of 1916, when several senior staff decided to return home rather than continue to work under such conditions. It says much for how US diplomats internalised their responsibilities as protecting power delegates that the doctors' objections found considerable support from the embassy staff, including the ambassador. Clearly by the summer of 1916 the need to 'bear witness' to the deteriorating conditions facing prisoners in Germany had begun to shift attitudes and undermine their willingness to comply with the Department's instructions. Gerard's deputy, Joseph Grew, engineered a reorganisation of the inspection teams over the autumn. He also induced Jackson to soften his approach sufficiently to alleviate the concerns of practising physicians and convince some to journey to Germany to continue the embassy's camp inspection work.[49]

Relations with other humanitarian actors

How did America's protecting power duties align with the activities of the wider humanitarian sector? Relations were inevitably closest with American organisations. Across Europe, US ambassadors, their spouses, and their staff sponsored charitable activities, chaired neutral commissions and hospital boards, and attended Red Cross and other fundraising events. Although they did not always see eye to eye, for the most part American ambassadors valued these relationships and happily promoted the activities of American nationals. With non-American organisations, however, whose work did not reflect on American prestige, relations were necessarily more complex and nuanced. Russia offers a particularly good case for exploring this facet of American diplomacy as the empire saw more intensive external humanitarian intervention than any other belligerent, and so it was here that US diplomats most frequently rubbed shoulders with other humanitarian agencies. The sparseness of America's consular network in Russia led the Central Powers to turn to the Swedish consul in Helsingfors and the Danish consul in Omsk to attend to German and Austro-Hungarian civilians and captured servicemen in these regions. By the time large-scale relief efforts were regularised in the winter of 1914–15, large parts of European Russia and western Siberia were, by agreement, handled through Swedish and Danish channels rather than American. Large-scale relief operations were run out of China, Denmark, and Sweden; the Scandinavians arranged for the repatriation of sick and wounded PoWs across their territories and arranged for the hospitalisation of tuberculosis patients in sanatoria. Vestiges of the earlier 'three emperors' league' were also evident in the voyages of German, Hungarian, and Austrian aristocrats – so called 'sisters of mercy' – who toured military camps to distribute alms and gauge prisoners' loyalty and patriotism.

As relative latecomers to a crowded scene, US diplomats in St Petersburg evidently struggled to establish a position commensurate to their status as the official custodians of German and Austro-Hungarian interests. Interactions with other agencies were outwardly civil, but American diplomats clearly felt ill at ease, both at a personal and a professional level, in working alongside their neutral counterparts. The motives of these 'humanitarian internationalists' were 'bewildering'. 'There is something curious about this prisoner business', Fred Dearing wrote on 6 April 1917. 'Everyone works at it as if possessed, but it begins to emerge, not selflessly at all, nor entirely for humanitarian purposes. Every man Jack and every woman Jane sees in it a chance to make a great name for himself, or herself; to acquire importance, influence, standing, entrée, fame among the Russians, among the Germans and Austrians, everywhere'.[50]

There were also, though, underlying constraints that played to others' advantage and impinged on the effectiveness of US operations. As Scandinavian operations spanned both sides of the battle lines, the Danes and Swedes were well positioned to find common ground in their negotiations with the belligerent governments. By contrast, although the Americans liaised with their Spanish counterparts in Berlin and Vienna, confidence in the Spaniards was never high, and such collaboration as there was was never wholehearted, and its achievements were meagre.[51] Furthermore, the Scandinavians' Red Cross societies supplied prisoners with the food, boots, clothing, and other items they desperately needed, and in the process relieved the Russian authorities of an irksome administrative and logistical burden.[52] The Americans channelled funds to military and civilian prisoners, but turned up at the camps empty-handed and then set about questioning the Russian camp or regional authorities. This hardly endeared them to their Russian hosts, who were responsible for implementing any improvements or suggestions arising from the visit. It was scarcely surprising that US delegates encountered so many obstacles whenever they ventured into the provincial governments. These structural differences put the protecting power at a significant disadvantage, and explains why, over the course of 1916, the Americans sought to shift the emphasis of their activities onto relief, hiring Edward Devine, a celebrated academic authority on the subject, to lead the embassy's 'second division', and recruiting staff with experience in running relief operations.

Figure 6.1 'Moscow January 11th 1917 Relief Division Conference', photographer unknown. Ambassador Francis (sitting third from left) with consul general in Moscow, Maddin Summers, on his right, and Basil Miles, director of the Second Division of the Embassy (in charge of German and Austrian War Relief) on his left. By this date the embassy had overcome Russian objections and built up a suitable complement of staff. Nevertheless, minutes of the meeting indicate that Miles 'emphasised the fundamental necessity for relations of absolute confidence between the Embassy Delegates and the authorities of the Imperial Government in whose jurisdiction they operate'

American interests clashed with the other humanitarian agencies in two additional areas. The first related primarily to the work of the itinerant aristocratic 'sisters of mercy'. Some of these individuals, Baroness Croy, Countess Üxküll, and Baroness von Walsleben among them, deeply impressed American observers. But in the main embassy staff resented these 'high born, ardent ladies', who were 'little better than high-grade spies', and whose unguarded utterances always threatened to upset the delicate balance in relations between the warring camps.[53] The young Countess Nora Kinsky was held in especially low regard – Dearing dismissed her as 'the most pestiferous small devil imaginable' – but it was ultimately criticisms of conditions in Germany, by the Russian 'nurse' Madam Sassanoff, that sowed discord in PoW relations in June 1916, and prompted Berlin to temporarily rescind the right, secured in Page's and Gerard's 'three point treaty', for neutral diplomats to conduct confidential interviews with camp inmates. There was, as Dearing wearily noted, 'more than just fire and a sense of injustice' to consider in managing camp visits. He would have much preferred to see the 'sisters of mercy' withdrawn and replaced with embassy agents.[54]

The second area where US interests collided with those of other agencies was in competing for the attention of the Russian authorities. The very existence of the Scandinavian relief operations allowed the Russians to justify withholding privileges from the US embassy that were routinely enjoyed by American diplomats in Berlin, Vienna, and elsewhere. This was especially apparent in the wake of Warfield's Stretensk report in early 1916, when the withdrawal of travel permits effectively reduced the embassy to a forwarding agent for money orders and official communiqués from the Central Powers. What particularly irked the Americans was that the German and Austro-Hungarian 'sisters of mercy' and Scandinavian diplomats and Red Cross personnel could draw on social and familial connections in the Russian court that were largely closed to representatives of the fledgling American republic. It was through this 'blackmail and corruption' that the Danish Red Cross secured access to labour companies along the Murmansk railway line, where prisoners suffered the highest mortality rates of the entire war.[55] The impact on US prestige was palpable. As Dearing noted in June 1916, 'it is intolerable that our functions should be nullified by the denial of any privileges to the Embassy and by concessions to other organisations. [...] We wish neither to supplant the Danes, nor merely to be put on a par with them. The Russians should rather suggest to the Danes that they approach the Embassy, the official custodian of the prisoners' interests. [We] will be glad to cooperate with them.'[56] The provision of humanitarian services was a competitive affair, and, in Russia at least, the Americans came up short. It left the US embassy in an uncomfortable position. As the official protecting power, America's good word had been pledged. Yet its capacity to fulfil its mandate ultimately hinged on the caprice of the Russian authorities, whose commitment to American involvement was partial at best. US diplomats lived under the constant fear of being supplanted by other agencies, who would make capital out of America's defeasance: 'the YMCA, the Swedes, the various red Crosses, [...] will assume the work [...] and we shall suffer in prestige'.[57]

Concluding remarks

When Gerard's staff handed over the Berlin embassy archives and keys to their Spanish counterparts in February 1917, few had any illusions about the challenges the Spanish would face in protecting US interests over the coming months. Spain's neutral credentials remained intact, but its powerlessness to effect improvements in Germany's treatment of prisoners, especially its Russian prisoners, had left Madrid so dispirited that it had come close to abandoning the task altogether. American expectations were so low that the US assigned the Spanish a relatively modest role in defending US interests after American entry into the war. Berne, not Madrid, was the central clearing-house for humanitarian matters once American servicemen arrived in Europe in the summer of 1917. Protests over Germany's ill-treatment of American prisoners were dutifully lodged in Madrid, but they were drafted with an eye to meeting domestic expectations and not in any hope of ameliorating conditions in Germany. Officials in Washington had equally little faith in neutral brokered 'humanitarian diplomacy' and looked instead to resolve disputes through direct talks with their German counterparts.[58]

The Great War was in many respects a missed opportunity for the international community to draw on the power and prestige of neutral governments to strengthen the humanitarian regime. America's diplomatic efforts on behalf of belligerent governments had been disappointing, but this was in large measure due to Washington's failure to invest its ambassadors with the necessary resources and autonomy to promote adherence to humanitarian norms in the belligerent capitals. The actions and expectations of American diplomats were shaped, indeed inhibited, by factors that were unique to their institutional settings; settings which prioritised state interests, viewed humanitarian issues through a political prism, and judged other actors as competitors, whose contributions threatened to detract from US prestige as official custodians of enemy interests. Individual diplomats may have aspired to promote humanitarian values throughout the course of their work, but they were ultimately more constrained by the institutions they inhabited than empowered by them.

Yet, if America's experiences between 1914 and 1917 led officials to question the efficacy of protecting powers, they also encouraged them to double down on state-based institutions as the wartime guardians of humanitarian standards. After the war Washington sought to augment the standing of the protecting power and confine the activities of the non-governmental sector, whether the YMCA or the Red Cross, to a supportive role. This development is important for understanding the context in which Washington sponsored the emergence of the League of Red Cross Societies in 1919; an organisation that refocused the attention of the Red Cross movement towards peacetime public health challenges, but implicitly undermined the primacy of the ICRC. The ICRC remained the principal Red Cross organ in times of war, but its diminished authority inevitably affected its ability to carry out its traditional functions. It also explains why

Washington was content to join the British government in trying to block voluntary organisations from attending the Geneva conference in July 1929, convened to update the 1906 Red Cross convention and forge a new code for prisoners of war. The Anglo-American intervention crushed the ambitions of the Sovereign Order of Malta to secure a seat at the conference. Had the Swiss government not spoken up strongly in its favour, the ICRC would surely have suffered a similar fate, and missed the opportunity to win international recognition for its status as a humanitarian actor. Historians are right to point to the 'patriotic humanitarianism' unleashed by the war, and stress how this allowed the voluntary sector to push the boundaries of humanitarianism, extend the definitions of war victim, and shape a nascent postwar 'international humanitarian order'.[59] But it is important not to lose sight of the fact that this momentum was checked, at least in part, by the actions of state authorities. While America was happy to assume the mantle of humanitarian superpower, its government was intent on limiting the scope of wartime humanitarianism, and craft a legal framework in 1929 that reinforced the privileges of traditional categories – prisoners of war and battlefield wounded – and confirmed traditional state-based actors as the principal mechanisms for overseeing and supervising the new conventions. In the process they constrained, and arguably arrested, the development of humanitarianism, and delayed the development of a more expansive human rights agenda for over two decades.

Notes

1. R. Stone, 'The American-German Conference on Prisoners of War, 1906', *American Journal of International Law*, 13:3 (1919), 434. The author would like to express his gratitude to David A. Langbart, senior historian at the NARA, for introducing him to the papers of the 'second division' of the US embassy in St Petersburg and thereby triggering his interest in the subject explored in this chapter.
2. See N. Wylie and L. Cameron, 'The Impact of the First World War on the Law Governing the Treatment of Prisoners of War, and the Making of a Humanitarian Subject', *European Journal of International Law*, 29:4 (2018), 1327–50, and N. Wylie and S. Landefeld, 'POWs, Civilians and the Post-War Development of International Humanitarian Law', in R. Kowner and I. Rachamimov (eds), *Out of Line, Out of Place: A Global and Local History of World War I Internments* (Ithaca: Cornell University Press, 2022), pp. 296–322.
3. M. Stibbe, 'The Internment of Civilians by Belligerent States during the First World War and the Response of the International Committee of the Red Cross', *Journal of Contemporary History*, 41:1 (2006), 5–19; U. Hinz, 'Humanität im Krieg? Internationales Rotes Kreuz und Kriegsgefangenenhilfe im Ersten

Weltkrieg', in J. Oltmer (ed.), *Kriegsgefangene im Europa des Ersten Weltkriegs* (Paderborn: Schöningh, 1998), pp. 216–36.
4 V. Moritz, '"In the Hand of the Enemy" – Prisoners of War in the First World War: Aid for Prisoners of War', accessed 2 April 2023, https://ww1.habsburger.net/en/chapters/aid-prisoners-war.
5 Agreement between the United States of America and Germany Concerning Prisoners of War, Sanitary Personnel, and Civilians, 11 November 1918, *Foreign Relations of the United States* (hereafter *FRUS*), *1918, Supplement 2: The World War* (Washington, DC: United States Government Printing Office, 1933), Doc. 148.
6 H. Jones, 'International or Transnational? Humanitarian Action during the First World War', *European Review of History*, 16:5 (2009), 697–713.
7 S. Neff, 'Prisoners of War in International Law: The Nineteenth Century', in S. Scheipers (ed.), *Prisoners in War: Norms, Military Cultures and Reciprocity in Armed Conflict* (Oxford: Oxford University Press, 2010), pp. 57–73.
8 C. Henn, 'The Origins and Early Development of the Idea of Protecting Powers' (PhD dissertation, University of Cambridge, 1986), pp. 135–227.
9 M. Abbenhuis, *An Age of Neutrals: Great Power Politics 1815–1914* (Cambridge: Cambridge University Press, 2014), pp. 144–77.
10 See D. L. Caglioti, *War and Citizenship: Enemy Aliens and National Belonging from the French Revolution to the First World War* (Cambridge: Cambridge University Press, 2020), pp. 17–104.
11 H. Jones, 'International Law and Western Front Prisoners of War in the First World War', in A.-M. Pathé and F. Théofilakis (eds), *Wartime Captivity in the Twentieth Century* (Oxford: Berghahn, 2016), p. 32.
12 Bryan (Washington) to Whitlock (Brussels), 5 August 1914, *FRUS, 1914 (Supplement)*, p. 736.
13 'Instructions to diplomatic and consular officers of the USA entrusted with the interests of foreign Governments at war', 17 August 1914. *FRUS, 1914 (Supplement)*, pp. 740–1.
14 Zimmermann (German Foreign Office) to Gerard (US embassy, Berlin), 3 January 1915. National Archives and Records Administration (NARA), RG84 St Petersburg, vol. 451.
15 See inter alia P. Gatrell, *A Whole Empire Walking: Refugees in Russia during World War 1* (Bloomington: Indiana University Press, 1999), pp. 15–34; P. Gatrell, *The Making of the Modern Refugee* (Oxford: Oxford University Press, 2013), pp. 25–31; M. Stibbe, *Civilian Internment during the First World War: A European and Global History, 1914–1920* (Basingstoke: Palgrave, 2019), passim.
16 J. Randolph, 'Report on German and Austro-Hungarian Relief Work of American Consulate General at Moscow', 18 September 1919, p. 1. NARA. RG59 Central File 1910–1929, Box 6437; W. B. McAllister, S. Rotramel, C. Hawley, and T. Faith, *War, Neutrality and Humanitarian Relief: The Expansion of US Diplomatic Activity during the Great War, 1914–1917* (Washington, DC: State Department, 2020), p. 144.

17 Penfield (Vienna) to Francis (St Petersburg), 25 September 1916, David Rowland Francis Papers, A0519. Missouri Historical Society, St Louis; H. E. Mattox, 'Technology and Foreign Affairs: The Case of the Typewriter', *American Diplomacy*, December 1997, https://americandiplomacy.web.unc.edu/1997/12/technology-and-foreign-affairs-the-case-of-the-typewriter/.
18 Penfield (Vienna) to Lansing (Washington) 14 February 1916, *FRUS, 1916 (Supplement)*, pp. 816–8.
19 Penfield (Vienna) to Washington, 15 September 1915, NARA, RG59 CDF 1910–1929, Box 6439; by this date, the embassy was charged with the interests of four powers, the consulate-general in Budapest seven.
20 Grant-Smith (Vienna) to Chase (Fiume). 1 June 1915, NARA, RG84 Budapest 1915, vol. 239, file 703.
21 For examples of emphatic language: Henn, 'The Origins and Early Development of the Idea of Protecting Powers', p. 240, and the US role in 'witnessing fair-play' between HMS *Doris* and the Ottoman authorities at Alexandretta in December 1914: E. Rogan, *The Fall of the Ottomans* (London: Penguin, 2015), pp. 96–7.
22 US embassy, Constantinople, Memorandum for the Sublime Porte, 4 December 1916, NARA, RG84 Constantinople 1916, vol. 732.
23 M. Judelsohn, 'Protection of Belligerent Interests in the Ottoman Empire', 22 September 1917, NARA, RG59 CDF 1910–1929, Box 6439.
24 The situation was compounded by the ambassador's lack of linguistic skills and social finesse, and the limited number of entrées into court circles provided by the handful of Americans married into the Russian aristocracy. For State Department criticism of Francis's approach to the Finance Ministry: Francis to William Phillips (State Department), 16 October 1916, Francis papers, Reel 2.
25 Penfield (Vienna) to State Department 24 August 1916, NARA, RG84 Vienna 1916, vol. 656.
26 Grew to Willing Spencer (US Legation, Panama), 29 December 1915 Grew Papers, MS Am 1687 vol. 6. Houghton Library, Harvard University; J. W. Gerard, *My Four Years in Germany* (Teddington: The Echo Library, 2008), ch. 15.
27 Wilson (St Petersburg) to Grant-Smith (Vienna), 5 January 1915, NARA, RG84 Vienna 1915, vol. 627.
28 Grant-Smith (Vienna) to Dearing (St Petersburg), 6 April 1916, and Laughlin (London), 6 April 1916, NARA, RG84 Vienna 1916, vol. 658; R. Nachtigal, 'Seuchen unter militärischer Aufsicht in Rußland: Das Lager Tockoe als Beispiel für die Behandlung der Kriegsgefangenen 1915/16?', *Jahrbücher für Geschichte Osteuropas*, 48 (2000), 363–87.
29 In the latter case the efforts ran afoul of Francis's desire to curry favour with the Russian authorities. The Entente did explore a common position on reprisals, which might have led to wider discussion over their treatment of prisoners, but the talks ran aground before agreement could be reached. See H. Jones, *Violence against Prisoners of War in the First World War: Britain, France and Germany, 1914–1920* (Cambridge: Cambridge University Press, 2011), p. 141.

30 Dearing diary, 9 April 1916, Papers of Frederick Morris Dearing, C2926, State Historical Society of Missouri.
31 It is not known whether the Department questioned Francis's judgement, though Penfield immediately cautioned Francis against pursuing the approach. Penfield to Francis, 25 September 1916, Francis papers, Reel 2.
32 For attempts to amend diplomatic notes, see Memorandum 6 October 1916. NARA, RG84 Vienna 1916 Vol. 659
33 Bryan (Washington) to Wilson (St Petersburg), 16 September 1914, *FRUS, 1914 (Supplement)*, p. 751.
34 Page to Arthur W. Page, 6 November 1914, in B. J. Hendrick (ed.), *The Life and Letters of Walter H. Page* (London: William Heinemann, 1922), vol. 2, p. 345.
35 For this episode see McAllister et al., *War, Neutrality and Humanitarian Relief*, pp. 60–1.
36 Henn, 'The Origins and Early Development of the Idea of Protecting Powers', p. 250.
37 Charles Wilson tellingly wrote in early January 1915, 'I am too jealous of Russia's good name, [...] to want her to incur any blame'. Wilson (St Petersburg) to Grant-Smith (Vienna), 5 January 1915, NARA, RG84 Vienna 1915 Vol. 627, File 711.44R.
38 See inter alia U. Hinz, *Gefangen im Großen Krieg: Kriegsgefangenschaft in Deutschland 1914–1921* (Essen: Klartext, 2006); J. Oltmer, 'Unentbehrliche Arbeitskräfte Kriegsgefangene in Deutschland 1914–1918', in J. Oltmer (ed.), *Kriegsgefangenschaft im Europa des Ersten Weltkrieges* (Paderborn: Ferdinand Schöningh, 2006), pp. 67–96; A. Kramer, 'Prisoners in the First World War', in Sibylle Scheipers (ed.) *Prisoners in War* (Oxford: Oxford University Press, 2010), pp. 75–90; I. Hull, *A Scrap of Paper: Breaking and Making International Law during the Great War* (Ithaca: Cornell University Press, 2014), pp. 67–88.
39 Jones, *Violence Against Prisoners of War*, pp. 130–4. Upwards of 16 per cent of Germany's PoWs were deployed behind front lines by August 1916.
40 Philip (Bogota) to State Department, 31 May 1919, NARA, RG59 CDF 1910–1929, Box 6437. For Philip's 'fine humanitarian spirit', and 'sympathy for the unfortunate, the sick, and the poor' that was 'innate in his character' see Henry Morgenthau, *Ambassador Morgenthau's Story* (New York: Doubleday, 1919), ch. 19.
41 See D. Rodogno, *Against Massacre. Humanitarian Interventions in the Ottoman Empire, 1815–1914* (Princeton: Princeton University Press, 2011).
42 McAllister et al., *War, Neutrality and Humanitarian Relief*, pp. 113–20.
43 J. Gerard, *Face to Face with Kaiserism* (New York: George H. Doran, 1918), ch. 7 (quoting from his diary); For Gerard's direct involvement see M. Stibbe, *British Civilian Internees in Germany: The Ruhleben Camp, 1914–1918* (Manchester: Manchester University Press, 2008), p. 59, p. 63, p. 66.
44 Draft letter to US ambassador (London), 6 December 1915, University of Montana, Mansfield Library, Correspondence of Judge James. W. Gerard, Series II, 13/35.

45 Grew, Diary entry, 20 June 1915. Grew Papers, MS Am 1687, vol. 6. A fortnight earlier Grew had noted 'mutual retaliation is the order of the day with POWs at present' (2 June 1915).
46 Rumbold to Mallet (Foreign Office), 5 September 1915, and Belfield (War Office), 19 October 1915; Sir Horace Rumbold papers, Bodleian Library, University of Oxford, vol. 19 and vol. 20.
47 Francis to Lansing, 16 May 1916, Francis Papers; Warfield to State, 17 January 1916, cited in A. (Iris) Rachamimov, *POWs and the Great War: Captivity on the Eastern Front* (Oxford: Berg, 2002), p. 128, note 45.
48 See D. J. McCarthy, *The Prisoner of War in Germany* (New York: Moffat, 1917), pp. 31–2.
49 Joseph Grew, Diary, 10 July 1916, and 'Report on activities of Berlin embassy, May 1916 to April 1917', no date, p. 59, MS Am 1687 vols 7 and 9; Gerard to E. M. House, 8 August 1916; McCarthy to Gerard, 13 October 1916, University of Montana, Mansfield Library, Correspondence of Judge James. W. Gerard. Series II, 16/12, 16/33.
50 Dearing, Diary, 6 April 1916, folio 117.
51 The US hoped that the opening of a Russian bureau in the Spanish embassy in Berlin in late 1916 might lead to a relaxation in the restrictions on US delegates in Russia. See J.-M. Delaunay, 'En toute discretion: L'Espagne protectrice des intérêts français en Allemagne, 1914–1919', in J.-M. Delaunay (ed.), *Aux vents des puissances: Hommages à Jean-Claude Allain* (Paris: PSN, 2009), pp. 195–208. See also M. Pérez de Arcos, '"Finding out whereabouts of missing persons": The European War Office, Transnational Humanitarianism and Spanish Royal Diplomacy in the First World War', *International History Review*, 44:3 (2022), 497–523.
52 See R. Nachtigal, 'Die dänisch-österreichisch-ungarischen Rotkreuzdelegierten in Rußland 1915–1918', *Zeitgeschichte*, 11–12:25 (1998), 366–74; G. H. Davis, 'National Red Cross Societies and Prisoners of War in Russia 1914–1918', *Journal of Contemporary History*, 28 (1993), 31–52; B. Blüdnikow, 'Denmark during the First World War', *Journal of Contemporary History*, 24 (1989), 683–703.
53 Dearing Diary, 11 April 1916, folio 141; 8 April 1916, folio 167; see Oberin Gräfin von Üxküll, *Aus einem Schwesternleben* (Stuttgart: V. Kohlhammer Verlag, 1957), pp. 11–59.
54 Dearing Diary, 13 April 1916, folio 148; 6 August 1916, folio 319. Gerard to Washington, 16 July 1916, NARA, RG84 St Petersburg, vol. 448; see A. (Iris) Rachamimov, '"Female Generals" and "Siberian Angels": Aristocratic Nurses and the Austro-Hungarian POW Relief', in N. Wingfield and M. Bucur (eds), *Gender and Wartime Violence in Twentieth-Century Eastern Europe* (Bloomington: Indiana University Press, 2006), pp. 23–46. Nora Gräfin Kinsky, *Russisches Tagebuch, 1916–1918* (Vienna: Seewald, 1976).
55 Dearing Diary, 5 June 1916, folio 270; see R. Nachtigal, *Die Murmanbahn 1915–1919. Kriegsnotwendigkeit und Wirtschaftsinteressen* (Grenzach-Wyhlen: BAG-Verlag, 2007).

56 Dearing Diary, 5 June 1916, folios 270–1.
57 Dearing Diary, 9 June 1916, folio 276.
58 Grew to Dresel (Berne), 25 January 1918, Grew papers, MS Am 1687, vol. 9; Grew to Dresel (Berne), 5 July 1917, Ellis L. Dresel papers, MS Am 1549 (160), Houghton Library, Harvard University.
59 D. R. Maul, 'The Rise of a Humanitarian Superpower: American NGOs and International Relief, 1917–1945', in M. B. Jerónimo and J. P. Monteiro (eds), *Internationalism, Imperialism and the Formation of the Contemporary World: The Pasts of the Present* (London: Palgrave, 2018), pp. 127–46 (p. 129, p. 131).

7

Blockaders as humanitarians? Connecting the Allied blockade of Germany and postwar humanitarianism

Phillip Dehne

Introduction

This chapter exposes the surprising connections between the Allied blockade during and immediately after the First World War, and the activities and institutions of humanitarian relief that developed along with the postwar peace. On the face of it these would seem to have been diametrically opposed. During the war the increasingly co-ordinated economic warfare policies of Britain, France, and the United States aimed to cut off Germany's access to all international trade, an effort denounced by the Germans as a 'hunger blockade'. But after the signing of the Armistice on 11 November 1918 those same mechanisms were employed for international relief efforts, looking to enhance Germany's access to foreign supplies of food and other critically needed resources.

As the Allies transitioned from war to peace, economic warfare became firmly linked to humanitarian relief. At the unprecedented Paris Peace Conference over the first six months of 1919, one-time economic warriors dominated the Supreme Economic Council (SEC), a Peace Conference organisation whose unheralded work helped to alleviate the destitution of Central Europeans. For Allied leaders in Paris humanitarian efforts were compelled by the political imperative of stabilising Germany to avert the spread of Bolshevism. For many of them these efforts to help Germany recover also fit nicely into their expectations for a strong postwar League of Nations focused on maintaining peace. The organisation and activities of the SEC marked a continuation of the 'inter-Allied' structure of the wartime blockade, and in turn became a critical model for many postwar international humanitarian efforts, especially those connected to the fledgling League.[1] For many involved in the development of relief efforts during the Peace Conference, the blockade was the bedrock on which the postwar 'humanitarian moment' was built.[2] By uncovering the synergies in Paris between economic warfare and emergency relief, this chapter provides a novel example of the 'remarkably diverse' roots of humanitarianism in the nineteenth and twentieth centuries.[3]

Connecting the blockade to humanitarianism cuts across the grain of most histories of the First World War. Usually, wartime humanitarianism and the blockade have been seen as fundamentally opposing forces, and this perception has also marked judgements of the Paris Peace Conference. For example, historians of the wartime relief of civilians in German-occupied territory, led by Herbert Hoover's Commission for Relief in Belgium (CRB), describe how civilian humanitarians from both the United States and Belgium argued not just with the German occupiers but also with the military-minded Allies who were reluctant to allow goods to flow into German-occupied territory.[4] In the words of the historian of wartime Belgium, Sophie de Schaepdrijver, 'the history of the relief effort was punctuated by British restrictions'.[5] Looking at it from the angle of the blockaders, Isabel Hull has shown that they were far from heartless; the ultimate decision of the British and French to allow relief shipments to Belgium in part reflected their concerns about the legality and morality of allowing the starvation of civilians.[6] But the view of Allied blockaders as only reluctantly yielding to plucky, neutral, civilian humanitarians has been more lasting. Historians of humanitarianism have largely adopted the judgements of the self-proclaimed humanitarians themselves. Both during the war and during the Paris Peace Conference, and then for decades afterwards, men like Hoover portrayed themselves as largely feeding the destitute populations of Europe only after pitched struggles against anti-German blockaders. For these humanitarians at the Peace Conference in Paris in 1919 the ultimate example of Allied vindictiveness was the fact that the blockade continued intact until the signing of the Treaty of Versailles at the end of June, as a means to coerce Germany to accept the peace terms. For critics of economic sanctions, this Armistice-era blockade has ever since provided a paradigmatic example of how sanctions can be driven by human spite and an immoral willingness to court catastrophic civilian death.

It might be argued that connecting the postwar humanitarian moment to the blockade mars the perception of the humanitarians as heroes. But looking at it from the perspective of the blockade, this chapter instead unveils a surprisingly constructive aspect of the undeniably destructive wartime blockade. In response to the humanitarian and political catastrophe facing Germany after the war, during the spring of 1919 the Allies adapted their wartime economic warfare efforts to now help feed Europe. Prominent internationalists bringing the League of Nations into operation during the Peace Conference were among those who worked the most on rebuilding the German economy, as they hoped to show how international sanctions and economic controls could be useful in the longer-term quest to eliminate war. For the Allies, critical political and practical imperatives linked the Armistice blockade to the development of humanitarian assistance to Germany.

Understanding the blockade

In 1914 the Allied blockade began as a fairly traditional type of naval siege, with the British Admiralty aiming to control the flow of goods travelling to and from northern German ports. However, economic warfare measures soon broke away from military strategy, steadily escalating and expanding throughout the war. In early 1915 the Allies began to regulate and 'ration' trade to neutral states contiguous to the Central Powers, with the aim of curtailing supplies that were getting through to Germany.[7] Britain deputised and outfitted a fleet of armed merchant ships to search for contraband cargo on ships steaming under any flag on the open ocean of the North Sea.[8] Allied governments confiscated and sold off German-owned property both at home and across their empires.[9] The Allied economic war stretched even beyond their own territories and the open seas. British and French communities in neutral countries overseas like Argentina prodded their home governments to create and install blacklisting measures against businesses perceived to be pro-German, thereby cutting off these targeted companies' access to international banking and shipping.[10] In Britain the government created a Cabinet-level Ministry of Blockade with dozens of employees and a global reach, and similar administrations of economic warfare developed in France and the United States.[11] In the process of uniting some of these varied national efforts into the international, 'inter-Allied' blockade especially over the last year of the war, the wartime allies, led by Britain, developed the basic institutions of modern international economic sanctions.

A widely held position is that the wartime blockades were unnecessarily cruel. When extended to the restive territories of the Ottoman Empire, the extension of blockade measures on all of Germany's allies appears as an unjust and self-serving tool of British and French imperial expansion.[12] But the economic war measures against Germany itself have also often been judged as overkill, with aims that went beyond the pale of ordinary warfare. It was one thing to attack the war-making capacity of the Second Reich. But did total war have to include measures that appeared to intentionally starve civilians? Blockade restrictions on imported food were an obvious problem, but even worse were the bans on fertilisers, which contributed to a collapse of food production in Germany between 1914 and 1918. The resulting lack of food translated into malnutrition and stunted growth for boys and girls across Germany during the war years, and a significantly higher than normal death rate among Germans of all ages.[13] The Allies' economic warfare efforts may have shortened the war, but theirs was a dark success. The civilian devastation caused by the Allied blockade during the Great War is central evidence for those who doubt whether economic war is ever legitimate.

However, it is also possible that the Allied blockade was not entirely to blame for wartime Germany's inability to feed its children. According to Cox, on top of the blockade 'poor government policy exacerbated shortages in the German food supply'.[14] The German government was surprisingly inefficient or even incompetent in controlling the distribution of the country's food, and, as the war wore on, overall dearth was probably inevitable for any country as cash and labour-strapped as Germany.[15] If the freedom of the seas and the neutral status of many of the world's nations had been respected by all the combatants, enabling anyone to purchase food, fertiliser, and ships, could Germany have possibly outbid the British or the French for these goods, let alone the Americans?

One might argue whether counterfactuals like these are ever appropriate for understanding history. However, in this case in particular, a First World War without the Allied blockade is so far outside the realm of the possibilities that existed in 1914–18 that it is barely worth considering. The imposition of a dominant naval blockade was at the core of Britain's prewar planning.[16] Highlighting their country's adherence to the strategy of economic warfare, Britain's army was only a 'dwarf force' compared to the armies of other European powers.[17] After the war began, the blockade continually escalated, as politicians and the public universally demanded that warfare become more comprehensive or 'total'. Everyone was looking for an edge, as war strategies shifted from a search for a military knockout blow to a war of attrition that aimed to wear down the enemy in every way possible.[18] In this war of attrition the blockade brought the Allies some obvious successes. The strictures of the blockade, and the failures of the Austrian and German governments to adequately supply their societies, wore down morale, led to social and political unrest, and delegitimised the institutions of the state. When combined with the long-term Allied military advantage, the blockade led to the collapse of both of these European empires.[19]

In the context of the brutal war, few in any political camp in any country believed that economic warfare was a particularly inhumane strategy. The blockade undoubtedly killed people including civilians, but, when judging its morality, the influential political scientist Edward Carr was only one of many who considered economic warfare as less cruel than other forms of combat.[20] Britain's blockade aimed to wreck Germany's economy and thus make it impossible to conduct the war.[21] There was a constant effort throughout the war to prove the other side's greater moral culpability, but even Germans doubted the claims of the *Berliner Tageblatt* in 1915 that German use of chlorine gas was morally equivalent to the starvation threatened by the British blockade; use of poison gas was then (as now) seen as particularly dastardly and inhumane.[22] Economic warfare was a strategy imposed by both sides. Germany's unrestricted submarine warfare against Allied merchant ships was on its face a military effort, as U-boats sank ships. But the targets of the U-boats were not the poor unsuspecting mariners on those ships but the consuming public in Britain and France. The goal was the economic one of clipping the Allied supply chain. Mass starvation was a foreseeable possibility, one that should lead to the final goal of political collapse and military capitulation. To all sides during the Great War the steady intensification of economic warfare measures appeared necessary, inevitable, and even just.

But what about during peacetime? Could tight wartime trade restrictions still be justified after the war ended, especially as widespread destitution became known? Despite the Armistice of 11 November 1918 that ended the bloodshed in the trenches, the wartime blockade continued into the peace-making era, officially lasting for seven and a half more months until the signing of the Treaty of Versailles on 28 June 1919. Rather than simply ending all blockade restrictions at the signing of the Armistice, Allied leaders meeting at the Paris Peace Conference throughout the first half of 1919 consciously decided to continue it. Verdicts about the continuation of the wartime blockade into this Armistice era have been less equivocal, and more censorious, than judgements about the wartime blockade.[23] The wave of civilian deaths in the months after November 1918 was notable for a war in which most casualties were military. These months have been perceived as a pivotal moment in the long history of economic warfare, particularly for critics who doubt that as a tactic of international coercion, blockade could ever be anything other than inhumane. As it no longer targeted the German state's ability to continue to wage war, the Armistice blockade clearly aimed at civilians, and undoubtedly hurt the poor most. No longer part of an armed struggle, economic warfare became more obviously a political tool, one that appeased some parts of the public in Allied countries thirsting for retribution against their enemies, even as it scarred the evolving politics of the new central European republics. The Armistice blockade corresponded with a few months when widespread dearth and political uncertainty plagued German civilians.[24] The blockade may have had a strategic purpose; in the judgement of the British historian Avner Offer, during the first six months of 1919 the 'blockade became decisive' in forcing Germany to sign the unfair, dictated Treaty of Versailles.[25] But how could the victors be so cruel as to intentionally starve the Germans who had given up the armed struggle? Viewed from this perspective, the continuation into 1919 of the blockade against Germany has faced denunciations as the most horrific cruelty perpetrated by the Allies during the entire wartime era. To historians like Paul Vincent, the Armistice blockade proved that vindictiveness and even cruelty drove the Allies who fashioned the peace in Paris.[26]

Sally Marks has since dismissed this idea of a 'hunger blockade' as a myth, but, like many myths, the one of intentional Allied cruelty continues to have a long life.[27]

Condemnations of this Armistice blockade place blame for it on a variety of things. Marshal Foch's demands to crush Germany through an indefinite continuation of the blockade are often cited as epitomising a more general French revanchism.[28] Desires to retain Germany's gold and other liquid assets for potential reparations payments, and wartime warnings about German plans to flood postwar global markets with cheap German-made goods that would crowd out their Allied competitors, made all the Allies wary of allowing Germany to reopen its borders to foreign trade. At Paris American delegates asserted that Britain's main reason for continuing the blockade was to assist their own economic revival by handicapping German trade rivals.[29] Members of the American delegation such as Herbert Hoover, who had become internationally famous as the head of the Belgian relief effort before the United States entered the war in 1917, complained throughout the Paris spring of 1919 (and then incessantly for decades afterward in his flurry of repetitive memoirs) about the selfish, unconscionable refusal of the British and French to immediately end the blockade. If it was selfish, it was also politically understandable. British liberal newspapers began squawking in March 1919 about the immorality of the continued blockade, but claiming to squeeze Germany until the pips squeaked remained popular among significant swathes of the Allied voters.[30] For most with this mentality, the squeeze meant not just in the terms of the final treaty but during the negotiation and drafting of the treaty. To some of the British and French delegates gathered in Paris in early 1919, continuing to cause hardship through economic warfare was necessary to coerce their German enemies into signing deservedly punitive peace treaties.[31] To some extent simple inertia may have fed the continuation of the blockade. In the overwhelming crush of business in Paris the 'Big Four' Peace Conference leaders (Woodrow Wilson of the United States, David Lloyd George of Britain, Georges Clemenceau of France, and Vittorio Orlando of Italy) never allocated enough time or political capital to decide that the blockade should stop.

To the Armistice blockade's critics such excuses simply prove that the humanitarian disaster of serious malnourishment and even starvation in Germany during early 1919 was avoidable, and thus particularly horrific both in the short-term wave of deaths, and in the longer term as it fed the resent-driven rise of the Nazis. Although issues like reparations and the 'war guilt clause' of the Treaty of Versailles have long been at the forefront of criticisms of the Allies' postwar peace-making efforts, the Armistice blockade has also long been seen as a core example of the Allies' supposed mistreatment of early Weimar Germany, of their overall botching of the opportunity for peace. In sum the 1919 Armistice-era blockade was immediately and broadly perceived as a black mark on the Allied war, and has remained so ever since.

Understanding postwar humanitarianism

In notable contrast with this harsh criticism of the Armistice blockade, historians of the novel international efforts to alleviate European destitution portray postwar humanitarian relief efforts as an unprecedented moral good. Mary Elisabeth Cox's excellent work quantifying the positive effects of relief efforts on German health is a recent example of how historians juxtapose the blockade against the relief. In this framework the efforts to feed and supply Germany in 1919 existed in fundamental opposition to the blockade, and were led by people who repudiated both the blockade and the blockaders at every turn. For example, throughout the spring of 1919, Eglantyne Jebb and the other founders of Save the Children bitterly denounced Lord Robert Cecil, who had been Britain's wartime Minister of Blockade, and who at the Paris Peace Conference was a leader both of the SEC and of the commission that was crafting the Covenant of the new League of Nations. Jebb judged Cecil as the prime reason the blockade still existed, lambasting him as an unrepentant economic warrior who rejected humanitarian relief.[32] Among righteous humanitarians, blockaders made for easy scapegoats for the deep difficulties facing Europeans.

People from countries around the world engaged in a variety of humanitarian efforts in Europe during the Armistice, but the particular Americanness of this humanitarian enterprise was notable then, and has remained so for historians since. The national characterisation of the Americans as 'volunteerist' do-gooders had been crafted during the war with the Belgian Relief effort. This carried over to perceptions during 1919, and after that postwar relief was also a US-dominated effort. American can-do benevolence has often been perceived in juxtaposition to the supposed intransigence of the British and French, who were more eager to turn the screws on Germany. In the historiography of famine relief and rebuilding efforts in Europe during 1919, the US repeatedly appears as the well-meaning philanthropist, lavishing money and precious food on irreconcilable Europeans who kept blockading Germany instead of helping it.[33] Again Hoover provides the best example – as the American Director of Relief, he is regularly portrayed as a tireless and selfless workaholic, as (in Cox's words) 'nothing short of heroic' in getting food through to Germany, despite the resistance of the sullen British and French.[34] Hoover played up this favourable perception of his wartime and postwar efforts to fashion a political career that led him all the way to the White House in 1929. This view of America's national humanitarianism fitted snugly with the country's slide toward isolationism during 1919 and into the 1920s, as isolationism relied on US distance from Europe, a distance both geographical and spiritual, as proof of the selflessness of American charity.

To some blockade critics it has always been truly vexing how efforts to rebuild Germany could coexist, seemingly at cross-purposes, with warfare measures against Germany's economy. But looking at the interaction between the Allies' Armistice-era economic war and simultaneous 'inter-Allied' efforts to relieve hunger in central Europe shows that it is a mistake to see these two efforts, the blockade and the relief, as opposites. Instead, when looking at the personnel and the policies, the vital and most successful initial efforts to rebuild the central European economies came from the people who had led the Allied wartime blockade.[35]

The Supreme Economic Council stood at the centre of these humanitarian efforts. It was created by peace conference leaders in late February 1919, and chaired by Britain's former Minister of Blockade, Lord Robert Cecil. During the war 'interallied' organisations like the Allied Maritime Transport Council (AMTC) had been central to augmenting the blockade against the Central Powers, in the AMTC's case by controlling Allied shipping resources. Now during the Peace Conference, these organisations of Allied economic control were recreated and repurposed as sections of the SEC. In the SEC these one-time blockaders now worked to supply the shipping and financing necessary for large-scale food shipments.

The SEC has been derided by Hoover and some historians as an inter-Allied 'façade' that obscured the Americans' actual control of European relief in early 1919.[36] But the SEC was the pivotal venue for negotiating agreements between the Allies and with Germany on supplying food. Efforts to open up food shipments began in earnest immediately after the SEC began operating, as the Council debated competing British, French, and American plans on how much food Germany could receive in return for gold and merchant ships. With global trade facing unprecedented turmoil due to a lack of shipping and finance, working to repair Europe's supply lines would not be easy. It is doubtful that simply declaring the blockade over would have solved anything; there was too much need for tricky diplomacy and economic coordination to clear the many bottlenecks in the systems of world trade. The SEC provided an institution where the Allies could debate and co-ordinate their efforts to reopen European trade. In SEC meetings in early March, the Allied delegates led by Hoover, Cecil, and Étienne Clémentel found a compromise that pleased neither the French or the Americans. Yet immediately after the resulting Brussels agreement was signed with

Germany on 14 March hundreds of thousands of tons of food began flowing to Germany from Rotterdam, with more food flooding in aboard merchant ships routed by the SEC from the United States and Argentina.[37]

Through the spring the blockade continued to exist as a possible lever to coerce Germany to sign the eventual Treaty of Versailles. Yet the regular meetings of the SEC and the daily activities of its subcommittees were instrumental in organising the de facto dismantling of much of the blockade well before the signing of the treaty. The SEC was the place during the conference where the Allies' conflicting views on blockade could be balanced, between the 'lift all war restrictions' Americans like Hoover and Vance McCormick, and the 'maintain many war restrictions' stance of the French. Over the spring months the leaders of the SEC worked with the 'Big Four' to chip away at specific strictures of the blockade. In meetings before the end of March the SEC ended Italy's blockade of trade in the Adriatic, and soon relaxed all the blockade measures on Poland and Estonia. By the start of May, in the words of the Superior Blockade Committee of the SEC, 'in effect Germany is now free to import all the food for which she can pay'.[38]

Crafting compromises between the most ardent pro-blockade and pro-humanitarian arguments allowed the SEC to effectively lessen the power of the blockade. It also enabled the SEC to make new innovations in the philosophy or rationale of economic warfare. On 14 May Cecil and other blockaders successfully argued to the 'Big Four' in favour of the coercive power of severely curtailing the existing blockade.[39] He argued that the mere threat of reinstating the blockade if German actions (such as a refusal to sign the treaty) mandated further Allied coercion was actually a more powerful coercive tool than continuing to maintain all economic warfare measures until the treaty signing. This idea of the coercive power of merely threatening sanctions lived on throughout the 1920s and beyond among those who hoped that a League of Nations wielding this power could help to maintain global peace.[40]

In other words, although the blockade of Germany was not officially lifted until the signing of the Treaty of Versailles on 28 June, for months it had been more of a potentially reintensified threat than a continuing harsh reality. One can even see this de facto drawdown of the blockade in evidence given by some historians who stress the dichotomy between the Allied blockade and armistice humanitarian efforts. For example, Mary Elisabeth Cox has shown that the weights of German children recovered quickly following the Armistice, and yet she chastises the blockaders for keeping up a stringent economic war. But do not the rising weights suggest instead that significant amounts of food were getting through despite the blockade?[41]

Beyond straightforwardly starving Germans, the Armistice blockade has also been criticised by humanitarians for unfairly stifling German and central European economic recovery after the war. Certainly the German economy did not rebound quickly in 1919 or 1920. But perhaps it was not the continuation of a porous blockade against Germany that hampered Central European economic recovery in 1919, but rather the jolt of the end of war seizing up trade, or the political chaos of the new central European states beset with proposed but undefined reparations demands. Perhaps the German economists who guided Weimar policy followed incorrect economic theories. The historian Adam Tooze explains the slow European recovery by pointing to the political situation of America, where 'assertive nationalism' led to an unnecessary, 'unilateral squeeze' on finance and global trade.[42] One should note the irony of potentially blaming the US for the difficulty of German recovery, an idea that does not fit well with the stories of the supposedly generous humanitarian relief that America extended toward the Germans.

Regardless of who was to blame for the halting postwar German economic recovery, it is worthwhile to reiterate that, during the Paris conference, the relationship between the blockade and the humanitarian relief of Central Europe was more symbiotic than antagonistic, with both connected within the oft-underestimated inter-allied agency, the SEC. It is only a slight stretch to suggest that the Armistice blockade was a targeted provisioning mechanism, rather than a simple curtailment of foreign trade.

Legacies of the Armistice era

The perception of the Armistice blockade as a unique horror rests on an overstatement of the tightness of this economic war through June 1919, and a resulting overestimation of the importance of its nominal continuation. And yet the opposite story about the Armistice blockade, as an episode that exemplified the Allies' cruelty and oppression, latched hold immediately. Through 1919 and later some of the humanitarians themselves who began to have a strong influence on international public discourse at the time of the signing of the Treaty of Versailles, like Herbert Hoover and Eglantyne Jebb, continued to lambast the blockade's supposed impact on the peace. Failure became the standard judgement of the Paris Peace Conference after John Maynard Keynes's *Economic Consequences of the Peace* came out at the end of 1919, and the story of the Armistice-era blockade likely became tainted by Keynes's portrayal of a diplomacy marked by a combination of torpor, indecision, and triumphalism.[43] Not surprisingly, the blockade was also portrayed as the greatest of all evils by the Germans. Immediately at the end of the war and periodically through the early 1920s Weimar officials invoked images of starving German children to indict

Allied policies and jockey for international sympathy.[44] The supposedly slightly-more-than three-quarters of a million dead due to the wartime blockade became a celebrated figure, a number that encapsulated the Allies' purported cruelty, and was used as a rhetorical cudgel across the political spectrum in Germany. Over time such rhetoric of Allied (and particularly French) perfidy favoured the Nazis.[45]

In part the failure of the blockader humanitarians to change the narrative was due to the difficult transition from the Peace Conference to the League. After the signing of the Treaty of Versailles in mid-1919 the authority and initiative of the SEC declined over the next six months, as did broader Allied unity when the US failed to ratify the treaty early in 1920. The partially successful international attempts to provide relief during the spring of 1919 did not immediately translate into continued efforts led by the League of Nations. The League created a commission on humanitarian aid only in late 1923. But between late 1919 and 1923 notable aid efforts to Russia, Poland, and Germany were private initiatives, many led by the now-private American Relief Administration (ARA) which was again helmed by Hoover. In Russia and Poland some co-operation developed between national organisations involved in international relief, but little in the way of the creation of any solid or lasting international organisation.[46] It is deeply ironic that it was the much-maligned SEC that did operate for a while in 1919 as a real international bureaucracy, providing a new paradigm for future international efforts.

These efforts in 1919 would not have lived up to twenty-first-century definitions of humanitarianism, such as the 'Humanitarian Principles' listed by the United Nations Office for the Co-ordination of Humanitarian Affairs.[47] For example the United Nations demands 'neutrality' in humanitarianism, but in 1919 none of the humanitarians could be seen as neutral, in terms of not taking sides in the political divide within the former Central Powers. Both blockaders and relief activists aimed to repulse the spread of Bolshevism in the defeated powers. Ignorant of another twenty-first-century guideline, the blockaders-turned-humanitarians of 1919 were definitely not 'impartial', as their food shipments prioritised Germany and Austria over destitute populations further to the east. The desire of humanitarians, especially Hoover, to sell the overproduction of US farms, and to have Germany pay in full for this food, made post-First World War humanitarianism far from 'independent' from the base, parochial desires of the giving party.

Yet people like Cecil in the SEC working in internationalist Paris during 1919 certainly saw themselves as humanitarians in the sense of alleviating suffering by providing relief to people in peril and planning for the rehabilitation of their shattered economies. As an organisation of the wartime allies, the SEC in particular helped to create lasting standards for post-conflict relief. The supplies provided to Germany in 1919 encouraged the expectation ever since that even defeated enemies must be treated with compassion rather than cruelty, an expectation held even by the defeated themselves.

Due to the Paris Peace Conference, the very idea of economic warfare gained what might be called a humanitarian side. In 1919 certain leaders hoped that future universal blockades could avert potential inhumanities by halting wars before they started, and thus keeping people out of peril. Threatening or engaging in an international blockade or trade war against a militarist aggressor might be an ultimately humanitarian enterprise. Among many League of Nations activists, this hope of an economic weapon for peace survived through the early 1930s.[48] As the organs of the blockade were being repurposed for humanitarianism, the crafters of the League of Nations were also embedding Great War-style economic warfare within Article 16 of the League Covenant and in the new institutions of the nascent League as the key to upholding peace, if the power to blockade could be wielded by a popular League of Nations. Considering the tremendous and painful role it played during the war, it was realistic to believe that economic warfare, including simple direct blockade but also more nuanced and targeted economic sanctions, could lead an aggressor to withdraw from a fight – or even that the mere threat of such sanctions might lead a would-be aggressor to forgo their potential aggression.

Over the last century, international economic sanctions have not always lived up to any of these goals. There are certainly some downsides to economic war. The most important charge against economic sanctions is that they hurt ordinary people, even while leaving unscathed the ruling elites whose policies the sanctions aim to change. However, since the earliest days of international economic warfare during and after the Great War, those waging economic campaigns have recognised the destructiveness of their blockades to the lives of ordinary enemy citizens. During the next World War, the United Nations Relief and Rehabilitation Administration was the first UN organisation to begin operations, in that case not just during the peace-making but before the war even ended.[49] In working to remedy German and Austrian starvation and restart their economies even before the Treaty of Versailles was signed in June 1919, the blockaders of the Great War set new norms for the humanitarian response that could be expected after military and economic sanctions led a foe to accept defeat.

Significant continuities link the Allies' wartime economic war and postwar international humanitarianism. The economic and trade policies followed by the Allies during the Paris Peace Conference in 1919 have often been understood in terms of conflict, as an unfortunate legacy of a lingering wartime enmity against Germany, and as something fundamentally out of step with the needs and realities of postwar recovery. Yet the Armistice blockade was so much more, as it provided inter-Allied capabilities and mentalities pivotal to the successes of postwar humanitarian relief efforts, while helping to sculpt the longer-term possibility of an effective, peacekeeping League of Nations.

Notes

1 These SEC influences on postwar humanitarianism overlap with the ways that SEC veterans nurtured international financial co-operation through the League of Nations, as described by P. Clavin, 'The Austrian Hunger Crisis and the Genesis of International Organisation after the First World War', *International Affairs*, 90:2 (2014), 274.
2 Phrase of B. Cabanes, *The Great War and the Origins of Humanitarianism, 1918–1924* (Cambridge: Cambridge University Press, 2014), p. 16.
3 D. Rodogno, *Against Massacre: Humanitarian Interventions in the Ottoman Empire, 1815–1914* (Princeton: Princeton University Press, 2011), p. 6; also see J. Irwin, 'Taming Total War: Great War-Era American Humanitarianism and Its Legacies', in T. W. Zeiler, D. K. Ekbladh, and B. C. Montoya (eds), *Beyond 1917: The United States and the Global Legacies of the Great War* (New York: Oxford University Press, 2017), pp. 136–7.
4 G. H. Nash, *The Life of Herbert Hoover: The Humanitarian, 1914–1917* (New York: W. W. Norton & Co., 1988); S. de Schaepdrijver, 'A Civilian War Effort: the *Comité National de Secours et d'Alimentation* in Occupied Belgium, 1914–1918', in *Remembering Herbert Hoover and the Commission for Relief in Belgium: Proceedings of the Seminar Held at the University Foundation on October 4, 2006* (Brussels: Foundation Universitaire, 2007); C. Druelle-Korn, *Food for Democracy? Le ravitaillement de la France occupée (1914–1919): Herbert Hoover, le Blocus, les Neutres et les Alliés* (Brussels: Peter Lang, 2018), as well as the English-language version: C. Druelle, *Feeding Occupied France during World War I: Herbert Hoover and the Blockade* (Cham: Palgrave Macmillan, 2019).
5 S. de Schaepdrijver, '"A Less-Than-Total Total War": Neutrality, Invasion, and the Stakes of War, 1914–1918', in F. Rash and C. Declercq (eds), *The Great War in Belgium and the Netherlands* (Cham: Palgrave Macmillan, 2018), p. 23.
6 I. V. Hull, *A Scrap of Paper: Breaking and Making International Law during the Great War* (Ithaca: Cornell University Press, 2014), pp. 117–19.
7 Among the many who have written on the blockade see A. C. Bell, *A History of the Blockade of Germany and of the Countries Associated with Her in the Great War, Austria-Hungary, Bulgaria, and Turkey, 1914–1918* (London: Her Majesty's Stationery Office, 1961); M. Parmelee, *Blockade and Sea Power: The Blockade, 1914–1919* (New York: Thomas Y. Crowell Co., 1924); C. P. Vincent, *The Politics of Hunger: The Allied Blockade of Germany 1915–1919* (Athens: Ohio University Press, 1985); E. W. Osborne, *Britain's Economic*

Blockade of Germany, 1914–1919 (London and New York: Frank Cass, 2004); A. Offer, *The First World War: An Agrarian Interpretation* (Oxford: Oxford University Press, 1989).

8 A. Hurd, *The Merchant Navy* (New York: Longmans, Green & Co., 1921).
9 N. Mulder, 'The Trading with the Enemy Acts in the Age of Expropriation, 1914–49', *Journal of Global History*, 15:1 (2020), 81–99.
10 P. Dehne, *On the Far Western Front: Britain's First World War in South America* (Manchester: Manchester University Press, 2009).
11 P. Dehne, 'The Ministry of Blockade and the Fate of Free Trade during the First World War', *Twentieth Century British History*, 27:3 (2016), 333–56.
12 Particularly instructive on this was the panel at the 2020 AHA meeting in New York on 'The World War I Blockade of the Ottoman Empire and Syria as War Crime and Precedent', with papers by Laura Robson, Mustafa Aksakal, and Elizabeth Thompson.
13 M. E. Cox, 'Hunger Games: or How the Allied Blockade in the First World War Deprived German Children of Nutrition, and Allied Food Aid Subsequently Saved Them', *Economic History Review*, 68:2 (2015), 600–31.
14 M. E. Cox, *Hunger in War and Peace: Women and Children in Germany, 1914–1924* (Oxford: Oxford University Press, 2019), pp. 79–83.
15 N. Ferguson, *The Pity of War* (New York: Basic Books, 1999), p. 276.
16 Offer, *The First World War*, 291–306; N. Lambert, *Planning Armageddon: British Economic Warfare and the First World War* (Cambridge, MA: Harvard University Press, 2012); Ferguson, *The Pity of War*, pp. 85–7.
17 Ferguson, *The Pity of War*, p. 102.
18 J. Leonhard, *Pandora's Box: A History of the First World War* (Cambridge, MA: The Belknap Press of Harvard University Press, 2018), p. 489.
19 Leonhard, *Pandora's Box*, p. 348, pp. 469–71, p. 831.
20 E. H. Carr, *The Twenty Years' Crisis, 1919–1939: An Introduction to the Study of International Relations* (London: Macmillan, 1962), p. 131; O. A. Hathaway and S. J. Shapiro, *The Internationalists: How a Radical Plan to Outlaw War Remade the World* (New York: Simon and Schuster, 2017), p. 395. The tendency to see economic warfare as less inhumane than other forms of warfare has lasted; on the wide variety of reasons that intentional starvation has, even a century later, only been 'conditionally' abolished under international law see N. Mulder and B. van Dijk, 'Why Did Starvation Not Become the Paradigmatic War Crime in International Law?', in I. Venzke and K. J. Heller (eds), *Contingency in International Law: On the Possibility of Different Legal Histories* (New York: Oxford University Press, 2021), pp. 370–88.
21 Hull, *A Scrap of Paper*, p. 167.
22 Leonhard, *Pandora's Box*, p. 264.
23 Druelle, *Feeding Occupied France*, pp. 107–8.
24 Cox, 'Hunger Games', 600–1.
25 Offer, *The First World War*, p. 78.
26 Vincent, *The Politics of Hunger*, pp. 115–23, pp. 158–60.

27 S. Marks, 'Mistakes and Myths: The Allies, Germany, and the Versailles Treaty, 1918–1921', *Journal of Modern History*, 85:3 (2013), 651.
28 For example see Cox, *Hunger in War and Peace*, p. 202, pp. 205–7. A strong rebuttal to a Foch-centric view of the French attitude toward peace-making is P. Jackson, *Beyond the Balance of Power: France and the Politics of National Security in the Era of the First World War* (Cambridge: Cambridge University Press, 2013), especially chapter 6.
29 K. Clements, *The Life of Herbert Hoover: Imperfect Visionary 1918–1928* (New York: Palgrave Macmillan, 2010), p. 4.
30 On British liberal opinion, see Hull, *A Scrap of Paper*, p. 5.
31 P. Dehne, *After the Great War: Economic Warfare and the Promise of Peace in Paris 1919* (London: Bloomsbury Academic, 2019), pp. 92–4.
32 Cabanes, *The Great War*, pp. 275–85.
33 F. M. Surface and R. L. Bland (eds), *American Food in the World War and Reconstruction Period: Operations of the organisations under the Direction of Herbert Hoover 1914–1924* (Stanford: Stanford University Press, 1931); Cox, 'Hunger Games', 624; Cabanes, *The Great War*, p. 212; K. Schwabe, *Woodrow Wilson, Revolutionary Germany, and Peacemaking, 1918–1919: Missionary Diplomacy and the Realities of Power* (Chapel Hill: University of North Carolina Press, 1985), pp. 191–210; E. Glaser, 'The Making of the Economic Peace', in M. F. Boemeke, G. D. Feldman, and E. Glaser (eds), *The Treaty of Versailles: A Reassessment after 75 Years* (Cambridge: Cambridge University Press, 1998), pp. 390–1; Irwin, 'Taming Total War', 123.
34 Cox, 'Hunger Games', 624.
35 See Cabanes on the continuities of people transitioning from wartime endeavours to peace, in *The Great War*, pp. 89–93.
36 Druelle, *Feeding Occupied France*, p. 321.
37 A. Mayer, *Politics and Diplomacy of Peacemaking: Containment and Counterrevolution at Versailles 1918–1919* (New York: Alfred A. Knopf, 1967), pp. 509–13; 17 March 1919 (10:00 am), 8th SEC meeting, *British Documents on Foreign Affairs (BDFA)*, Reports and Papers from the Foreign Office Confidential Print, Part II, Series I: The Paris Peace Conference of 1919, Volume 12 (Frederick, MD: University Publications of America, 1989-), vol. 12; 26 May 1919, Report of Enemy Tonnage Sub-Committee, 20th SEC meeting, *BDFA*, vol. 12.
38 13 May 1919, Superior Blockade Council memo, Bernard M. Baruch Papers, Box 387, Public Policy Papers, Department of Rare Books and Special Collections, Princeton University Library.
39 14 May 1919, Council of Four meeting (11:45 am), *Papers Relating to the Foreign Relations of the United States, The Paris Peace Conference, 1919*, vol. 5 (Washington, DC: US Government Printing Office, 1946), vol. 5, Doc. 64.
40 Mulder and Van Dijk, 'Why Did Starvation', pp. 376–7.
41 Cox, 'Hunger Games', 615–16.
42 A. Tooze, *The Deluge: The Great War, America and the Remaking of the Global Order, 1916–1931* (New York: Viking, 2014), pp. 349–50.

43 A. Lentin, *General Smuts: South Africa* (London: Haus, 2010), p. 96; P. Cohrs, *The Unfinished Peace after World War I: America, Britain and the Stabilisation of Europe, 1919–1932* (Cambridge: Cambridge University Press, 2006), p. 17.
44 E. Piller, 'German Child Distress, US Humanitarian Aid and Revisionist Politics, 1918–24', *Journal of Contemporary History*, 51:3 (2016), 453–86.
45 N. Patin, 'Histoire d'un chiffre: Réflexions autour des victims allemandes du blocus de 1914–1918', *UMR Sirice*, 26:1 (2021), 95–107.
46 Cabanes, *The Great War*, p. 245; D. Rodogno, F. Piana, and S. Gauthier, 'Shaping Poland: Relief and Rehabilitation Programmes by Foreign Organisations, 1918–1922', in D. Rodogno, B. Struck, and J. Vogel (eds), *Shaping the Transnational Sphere: Experts, Network and Issues from 1840s to the 1930s* (New York: Berghahn, 2015), pp. 259–78.
47 'OCHA on Message: Humanitarian Principles', OCHA, July 2022, www.unocha.org/research-and-reports. The author is indebted to Ronan Macnamara for illuminating the differences between historical definitions of humanitarianism and those followed by international organisations now.
48 Mulder and Van Dijk, 'Why Did Starvation', pp. 374–7.
49 S. Porter, 'Humanitarian Diplomacy after World War II: The United Nations Relief and Rehabilitation Administration', in R. Hutchings and J. Suri (eds), *Foreign Policy Breakthroughs: Cases in Successful Diplomacy* (New York: Oxford University Press, 2015).

8

Better fed than red: international famine relief, 1921–22

Kimberly Lowe

Introduction

In 1921 a famine in the Volga region of central and southern European Russia threatened as many as thirty million individuals with death by starvation. The famine became the latest humanitarian disaster affecting communities that since 1914 had been ravaged by war, revolution, and epidemic disease. The Volga region had seen some of the most fierce fighting on the Eastern front during the Great War. Since 1918 the civil wars and border conflicts that erupted in the wake of the Russian Revolution had created a host of challenges: thousands of prisoners of war with no clear path to their homes in Central and Eastern Europe and Russia; millions of refugees driven from their homes; a typhus epidemic that threatened to spread to Western Europe; and new civilian and combatant victims of internal conflicts. All of these crises prompted international humanitarian responses that created lasting changes in interwar humanitarian aid.[1]

Even within this landscape contemporary observers viewed this famine as a humanitarian crisis of monumental proportions. As soon as news of the famine reached Western Europe and the Americas, private humanitarian organisations, government leaders, and officials at the League of Nations began to discuss ways to bring food and seed to the starving inhabitants of the Volga. Initially both private and governmental conferences envisioned the creation of a massive international famine relief effort, capable of feeding at least twenty million children and adults. This food aid would have been the largest intergovernmental aid operation of the interwar period. It also would have represented the first time that European governments used food as a co-ordinated tool of foreign policy. Yet it never materialised. This chapter investigates why the Volga famine elicited such fervent intergovernmental plans for humanitarian relief, and why these plans fell apart.

On the basis of an analysis of the negotiations among governments and private organisations about famine relief, I argue that it was the anti-Bolshevik possibilities for food aid that elevated the famine beyond the realm of humanitarian suffering and into the arena of geopolitics. While all proponents of relief recognised the tremendous humanitarian need created by the famine, and the high likelihood of epidemics spreading beyond Russia, this was not the main justification given for an international aid operation. The focus was on combating Bolshevism. While the material relief brought by the famine aid operations had clear 'non-political' impacts, the motivations for this relief were political from the start. Even more importantly, the Western European Allies ultimately refused inter-governmental funding for famine relief, despite recognising the magnitude of the humanitarian crisis, because they concluded that relief could not be delivered in a manner consistent with an anti-Bolshevik foreign policy. This is a clear example of political considerations, not objective need, determining where, how, and why aid was both given and withheld.

The British and Allied governments saw food aid as a non-military response to the Bolshevik threat, at a time when it was clear that the Allied military intervention in Russia had failed. After taking power in Moscow in 1917, the Bolshevik party called openly for communist revolutions to overthrow liberal-democratic and capitalist governments around the world. The Bolsheviks had also violated basic principles of international law by repudiating the treaty and financial obligations of the former imperial state. They were openly hostile to what Western European governments considered the 'rule of law' and 'Western civilization'. By 1921 the post-revolutionary military attempts to overthrow the new regime had failed. The White Armies had suffered their final defeat from the Red Army at the end of 1920. In March 1921 the Polish and Soviet Russian governments signed the Treaty of Riga, bringing an end to fighting between the Red Army and Polish, Ukrainian, Latvian, Lithuanian, and Belarussian nationalists.

At the same time, the future of the Soviet state was still uncertain. To many Western observers, it did not seem unrealistic to think a devastating famine might force the Bolsheviks to further compromise their radical communist political and economic policies. Russian agriculture and industry were in dire straits, and Moscow had recently taken steps to introduce a mixed economy and foreign investment. In March 1921 Vladimir Lenin introduced the New Economic Policy, which allowed for a greater degree of free trade and private ownership. Leonid Krasin, the Commissar of Foreign Trade, signed the Anglo-Soviet Trade Agreement that same month. This ended the British blockade of Russia and opened Russian ports to British ships.

Food aid provided the British and Allied governments with a non-military hope of moderating the political regime of Soviet Russia. British officials based their hope on a belief that the famine had transformed Soviet Russia into a territory of low sovereignty, ripe for political change.

Intelligence reports described the Soviet economy on the brink of collapse and a countryside on the brink of anarchy. The Supreme Allied Council initially planned to use food to directly empower a committee of political moderates to take power from the Bolsheviks. When it became clear that intelligence reports had underestimated the extent of Bolshevik control, the governments instead made food aid contingent on the Soviet regime recognising the international debts of the Tsar. This was the same issue that had proved a sticking point in the negotiations over the Anglo-Soviet Trade Agreement and would also dominate the Genoa Conference negotiations in 1922. Soviet recognition of these debts had both financial and political implications: it would have been a significant sign that the Bolsheviks were willing to integrate into the capitalist international system. When Moscow refused, European governments abandoned their plans for international relief.

Instead of an international intergovernmental effort, national, ideological, and financial divisions resulted in five famine relief operations from both the right and left of the political spectrum. On the left, the Soviet government's official famine relief committee fed five million.[2] Two international workers' solidarity networks, the International Trade Union Federation (or Amsterdam Union) and Foreign Committee for the Organising of Workers' Relief for the Starving of Russia (directed by the Comintern), mounted operations that fed around 120,000.[3] On the right, the American famine relief effort led by Herbert Hoover's American Relief Administration (ARA) fed ten million individuals at its height in mid-August 1922. Finally, over twenty private organisations from across Europe co-ordinated their efforts under the loose oversight of the International Committee for Russian Relief (ICRR), led by Fridtjof Nansen. Through a combination of government and private charitable donations, this pan-European effort fed one and a half million Russian children and adults. The ICRR was itself noteworthy for the number of organisations involved and the fact that international aid was furnished to a country that was neither an ally nor part of a common imperial structure. Yet it also fed a fraction of the number planned for in the aborted intergovernmental aid plans.

Existing research on foreign aid operations during the Volga famine has focused primarily on how these efforts represented humanitarian innovations, not political tools. Much research focuses on how the ARA operation illustrated a modern approach to humanitarian aid focused on large-scale, scientific, unilateral aid operations abroad. Herbert Hoover's belief that food aid could combat Bolshevism is noted by most histories of the ARA's famine operations, including Bertrand Patenaude's and Bruno Cabanes's recent work.[4] Research on European operations make no mention of anti-Bolshevism as a motivation for famine relief. Cabanes calls attention to the ways that anti-Bolshevik public sentiment damaged Nansen's efforts to raise money for the ICRR, but argues that Nansen's own motives were purely humanitarian.[5] Tehila Sasson shows that British imperial expertise garnered from famines in India dominated the technical approach to relief pursued by both British and international relief workers.[6] Similarly, Norbert Götz, Georgina Brewis, and Steffen Werther note that American and European relief organisations found it difficult to raise money to aid 'a foreign power with a hostile ideology', and therefore sought to distinguish between the Russian people and the Bolshevik regime.[7] The authors also show that aid organisations tried to argue that famine relief had domestic economic benefits or would bolster national prestige abroad, to varying degrees of success.[8] Working from the Russian state archives, Marin Coudreau demonstrates that Bolshevik authorities used their co-operation with Nansen's famine relief to bolster their own goals for domestic aid and reconstruction. From the Russian Soviet perspective Nansen's operations also supported Moscow's desire to receive official international recognition and financing.[9] Finally, the ideology and operations of the workers' solidarity networks are an area worthy of further research.[10]

In this chapter I examine the aborted intergovernmental plans for food aid and the motivations of Nansen and his deputies within the ICRR. This history makes clear that for both private and governmental actors, anti-Bolshevism pervaded plans for humanitarian aid to Russian famine victims. Not only Hoover but also Fridtjof Nansen believed that full bellies could turn the Russian people away from political extremism and towards the liberal-democratic principles of Western Europe and the United States. For both men this belief coexisted with a neutral approach to aid delivery focused only on the humanitarian need of the recipients. The British and Allied governments were also interested in food as a tool of foreign policy. Yet, unlike Hoover or Nansen, they sought to use famine relief to directly influence the political and economic policies of Soviet Russia. Nansen and Hoover were convinced that humanitarian aid brought to Russians in the Volga was enough to sow the seeds of moderate political leanings, but the British government required a more direct connection between food and politics.

News of the famine reaches the West

The Volga famine had both natural and human-made causes. Fighting on the Eastern front during the First World War and Russian Civil War had centred on the Volga and trans-Volga regions. The Bolshevik policy of grain requisitioning during the Russian civil war further decreased the seed available to farmers for planting. All of this was disastrous for the crop yields of what had been some of the most fertile regions of the Russian Empire. By 1920 corn production had decreased 75 per cent compared to the 1913 harvest. A drought from October 1920 to June 1921 then transformed a growing food crisis into a full-scale famine. The entire Volga and trans-Volga regions lost their harvest. In response Bolshevik authorities requisitioned twice the normal amount of grain from non-famine provinces, spreading the food crisis to Crimea and Ukraine. By July two-thirds of the country faced famine. Widespread malnourishment also produced epidemics of typhus and cholera, which threatened to spread across Russia into the bordering states of Eastern Europe. Left unchecked, the famine had the potential to produce more deaths than the First World War, and as many as the worldwide flu pandemic of 1918.[11]

Although Bolshevik policies of grain requisition had contributed to the food crisis, when the scale of the famine became apparent the Soviet government actively solicited substantial foreign aid. Moscow allocated 12 million gold rubles to purchase seed abroad, and transferred ninety thousand people out of the famine-stricken areas.[12] On 2 August Georgy Chicherin, the People's Commissar for Foreign Affairs, sent an official note to all governments requesting foreign aid. He assured them that all relief would be accepted, irrespective of the political source.[13] Unlike Joseph Stalin during the famine of 1932–33, Vladimir Lenin did not pursue a deliberate policy of starvation, even though Bolshevik authorities focused aid efforts on eastern Russia to the detriment of Ukraine and Crimea.[14]

For many Western observers, the most surprising aspect of Moscow's reaction to the Volga famine was the creation of the All-Union Russian Public Committee for Relief of the Starving. This committee was given official responsibility to solicit foreign aid and direct assistance to the famine area. Its charter stated that it was independent from government oversight. Its membership included prominent scientists, artists, intellectuals, and other figures with international reputations and moderate political views.[15] Tikhon of Moscow, the Eleventh Patriarch of Moscow and of all Russia, and one of the most prominent leaders of the Russian Orthodox Church, was a member. Another member was Maxim Gorky, the world-renowned Russian author, who in 1918 had denounced Lenin and Leon Trotsky for their censorship of the press and arbitrary arrests. On 11 July Patriarch Tikhon sent a telegram to the Anglican Archbishop of Canterbury and the Orthodox Archbishop of New York warning that a great part of Russia's population faced death if food and medicine were not sent abroad. Two days later Maxim Gorky sent a similar telegram appeal to all 'cultured European and American people'. He appealed to the common heritage of Western civilisation and argued famine relief was an opportunity to show that 'humanitarian ideas and feelings' were still alive and well after the devastating war and terror of the preceding years.[16]

Reports from the handful of non-Russian observers allowed into the country also confirmed the dire situation. Representatives of the British Quaker Relief Mission found that in the province of Samara the harvest had been 7 per cent of its normal yield.[17] The head of the British trade delegation in Moscow, Sir Robert MacLeod Hodgson, reported that children were being abandoned by their parents without clothing or food, and the people were eating grass, bread made from roots, horses, and rubbish.[18]

Outside observers also believed that the crisis necessitated intergovernmental action. Philip Noel-Baker, the British assistant to Eric Drummond, the Secretary General of the League of Nations, argued that large-scale foreign aid was necessary to prevent the complete economic and political collapse of Russia. In his view private charities could handle other postwar humanitarian crises like the care of refugees, but 'the Famine absolutely demands Government action'.[19] He warned that anarchy in the famine areas would spread to the whole of Russia, which would make it impossible to re-establish political or economic relations with the rest of Europe for a very long time. This view was shared by Harold Nicolson and Sir Owen St Clair O'Malley of the British Foreign Office, as well as John Gorvin, General Secretary of the International Committee for Relief Credits, and Arthur Salter, General Secretary of the Reparations Commission.[20]

International planning for intergovernmental relief

By early August 1921 both private organisations and governments were actively contemplating an intergovernmental relief action to combat the famine. The Supreme Allied Council, with representatives from the United States, Great Britain, France, Italy, Belgium, and Japan, was the first to act. On 10 August the French Prime Minister Aristide Briand and British Prime Minister Lloyd George opened the meeting with strong statements regarding the moral and political need for an intergovernmental operation to fight the famine. The Italian Prime Minister Ivanoe Bonomi agreed, stating that 'it was in the political interest of Europe to [show] that the Bolshevik regime was not an earthly paradise and had now reduced Russia to seeking the help of other countries'.[21]

The Supreme Allied Council had a specific goal for international famine relief: political moderation. Since July the British Foreign Office had been collecting secret intelligence indicating that anti-Bolshevik activities and peasant uprisings were taking place throughout the country. By August British military intelligence had concluded that the Soviet regime was on the brink of collapse and that foreign intervention in the form of food aid could be used as a cover for a peaceful transfer of power.[22] In Moscow Hodgson reported that 'the Bolshevik Government is largely responsible for the present catastrophe [...] It is now obliged to have recourse to help of moderate political elements whose position is accordingly strengthened.'[23] He also warned that doing nothing in the face of such suffering would give credence to the anti-British communist propaganda fomented by the Bolsheviks both in Russia and abroad. Hodgson recommended that the British government sponsor a relief action, and direct aid to the All-Union Russian Public Committee. The aim was to transform the committee into a viable political alternative to the Bolshevik authorities in Moscow.

This was the policy recommended to the Supreme Allied Council by the British Secretary of State for Foreign Affairs, Lord Curzon. Curzon, who had been Viceroy of India during the 1899 famine, strongly advocated for an international relief effort that would include both the Allies and countries adjacent to Russia such as Czechoslovakia and Estonia. The council concluded their 10 August meeting by establishing a commission to investigate the possibilities for an international, intergovernmental famine relief effort.

Five days after the Council met, the International Committee of the Red Cross and League of Red Cross Societies hosted a conference on famine relief. Representatives of twelve governments, twenty-two national Red Cross societies, and twenty-seven other organisations, including the League of Nations Epidemic Commission and All-Union Russian Public Committee, convened in Geneva to discuss sending food aid to Russia. Accordingly, the conference quickly agreed that, to be effective, aid needed to be organised by 'a powerful international organisation' recognised by all governments, especially that of Soviet Russia.[24] The delegates voted to create the International Committee for Russian Relief. Yet, disagreement arose over who should direct the ICRR. Some delegates argued in favour of the League of Nations, because of its international character and technical expertise. Others considered American supplies and money necessary for success, and feared that leadership by the League of Nations would alienate the United States, which had not joined the League.

In the end the conference compromised and decided to ask both a European, Fridtjof Nansen, and an American, Herbert Hoover, to lead the operation. Hoover and Nansen were obvious choices because of their celebrated reputations as humanitarians. Hoover had gained international renown from his ambitious and successful feeding of German-occupied Belgium during the Great War. This mission served as the technical template for the ARA's eventual food aid to the Volga. Nansen had just recently overseen the League of Nation's repatriation of prisoners of war from

Siberia. He had direct experience negotiating with Bolshevik leaders and had proved he could operate effectively despite the political, logistical, and transport challenges posed by Soviet Russia.

These two men also shared a long-standing interest in food as a tool of political moderation. In 1918 Hoover made clear that he considered a stable food supply to be a key method to 'stem the tide of Bolshevism'.[25] A year later US President Woodrow Wilson supported Hoover's proposal to offer the Bolsheviks food in exchange for ceasing hostilities against the White Armies. Hoover enlisted the support of Fridtjof Nansen, who convinced the British, French, and Italian prime ministers to support the proposal. When Nansen approached the Soviet government, however, they made clear they had no interest in the exchange.[26] Undaunted, Hoover went on to use private ARA resources to feed the White Armies, to encourage an uprising against the communist government of Béla Kun in Hungary, and to quell socialist revolutionary unrest in Vienna.[27] Neither he nor Nansen abandoned their belief in the ability of food to maintain political stability and discourage people from political extremism.

American funding for famine aid

Hoover had no intention of joining an international relief operation. He preferred to control a national operation undertaken by the ARA and branded as clearly American. He refused to join the ICRR, citing his role as US Secretary of Commerce.[28] To concentrate American efforts in Hoover's hands, US President Warren Harding designated the ARA as the sole source of American relief to Russia. He instructed the US State Department to issue passports to Russia only for individuals in the service of the ARA.[29] This required all other American charities, including the American Red Cross and American Quakers to sever ties with sister organisations across the Atlantic and funnel their supplies through the ARA.

The US and Soviet Russian governments paid directly for $30 million worth of the grain purchased by the ARA.[30] Hoover obtained special permission from the Presidential Cabinet to sidestep the trade embargo with Russia and use the Soviet government's last remaining gold reserves to buy $10 million worth of grain from American farmers. President Harding also asked Congress for a $20 million appropriation of funds to purchase corn from American farmers and fund the relief operation.

To both the Presidential Cabinet and US Congress Hoover framed famine relief as an opportunity to build the reputation of the United States abroad and bolster the domestic economy. Within Harding's cabinet Hoover had the support of the Secretary of War, John W. Weeks; Secretary of the

Navy, Edwin Denby; and the Secretary of State, Charles Evans Hughes. For Hughes, Hoover's highly visible form of American charity served to combat anti-American communist propaganda. The ARA operation also allowed the US to maintain its official policy of nonrecognition while gaining quasi-consular services through ARA agents. Once in Moscow, the ARA's head of operations regularly sent trade and economic information, as well as political observations, back to the Department of Commerce. This information was then forwarded to the State Department. Hoover and numerous agricultural groups also lobbied members of Congress to support the $20 million appropriation. They argued that it would immediately boost the depressed price of grain and keep open the possibility of future trade with Russia. The support of the agricultural lobby and Hoover's own impeccable anti-Bolshevik reputation overcame Senators' objections about spending government money to aid Bolshevik Russia. The appropriation passed both the House and Senate with relatively little objection, although support was almost entirely from Harding's own Republican Party.[31]

European funding for famine aid

The lack of American involvement was not deemed a fatal blow by those supporting an intergovernmental action. Philip Noel-Baker saw the removal of the United States as an opportunity for the League of Nations to lead the operation. Nansen immediately accepted the offer to become High Commissioner of the ICRR. To direct the resources of the League of Nations Secretariat towards famine aid, Nansen also accepted the League's outstanding invitation to become its High Commissioner for Russian Refugees.[32] Nansen had refused this post in June, but news of the famine in July changed his mind.[33]

After accepting the ICRR post, Nansen assembled a small team of men who had prior experience working in Russia. John Gorvin (British), Thomas Lodge (British), Moritz Schlesinger (German), and Edouard Frick (Swiss) had all been intimately involved with the repatriation of prisoners of war from Siberia. Frick was also the International Committee of the Red Cross's delegate to Eastern Europe. Finally, William Andrew Mackenzie was the Secretary-General for the Save the Children International Union, which had operations in Soviet Russia. These five men accompanied Nansen to Moscow to negotiate with Chicherin. Walter Lyman Brown, the Director of ARA operations in Europe, had been in Riga negotiating with Maxim Litvinov, the Assistant People's Commissary for Foreign Affairs, since 10 August.[34] In less than a month the Soviet government signed two different agreements permitting foreign famine relief: one with the ARA on

20 August, and the other with Nansen on 27 August.[35] The two agreements ensured that almost all foreign food aid had to be funnelled through one of these two organisations.

In Moscow Nansen agreed to seek a £10 million ($40 million)[36] loan on behalf of the Soviet government from the governments of Western Europe. As collateral Chicherin offered only his promise that these bonds would have priority over any debts previously incurred by the Soviet government.[37] None the less, Nansen and his colleagues believed that they could secure £10 million through unused Relief Credits to fund their operation. These credits had already been approved by European governments for the reconstruction of Eastern Europe. They had been used to fund the repatriation of prisoners of war from Russia without traditional collateral. According to the records of the International Committee for Relief Credits, which co-ordinated these funds, between £5 million and £6 million of British credits remained unused and could be directed towards famine relief with Parliamentary sanction. Philip Noel-Baker, Arthur Salter, and Edouard Frick all expected that if the British authorised £5 million, the Germans, Italians, and Czechoslovakians would all contribute more than £5 million to the cause.[38]

The fatal blow to securing European governmental funding was caused by the dissolution of the All-Union Russian Public Committee. On 27 August the Cheka arrested all its members.[39] The British Secret Intelligence Service reported to the Foreign Office that, while the official claim was that the committee was abusing its position, they now suspected that Lenin's only purpose for the committee had been to bring foreign attention to the famine.[40] The Bolsheviks transferred the powers of the independent committee to the Central Commission for Relief of the Starving (or Pomgol), run by the government and composed entirely of Bolsheviks. This committee raised money for government-sponsored famine relief through a lottery, a food tax, and the confiscation of property from the Russian Orthodox Church.[41] In late October 1921 the Pomgol began direct distributions of food to union members, government workers, and the sick. Intellectuals, members of the clergy, and small tradesman or peasants deemed enemies of the revolution were excluded.[42]

The dissolution of the All-Union Russian Public Committee sent a clear message: the Bolshevik regime continued to hold power in Russia. It also fundamentally changed the calculus for foreign relief, because aid could no longer be directed through a non-Bolshevik body. The British Foreign Office concluded in September that the dissolution of the committee, combined with Soviet violations of the Anglo-Soviet Trade Agreement, meant that the hoped-for 'gradual evolution of the Soviet Government towards something resembling democracy' had failed to materialise.[43]

The idea of empowering political moderates in Moscow through food was replaced by a plan to force the Soviet government to recognise the debts of the Tsarist regime in exchange for food. This became the focus of the international commission created by the Supreme Allied Council. The International Commission on Russian Relief met twice: 30 August to 1 September, and 6 to 8 October. The August meeting included only representatives from the governments of France, Britain, Japan, Italy, Belgium, and the United States. Twenty-one governments, the Joint Commission of the Red Cross, and the Belgian Red Cross sent representatives to the October meeting. In their discussions at both these meetings the delegates acknowledged that the charitable work of private organisations, even subsidised by governments, could not hope to make a dent in either the immediate food crisis or the underlying economic devastation that had caused it. Yet, after days of debate, the delegates endorsed the French and British policy that no credit would be awarded to Russia unless the Soviet government recognised existing debts, nationalisations, and requisitions of private property, and provided adequate collateral for new loans. Only the Italian delegation refused to support the condition, while the delegates of Denmark and Germany abstained from voting.[44] Chicherin, who had already in late September accused the Allies of using famine relief as a pretext to foment counter-revolution,[45] did not deem the October meeting worthy of an official response.

The Second Assembly of the League of Nations also refused Nansen's request to provide credit to fund a large-scale relief effort. In September the League Assembly's Sixth Committee for Political Questions underscored the gravity of the famine and its importance from both a humanitarian and an economic point of view. It then declined to grant any funds to the operation.[46] Nansen could not believe that the League would do nothing to prevent millions of human beings from starving to death, even if it meant strengthening the Soviet government. He would later recount that a Yugoslavian delegate responded, 'without any appearance of shame, that it was better for ten million Russians to starve to death rather than to risk supporting Lenin's régime'.[47]

Nansen's direct efforts to convince the British government to authorise use of its relief credits for famine aid met with a similarly chilly reception. The British Foreign Office and British Treasury were sceptical that the necessity of feeding the starving justified ignoring 'the elementary principles upon which credit is given all the world over'.[48] In January 1922, when the beginning of relief work had provided ample evidence that the food emergency was even greater than previously believed, Nansen met with the British Prime Minister. Lloyd George was especially interested in the argument that £5 million in relief credits for famine relief could help assure the success of the upcoming negotiations at Genoa. It would put the Soviet government under obligation to pay a debt 'which they had definitely accepted and which there was no possibility of their wishing to repudiate'.[49] Lloyd George could not act, however, without the support of the House of Commons.

Philip Noel-Baker enlisted the help of Lord Robert Cecil and the Liberal Member of Parliament Sir Donald Maclean to garner support for the issue among Members of Parliament.[50] The House of Commons debated the issue on 9 March. Austen Chamberlain, the Conservative speaker of the House, fielded criticisms from Labour and Liberal MPs about the government's continued refusal to provide aid to Russia. They questioned both the country's honour as a humanitarian nation, as well as the economic benefit of preventing twenty million 'potential customers' from dying. Chamberlain held firm to the position that the British government was not responsible for providing relief, and therefore should not spend public money to aid foreigners.[51] Lloyd George's coalition government was not swayed, neither by the Parliamentary debate, nor the petition being signed by the various famine funds working in Britain.

Without substantial governmental backing, the International Committee for Russian Relief was reliant on charitable donations to fund its work. The organisations collaborating with Nansen raised approximately $5 million through a combination of private and governmental donations to national charities. Governments represented the largest donors to the private organisations working under the ICRR. The British gave £250,000 ($1,216,625) to their nation's Red Cross. Czechoslovakia spent 3,000,000 F ($579,000) on famine relief, while Germany, Sweden, Norway, and the other fourteen governments supporting national famine relief efforts each spent less than $500,000.[52] The French government made 6,000,000 F ($1,158,000) available to the French Red Cross for famine relief, but refused to collaborate with Nansen's organisation.[53] These donations allowed the organisations of the ICRR to mount the third largest famine relief operation, behind that of the ARA and the Russian Soviet government. At the same time these organisations fed less than 10 per cent of the number that the original intergovernmental plans had envisioned.

Distribution of relief in Soviet Russia

The ARA and ICRR operations co-operated similarly with the Bolshevik authorities in order to distribute relief during the famine. This contradicts past and present perceptions that Hoover operated independently, while Nansen co-operated with the Bolshevik authorities. Nansen's and Hoover's agreements with the Bolsheviks were strikingly similar: seventeen of the twenty-seven clauses were the same. In both cases the Soviet authorities agreed to provide transportation of supplies from Russian ports to the interior at their own expense. These supplies were given top priority when it came to transport and were protected from seizure or requisition. The Soviets also granted immediate entry and exit of all personnel belonging to Nansen or Hoover's operation, as well as full liberty of movement while in the country.[54] Contrary to Hoover's wishes, ARA personnel (like those of Nansen) possessed only normal diplomatic protection, not extraterritorial rights, and could be expelled if found to be engaged in illegal activity.[55] In short the Soviet authorities sought to both facilitate the distribution of relief by both Hoover and Nansen, while also retaining the ability to ensure that neither operation became a source of counter-revolutionary activity.

There were two minor but important differences between Nansen's and Hoover's agreements with the Soviet government. First, the ARA was also granted full autonomy regarding the distribution of supplies. Under the Nansen agreement all supplies imported by the ICRR remained its property, but decisions about distribution were shared with a representative of the Soviet government. Second, during the negotiations with Brown, the Soviets released American prisoners detained within Soviet territory and facilitated their departure from Russia.[56] Nansen's agreement asked for no concessions, contrary to the wishes of many states bordering Russia who had fought wars against the Red Army and still had prisoners held by the Soviet government. These states wanted to make the repatriation of these men a precondition for relief. Other delegates of the August conference in Geneva rejected this proposal because it would make humanitarian relief contingent on a political issue.[57]

These two differences between the ARA and ICRR agreements led to claims that the ARA operated independently within Russia, while Nansen's organisation supported the Soviet government.[58] Critics of Nansen's agreement warned that the Soviet authorities could not be trusted to distribute food to those most in need and praised Hoover's insistence on sole control of all supplies. Nansen defended the lack of concessions as humanitarian, and argued that the policy of joint control was a response to the practical difficulties of operating in Soviet territory. His previous experience had shown him that it was preferable to have dealings with one empowered representative of the Soviet regime, as opposed to ten or twenty local officials who did not have the power to make decisions.[59]

In fact, once in Russia the ARA found that it could not provide effective relief without the aid of the central government in Moscow. On 2 September 1921 Philip Carroll, the head of the ARA's advance team, requested a liaison officer from Lev Kamenev, head of the Pomgol.

Figure 8.1 Dr Fridtjof Nansen and Dr Reginald Farrar among a crowd of local residents, Saratov, Russia, circa December 1921 / January 1922

Accordingly, Aleksandr Eiduk, a member of the Cheka and the same official working with Nansen, was appointed as government representative to the ARA.[60] Both Nansen and the ARA relied on Eiduk and his successor Karl Lander to ensure that transports ran safely and smoothly, visas were issued promptly, and local employees were safe from arrest. Nansen took considerable pride in the fact that 'in reality, it is our agreement that has demonstrated itself to be the most practical'.[61] Unlike Hoover, Nansen had prior experience of working in Russia and knew that it was not a territory in which aid organisations could operate unilaterally.

Although the International Committee for Russian Relief combined the operations of multiple national organisations, some participants wanted their work to garner the same national prestige afforded to the ARA. Nansen oversaw a small High Commissariat of five delegates who were responsible for the transport of supplies from Russian ports to the interior, obtained visas for relief workers, and handled negotiations with the Soviet authorities. Without Nansen's support, other foreign organisations found it all but impossible to obtain the visas and other permissions necessary to operate on Soviet territory.[62] Nansen's contacts with Eastern European governments also gave him an advantage in purchasing grain, which organisations like the British Quakers made use of to procure supplies from Poland instead of London or elsewhere. The Quakers also reported that fewer thefts had occurred in Russia than in any other country where they had worked, since the Nansen agreement required the Soviet authorities to reimburse aid organisations for any supplies lost en route.[63] However, Nansen's delegates did not possess large quantities of their own supplies or run distribution centres.

For this reason some observers from the British Empire criticised Nansen's High Commissariat as inefficient and superfluous.[64] Many British organisations, having collectively raised almost half of the total relief funds of the ICRR, and with the largest operations on the ground, believed their nation's reputation was being overshadowed by Nansen's name.[65] They wanted clear national branding for their work. In September 1922 the British organisations decided to form their own national relief effort, leading to the dissolution of the ICRR. However, the Soviet government refused to conclude an agreement with the British organisations, forcing them to continue to work under the Nansen agreement even after the formal dissolution of their ties with Nansen's office.[66]

In fact, by September 1922 the Bolshevik authorities had concluded that the food emergency had passed. Moscow abolished the Pomgol and replaced it with the Committee for the Struggle Against the Consequences of the Famine (Posledgol). This new committee focused on economic reconstruction of the famine regions.[67] In May 1923 the Soviet government stopped covering the costs of transportation.[68] This effectively ended foreign famine relief in Russia. Nansen used the funds remaining in the budget of his organisation to assist Russia's economic reconstruction by establishing two agricultural co-operatives for the importation of tractors.[69] By August 1923 his famine work had been completely liquidated.

Conclusion

Had the intergovernmental famine relief operation been realised, it would have represented the largest government-funded, international aid effort of the interwar years. For the British and Allied governments after the Great War this aid was first and foremost a political tool. When British secret intelligence suggested that the All-Union Russian Public Committee was a viable alternative authority to a besieged Bolshevik regime, the Supreme Allied Council made optimistic plans for a government-funded relief effort. After the Bolsheviks arrested the members of the All-Union committee and intelligence reports confirmed that the regime remained in control, Allied interest in famine relief quickly dissipated. Humanitarian aid was not ultimately used as an anti-Bolshevik tool of foreign policy during the Volga famine, but the idea of combating communist political movements through humanitarian aid did not disappear. During the Cold War this idea came to exert a much greater influence than when it was first introduced during the interwar years. Further research is needed to trace these connections from the aftermath of the Great War to the advent of the Cold War.

In the absence of a co-ordinated foreign policy, the Western famine relief operations in Russia competed with one another for national prestige. Herbert Hoover insisted on controlling all American efforts and ensured that the ARA's distribution of food was accompanied by propaganda that enhanced America's reputation abroad and combated anti-American Bolshevik propaganda. The British organisations ultimately left the ICRR because they wanted their efforts to similarly glorify the British Empire, not Fridtjof Nansen. All of these organisations valued the moral prestige created by a nationally branded humanitarian operation.

At the same time, Hoover, Nansen, and their deputies shared a belief that, if hungry people were fed, they would not become red. Gorvin wrote to Nansen in June 1923 predicting that those who had worked with the ICRR would forsake radical politics and 'accept the idea of a sane democracy on which alone Russia will be built up'.[70] The Director of the ARA in Russia, Colonel William N. Haskell, pronounced the death of communism in his August 1923 final review of the famine relief operation.[71] There is little evidence to suggest that either man was correct. In the end the greatest excitement surrounding famine relief in 1921 was not humanitarian but political. Yet the legacy of both the ARA and ICRR was not political but humanitarian: millions of people fed during one of the largest famines in Europe during the twentieth century.

Notes

1 See K. Lowe, 'The International Committee of the Red Cross and the Reconstruction of the New Europe, 1918–1923', in B. Dziewanowski-Stefańczyk and J. Winter (eds), *A New Europe, 1918–1923: Instability, Innovation, Recovery* (London: Routledge, 2022), pp. 161–80.

2 All figures in this paragraph are from 'Feeding of the Starving Russian Population on the 15th August 1922', Nansen Archive, Ms. fol. 1988, R:3-A, Nasjonalbiblioteket, Oslo, Norway (henceforth NB).
3 The Amsterdam Union collected money from social democrats and trade unionists. The Foreign Committee for the Organising of Workers' Relief for the Starving of Russia attracted support from communist workers and left-leaning intellectuals. Its secretary was the German communist Willi Münzenberg. Attempts to create a united front between these two solidarity networks failed, but they did co-ordinate with one another. In his speech to the Fourth Congress of the Comintern Münzenberg reported that these two organisations fed 240,000–260,000. See W. Münzenberg, 'Report on Workers' Relief', *International Press Correspondence*, 2:116 (1922), 976–9.
4 See B. M. Patenaude, *The Big Show in Bololand: The American Relief Expedition to Soviet Russia in the Famine of 1921* (Stanford: Stanford University Press, 2002), pp. 33–4; B. Cabanes, *The Great War and the Origins of Humanitarianism, 1918–1924* (Cambridge: Cambridge University Press, 2014), p. 195; see also N. Cullather, 'The Foreign Policy of the Calorie', *The American Historical Review*, 112:2 (2007), 349–52; B. Weissman, *Herbert Hoover and Famine Relief to Soviet Russia, 1921–1923* (Stanford: Hoover Institution Press, 1974), pp. 17–45; H. H. Fisher, *The Famine in Soviet Russia, 1919–1923: The Operations of the American Relief Administration* (New York: Macmillan, 1927), pp. 10–27.
5 Cabanes, *Origins of Humanitarianism*, pp. 192–4.
6 T. Sasson, 'From Empire to Humanity: The Russian Famine and the Imperial Origins of International Humanitarianism', *Journal of British Studies*, 55:3 (2016), 519–37.
7 N. Götz, G. Brewis, and S. Werther, *Humanitarianism in the Modern World: The Moral Economy of Famine Relief* (Cambridge: Cambridge University Press, 2020), p. 96.
8 Götz, Brewis, and Werther, *Moral Economy of Famine Relief*, pp. 103–7.
9 M. Coudreau, 'Le Comité international de secours à la Russie, l'Action Nansen et les bolcheviks (1921–1924)', *Relations Internationales*, 151:3 (2012), 49–61.
10 See K. Braskén, 'In Pursuit of Global International Solidarity? The Transnational Networks of the International Workers' Relief, 1921–1935', in H. Weiss (ed.), *International Communism and Transnational Solidarity* (Leiden: Brill, 2017), pp. 130–1; and Götz, Brewis, and Werther, *Moral Economy of Famine Relief*, pp. 110–13.
11 Information Bureau of the Russian Trade Delegation in London, 'Memorandum on the Famine in Russia', 6 August 1921, R656/12/14983/14182, League of Nations Archives (henceforth LNA), Geneva; and N. Yarovoff, 'The Present Day Food Position of Russia', 25 September 1922, Nansen Archive, Ms. fol. 1988, R:3-A, NB.
12 Information Bureau of the Russian Trade Delegation in London, 'Memorandum on the Famine in Russia', 6 August 1921, R656/12/14983/14182, LNA.

13 Chicherin to Utenriksdepartementet, telegram, 2 August 1921, Nansen Archive, Ms. fol. 1988, R:1(5), NB.
14 The Soviet authorities continued to send bread from Ukraine and Crimea to the Volga, despite the food crisis in those regions. They also discouraged the ARA from including Ukraine in its relief operations. See Fisher, *The Famine in Soviet Russia*, p. 266.
15 Direction of Military Intelligence, 'Russian Famine Relief Committee', 10 August 1921, FO 371–6919, National Archives, United Kingdom (henceforth NA); Information Bureau of the Russian Trade Delegation in London, 'Memorandum on the Famine in Russia', 6 August 1921, R656/12/14983/14182, LNA.
16 M. Gorky to F. Nansen, telegram, 13 July 1921, Nansen Archive, Ms. fol. 1988, R:1(4), NB.
17 M. Asquith, *Famine: Quaker Work in Russia 1921–23* (New York: Oxford University Press, 1943), pp. 13–15.
18 No. 391: Mr Hodgson (Moscow) to the Marquess Curzon of Kedleston (received 19 August, 10:30 a.m.) [N 9511/8614/38], *Documents on British Foreign Policy 1919–1939* (henceforth DBFP), First Series: vol. 20 (London: H. M. Stationery Office, 1976).
19 P. Noel-Baker to F. Nansen, 16 March 1922, NBKR 9/101, Churchill Archives Centre, Churchill College, Cambridge (henceforth CAC).
20 P. Baker to E. Drummond, 'Relief of Famine in Russia', memorandum, 12 August 1921, NBKR 4/610, CAC.
21 No. 95: British Secretary's Notes of an Allied Conference held at the Quai d'Orsay, Paris, on Saturday, 13 August 1921, at 10.30 a.m., DBFP 1: vol. 15.
22 Direction of Military Intelligence, 'Appendix III: Memorandum on the Situation in Russia', 10 August 1921, FO 371–6919, NA.
23 R. Hodgson (Moscow) to Marquess Curzon of Kedleston, telegram, 11 August 1921 (received 12 August 1921), FO 371–6920, NA.
24 Commission Mixte du Comitéé International de la Croix-Rouge et de la Ligue des Sociétés de la Croix-Rouge, 'Pour la Russie', 4 August 1921, Nansen Archive, Ms. fol. 1988, R:1(5), NB.
25 H. Hoover, 'Memorandum on Reconstruction', 22 November 1918, in S. L. Bane and R. H. Lutz (eds), *Organisation of American Relief in Europe, 1918–1919: Including Negotiations Leading up to the Establishment of the Office of Director General of Relief at Paris by the Allied and Associated Powers* (Stanford: Stanford University Press, 1943), p. 52.
26 Dr Fridtjof Nansen to President Wilson, 3 April 1919; Messrs Wilson, Clemenceau, Lloyd George, and Orlando to Dr Fritdtjof Nansen, 17 April 1919; The Representative at Copenhagen of the American Relief Administration (Swenson) to the Commission to Negotiate Peace, 14 May 1919, in *Papers Relating to the Foreign Relations of the United States* (henceforth FRUS) 1919: Russia (Washington: United States Government Printing Office, 1937), p. 102, p. 108, p. 111. For accounts of this 1919 relief plan see Fisher, *Famine in Soviet*

Russia, pp. 10–27; Patenaude, *Big Show in Bololand*, pp. 33–5; Weissman, *Herbert Hoover and Famine Relief*, pp. 29–34.
27 Weissman, *Herbert Hoover and Famine Relief*, pp. 40–2.
28 Fisher, *Famine in Soviet Russia*, pp. 64–5.
29 Weissman, *Herbert Hoover and Famine Relief*, p. 61.
30 Approximately $503 million in 2023 currency. Fisher, *Famine in Soviet Russia*, p. 553.
31 Weissman, *Herbert Hoover and Famine Relief*, p. 94, pp. 102–10.
32 Baker to Nansen, letter, 6 August 1921, Nansen Archive, Ms. fol. 1988, F:1, NB.
33 See F. Nansen to E. Frick, letter, 24 June 1921, Nansen Archive, Ms. fol. 1988, K.10.C, NB; F. Nansen to J. H. Gorvin, letter, 27 July 1921, R656/12/14510/14182, LNA.
34 For detailed accounts of the negotiations between the ARA and Soviet government see Patenaude, *Big Show in Bololand*, pp. 39–46. Weissman, *Herbert Hoover and Famine Relief*, pp. 58–73; Fisher, *Famine in Soviet Russia*, pp. 59–62.
35 'Agreement between the American Relief Administration and the Soviet Authorities in Russia, signed 20 August 1921', *FRUS* 1921, vol. II, 813–17; 'Agreement between Dr. Fridtjof Nansen, High Commissioner for Russian Relief, appointed by the Geneva Conference, and George Tchitcherine, People's Commissary for Foreign Affairs of the Russian Socialist Federative Soviet Republic', 27 August 1921, Nansen Archive, Ms. fol. 1988, R:1(4), NB.
36 Approximately US$672 million in 2023 currency. All currency conversions to US dollars are based on 1921 exchange rates, as recorded in L. H. Officer, 'Exchange Rates', in S. B. Carter, S. Gartner, M. Haines, A. Olmstead, R. Sutch, and G. Wright (eds), *Historical Statistics of the United States, Earliest Times to the Present* (New York: Cambridge University Press, 2006), pp. 5-567–72.
37 'Agreement between Dr. Fridtjof Nansen'.
38 P. Noel-Baker to E. Drummond, 'Relief of Famine in Russia', memorandum, 12 August 1921, NBKR 4/610, CAC.
39 No. 408: Lord Hardinge (Paris) to Sir E. Crowe (received 11 August) No. 591 Telegraphic [N 9220/8614/38], DBFP 1, vol. 20.
40 Captain M. Woolcombe to Mr Gregory, 19 September 1921, FO 371–6923, NA.
41 Fisher, *Famine in Soviet Russia*, p. 315.
42 Charles M. Edmonson, 'The Politics of Hunger: The Soviet Response to Famine, 1921', *Soviet Studies*, 29:4 (1977), 515; Weissman, *Herbert Hoover and Famine Relief*, p. 123.
43 No. 417: Memorandum by Mr Leeper on the Political Aspects of the Russian Famine [N10364/4/38], DBFP 1, vol. 20.
44 The minutes of the August meeting are available at International Commission on Russian Relief, 23 September 1921, FO 371–6923, NA. The October meeting minutes are found at International Commission for Russian Relief, 15 December 1921, FO 371–6927, NA.
45 See G. Chicherin to the governments of Great Britain, France, Italy, and Belgium, telegram, 19 September 1921 (received 20 September 1921), FO 371–6923, NA.

46 Report of the sub-committee 'C', Famine in Russia, 27 September 1921, R656/12/16158/14182; G. Motta, 'Relief Work in Russia', report presented to the Assembly by the Sixth Committee, 29 September 1921, R656/12/16234/14182, LNA.
47 F. Nansen, 'New Year Thoughts', 22 December 1921, Nansen Archive, Ms. fol. 1988, R:3-A, NB.
48 No. 417: Memorandum by Mr Leeper on the Political Aspects of the Russian Famine [N10364/4/38], DBFP 1, vol. 20.
49 P. Noel-Baker to E. Frick, letter, 2 February 1922, NBKR 4/617, CAC.
50 P. Noel-Baker to L. Maudsley, letter, 25 February 1922, Nansen Archive, Ms. fol. 1988, R:1(8), NB.
51 'House of Commons Deb 9 March 1922', *Parliamentary Debates (Hansard) Official Report* (London: H. M. Stationery Office), pp. 1462–5.
52 Comité International de Secours à la Russie, procès-verbal, 25–26 January 1922, CR87, Archives du Comité International de la Croix-Rouge, Geneva, Switzerland (henceforth ACICR).
53 G. Vaucher, 'Le Comité international de secours à la Russie et son haut commissariat', *Revue Internationale de la Croix-Rouge*, 4:37 (1922), 4. The $5 million assembled for Nansen's efforts equates to approximately $75 million in today's currency.
54 'Agreement between the American Relief Administration', *FRUS* 1921, vol. II, pp. 813–17; 'Agreement between Dr. Fridtjof Nansen', Nansen Archive, Ms. fol. 1988, R:1(4), NB.
55 Weissman, *Herbert Hoover and Famine Relief*, p. 94.
56 Ibid., p. 52, p. 59.
57 'Pour la Russie', procès-verbal de la conférence convoquée par la Commission mixte du Comité International de la Croix-Rouge et de la Ligue des Sociétés de la Croix-Rouge, Genève, 2nd plenary session, 16 August 1921, R656/12/14324/14182, LNA.
58 For example, at the October meeting of the International Commission for Russian Relief, government representatives discussed at length the benefits of Hoover's 'sole control' of relief and criticised Nansen for co-operating with Soviet officials. P. Lloyd-Greame, 'Report on Meeting of International Commission for Russian Relief at Brussels', 11 October 1921, CAB 24–128–97, NA.
59 Comité international de secours à la Russie, procès-verbal, 25–6 January 1922, CR87, ACICR.
60 Patenaude, *Big Show in Bololand*, p. 108.
61 Comité International de Secours à la Russie, procès-verbal, 25–26 January 1922, CR87, ACICR; 'Deuxième conférence internationale de secours aux affamés', *Izvestia* [translation], 19 July 1922, Nansen Archive, Ms. fol. 1988, R:3-A, NB.
62 P. Noel-Baker, draft newspaper opinion, [undated], NBKR 4/610, CAC.
63 Note on conversation between Dr Nansen and Mr. Harrison Barrow, Miss Alice Clock, and another, representing the Friends' War Victims Emergency Fund, 1 February 1922, NBKR 4/617, CAC.

64 See M. Atkinson, 'Soviet Russia and the Famine', *The Nineteenth Century and After*, XCI:542 (1922), 603–12.
65 'Note on conversation between Lord Emmott, Sir B. Robertson, F. Nansen, Maudsley, Dyer, Saunders', [January 1922?], NBKR 4/610, CAC; 'Minutes of a Meeting held on May 12th, 1922 at the offices of the Haut Comissariat, Geneva, between the representatives of the British relief organisations and Dr. Nansen', Nansen Archive, Ms. fol. 1988, R:3-A, NB.
66 J. Gorvin to E. Frick, letter, 18 September 1922, Nansen Archive, Ms. fol. 1988, R:6-C(1–2); Gallati, 'Action du Dr. Nansen pour le secours a la Russie, bureau de Riga, rapport pour le mois d'octobre 1922', Nansen Archive, Ms. fol. 1988, R:3-A, NB.
67 Fisher, *Famine in Soviet Russia*, p. 310.
68 Secrétariat de l'Action du Docteur Fridtjof Nansen pour le Secours à la Russie, memorandum, 24 March 1923; K. Lander to German, Dutch, Danish, Swiss, and Serbian Red Crosses, letter, 8 May 1923, Nansen Archive, Ms. fol. 1988, R:3-A, NB.
69 F. Nansen, circulaire, 22 May 1923, Nansen Archive, Ms. fol. 1988, R:6-C(3), NB.
70 J. Gorvin to F. Nansen, letter, 6 June 1923, Nansen Archive, Ms. fol. 1988, R:6-C(3), NB.
71 Weissman, *Herbert Hoover and Famine Relief*, p. 189.

Part III

The legacies and limits of Great War-era relief

9

Abandoning Poland: Great War humanitarianism as a history of failure

Elisabeth Piller

> When the history of Poland during the war comes to be written the world will stand aghast at the story of her sufferings.[1]

This chapter focuses on the Commission for Relief in Poland (CRP), an American humanitarian organisation which intended to mitigate civilian suffering in German-occupied Poland during the Great War.[2] The CRP was incorporated in early 1915 following an agreement between the Rockefeller Foundation and German authorities. Yet its projected relief work, to be patterned on similar food aid operations in occupied Belgium, soon foundered on the diverging interests of the belligerent great powers. In fact the single most salient fact about the CRP was that it never really existed at all, that it remained, in Branden Little's words, a 'skeleton organisation'.[3] Despite years of public appeals and intense negotiations between heads of state, foreign ministries, merchants, and relief workers, the CRP never managed to send more than a smattering of supplies into Poland. As one of its key advocates at the Rockefeller Foundation noted wearily: 'we have devoted more time and thought, without accomplishing any results, to this question of Polish relief than to any other [...]'.[4] As long as the war lasted, the Commission for Relief in Poland was an idea – and a powerful one at that – but it never became a reality.[5]

The chapter explores the reasons for this failure. Why, despite so much effort, did the Commission for Relief in Poland never come into existence? Why did it prove impossible for US relief workers to re-victual Poland as they had Belgium? And should this failure influence how historians write and think about the history of humanitarianism in the era of the Great War? These questions have never been fully answered. There has been little scholarly attention to the CRP. The comparatively many studies written on American relief in *postwar* Poland usually mention the fruitless efforts during the war but do not go into detail.[6] In his forthcoming monograph, Branden Little also looks briefly into Rockefeller efforts on behalf of Poland, especially the first round of negotiations in 1915, and attributes the end of the negotiations to US–German tensions following the sinking of the *Lusitania* in May of that year.[7] The most detailed accounts so far have been written by M. B. Biskupski. He has underlined the disparity in large-scale humanitarian aid to Belgium as compared to a dearth of aid provided to Serbia and Poland and has attributed this situation in part to the consolidation of Great Britain's blockade strategy by 1916. He has also traced the negotiations and public pressure regarding Polish wartime relief but has been primarily concerned with its impact on US support for Polish independence after the war.[8] The relative neglect of the topic is partly a result of contemporary silences. Even profuse writers like the US businessman, humanitarian, and later president Herbert Hoover (the projected director of the CRP) grew tight-lipped when it came to Polish relief. Moreover, contemporary statements made by representatives of the Entente and the Central Powers have to be approached with great caution as both sides sought to deflect the blame for the relief organisation's failure. To this day, the smoke and fog of the Great War's propaganda battles obscures the CRP's story.

One might argue, of course, that the CRP has drawn little attention because it was just not that important. Yet Polish relief mattered greatly to contemporaries and should matter, too, to historians. In particular the fate of the CRP is notably at odds with the historiographical tendency to see the war and postwar period as a humanitarian 'success story'. The era of the First World War is widely regarded as a defining moment in the development of US humanitarianism. Julia Irwin identifies it as the American nation's 'humanitarian awakening', while Keith Watenpaugh considers US relief work in the Middle East pivotal to the making of 'modern', that is, large-scale, bureaucratic, and professional, humanitarianism at the time.[9] And nothing so embodies the alleged triumph of US humanitarianism as the organisation the CRP was modelled on: the American-led Commission for Relief in Belgium (CRB). Founded in the fall of 1914, it quickly became one of the largest and most accomplished relief organisations of its time, providing $1 billion worth of food and provisions to nine million civilians in the German-occupied parts of Belgium and northern France. Its organisational principles, mission, and personnel inspired large-scale US aid programmes after the First World War, and again after the Second World War. Already during its lifetime from 1914 to 1919, the CRB was hailed as the epitome of American common sense, efficiency, and voluntarism; its many accomplishments carried its director, Herbert Hoover, into the global limelight and eventually into the White House.[10]

And yet these widely celebrated achievements obscure the Great War's less successful humanitarian undertakings, including those for occupied Poland. This chapter adopts a comparative approach to ponder the fate of the CRP, contrasting the conditions for the success of the Commission for Relief in *Belgium* with those that doomed the Commission for Relief in *Poland*. The chapter first analyses the factors that allowed the CRB to create and maintain a humanitarian corridor into Belgium for the entirety of the war. It then turns to the CRP and tries to assess why the humanitarian operations in Belgium could not be replicated on the Eastern front. Finally, the chapter considers the implications of the Polish case for how we understand and write the history of humanitarianism in the era of the Great War.

The Commission for Relief in Belgium: creating a humanitarian space

Any assessment of the CRP and its failure must begin with an assessment of the CRB and the factors that conditioned its success.

The CRB was founded in October 1914 by a group of London- and Brussels-based American and Belgian businessmen in order to arrange food deliveries to German-occupied Belgium. While the non-state CRB began as an ad-hoc venture of modest proportions, it soon grew into a food administration of enormous scale. From early 1915 onward, it oversaw the purchase, import, and distribution of most food supplies in Belgium.[11] The need for an organisation like the CRB arose from the dual challenge posed by the German occupation and the British blockade. Not only had the Belgian food supply been disrupted and depleted by the German invasion and occupation in the months prior to the 1914 harvest but from October 1914 the British sea blockade cut off German and German-controlled lands, including the heavily import-dependent Belgium, from outside food deliveries. The question of who was to feed Belgium soon descended into a fruitless squabble between British blockaders and German occupiers. London argued that Germany as occupying force was legally obligated to feed Belgium, while Berlin argued that it could not be expected to live up to its obligation as long as Great Britain maintained its illegal food blockade. The non-state and neutral-run Commission for Relief in Belgium provided a solution to this seemingly intractable issue. Staffed with American (and after 1917, Spanish and Dutch) volunteers and guaranteed by Spanish, Dutch, and American diplomats, it managed to create a humanitarian corridor through the blockade and into occupied Belgium.

The CRB and its accomplishments have been celebrated, and for good reason. As a private organisation that negotiated with governments and fed large parts of a nation, the CRB held a truly unprecedented role. Accordingly, its directors had to overcome a near endless row of obstacles, including how to convince the belligerents to let them operate in the first place, how to purchase and ship food in a tight wartime market, and how to finance its expansive operations.[12] The first of these questions – how to gain access to Belgium and to secure the consent of the belligerent great powers – was fundamental to its work. So how did the CRB construct and maintain a 'humanitarian space', that is, an operational environment for the delivery of provisions, in Belgium?[13] It bears noting that the CRB's operations owed little to international law or precedent. Contemporary international law provided few safeguards for civilians, including occupied populations, and nutritional deprivation was not considered a war crime until the 1970s.[14] Rather, the CRB's operations rested on an elaborate system of mutual guarantees, which Hoover and neutral diplomats painstakingly negotiated with British and German authorities in late 1914 and early 1915. Pivotal to the CRB's operation was the German pledge not to requisition local or imported foodstuffs in Belgium and to grant the CRB full oversight over food distribution. This arrangement helped assure the British that the Germans would not syphon off relief supplies, thereby improving their own food situation and undermining one of the blockade's major objectives. On the basis of the German guarantee the British thus consented to the CRB's operations, helped subsidise its relief operations, and provided CRB-chartered ships with safe passage and expedited customs clearance. Although these guarantees had repeatedly to be renegotiated, the main parameters of the humanitarian space in Belgium remained intact for the duration of the war.

But what led the two belligerents to accept, in the German case, the inconvenience of an international presence in the occupied area, and, in the British case, a 'de facto breach of the blockade'?[15] In other words, what factors conditioned the success of these negotiations and the creation of the CRB?

First, and most importantly, the CRB came into being because it accorded with German and, to some degree, British interests. In the German case, having an Allied-funded and American-run organisation feed the Belgian population was an obvious military and political advantage. While an international presence made German occupation authorities less free to exploit Belgium's material and human resources, it absolved them from having to use Germany's own sparse food reserves for the Belgian population, or to have to face massive international criticism had they failed to do so. Moreover, keeping the population fed and having a few sympathetic Americans roam the country was a check on Belgian discontent and helped stabilise the occupation regime and nearby military operations.[16] By contrast, the benefits of the CRB were less apparent to British authorities. Hoover encountered significant British opposition to raising the blockade even for the well-defined purpose of provisioning Belgium. The British admiralty in particular was hostile to the CRB because neither the pacification of the Belgian population nor the loosening of the blockade seemed in the British interest. The international relief of Belgium, they realised early on, would save German resources and weaken the blockade's overall effect.[17] Still, the Foreign Secretary Sir Edward Grey, the Foreign Office, and members of the Cabinet repeatedly overruled military opposition in order to open a humanitarian corridor into Belgium. Humanitarian and political concerns played a defining role as Great Britain could ill-afford to help starve the very country over whose neutrality and treatment it had entered the war. Allaying Belgian hunger was a matter of British credibility and also made it easier to deflect critical questions about the legality of the food blockade.[18]

These national interests were closely connected to another major factor: the power of public opinion. Both the British and the German government were highly sensitive to public sentiment at home and abroad. The German invasion of August 1914 had turned Belgians into the war's quintessential innocent victims and Belgian hardship inspired an outpouring of global sympathy and donations.[19] Among the British public the Belgian situation evoked great concern and placed considerable pressure on the government to aid 'poor little Belgium'.[20] All compassion aside, in this climate of opinion neither side wanted to *appear* responsible for a Belgian famine. As Berlin and London competed for international sympathy and support in the first few years of the war, their treatment of Belgian civilians came to stand for the humanity and righteousness of their cause, or the lack thereof.[21] This applied to Germany, of course, whose reputation was severely tarnished by the illegal invasion of Belgium and the German army's subsequent atrocities; but it was equally true for the British, who had declared the protection of Belgium and other small powers a war aim.[22] Hoover himself masterfully wielded 'the club of public opinion', as he called it, to get the two governments to toe the line. He carefully cultivated the CRB's public relations and kept alive worldwide charity for Belgium.[23] The world's interest, Hoover remembered, 'became our effective armor against the periodic attempts of both the British and German militarists to suppress or restrict our activities'.[24]

Finally, the CRB hinged on the concept and practice of neutrality in a number of ways. For one it was the involvement of representatives of neutral countries, especially Spain, the Netherlands, and the United States, that allowed the CRB to operate in the first place. Neutral oversight was crucial to even the most basic of its functions. For example, since there were no direct lines of communication between the belligerents, all of the CRB's extensive negotiations had to be relayed through neutral embassies, relief workers, or merchants. No less important, the relative trust that

Great Britain and Germany placed in certain neutrals sustained the CRB's intricate web of guarantees. This was true for the American, Dutch and Spanish diplomats, who guaranteed the CRB's operations, as well as for the relief workers on the ground. It is hard to imagine, for example, that the British would have trusted the Belgians – all too easily coerced by the occupier – with monitoring the CRB's food distribution. For this reason, the CRB carefully cultivated its image of impartiality and neutrality and repeatedly removed relief workers accused of unneutral behaviour.[25] At a time of soaring mutual suspicions, the CRB's efforts at exacting neutrality help explain its many privileges, including expedited customs clearance for its food ships and the freedom of movement its relief workers enjoyed in an otherwise locked-down zone of occupation.[26] Finally, neutrality was a significant factor regarding the war's international constellations. Because Great Britain and Germany competed for neutral and especially US favour and support, they were sensitive to neutral disapproval. In fact the influence of international public opinion on London and Berlin rested largely on their hopes to draw the United States on their side.

To be sure, this brief sketch of the factors conditioning the CRB's success is highly reductionist. National interest, public opinion, and questions of neutrality played together in complex ways in the decision-making of belligerent governments. And still, a schematic approach *is* useful when trying to think comparatively about the CRP. If above-mentioned factors account for the success of the CRB in Belgium, why did they, or any combination of them, fail to foster a humanitarian space in occupied Poland?

The relief organisation that never was: The Commission for Relief in Poland

Before turning to the CRP, the conditions in occupied Poland should be briefly considered.[27] From December 1914 onward the Central Powers began to occupy successive parts of what (after the Third Polish Partition in 1795) had become Russian Poland. By August 1915 Germany and Austria-Hungary held the entirety of Russian Poland and established occupation governments, seated in Warsaw and Lublin respectively. Germany's Government General Warsaw controlled a population of 7.5 million, of which about 2.5 million lived in densely settled industrial centres like Warsaw and Lodz, then the third and fourth largest cities of the Russian Empire. Although it is difficult to generalise about Polish living standards during the war, the urban population suffered very considerable hardship. Already in the spring of 1915 official German reports on the city of Lodz, occupied since December 1914, spoke of 'extreme distress' among

Figure 9.1 Exhibition poster, Polish Victims' Relief Fund, E. Verpillevy 1915: The homeless women and children of Poland are far, but need they be far from your hearts? Pray help us to help them!'

the largely unemployed population.[28] A German relief committee warned that 'the poorer population, beset by hunger and privations, is in danger of falling prey to epidemics'.[29] Robert Blobaum's recent study of wartime Warsaw also testifies to plummeting living standards, widespread food and coal shortages, and the spread of contagious disease.[30]

Polish distress arose from a combination of factors. The first was the fighting itself. Warsaw's proximity to the front meant that the city had to contend with a diminished harvest, interrupted supply lines, and the arrival of hundreds of thousands of refugees. Russia's scorched earth policy in the summer of 1915 increased Polish hardship: as the Russian army retreated, it razed villages and critical infrastructure, drained the country of supplies and livestock, removed experienced administrators, and emptied charity and pension coffers. The German occupiers not only failed to fully ameliorate the subsequent suffering but also aggravated the situation. While the German occupation authorities sought to restore critical infrastructure and increase the efficiency of agricultural production, they also requisitioned scarce resources and dismantled industries.[31] The food rationing system they introduced proved insufficient to sustain those without recourse to additional provisions, including the ever-rising number of urban unemployed. While living standards dropped all over wartime Europe, no other city (except Vilnius in the German-occupied Ober Ost) had a death rate comparable to Warsaw.[32] US relief workers would later record Polish statements that 'when the Russians are here, they hang us. Now that the Germans are here, we hang ourselves.'[33]

The Polish plight roused the sympathy of ethnic and religious kin as well as humanitarians abroad. Local Polish organisations like the Warsaw Citizens Committee not only improvised extensive welfare provisions on the spot but also alerted the world to Polish distress.[34] In the United States, in particular, these appeals found a strong resonance. In the autumn of 1914 the US Polonia began collecting funds, often coupling calls for Polish relief with calls for Polish independence. Prominent Polish expats, like the famous pianist and later Polish prime minister Ignacy Paderewski campaigned tirelessly and successfully on behalf of Polish war sufferers in the United States.[35] As early as December 1914 the Rockefeller Foundation also turned its attention from Belgium, where it had just given $1 million to the CRB, to occupied Poland. A Rockefeller fact-finding mission visited the country in late 1914 only to conclude that 'probably three million persons fac[e] immediate famine'.[36] In public appeals and internal reports alike, Belgium featured as a powerful point of reference. Wycliffe Rose, Chairman of the Rockefeller War Relief Commission, informed Washington in late January 1915 that 'distress in Poland [is] more acute than in Belgium',[37] and Edward House, President Woodrow Wilson's influential adviser, later claimed 'that Belgium [... is] a garden spot in comparison [to Poland]'.[38] Such comparisons served to establish Polish distress vis-à-vis the war's humanitarian *cause célèbre* just as they suggested a clear solution: a Commission for Relief in Poland, to be patterned on the CRB. As Jerome Greene of the Rockefeller Foundation explained to the US State Department in May 1915: 'the fact [remains] that millions of human beings now starving can be saved if the administrative machinery can be set up for Relief in Poland on exactly the same principles that have been tolerated by the belligerents in the case of Belgium'.[39]

Just how to establish such 'administrative machinery' for the relief of Poland occupied American, German, and British diplomats, humanitarians, and journalists through 1915 and 1916. A first round of negotiations took place from February to May 1915, and initially promised quick success under the aegis of the Rockefeller Foundation. Already in February 1915 Foundation officers as well as the American ambassador to Berlin, James W. Gerard, and German officials agreed to form an International Commission for Relief in Poland.[40] Berlin pledged to abstain from requisitioning food in the to-be-provisioned area and granted CRP delegates full oversight, the free use of German transportation, and a monthly subsidy of 2 million marks.[41] The Rockefeller Commission for its part offered $10,000 a month for overhead expenses and helped assemble a neutral committee – chaired by Ambassador Gerard and guaranteed by neutral ambassadors – to purchase and distribute the foodstuffs. Despite these promising developments, Polish relief soon foundered on the Rockefeller Foundation's inability to secure food from 'nearby' European countries (including Sweden, Romania, and Russia). This dashed initial hopes that the CRP might be organised without the permission of the British blockade authorities and prompted US foundation officers and diplomats to turn, albeit pessimistically, to secure London's approval for transatlantic shipments to Poland in April 1915.[42] As Branden Little points out, the German sinking of the British ocean liner *Lusitania* a few weeks later, with nearly 1,200 civilians on board, including over one hundred Americans, derailed these efforts. It further hardened the British position, and – with US neutrality in the balance – led the Department of State to abandon all negotiations for the moment.[43]

Following a new set of Polish appeals and an alarming survey of Polish conditions by the CRB's chief nutritionist Vernon Kellogg, international negotiations resumed in December of 1915. However, the CRP was now intended to re-victual the much larger territory since occupied by the Germans and to be organised directly by Herbert Hoover. In February 1916 Hoover presented the British government with a proposal agreed on with German authorities. The proposal reiterated German guarantees not to requisition most local and imported food (although there were notable exceptions with regard to the German constabulary force) and agreed to supply the Polish population with minimum rations, to be complemented by CRP food. The British response in May 1916 rejected any exception for the German constabulary and asked for a number of further clarifications and assurances. More importantly, British consent was made conditional on a joint German-Austrian administration of food in occupied Poland, as well as in other areas occupied by the Central Powers. British authorities argued that the Austrian-occupied agricultural regions were the 'natural hinterland' of the German-occupied cities and that there ought to be one food regime for all of occupied Poland.[44] Hoover and US diplomats were rightly pessimistic whether this would be acceptable to Germany.[45] As Walter Hines Page, the US ambassador to London, informed the Rockefeller Foundation, 'it looks very doubtful whether the international arrangement necessary for Polish relief will go through. The Germans and the Allies I fear have reached a deadlock, but we are doing all we can to bring them to an agreement. But you must not be surprised if nothing comes to pass.'[46] Page's pessimism turned out to be well-founded. Significant US efforts to break this deadlock, including a one-million-dollar pledge by the Rockefeller Foundation and the intervention of President Woodrow Wilson, proved of no avail.[47] In late July 1916 London restated its demand that international relief ought to apply to all of occupied Belgium, northern France, Poland, Serbia, Montenegro, and Albania and that the Central Powers should reserve to these areas 'the entire produce of the[ir] soil, all livestock, and all stocks of food, fodder, or fertilizers'.[48] In effect the British proposal demanded that Germany and Austria should develop a joint food account for occupied Europe, thereby rendering most of occupied Europe's food resources off limits to the Central Powers. Given Austro-German frictions and the increasing plight of their own populations, the proposal stood no chance of success.[49] In August 1916 the German government announced that, with the harvest fast approaching, relief to Poland was no longer needed.[50] For all intents and purposes this spelled the end of the CRP.

The twists and turns of these negotiations are less interesting than why they ultimately came to naught. Put in comparative terms, why did the factors that allowed for the CRB to function successfully fail to accomplish the same thing with regard to Poland?

As could be expected, national interests played a significant role. German authorities were clearly interested in an arrangement similar to that practised in Belgium. The nascent CRP thus enjoyed the support of German military and political authorities. In early 1915 Paul von Hindenburg and Erich Ludendorff were quick to guarantee the safety of relief workers and the non-requisitioning of imported foods.[51] German authorities in Berlin facilitated the movement of Rockefeller delegates around Europe and instructed their diplomatic missions abroad to try and sustain Rockefeller interest in Poland.[52] In April 1915, when funds for food purchases seemed to be lacking, the German Chancellor immediately offered a monthly subsidy of 2 million marks.[53] All humanitarian concerns aside, Germany was clearly interested to avoid hunger, disease, and chaos behind the front lines and, potentially, to win over the Polish population.[54] As in Belgium, the CRP would also have absolved Germany from sharing its own increasingly scarce resources to this end. Theodor Lewald, the German official in charge of both occupied Poland and occupied Belgium at the German Ministry of the Interior, noted already in February 1915: 'The question of the victualing of Belgium and Russian Poland is growing more difficult each day. If we have to feed 7 million Belgians, 4 million Frenchmen and 9 million Poles, there is no saying what will happen.'[55] At least for the first year of negotiations, Berlin went to considerable lengths to bring the CRP into existence.

By comparison, as Biskupski has emphasised, the British had little interest in Polish aid, given strategic priorities as well as prior experiences in Belgium.[56] Already before the sinking of the *Lusitania*, American humanitarians and diplomats had been pessimistic about securing British approval and by 1916 British authorities were still reluctant about the CRP. Judging by the course of negotiations, London's primary objective was to stall the development of Polish relief while at the same time trying to avoid offending US sensibilities. For example, the Foreign Office took nearly three months to respond to the US–German proposal of February 1916 – a very long time for a humanitarian emergency. This reluctance was born of several reasons. For one the British government was wary of German guarantees. Just when the Polish relief negotiations resumed in early 1916, the British were investigating German requisitions, in violation of the CRB agreement, in Belgium;[57] until a more satisfactory set of guarantees for Belgium had been negotiated, another relief operation was out of the question. Besides, there remained the fundamental problem that international relief ultimately benefited the enemy by conserving German resources. The British admiralty, in particular, vehemently opposed opening yet another 'blockade hole' at a time when it was otherwise making strenuous, and ever more successful efforts to seal off the continent.[58] It was entirely consistent with its interests, then, that London demanded that the local resources of *all* occupied territories – including surplus regions – should be pooled and placed off limits to the Central Powers.[59] Under this arrangement, international relief would have strengthened rather than weakened the blockade regime and would have shifted the strategic burden of humanitarian aid from the Allies to the Central Powers. Accordingly, the German government rejected the proposal, seeing it as an attempt to incorporate the occupied regions into Britain's 'all-unlawful proclaimed system of starving out Germany'.[60] Berlin's negative response was also in line with its own changing priorities. By the autumn of 1916 Berlin hoped that destitution would be one factor compelling the Poles to work or fight for Germany.[61] As one Rockefeller delegate surmised in October 1916: 'Germany wants to keep the curtain drawn, so that she can rapidly Germanize a country that will prove of great value to Germany. She can do in two or three years by starvation what has taken one hundred and fifty years to do in German Poland, now East Prussia [sic!], provided she can keep the curtain drawn, so that there will be no protest from the rest of the world.'[62] By mid-1916, in short, the CRP was all out of chances of success because it no longer served either belligerent's strategic interest.

Nor did public opinion prove as decisive a factor in the Polish case as it had with regard to Belgium. American humanitarians' efforts to invoke 'the court of public opinion' in order to prise open a way into Poland proved comparatively unsuccessful.[63] Poland was simply less visible and familiar to Western audiences. The suffering of Warsaw or Lodz did not resonate as strongly with Anglophone audiences as did that of Louvain or Brussels. As one American proponent of Polish relief acknowledged, 'all of us are familiar with the point of view of the Western nations of Europe and with their history. We vibrate with sympathy with the unparalleled heroism of the Belgians. [...] We have all seen Rheims, Antwerp, Louvain; they are our personal possessions, and form part of our lives, but few of us know much about Poland.'[64] Of course there were also circumstances working in Polish favour. In the United States Polish Americans were a vocal, well-organised, and sizeable minority group, whose votes were far from negligible.[65] It was partly for that reason that in 1916, an election year, President Wilson designated 1 January as Polish relief day and in June personally intervened with the belligerents on behalf of Polish relief.[66] Yet Polish American interest also weakened the relief effort because it made Polish relief seem a partisan, ethnic endeavour (as compared to the allegedly universal cause of Belgium) and exposed it to anti-Polish prejudice. Nor, of course, did Poland ever carry the same symbolic value as 'brave little Belgium'. This was particularly true for the Anglophone world, but also for the Dutch, Swedish, or Swiss public. Whereas the plight of invaded Belgium inspired considerable solidarity among other small neutrals, Poland was not even a state in 1914.

But the comparatively limited resonance of Polish appeals was also and especially a matter of timing. The truth of the matter was that the kind of violations of international law, and the inhumane treatment of civilians that had inspired public outrage in the summer of 1914, no longer made headlines a few years into the war. Already in May 1915 an officer of the Rockefeller Foundation had to conclude that 'the emotional appeal of starving millions makes comparatively little impression upon a public that has become used to hearing of horrors on a tremendous scale'.[67] This was especially apparent in Great Britain, where government support for the CRB rested on the public sympathy for Belgium at home and abroad. Yet in the second and third year of the war, the British public's own hardships cooled compassion for 'distant others', especially when it came at the detriment of British interests. By 1916 the British public clamoured for a tough stance on the blockade and generally blamed Polish plight on German actions.[68] German authorities, too, felt little pressure to act because Polish distress was generally attributed to either Russian actions or the British blockade and hence considered an Allied responsibility.[69] Under these circumstances public opinion forced no concessions similar to those in Belgium.

In fact it could be argued that the dynamics of public and published opinion made the CRP less – not more – likely. The 1916 negotiations, in particular, were followed closely in the European and US press. The belligerents' main news agencies, Reuters and Wolff Telegraphisches Bureau, shared official correspondence, which newspapers then readily printed and dissected. The abortive negotiations were accompanied by a flurry of public accusations and counter-accusations as Berlin and London both sought to wash their hands of Polish distress. Responding to British demands for wide-ranging guarantees, German and Austrian newspapers accused Great Britain of deliberately sabotaging the relief work and renewed the popular charge of British hypocrisy, casting it as a country that only 'pays lip service to humanity'.[70] The British responded in kind. When the British government suggested a blanket agreement for occupied Europe in July 1916, it announced that, if conditions were not met, it would 'hold [the Central Powers] responsible [...] for every civilian life lost through insufficient nourishment in every territory occupied by the[ir] armies'.[71] In this statement, retorted the German news agency, 'British hypocrisy [...] exposes itself with peculiar transparency'.[72] According to the *Norddeutsche Allgemeine Zeitung*, 'not Germany, as is mendaciously asserted by the Entente, but Russia has sentenced Poland to starvation; by the prevention of neutral importation contrary to international laws England has supported Russia in starving Poland. Germany alone has protected Poland from want.'[73] Such accusations were readily taken up in the neutral press, too.[74] By 1916 public opinion no longer exerted pressure to ignore military necessity for humanitarian concerns, but provided only a forum to accuse the respective other of inhumanity. Throughout, all belligerents seemed less invested in ensuring Polish relief than in making sure they would not be blamed for its predictable failure. Behind all this public posturing, of course, stood the unpleasant truth that Great Britain was indeed trying to starve Germany and that Germany, in turn, was starving the Poles.[75]

Finally, if national interest and public opinion did not favour Polish relief work, neither did neutrality and international constellations. In 1914 both London and Berlin had been careful not to offend neutral and especially US sensibilities. But by 1916 the neutrals no longer commanded the same caution. For one, the influence and independence of the European neutrals gradually declined, as they were 'caught in the middle' of two ever less considerate power blocs.[76] And while the United States still mattered, the belligerents were now more willing to test the limits of its forbearance. If in 1914 they had been unsure what might trigger US intervention, by 1916 they had a more realistic grasp of US interests in the conflict. German authorities, for example, could be quite sure that, if the United States had not entered the war over submarine warfare in 1915, it would not enter over Polish relief. In a similar vein the British must have been certain that their intransigence with regard to the CRP could place no worse strain on Anglo-American relations than had their repression of the Irish Easter Rising earlier that year.[77] While the United States was still courted for its sympathy and support, the belligerents had a much better idea of what actions might tip the scale – and Poland was not one of them.

So, after all that has been said, why did US humanitarians fail to create a humanitarian space in Poland? Ultimately, the answer lies in a combination of geography and timing. Simply put, Poland was not Belgium. It lacked Belgium's symbolic value as well as its familiarity and accessibility.[78] The different nature of the war on the Eastern front, primarily the fact that it was a moving war, complicated the planning process and repeatedly recast the population and territory to be provisioned. Programmes designed to feed three million people in February 1915 had to be renegotiated to feed eight million a year later. Yet by 1916 much had changed. At that time the totalising logic of the war had already radicalised its conduct and aims.[79] Unlike the CRB, the CRP was thus negotiated in a most unfavourable context. By 1916 belligerents had become determined to win at all cost, whether that meant fully exploiting occupied territories or starving the enemy into submission.[80] Put differently, the delicate balance between moral and military imperatives that the CRB had rested on since 1914 had irrevocably tipped towards the latter.[81] In fact the failure of the CRP might have had less to do with Poland than with the shrinking of the humanitarian space during the Great War. While some humanitarian efforts, especially those based on reciprocity and mutual interests, grew more comprehensive (including regulations regarding PoWs), this was not the case for occupied populations. Although Germany and Great Britain reluctantly honoured earlier commitments in Belgium, they refused to take on new commitments. In fact it is highly doubtful whether Germany and Great Britain would have ever committed to Belgian relief if it had been negotiated in 1916. Had the CRB not been created in late 1914, it might never have been created at all.

Conclusion: the history of humanitarianism as a history of failure

So what does the Commission for Relief in Poland tell historians about the history of Great War humanitarianism, and what does it mean for how we write that history?

At its most fundamental the fate of the CRP reminds us of the very different conditions on the Eastern front versus the Western front, in terms of both warfare and humanitarian efforts to mitigate its consequences. This is not necessarily to suggest that the Great War's Eastern front was a prelude to the war of extermination during the Second World War, a question hotly debated among historians.[82] Rather, it is to note that the military status quo frequently changed on the Eastern front, that it was an area of complicated logistics, and that the joint occupation of Russian Poland by Germany and Austria-Hungary further aggravated these problems. It was also considerably more remote in terms of media coverage and international attention. These basic differences made it more difficult to negotiate and administer relief in Poland than in Belgium. What is more, occupied Serbia, Montenegro, Romania, and Albania to some degree all shared Poland's fate. To this day comparatively little is known about the efforts to aid their populations. In terms of humanitarianism the war in the East remains a 'forgotten front' (Gross).[83]

The Polish case should also caution against generalising from the Belgian 'success story'. Arguably, the fate of Polish civilians was more representative of Great War humanitarianism than was that of Belgian civilians. Historians have cited the CRB's continued operations as an example that 'military priorities did not hold absolute sway'.[84] But looking beyond Belgium offers a different picture, one defined by tight and ever tightening parameters of civilian relief. It is important to remember that humanitarian endeavours after 1914 had very clear limits and that they succeeded only relatively rarely. In the end Belgium – not Poland – proved the exception to Great War humanitarianism.

The Polish case also serves as a reminder that historians still write all too little about failure. This probably owes something to the demands of effective storytelling: failed organisations like the CRP afford no compelling images of heroic relief workers or grateful beneficiaries.

Moreover, retelling negotiations is a tedious business, and retelling failed negotiations more tedious still. More importantly, it points to distinct silences in the sources that historians use. In fact contemporaries rarely admitted to failure. Businessmen like Herbert Hoover would have been nothing but bewildered by today's corporate ideas of 'celebrating failure'. In a note that Hoover left for future biographers in his personal papers (that action alone should give us pause!) he wrote: 'When all is said, and done, accomplishment is all that counts. Record of failure may be warning, guiding information or vicarious sacrifice but it is the progress reached that counts'.[85] Accordingly, Hoover and his associates systematically built a reputation of efficiency and success. Will Irwin, muckraking journalist, CRB delegate, and ardent Hooverite, called Hoover's Great War-era relief work 'an accomplishment without stain'.[86] It is telling that in the three massive volumes that Hoover himself devoted to his humanitarian exploits in the era of the Great War he spared only one line for wartime Poland. As Meredith Hindley has rightly observed, Hoover's memoirs tend 'to emphasise great triumphs and play down problems'.[87] And so did Hoover's associates.[88] For historians this raises fundamental methodological questions about the primary sources and archival collections we consult. For instance, the Hoover Institution Archives with their rich, perfectly accessible and beautifully inventoried collections constitute one of the major resources for historians interested in Great War-era humanitarianism. But they were founded, organised, and maintained by the very men who so abhorred and downplayed failure.[89] These collections may thus lead us to overemphasise certain aspects of Great War humanitarianism (such as US contributions or humanitarian successes) and to de-emphasise others (such as international and local contributions or humanitarian failures). The forgotten history of the CRP should encourage us to go in search of these archival silences.

Finally, understanding the CRP is relevant to understanding Great War-era humanitarianism more generally. The outpouring of humanitarian aid after the war's end is often attributed to waning nationalist resentment and ideological objectives. Men and women like Herbert Hoover or Eglantyne Jebb saw postwar aid as a means to combat the spread of Bolshevism and/or work towards international reconciliation;[90] but postwar aid was also about opportunity. The Armistice finally put within reach the kind of operations that humanitarians had long felt impossible to accomplish. After the war they prioritised the countries they had previously failed to aid, not only because conditions there were often especially bad but also because wartime frustration had created a focus on these regions. In that sense the clear limits of Great War humanitarianism also defined its legacy. It was precisely because failure was unacceptable to men like Hoover that they poured their resources into postwar Poland. In the Polish case this not only made Poles primary beneficiaries of postwar US aid but also compounded US support for Polish independence at the peace negotiations.[91]

Notes

1 J. W. Gerard, *My Four Years in Germany* (New York: Grossert & Dunlop, 1917), p. 217.
2 My sincerest thanks go to the archivists of the Hoover Institution Archives and the Rockefeller Archive Center, who went out of their way to provide missing archival materials in the midst of the pandemic. Without them this chapter could not have been finished.
3 B. Little, 'Band of Crusaders: American Humanitarians, the Great War, and the Remaking of the World' (PhD Dissertation, University of California Berkeley, 2009), p. 241.
4 Jerome D. Greene to William Phillips, Dept of State, 18 July 1916, Rockefeller Archives Center (RAC), RF RG1–1 Series 100N, FA386a, Box 72, Folder 688, Negotiations.
5 This does not mean that no aid was given to Poland. As Jacelyn Granick shows, American Jewish humanitarians managed to send $2.5 million to Polish Jews, helping them afford some of their daily necessities. Yet compared to the $1 billion sent to Belgium, this was – as contemporaries realised – completely inadequate; see J. Granick, *International Jewish Humanitarianism in the Age of the Great War* (Cambridge: Cambridge University Press, 2021), p. 40.
6 M. L. Adams, 'Herbert Hoover and the Organisation of the American Relief Effort in Poland (1919–1923)', *European Journal of American Studies*, 4:2 (2009), 1–20, 2; C. Blackburn, 'The Rebirth of Poland: American Humanitarianism after the Great War', *Studia Historyczne*, 4:228 (2014), 521–39; D. Rodogno, F. Piana, and S. Gauthier, 'Shaping Poland: Relief and Rehabilitation Programmes by Foreign Organisations, 1918–1922', in D. Rodogno, B. Struck, and J. Vogel (eds), *Shaping the Transnational Sphere: Experts, Network and Issues from 1840s to the 1930s* (New York: Berghahn, 2015), pp. 259–78.
7 B. Little, *Band of Crusaders: American Humanitarians and the Remaking of the World, 1914–1964* (book manuscript); the author would like to thank Branden Little for sharing this part of his book manuscript with her; see also 'Why the Plan for Relief in Poland Failed', *The Christian Science Monitor*, 31 October 1916, p. 3.
8 M. B. Biskupski, 'Strategy, Politics and Suffering: The Wartime Relief of Belgium, Serbia and Poland, 1914–1918', in M. B. Biskupski (ed.), *Ideology, Politics and Diplomacy and East Central Europe* (Rochester NY: Rochester Press, 2003), pp. 31–57; M. B. Biskupski, 'The Diplomacy of Wartime Relief: The United States and Poland, 1914–1918', *Diplomatic History*, 19:3 (1995), 431–51.

9 J. Irwin, *Making the World Safe: The American Red Cross and a Nation's Humanitarian Awakening* (New York: Oxford University Press, 2013); K. Watenpaugh, *Bread from Stones: The Middle East and the Making of Modern Humanitarianism* (Oakland: University of California Press, 2015).

10 G. Nash, *The Life of Herbert Hoover: The Humanitarian, 1914–1917* (New York: W. W. Norton, 1988).

11 The literature on the CRB is growing: see Nash, *The Life of Herbert Hoover*; Little, 'Band of Crusaders'; J. den Hertog, 'The Commission for Relief in Belgium and the Political-Diplomatic History of the First World War', *Diplomacy and Statecraft*, 21:4 (2010), 593–612; C. Druelle, *Feeding Occupied France During World War I: Herbert Hoover and the Blockade* (London: Palgrave Macmillan, 2019); T. Westerman, 'Rough and Ready Relief: American Identity, Humanitarian Experience and the CRB, 1914–17' (PhD Dissertation, University of Connecticut, 2014); S. Farré, 'La Commission for Relief in Belgium: neutralité, action humanitaire et mobilisations civiles durant la Première Guerre mondiale', *Relations internationales*, 3:159 (2014), 69–82. Also *Remembering Herbert Hoover and the Commission for Relief in Belgium: Proceedings of the Seminar Held at the University Foundation on October 4, 2006* (Brussels: Foundation Universitaire, 2007).

12 H. Hoover, *An American Epic. Vol. 1: The Relief of Belgium and Northern France, 1914–1930* (Chicago: Henry Regnery, 1959).

13 An operational environment in which to provide humanitarian assistance; a good recent collection on the topic is M. Acuto (ed.), *Negotiating Relief: The Politics of Humanitarian Space* (New York: Hurst, 2014).

14 T. Graditzky, 'The Law of Military Occupation from the 1907 Hague Peace Conference to the Outbreak of World War II: Was Further Codification Unnecessary or Impossible', *The European Journal of International Law*, 29:4 (2019), 1305–26; see N. Mulder and B. van Dijk, 'Why Did Starvation Not Become the Paradigmatic War Crime in International Law?', in I. Venzke and K. J. Heller (eds), *Contingency in International Law: On the Possibility of Different Legal Histories* (Oxford: Oxford University Press, 2021), pp. 370–88.

15 Druelle, *Feeding Occupied France*, p. 19.

16 German officials in Belgium considered the food aid of extreme importance: see Oscar Freiherr von der Lancken Wakenitz, *Meine Dreissig Dienstjahre 1888–1918* (Berlin: Verlag für Kulturpolitik, 1931), p. 166, p. 200.

17 For British arguments see the conversation between Lloyd George and Hoover in January 1915 (as recorded by Hoover), L. P. Lochner, *Herbert Hoover and Germany* (New York: Macmillan, 1960), p. 13.

18 H. Hoover, *The Memoirs of Herbert Hoover Vol. 1: Years of Adventure, 1874–1920* (New York: Macmillan, 1951), 168.

19 N. Gullace, 'Sexual Violence and Family Honor: British Propaganda and International Law during the First World War', *American Historical Review*, 102:3 (1997), 717–18; J. Horne and A. Kramer, *German Atrocities, 1914: A History of Denial* (New Haven: Yale University Press, 2001); see also Chapters 1 and 3 above.

20 R. Gill, '"Brave little Belgium" Arrives in Huddersfield ... Voluntary Action, Local Politics and the History of International Relief Work', *Immigrants & Minorities*, 34:2 (2016), 132–50.
21 S. de Schaepdrijver, 'Occupation, Propaganda and the Idea of Belgium', in A. Roshwald and R. Stites (eds), *European Culture in the Great War: The Arts, Entertainment and Propaganda, 1914–1918* (Cambridge: Cambridge University Press, 1999), p. 268.
22 On the connection of strategy and public opinion in the defence of Belgium see also Biskuspki, 'Strategy, Politics, and Suffering', pp. 35–6.
23 Hoover, *Years of Adventure*, p. 155; Hoover, *American Epic*, vol. I, p. 23.
24 Hoover, *Years of Adventure*, p. 159.
25 See Hoover, *American Epic*, vol. I, p. 149; Gates to Rockefeller Jr, 15 February 1917 RAC, Office of the Messrs Rockefeller records, Rockefeller Boards, Series O (FA324), Box 39, Folder 393 War Relief Commission-Poland.
26 For an impressive testament to this relative freedom of movement see the travel documents of Charlotte Kellogg, Box No. 1 Folder 19, Relief Work File: Passport and Travel Documents, Hoover Institution Library & Archives (HIA).
27 See Stephan Lehnstaedt, 'Occupation during and after the War (East Central Europe)', in U. Daniel, P. Gatrell, O. Janz, H. Jones, J. Keene, A. Kramer, and B. Nasson (eds), *1914–1918-online. International Encyclopedia of the First World War*, October 2014, DOI: http://dx.doi.org/10.15463/ie1418.10395, https://encyclopedia.1914-1918-online.net/article/occupation_during_and_after_the_war_east_central_europe?version=1.0; in greater detail: S. Lehnstaedt, 'Besatzungswirtschaft im Generalgouvernment Warschau und in Osteuropa', in M. Boldorf (ed.), *Deutsche Wirtschaft im Ersten Weltkrieg* (Berlin: de Gruyter, 2020), pp. 575–98.
28 Kaiserlich Deutsches Polizei-Präsidium Lodz, 11 March 1915, Bundesarchiv Berlin (BArch), N2176 Theodor Lewald Papers, 60.
29 German Press announcement (probably March 1915), BArch, N2176, Theodor Lewald Papers, 60.
30 R. Blobaum, *A Minor Apocalypse: Warsaw during the First World War* (Ithaca: Cornell University Press, 2017).
31 A. Stempin, *Das vergessene Generalgouvernment: Die deutsche Besatzungspolitik in Kongresspolen 1914–1918* (Paderborn: Ferdinand Schöningh, 2020), p. 54.
32 Blobaum, *A Minor Apocalypse*, p. 99; on Vilnius see T. Balkelis, 'Humanitarian Crisis in German Occupied Vilnius, 1916–1917', *First World War Studies*, 13:1 (2022), 67–83.
33 Frederic C. Walcott to Vance McCormick (State Dept), 6 October 1916, RAC, RF RG1–1 Series 100N, FA386a, Box 72, Folder 688, Negotiations.
34 Blobaum, *A Minor Apocalypse*, p. 86; see also Warsaw 'Petition to the Commission for Relief in Belgium' of December 1915 on the necessity of feeding occupied Poland, HIA, CRB Collection, Box 83, Folder 4.
35 L. L. Gerson, *Woodrow Wilson and the Rebirth of Poland, 1914–1920: A Study in the Influence on American Policy of Minority Groups of Foreign Origin* (Hampton: Archon Books, 1972), p. 49.

36 Copy of Night Letter, Wycliffe Rose to Rockefeller Foundation (via US Embassy Berlin to State Department), 27 January 1915, RAC, Office of the Messrs Rockefeller records, Rockefeller Boards, Series O (FA324), Box 39, Folder 393 War Relief Commission-Poland.
37 Ibid.; the annual report noted that suffering 'seemed more extreme than it had been at any time in Belgium'. Rockefeller Foundation, *Annual Report 1915*, p. 320.
38 Quoted from Gerson, *Wilson and Poland*, p. 68.
39 Jerome D. Greene to Wm Phillips, Department of State, 19 May 1915, RAC, RF RG1–1 Series 100N, FA386a, Box 72, Folder 688, Negotiations.
40 Gerard, *My Four Years in Germany*, p. 216; the negotiations are documented in RAC, Office of the Messrs Rockefeller records, Rockefeller Boards, Series O (FA324), Box 39, Folder 393 War Relief Commission-Poland; for the set-up see Lewald to American Relief Committee of the Rockefeller Foundation for the destitute in Russian Poland, 19 April 1915, and John van Schaik to Wickliffe Rose, 19 April 1915, in RAC, RF RG1–1 Series 100N, FA386a, Box 72, Folder 688, Negotiations.
41 Memorandum, Agreement Baron Heymerke and RF, 1 May 1915, BArch, N2176 Theodor Lewald Papers, 60.
42 Wickliffe Rose to John Van Schaick, 8 May 1915, RAC, RF RG1–1 Series 100N, FA386a, Box 72, Folder 688, Negotiations.
43 A closer look at the American reaction and its impact on the CRP in Little, *Band of Crusaders* (book manuscript, not yet numbered).
44 The Ambassador in Great Britain (Page) to the Secretary of State, 7 July 1916, Subenclosure: Memorandum (Grey), *Papers Relating to the Foreign Relations of the United States (FRUS) 1916 Supplement* (Washington: United States Printing Office, 1929), Doc. 1177; The Ambassador in Great Britain (Page) to the Secretary of State London, 16 June 1916; Enclosure: The British Secretary of State for Foreign Affairs (Grey) to the American Ambassador (Page), 15 June 1916, *FRUS 1916 Supplement*, Doc. 1175.
45 Hoover to Walcott, 26 May 1916, RAC, RF RG1–1 Series 100N, FA386a, Box 72, Folder 688, Negotiations. Having returned from Belgium and Germany by the middle of the month Hoover cabled: 'YOU MAY ABANDON ALL HOPE POLISH RELIEF', CRB to Greene, 19 June 1916, RAC, RF RG1–1 Series 100N, FA386a, Box 72, Folder 688, Negotiations.
46 Walter H. Page to Greene, 8 June 1916, RAC, RF RG1–1 Series 100N, FA386a, Box 72, Folder 688, Negotiations.
47 The President of the United States to the Sovereigns of Austria-Hungary, Germany, Great Britain, and Russia, and the President of France Washington 20 July 1916, *FRUS 1916 Supplement*, Doc. 1178.
48 British Foreign Office to Ambassador Page, 26 July 1916, RAC, RF RG1–1 Series 100N, FA386a, Box 72, Folder 688, Negotiations.
49 On Austro-German frictions over Polish food see Lehnstaedt, 'Besatzungswirtschaft im Generalgouvernment', p. 587; on the nutritional situation in Germany, M. E. Cox, *Hunger in War and Peace: Women and Children in Germany 1914–1924* (Oxford: Oxford University Press, 2019).

50 The Ambassador in Germany (Gerard) to the Secretary of State [Telegram] 29 July 1916, *FRUS 1916 Supplement*, Doc. 1181.
51 Henry James, Jr, Memorandum as to Developments in the plan for the relief of Poland (March 1915), RAC, Office of the Messrs Rockefeller records, Rockefeller Boards, Series O (FA324), Box 39, Folder 393 War Relief Commission-Poland; on Ludendorff's opinion see Ludendorff to Lewald, 22 March 1915, BArch N2176 Theodor Lewald Papers, 57.
52 Lewald to Bussche-Haddenhausen (Bukarest), 9 February 1915, BArch, N2176 Theodor Lewald Papers, 60.
53 Lewald to Oberquartiermeister Ost, Oberst von Eisenhart-Rothe, 15 March 1915, BArch, N2176 Theodor Lewald Papers, 60.
54 For a range of German arguments see Herbert Gutmann to Stadtdirektor Tramm, 24 February 1915, BArch, N2176 Theodor Lewald Papers, 60.
55 Lewald to Bussche-Haddenhausen (Bukarest), 9 February 1915, BArch, N2176, Theodor Lewald Papers, 60
56 Biskupski, 'Strategy, Politics and Suffering', p. 53.
57 The Ambassador in Great Britain (Page) to the Minister in Belgium (Whitlock), London, 11 January 1916 enclosed in The Minister in Belgium (Whitlock) to the Secretary of State, 18 April 1916, *FRUS 1916 Supplement*, Doc. 1148; The Ambassador in Great Britain (Page) to the Secretary of State, 11 January 1916, *FRUS 1916 Supplement*, Doc. 1153.
58 The Ambassador in Great Britain (Page) to the Secretary of State, 6 March 1916, *FRUS 1916 Supplement*, Doc. 1158.
59 The suggestion originally included only Poland: The Ambassador in Great Britain (Page) to the Secretary of State, 12 May 1916, *FRUS 1916 Supplement*, Doc. 1166.
60 Wolff announces, Berlin, 28 July 1916, RAC, RF RG1–1 Series 100N, FA386a, Box 72, Folder 688, Negotiations. The British government later believed the entire negotiations were just a German 'move [...] of exciting public opinion against the legitimate use of sea power'. See 'Why the Plan for Relief in Poland Failed', *The Christian Science Monitor*, 31 October 1916, p. 3.
61 See Lehnstaedt, 'Besatzungswirtschaft im Generalgouvernment'; also A. R. Hofmann, 'Die vergessene Okkupation: Lodz im Ersten Weltkrieg', in Andrea Löw, K. Robusch, and S. Walter (eds), *Deutsche-Juden-Polen: Geschichte einer wechselvollen Beziehung im 20. Jahrhundert* (Frankfurt: Campus, 2004), p. 68.
62 Frederic C. Walcott to Vance McCormick (State Dept), 6 October 1916, RAC, RF RG1–1 Series 100N, FA386a, Box 72, Folder 688, Negotiations; for a recent scholarly treatment of Germanisation plans see M. T. Kettler, '"Incurable Megalomania" and "Fantasies of Expansion": The German Army Reimagines Empire in Occupied Poland, 1915–1918', *Central European History*, 54:4 (2021), 621–45.
63 On these efforts see The Acting Secretary of State (Polk) to the Ambassador in Germany (Gerard), 27 May 1916, *FRUS 1916 Supplement*, Doc. 1169; Statement to press, 12 May 1916 (War Relief: Poland), RAC, RF RG1–1 Series 100N, FA386a, Box 72, Folder 688, Negotiations.

64 Brochure, The American Polish Committee, Address on 10 February 1915 by Mrs George Montgomery Tuttle at the Colony Club at the Conference of the War Relief Committees, copy in: RAC, Office of the Messrs Rockefeller records, Rockefeller Boards, Series O (FA324), Box 39, Folder 393 War Relief Commission-Poland.

65 On the contours of Polish American lobby work twenty years later see A. Jaroszyńska-Kirchmann, 'The Mobilisation of American Polonia for the Cause of the Displaced Persons', *Polish American Studies*, 58:1 (2001), 29–62.

66 Gerson, *Wilson and Poland*, pp. 63–4.

67 Jerome D. Greene to Wm Phillips, Dept of State, 19 May 1915, RAC, RF RG1–1 Series 100N, FA386a, Box 72, Folder 688, Negotiations.

68 Arnold Toynbee, *The Destruction of Poland: A Study of German Efficiency* (London: T. Fisher Unwin, 1916); for the British shift in strategy and its increasing emphasis on the blockade see Biskupski, 'Strategy, Politics and Suffering', p. 53.

69 For a summary of arguments see 'Die "Aushungerung" der Polen', *Frankfurter Zeitung*, no. 299 (19 August 1916), p. 1; *Zwei Jahre deutscher Arbeit im Generalgouvernement Warschau* (Berlin, 1917), p. 6, pp. 39–40, copy in: Barch, N2176 Theodor Lewald Papers 59; The Provisioning of Poland. Germany's Work, Berlin, 22 August 1916 (translation for Rockefeller Foundation), RAC, RF RG1–1 Series 100N, FA386a, Box 72, Folder 688, Negotiations.

70 'England und die amerikanische Hilfsaktion für Polen', *Wiener Abendpost, Beilage zur Wiener Zeitung*, no. 128 (5 June 1916), p. 6.

71 British Foreign Office, 26 July 1916, to US Ambassador Page, RAC, RF RG1–1 Series 100N, FA386a, Box 72, Folder 688, Negotiations.

72 Wolff announces, Berlin 28 July 1916, RAC, RF RG1–1 Series 100N, FA386a, Box 72, Folder 688, Negotiations.

73 The Provisioning of Poland: Germany's Work, Berlin, 22 August 1916, RAC, RF RG1–1 Series 100N, FA386a, Box 72, Folder 688, Negotiations. These sentiments were echoed in the official statement by the German Foreign Ministry and German Emperor, Wilhelm II, to President Wilson, 22 August 1916, see FRUS 1916 Supplement, Doc. 1186.

74 For some examples see 'Suffering Poland and English Politics. A Stockholm Initiative', *Nya Dagligt Allehanda*, 1 August 1916; reply by the British Minister in Stockholm, to the Editor of the *Nya Dagligt Allehanda*, 4 August 1916; copies in: RAC, RF RG1–1 Series 100N, FA386a, Box 72, Folder 688, Negotiations.

75 The actual nutritional impact of the blockade continues to be debated. Mary Cox's recent monograph makes a strong case for the impact of the blockade on German women and children: see Cox, *Hunger in War and Peace*; during the war German authorities systematically hid the nutritional effects of the blockade, see E. Piller, 'German Child Distress, American Humanitarian Aid and Revisionist Politics, 1918–1924', *Journal of Contemporary History*, 51:3 (2016), 453–86; on the meaning of the allegedly almost eight hundred thousand German blockade victims see N. Patin, 'Histoire d'un chiffre: Réflexions autour des victimes allemandes du blocus de 1914–1918', *Les Cahiers Sirice*, 26:1 (2021), 95–107.

76 J. den Hertog and S. Kruizinga (eds), *Caught in the Middle: Neutrals, Neutrality and the First World War* (Amsterdam: Amsterdam University Press, 2011).

77 R. Schmuhl, *Ireland's Exiled Children: America and the Easter Rising* (New York: Oxford University Press, 2016).
78 The case was also stark for Serbians, as Biskupski shows. M. B. Biskupski, 'Strategy, Politics and Suffering', p. 45.
79 J. Horne, 'Atrocities and War Crimes', in J. Winter (ed.), *Cambridge History of the First World War*, vol 1, *Global War*, pp. 561–84, p. 573.
80 This point, especially the increasing strategic commitment of London to the blockade, is made strongly by Biskupski, 'Strategy, Politics and Suffering', p. 53.
81 In 1916 Hoover and Kellogg went to Berlin and saved the CRB at the expense of Poland; see W. Irwin, *Herbert Hoover, A Reminiscent Biography* (New York: Century, 1928), pp. 159–62; V. Kellogg, *Fighting Starvation in Belgium* (New York: Doubleday, Page & Company, 1918), pp. 61–5. Branden Little rightly notes, '"Saving" Belgium absorbed so much humanitarian attention that much less was available for Poles, Serbs, and Armenians.' Little, *Band of Crusaders*, n.p.; Biskupski likewise observes that 'the exception of Belgium, in effect, made London far less willing to entertain other exceptions'. Biskupski, 'Strategy, Politics and Suffering', p. 37.
82 See Vejas Gabriel Liulevicius, 'From Ober Ost to Ostland?', in Gerhard P. Gross (ed.), *The Forgotten Front: The Eastern Theater of World War I, 1914–1915* (Lexington: University Press of Kentucky, 2018), pp. 245–62.
83 Gross, *The Forgotten Front*.
84 Den Hertog, 'The Commission for Relief in Belgium', 594.
85 Herbert Hoover Presidential Library, Herbert Hoover, Pre-Commerce Papers, box 46, Information for Biographers, quoted from Druelle, *Feeding Occupied France*, p. 66.
86 Irwin, *A Reminiscent Biography*, p. 169.
87 M. Hindley, 'Blockade Before Bread: Allied War Relief for Nazi Europe, 1939–1945' (PhD Dissertation, American University, Washington, DC, 2007), p. 27.
88 F. Surface and R. Bland, *American Food in the World War and Reconstruction Period: Operations of the Organisations under the Direction of Herbert Hoover 1914 to 1924* (Stanford: Stanford University Press, 1931), p. 23.
89 Hoover himself collected everything to do with the CRB and arranged for six hundred boxes of records to be deposited at Stanford University. This laid the foundation for the Hoover Library of War, Revolution and Peace, inheriting its compiler's assumptions and priorities. The archivists and librarians continued to work closely with Hoover. A first finding aid, published in 1940, included a piece on the development of the library written by Hoover, see N. Almond and H. H. Fisher, *Special Collections in the Hoover Library on War, Revolution, and Peace* (Stanford: Stanford University Press, 1940), pp. ix–xi.
90 B. Cabanes, *The Great War and the Origins of Humanitarianism, 1918–1924* (Cambridge: Cambridge University Press, 2014).
91 For this argument see H. H. Fisher and S. Brooks, *America and the New Poland* (New York: Macmillan, 1928), pp. 90–1; G. J. Lerski, *Herbert Hoover and Poland* (Stanford: Hoover Institution Press, 1977), p. 5; and especially Biskupski, 'The Diplomacy of Wartime Relief'.

10

Children and the 'hunger politics' of 1919–20: food aid to German children and the founding of the international Save the Children movement

Tatjana Eichert and Rebecca Gill

During the interwar era, aid to children emerged as a symbol of humanitarian universalism and became a specialist area of international welfare. As Ellen Boucher notes,

> For advocates of internationalism, the figure of the child served a dual purpose. It transcended the political divisions of the war by highlighting the innocence and vulnerability of all young people, and it simultaneously evoked the struggles that confronted embattled European nations.[1]

This development is conventionally told through the international organisations involved, particularly the Save the Children International Union (SCIU),[2] and scholarly emphasis is placed on the mid-1920s when the child was adopted as an object of international relations in the 1924 Declaration of the Rights of the Child.[3] Yet this focus obscures two crucial aspects of the story of children and humanitarianism. Firstly, it marginalises the very immediate postwar period's politics of child-centred food aid, including rivalry between Berne and Geneva, and secondly, it undermines the role of German welfare specialists and existing networks of feminist activists. This chapter foregrounds the 'hunger politics' of 1919–20. As Alice Weinreb observes, 'food brings modern bodies into contact with political strategy'.[4] In postwar Germany food scarcity produced not simply a biological need for nourishment, but also an international politics of hunger involving competing humanitarian projects. The feeding of German children was viewed variously as a source of national efficiency, as a moral injunction against the starving of enemy civilians, as a form of solidarity with regional German-language speakers, and as a means of securing European peace and stability.

In this chapter we detail these interconnections and competitions through the untold story of Emily Hobhouse's involvement in the early days of the Save the Children movement (the British Save the Children Fund (SCF) was launched in May 1919 and the SCIU in January 1920) and the Leipzig school-feeding scheme she set up in parallel. This scheme was run by a local committee of German child-welfare experts and municipal officials. Feeding children in Leipzig was, for the suffragist and pacifist Hobhouse and her supporters in the early SCF, a practical intervention in political debates about the making of the peace in Europe and the victimisation of Germany. Leipzig was SCF's biggest financial commitment. However, by August 1920, SCF had undergone a split and had reneged on its support for the project. In analysing the links made between children, nutrition, and peace, we track the forgotten tensions at the foundation of the SCF and SCIU to highlight the impact of controversies over relief to German children in 1919–20 on the permutations of the cause of the child in the immediate postwar period. In doing so we highlight how the Genevan diplomacy and legalism of the interwar SCIU and the 1924 Declaration – a form of collective rights akin to those overseen by the International Committee of the Red Cross (ICRC) – represented a superseding of the 1919–20 credo of gender-based peace activism rather than the straightforward expansion of sympathy suggested by Dominique Marshall or the linear development plotted by Bruno Cabanes.[5]

Emily Hobhouse and the 'enemy' child

The archive of the British SCF reveals little about the history of its early work in Germany. This was a politics of child hunger deliberately withheld from organisational archives. This omission is reproduced in histories of humanitarianism which rarely examine relief to German children following the First World War; indeed, the history of food aid and interwar humanitarianism in general is only recently being established.[6] In January 1919 Dorothy Buxton had founded the Fight the Famine Council from overlapping circles of radical liberals, socialists, suffragists, and anti-militarists in Britain who had filled the ranks of the wartime Union of Democratic Control, the Women's International League (WIL), and the Independent Labour Party.[7] Hobhouse, who had close ties to the leaders of all of these organisations, and had written for their press, was an early supporter. To administer relief in the famine zone, Buxton established the SCF, to which Hobhouse affiliated the relief agencies she had herself set up at the close of the war. Hobhouse received one of the first SCF grants in order to initiate the Leipzig scheme. Children, one of the demographic groups most vulnerable to food shortage, were to be a particular target of relief.

For Hobhouse and the early SCF, the feeding of German children was a refutation of the iniquities of the continuance of the British wartime blockade into the Armistice and of the terms of the peace, particularly the level of German reparations. This inaugural act of political protest runs counter to the narrative of origins favoured until recently by the movement itself in much of its publicity.[8] In their article on Dorothy Buxton, Emily Baughan and Juliano Fiori argue that the SCF archive was curated in a deliberate attempt to foster a non-political myth of origins to publicise its increasingly impartial humanitarianism.[9] In contrast, Hobhouse's desire to preserve the record of her peace activism in the face of considerable public controversy has resulted in a personal archive, now at the Bodleian Library in Oxford, deliberately more comprehensive in its documentation of the politics of bilateral aid to German children than the filleted records of the SCF. This documentation is supplemented by the personal papers of Buxton and her sister Eglantyne Jebb at the London School of Economics. As Honorary Secretary of the SCF, Jebb was instrumental in its affiliation to the new SCIU and the termination of its support for school feeding in Leipzig, leading to disagreement between the sisters. By the autumn of 1920 Buxton had publicly distanced herself from the movement she had founded, along with other early supporters.

Examining Hobhouse's relief work as a practical intervention in debates about the making of the peace expands the focus of existing accounts of feminist internationalism in this era, which centre on the formation of feminist organisations such as the Women's International League for Peace and Freedom (WILPF), founded 1915, and diplomatic gestures of reconciliation.[10] Linking the historiography of 'hunger politics' and food aid with the historiography of feminist internationalism offers a new perspective on women's postwar peace activism and its demonstrable effects on women and children in war-torn Europe.[11] For if, as Ingrid Sharp notes, 'it was no longer credible to simply state that women had a natural affinity for peace due to their nurturing roles or maternal natures', then Hobhouse and the early SCF's relief work was a means to address the 'linked ideas of internationalism, pacifism and suffrage', and clarify 'women's connection with war and peace'.[12] Certainly, Hobhouse's experiences of activism and relief in the South African War (1899–1902) and the First World War led to her commitment to expose the effects of wartime violence on civilians through the 'propaganda of the deed' in postwar Germany.[13] Sarah Hellawell has demonstrated that much of the gender-based advocacy after the First World War, particularly the work of the WIL, which became the British section of the WILPF, drew on networks from the days of protesting against the South African War and providing aid to women and children in the British-run concentration camps.[14]

Hobhouse, like Buxton, worked with WIL and Quaker groups to enquire into the effects of the blockade at the end of war.[15] Indeed, it was in response to appeals for aid from German and Austrian feminists that members of WIL first began to organise relief. Hobhouse mobilised her friendships from the days of the South African War, pressing South African statesman Jan Smuts to 'get round [British Foreign Secretary] Balfour' in order to send rubber teats to feed starving babies as part of WIL's work.[16] In the midst of organising the Leipzig scheme, Hobhouse wrote the preface for the Afrikaans edition of her book *The Brunt of the War and Where It Fell* on the suffering of Boer women and children in the South African War. Here she made explicit the links between the effects of war on civilian populations and the feminist activism necessary to propagate the message of peace: '[e]verything points to the great mission that lies open to women in preparing the mind and conscience of the world for permanent peace'.[17]

In terms of scale, the Miss Hobhouse Hilfe (Miss Hobhouse Relief) school-feeding scheme in Leipzig was dwarfed by American attempts to feed German school children in the city and elsewhere in Europe. Yet precisely owing to its small size and precarious funding arrangements (Hobhouse was forced to appeal to her contacts in Britain, America, Austria, Switzerland, Germany, and South Africa), her archive creates a fascinating record of the fluctuating reputations, feminist activism, and forgotten controversies that determined the nature of international child welfare in the immediate interwar period.

The Miss Hobhouse Hilfe in Leipzig

As Elisabeth Piller demonstrates, the visibility of German suffering after the Armistice was the result of an attempt by German doctors and propagandists to appeal to international public opinion to revoke the blockade and the terms of the Versailles Treaty, where previously they had sought to play down the extent of malnutrition to maintain home-front morale.[18] Certain demographics were shown to be particularly susceptible to food shortages: children, women, and older people faced increased mortality, and young people faced higher rates of deficiency disease.[19] Scholarship on food in First World War Germany has been limited.[20] However the extent to which excess civilian mortality can be attributed to the wartime blockade has been subject to lengthy debate.[21] In *Hunger in War and Peace*, Mary Cox uses conditions in Leipzig, as documented in the reports of Kruse and Hintze, as her main case study of the effects of wartime food shortages on an urban population. 'German residents in Leipzig', she surmises, 'suffered extraordinary nutritional deprivation', resulting in a stunting of children's development among other indicators.[22] As Cox shows, on the basis of Kruse and Hintze's reports, in 1917 'one out of seven Leipzigers lacked sufficient calories [...] to even leave their rooms, let alone go to school or a place of employment'.[23]

Hobhouse's archive reveals some of the drawing of lines of international responsibility at this moment of arbitrating the different relief programmes in war-torn Europe and the building up of spheres of operation for Swiss, American, and British agencies. At the same time, food aid was fitted into prevailing priorities and practices, and local committees managed this as an aspect of public relationships on the ground, determining the meaning of food aid within the culture and politics of hunger in the period, particularly evolving narratives of German victimisation.[24] Paul Weindling has demonstrated that this narrative of victimhood gave impetus to welfare eugenics, including the feeding and treatment of school children, out of a wider concern for national survival.[25] The continuation of existing social welfare initiatives, and the application of pioneering nutritional research, often deriving from Central European universities, was a common feature of both local welfare and international humanitarian projects of this period. It was under the direction of Professor Kruse, an eminent German nutritionist at Leipzig University's Institute of Hygiene, that Hobhouse's feeding scheme provided nutritionally standardised meals. Another example was Professor Abderhalden, a Swiss-born medical professor in the neighbouring city of Halle, who was instrumental in promoting relief for Leipzig and would arrange for some of the underweight children in the Leipzig school-feeding scheme to convalesce in Switzerland.[26] Although historians recognise that food aid and humanitarian assistance in First World War Germany had a transnational dimension, the intersection of this German welfare work with international aid has received limited attention, in particular the role of local populations targeted by this relief. Here were grounds for both mutual interest and tension. In the context of postwar Germany, where the availability of food was key to both national recovery and bitter recrimination, Hobhouse herself could be thanked for her radical repudiation of British governmental policy, but her gift of food as a gesture of peace and solidarity was not always received in kind.

Hobhouse was first alerted to suffering in Leipzig by German scientific experts, particularly Richard Woltereck.[27] Woltereck, a zoology professor in Leipzig, headed the department of welfare at the German embassy in Berne. After the war he got involved in several small welfare schemes aimed at fostering German reconstruction, including a Swiss and German Relief Commission for Suffering Children based in Berne and Leipzig.[28] Hobhouse quickly realised that Switzerland constituted the ideal channel to purchase and ship relief and she co-founded the small Fund in Aid of Swiss Relief to raise money in Britain for Swiss relief programmes for starving children in Central Europe.[29] Here she drew on the precedent of Swiss committees which had already launched relief in Austria, as well as Switzerland's political neutrality and tradition of convalescent care. Hobhouse's network, which included Swiss supporters of her previous work in South Africa such as Lady Clare Annesley, became vital in setting up the Miss Hobhouse Hilfe in Leipzig. In England the work of these local Swiss committees had also caught the attention of Buxton and Jebb of the Fight the Famine Council who sought to raise funds for children in Austria and Germany. In spring 1919, Buxton visited the Hilfsaktion office in Berne to discuss how the pioneering Swiss relief work in Vienna could be expanded across Central Europe, including Germany, by establishing an international scheme that would raise funds in Allied countries, especially Great Britain and the United States.[30] The talks resulted in the foundation of a relief organisation in Berne with particular focus on children, the Comité international de secours aux enfants (CISE), in late March 1919, in parallel with the foundation of the SCF in London.[31] Hobhouse, building on her friendship with Buxton, became an important link between the CISE and the SCF as both women collaborated with the CISE to organise child relief in Vienna.[32]

In November 1919, Woltereck had contacted the city mayor to propose Hobhouse's idea of a feeding scheme.[33] At the beginning, he suggested, a

Figure 10.1 School children receiving milk from the Miss Hobhouse Hilfe, photograph preserved in Emily Hobhouse's Leipzig scrapbook

small group of children should be fed for six months in the hope that positive results would encourage similar schemes in fifteen other large German cities. In Leipzig alone, Woltereck estimated, at least thirty thousand severely malnourished children needed food relief.[34] After previous visits during autumn 1919, Hobhouse returned to Leipzig in December with medical doctor Fritz Schwyzer from Lucerne to undertake more research into the situation of children on behalf of the CISE and the SCF.[35] In Leipzig they were given statistical figures on child health by Kruse. They compiled a report for the Berne Committee, later published by the SCIU, which compared conditions for children in Vienna, where American and British Quakers were working to mitigate conditions, and Leipzig, where the suffering was less well-known, and visited Vienna to observe American child-feeding.[36] In Leipzig Hobhouse, Woltereck and Schwyzer set up a local committee, the Komitee für Speisung unterernährter Leipziger Schulkinder [Committee for the Feeding of Malnourished School Children in Leipzig] in December 1919. Chaired by Dr Ackermann, head of the Leipzig city school office, the committee met for the first time on 15 January 1920.[37] It was supposed to administer the scheme, bringing together city officials, local dignitaries, and physicians under the auspices of the Leipzig City Council's school administration.[38] In its first months the Leipzig scheme relied on food donations collected by the Berne Committee and the Danish Red Cross and its activities quickly expanded. The first meals to around one thousand children were provided on 22 January 1920 in four Leipzig schools.[39] In February the Quakers started preparations for a feeding scheme in Leipzig covering between twenty thousand and thirty thousand children with a focus on the western areas of Leipzig to avoid disrupting Hobhouse's scheme, which was active in eastern areas.

By August 1920, the Quakers were feeding around 29,000 people including mothers and babies in the city and the Hobhouse scheme covered around 11,000 school children. Although Woltereck had initially referred to Professor von Pirquet's NEM milk unit-based system to calculate food rations, which was also favoured by Hobhouse, the Leipzig committee calculated the amount of distributed food on the basis of calories.[40] Meals were to contain around 700 calories and Schwyzer developed flexible recipes containing possible amounts of different food items to achieve this calorific ration.[41] At this point, scientists differed in their theories on diet, with Kruse and Hintze declaring that calories mattered more than the percentage of protein and fats in the diet.[42] The children were selected on the basis of their health by the school doctors and weighed regularly to monitor progress.[43] Hobhouse established the food aid through co-operation with local institutions – a feature of the Quakers' work in Vienna.[44] She acted as fundraiser and international figurehead while local experts such as Kruse had scientific oversight and controlled the implementation of the scheme. This was a two-way relationship, with the Germans aware that they needed help to secure food from outside of Germany in these early days, not least because of continuing currency inflation. School-feeding schemes had existed in public Leipzig schools since 1909 and strong linkages to prewar and wartime welfare structures and expertise existed.[45] Ida Mansfeld, for instance, took the practical lead to organise communal and school kitchens – a continuation of her work in the city's 'war kitchens'.[46] At times this localised arrangement caused tensions. Hobhouse emphasised early on that she wished to follow the Vienna scheme in Leipzig. This meant that children were required to pay a small sum to participate (she suggested 20 Pfennig) and children were banned from taking food home.[47] Hobhouse strongly rejected the suggestion of the Leipzig Komitee to prioritise children considered to be of particular need, namely children of prisoners of war or war widows, children with potential tuberculosis, and 'nervous' children, illuminating divergent adjudications of deservingness based on degrees of victimhood and social welfare on the one hand, and anthropometric observations on the other.[48] Another issue causing friction was the portion size, which Hobhouse considered too large. Kruse and other local doctors argued that the children were used to larger portions of food with low calorie density such as soups and did not feel full after small portions even if they contained the agreed 700 calories.[49] Most of all, Hobhouse emphasised that the feeding scheme should ensure continuity. Against the wishes of the Komitee, who pointed to problems in staffing, she insisted that children receive food during the summer breaks. She preferred children who were already part of the programme but who had not yet reached their weight goals to be kept in the programme rather than adding new children in need of food support. In Hobhouse's view, continuous feeding would improve their health in such a way that their growth measurements would document the success of the feeding scheme and stimulate similar projects.[50]

Gestures of solidarity and reconciliation also carry their own hierarchies. Hobhouse's delineation of children over adults for their promise of national revival was paralleled in her class-based aid to bourgeois Germans, fellow women pacifists, and students.[51] These gifts were also (sometimes deliberately) misrepresented. In Leipzig, Hobhouse's food relief was seen as a singular act by a foreigner who did not close her eyes to the impact of the blockade. In January 1920, a local Leipzig newspaper reprinted Hobhouse's appeal for children in Leipzig from the *Manchester Guardian*.[52] The newspaper saw this as a sign 'that there are people in those countries that remain until today enemy countries who see us also as humans', but gratitude was directed at Hobhouse and not the British people. Local newspapers noted that it was 'German-English' who donated.[53] Likewise, later speeches given in Leipzig at Christmas 1921 to thank South Africans for their donation stressed the affinities between Germans and Boers, citing former German South West Africa.[54] Such depictions clearly sought to make accepting aid more palatable at a time when many Germans struggled to express gratitude to the former enemy.

On 8 July 1922, the Miss Hobhouse Hilfe came to an end in light of decreasing donations after delivering over five million portions of food. The remaining funds of the Leipzig Hilfe were distributed between two small funds in Hobhouse's name, the first to benefit Leipzig children with a holiday, and the second to support middle-class families, particularly those affected by continuing inflation.[55] Hobhouse continued to send donations to support Quaker school-feeding in the city.[56] By early 1923, the city's youth office had taken over administration of school-feeding.[57]

Competing humanitarian visions: controversies over the founding of Save the Children International Union (SCIU)

In late 1919, while Hobhouse was negotiating with the Komitee in Leipzig, a bitter dispute emerged between London and Berne over the founding of the SCIU. Hobhouse's Swiss affiliation drew her into this conflict, aggravating the growing distance between Jebb and Hobhouse that eventually led the SCF to terminate its funding for Leipzig. In her study of the League of Nations' Child Welfare Committee, Joëlle Droux argues that studying the role of individuals rather than organisations per se can help us understand the interplay among international networks and civil society movements, particularly because it was on the level of individuals that initial rivalries among actors in the field of child welfare could be overcome.[58] However, the history of the establishment of the SCIU illustrates that individuals also played a pivotal role in sustaining these rivalries. Correspondence between Oscar Bosshardt, Chair of the CISE in Berne, and Eglantyne Jebb of the SCF, reveals lengthy negotiations over the structure and seat of the SCIU.[59] Archival sources allow us to trace the involvement of individuals in this dispute in order to demonstrate the personal, professional, and political rivalries and negotiations that led to the split in the SCF movement and the relegation of the Leipzig scheme. Informing these schisms was a contest over the role of Berne, the federal capital, in co-ordinating existing Swiss relief schemes and the position of Geneva, as an international city, strengthened by the presence of the ICRC. In addition, the links made between children, nutrition, and peace inspired competition over the very purpose of international humanitarianism. Hobhouse, and the anti-militarists of the early SCF, who had organised a moral campaign to feed 'enemy' children as a singular act of political restitution and recrimination, were increasingly at odds with those such as Jebb who envisaged impartial needs-based child-feeding as an act of collective security, engendering peaceful domestic and international relations and able to thwart the appeal of Bolshevism.

Initially, Jebb saw the CISE as an international partner for the SCF that would allow the SCF to no longer have to limit itself to 'English channels'.[60] In July 1919, she approached CISE members with the suggestion that they transform the CISE into a central international relief agency to which SCF and relief agencies in other countries would affiliate. In this new form, the CISE would serve as 'a kind of central clearing house for information in regard to the relief movement'.[61] The CISE unanimously accepted and agreed.[62] But soon Jebb proposed a different plan. The SCF and CISE should establish an international relief agency together to which the CISE would affiliate, rather than lead.[63] Feeling marginalised, the principal bone of contention for the CISE was Jebb's plan to establish the international child relief agency in Geneva instead of Berne. While Bosshardt emphasised the presence of foreign diplomatic missions in Berne, Jebb wanted to ensure proximity to the ICRC and avoid the organisation from being perceived as 'pro-Germany' among donors. Her proposal fed into underlying Swiss political rivalries between German-speaking Berne and French-speaking Geneva.[64] In the eyes of German-speaking Swiss like Dr Schwyzer, the 'Ferrière-d'Arcis crowd' in Geneva was anything but neutral and was perceived as anti-German as well as anti-Swiss-German.[65] Deeply offended, the CISE members insisted on locating the agency in Berne.

Against the background of stalled discussions, the British SCF members pursued a backup plan.[66] Unbeknownst to the CISE, Jebb and fellow SCF members established an alternative organisation in Geneva in November 1919 named the International Save the Children Fund.[67] A last attempt to reach an agreement between CISE and SCF members – a meeting including Jebb, Buxton, Bosshardt, and Hobhouse in Berne – ended in a fiasco. Buxton described the negotiations as 'really awful', 'complicated', and 'unpleasant'.[68] Hearing that the SCF had already established an international agency, the CISE members threatened to do the same but underestimated how progressed the SCF's plan was.[69] In December 1919, Herbert Hoover, head of the American Relief Administration, was informed of the foundation of the Geneva-based SCF organisation.[70] Now faced with the threat of being excluded, the CISE members finally gave in and agreed to co-found an international child-relief agency with the SCF in Geneva and to join it as an affiliated Swiss committee.[71] On 6 January 1920, the SCIU was officially founded in Geneva with ICRC president Gustave Ador chairing the executive committee. In the coming weeks the CISE began to transform itself into the Comité Suisse de Secours aux Enfants, also known under its German name as Schweizer Kinderhilfskomitee.[72] The creation of the 'non-political' SCIU in Geneva also allowed British and imperial statesmen such as Lord Robert Cecil, former Minister of Blockade in London, and the South African President Jan Smuts to offer their patronage to a venture which accorded closely with their own internationalism.[73]

Correspondence between Jebb and Bosshardt reveals not only deep confusions and misunderstandings between the SCF and the CISE but also ultimately different understandings of 'internationalism' between London and Berne. The CISE members saw their committee as international on the basis of the fact that they received funds from abroad and provided relief in different countries. Several of its members were part of a regional transnational German-speaking network of child welfare experts, who propagated school and child-feeding intervention. In Switzerland measurements of school children had been conducted already prior to the war. Efforts to measure the impact of food scarcity increased in Switzerland during the war including a large-scale screening of ten thousand school children in Berne.[74] Measures to mitigate the anticipated impact in Switzerland consisted mainly in organised stays of children in the countryside during the summer and school feeding schemes during the winter.[75] It was through these German-language contacts in Berne such as Bosshardt and Woltereck that Hobhouse had first started her work for Austrian and then German children. Through establishing an international child-relief agency, the CISE mainly hoped to expand the number of donor and project countries but wanted to keep the administration and distribution of funds in its own hands. Jebb was concerned that the CISE would gain 'too much power' if it had control over the funds.[76] The SCF envisioned an international union which the CISE would join as a national section – a federated model that Jebb compared to the Red Cross. Unlike the ICRC, which operated as a private Swiss charity, the SCIU had an honorary committee, executive committee, and council composed of international representatives.

For Hobhouse, the new internationalist outlook of the SCF represented a dereliction of its founding principles and its earlier peace activism. Though the SCF continued to fund relief in Germany, it decided henceforth only to refer to 'Central Europe' in its publicity.[77] As she complained to Buxton following the foundation of the SCIU, sympathy for former enemies was waning:

> there has been for some time a tendency in the S/C Fund [sic] towards a change of policy – a narrowing of sympathies and of the broader humane views with which the movement started – [...] this tendency has increased very rapidly of late and is showing itself in many ways which make those of us, who felt one with it at first, out of touch now.[78]

At the SCF–CISE meeting in Berne in November 1919, Hobhouse's alienation from the SCF was obvious. Jebb had not informed her of the foundation of an alternative international agency, and Hobhouse, who referred to herself during the meeting as a CISE member, sided with Bosshardt's proposal of Berne as a seat.[79] After the foundation of the SCIU, Hobhouse remained a member of the Berne Committee and worked with Bosshardt to co-ordinate food shipments to Leipzig.[80] Hobhouse argued that the feeding of German children ought to be guaranteed by the SCF, in order to 'hold the Scales of Justice true'; that this was English money coming from the country which had instated the blockade ought to be explicit for it was having an effect 'morally and spiritually [which] is *very* great'.[81] Buxton advocated Hobhouse's position to Jebb in a correspondence of September that year following the SCF's decision to terminate the Leipzig grant.

Jebb summarily refuted point-by-point Buxton and Hobhouse's objections in a long letter in September 1920 in which she defended the SCF committee. 'They are actuated of course by a desire not to allocate more than strictly necessary to Germany owing to the fact that we undoubtedly lose by it', referring to the negative publicity they had received for feeding German children. In Germany, she stated, 'we are at present engaged in collecting data re relative needs', but, in a reference to Hobhouse's activism, 'we are not going into any more arrangements with people wishing to push particular isms'. 'We now regret the large sums we spent on the feeding centre in Leipzig', she continued, '[n]ot that this centre was not excellently run, but we ought to have left school feeding in Germany to the Municipal authorities and to Hoover'.[82] Ultimately Jebb wanted the SCIU to go beyond food relief and focus more on strengthening national child-welfare institutions.[83] The need was now to extricate themselves from political protests in order to secure international co-operation and influential patrons.

Hobhouse turned to her South African friends for support. 'I had written to my old friends who 20 years ago had themselves drunk to the full the cup of suffering brought by war and famine. They still feel confidence in one who helped them in their own deep distress.'[84] These friendships, emotional connections, and emerging political networks can be gleaned from her correspondence with Mrs Steyn (wife of the former President of the Free State, Martinus Steyn), who raised money for the Leipzig scheme through Afrikaner women's groups. Of the SCF in London, Hobhouse complained to Mrs Steyn that she had insisted they 'correct the statement in their bulletin saying that the money had been sent to them. They are determined to suppress my name if possible.'[85] Hobhouse's letters track not only the history of the shifting positions taken by SCF but also the imperial-internationalism of Smuts, and the anti-imperialism of Afrikaner women's politicking. For these women, solidarity with German children was part of a growing anti-British stance and reignited the public memory of the concentration camps as a critical force in Afrikaner nationalism.[86] This was a further politicisation of the child at a local level not accounted for in conventional histories of the ideals of interwar internationalism.

Conclusion

This chapter argues that the emergence of the child as the universal humanitarian subject in the interwar period arose in response to the politics of feeding German children in 1919–20. This was not simply an expansion of sympathy. Rather, it was a particular, and pragmatic, configuration sought by Jebb as she worked to extract herself from the Leipzig scheme and orientate the SCF away from bilateral interventions and political controversy. This was grounded in pacifism, though of a kind very different from the anti-militarist political activism of Hobhouse and the early SCF. '[T]he most certain way to give humanity a new growth', noted a later SCIU memorandum, 'was to unite men in a common cause founded on a new consciousness of the supreme value of the child, representing the future of our race.'[87] This expansion of the national efficiency and pronatalism movements of the prewar period into the international realm rested on the promise of child development for a new world order. Hobhouse, estranged from the Save the Children movement, offered her name instead to the newlyformed German Distress Committee along with other prominent anti-militarists.[88]

A focus on the aftermath of the First World War in Europe challenges the preponderance in recent historiography to privilege the imperialism of American intervention in the Near East as the 'origin' of modern humanitarianism, where sovereignty was not the issue it was in Central Europe.[89] This ignores the competing humanitarian programmes in Europe, and the foundation of the international Save the Children movement, whose co-ordination of research on minimum national standards and its promotion of the Declaration of the Rights of the Child was grounded on – and limited by – national sovereignty. In its appeal to nation-states as guardians of children as productive citizens of the future, the SCIU reflected the popularity of welfare eugenics in post-First World War Europe, as evident in SCF collaborations in Germany and Austria in 1919–20, as well as the influence of the ICRC's state-based internationalism in Geneva.[90] This meant, however, that it lacked a blueprint for protecting the rights of ethnically undesirable, 'stateless', or refugee children.[91] Able to draw on its networks and collaborators, in the postwar period the SCIU jostled for influence at the League of Nations.[92] It recommended, for instance, the NEM system for feeding refugee children to the League's Health Organisation, and it remains an important norm-setting movement in international child health.[93]

Though the direct appeal of the suffering child was ubiquitous in fundraising and publicity images, the reality of the SCIU's work thus involved collaboration with intermediaries in national governments, organisations, and civil society. The interplay of the local, national, imperial, and international realms was never harmonious and continued to involve different models: peace building, reconciliation, and national welfare. In the Second World War the internationalism of the SCIU, like that of the ICRC, failed to meet the challenge of the belligerent nationalism of the fascist states, or overcome the strategic foreign policy and military interests of the Allies.[94] As Chelsea Sambells argues, only for reasons of propaganda did the Nazis allow undernourished children in occupied Europe to be evacuated by a coalition of Swiss charities for convalescence in Switzerland, starting in 1940.[95] This coalition included the SCIU. As Joëlle Droux shows, the decision to reactivate the by-now-outmoded policy of family separation in order to evacuate Belgian and French children was a response to British insistence that no direct relief be provided by the SCF or SCIU to enemy-occupied countries.[96] Screening policies by the Swiss Red Cross and the Swiss and German authorities excluded Jewish children.[97] Here lay the intersecting legacies of the 'hunger politics' of 1919–20 on the constitution of the SCIU, interwar welfare eugenics, Swiss humanitarianism, and British economic warfare policies, and thus on the 'successive transformations of the cause of the child' in the twentieth century.[98]

This history points to the need for deep contextual knowledge of 'hunger politics' in any rendering of humanitarian action, including symbolic representation of hunger and the management of public opinion, but also the personal and collective memory and meaning of food and malnutrition in any given location and context, and the perspective and agency of children. Only oblique references to the experience of children are contained in the Leipzig archive: used to bulking up on low-nutrition but high-density meals of cabbage, they complain at the standardised but smaller portions of school meals; conditioned by their experience of hunger, they horde food or wish to keep it for family members; approving of the breakfast, they find the lunch boring and repetitive; though nourished at school, they initially gain little weight, owing possibly to poor diet at home or perhaps the lost claim to a family meal. In exploring the political and cultural negotiation of health needs, including personal histories of child hunger, historians of humanitarianism can expand a more conventional historiographical focus on organisational ideals and priorities.

Notes

The authors would like to acknowledge the support of the AHRC for funding the project 'Emily Hobhouse Letters: South Africa in International Context, 1899–1926', AH/M011119/1. They would also like to thank Alina Müller for her research assistance in the Stadtarchiv in Leipzig.

1. E. Boucher, 'Cultivating Internationalism: Save the Children Fund, Public Opinion and the Meaning of Child Relief, 1919–24', in L. Beers and G. Thomas (eds), *Brave New World: Imperial and Democratic Nation-Building in Britain between the Wars* (London: University of London Press: Institute of Historical Research, 2011), p. 15.
2. The SCIU is also known under its French name Union Internationale de Secours aux Enfants (UISE).
3. D. Marshall, 'The Construction of Children as an Object of International Relations: The Declaration of Children's Rights and the Child Welfare Committee of League of Nations, 1900–1924', *The International Journal of Children's Rights*, 7:2 (1999), 103–48; P. T. Rooke and R. L. Schnell, '"Uncramping Child Life": International Children's Organisations, 1914–1939', in P. Weindling (ed.), *International Health Organisations and Movements, 1918–1939* (Cambridge: Cambridge University Press, 2009), pp. 176–202.
4. A. Weinreb, *Modern Hungers: Food and Power in Twentieth-Century Germany* (New York: Oxford University Press, 2017), p. 4.
5. Marshall, 'Construction of Children', 134–5; B. Cabanes, *The Great War and the Origins of Humanitarianism, 1918–1924* (Cambridge: Cambridge University Press, 2014), pp. 289–95.
6. T. Proctor, 'An American Enterprise? British Participation in US Food Relief Programmes (1914–1923)', *First World War Studies*, 5:1 (2014), 29–42; G. Aiken, 'Feeding Germany: American Quakers in the Weimar Republic', *Diplomatic History*, 43:4 (2019), 597–617.
7. P. Dunstan, *Campaigning for Life: A Biography of Dorothy Frances Buxton* (Cambridge: Lutterworth Press, 2018), pp. 105–30.
8. L. Mahood, 'Eglantyne Jebb: Remembering, Representing and Writing a Rebel Daughter', *Women's History Review*, 17:1 (2008), 1–20.
9. E. Baughan and J. Fiori, 'Save the Children, the Humanitarian Project, and the Politics of Solidarity: Reviving Dorothy Buxton's Vision', *Disasters*, 39:S2 (2015), 131.
10. L. Rupp, 'Constructing Internationalism: The Case of Transnational Women's Organisations, 1888–1945', *The American Historical Review*, 99:5 (1994), 1571–600.
11. For example Hobhouse's extensive connections included Jane Addams, Aletta Jacobs, Elisabeth Rotten, Lida Gustava Heymann, Clare Annesley, Kate Courtney, Hilda Clark, Ruth Fry, and Edith Durham.
12. I. Sharp, J. Acsády (on Hungary), and N. Vukov (on Bulgaria), 'Internationalism, Pacifism, Transnationalism: Women's Movements and the Building of a

Sustainable Peace in the Post-War World', in I. Sharp and M. Stibbe (eds), *Women Activists between War and Peace: Europe, 1918–1923* (London: Bloomsbury, 2017), p. 79.

13 This expression was used by Jane Addams, inaugural President of the WILPF, quoted in B. Bianchi, '"The Massacre of the Innocents Has Haunted Us for Years": Women Witnesses of Hunger in Central Europe', in B. Bianchi and G. Ludbrook (eds), *Living War, Thinking Peace (1914–1924): Women's Experiences, Feminist Thought, and International Relations* (Cambridge: Cambridge Scholars Publishing, 2016), p. 85.

14 S. Hellawell, 'Antimilitarism, Citizenship and Motherhood: The Formation and Early Years of the Women's International League (WIL), 1915–1919', *Women's History Review*, 27:4 (2018), 551–64.

15 See, for instance, 'The Starving Children of Austria: Mrs C. R. Buxton's Pictures', *Manchester Guardian*, 8 May 1919.

16 Hobhouse to Jan Smuts (copy), 28 December 1918, Hobhouse archive, Bodleian Library (BL), Oxford, Box 15.

17 E. Hobhouse, MS, preface for the Afrikaans translation of *The Brunt of the War and Where it Fell*, 1922, BL, Box 15, p. 6.

18 E. Piller, 'German Child Distress, American Humanitarian Aid and Revisionist Politics, 1918–1924', *Journal of Contemporary History*, 51:3 (2016), 453–86.

19 C. P. Vincent, *The Politics of Hunger: The Allied Blockade of Germany, 1915–1919* (Athens: Ohio University Press, 1985), p. 137; M. E. Cox, *Hunger in War and Peace: Women and Children in Germany, 1914–1924* (Oxford: Oxford University Press, 2019), p. 130.

20 H. M. Benbow and H. R. Perry, 'Hunger Pangs: The Contours of Violence and Food Scarcity in Germany's Twentieth-Century Wars', in H. M. Benbow and H. R. Perry (eds), *Food, Culture and Identity in Germany's Century of War* (Basingstoke: Palgrave Macmillan, 2019), p. 3.

21 See A. Offer, *The First World War: An Agrarian Interpretation* (Oxford: Clarendon Press, 1989); S. Marks, *The Illusion of Peace: The International Relations in Europe, 1918–1933* (New York: Palgrave Macmillan, 2003). For the discussion on the blockade's death toll see N. Patin, 'Histoire d'un chiffre: Réflexions autour des victimes allemandes du blocus de 1914–1918', *Les Cahiers Sirice*, 26:1 (2021), 95–107.

22 Cox, *Hunger in War and Peace*, p. 132.

23 Ibid., p. 113.

24 For narratives of victimisation see C. Siebrecht, 'Sacrifice Defeated: The Armistice and Depictions of Victimhood in German Women's Art, 1918–24', in T. Tate and K. Kennedy (eds), *The Silent Morning: Culture and Memory after the Armistice* (Manchester: Manchester University Press, 2015). For insight into the cultural history of hunger see J. Vernon, *Hunger: A Modern History* (Cambridge, MA: Belknap, 2007), p. 2.

25 P. Weindling, *Health, Race and German Politics between National Unification and Nazism: 1870–1945* (Cambridge: Cambridge University Press, 1993), pp. 303–4.

26 Hobhouse to C. E. Maurice, 10 October 1923, and Hobhouse to Ackermann, 8 May 1921, BL, Box 15. Abderhalden was the head of the Zentralstelle zur Unterbringung deutscher Kinder in der Schweiz (Central Office for Hosting German Children in Switzerland) that organised recuperation stays in Switzerland, mostly in the German-speaking part: see D. Steiner, *'Dem fremden kleinen Gast ein Plätzlein decken.' Julie Bikle und die Beherbergung deutscher Kinder in der Schweiz, 1919–1924* (Zurich: Chronos, 2016).
27 Letter, Woltereck to Leipzig mayor, 22 November 1919, Leipzig City Archives (LCA), SchuA 892.
28 J. Harwood, 'Weimar Culture and Biological Theory: A Study of Richard Woltereck (1877–1944)', *History of Science*, 34:3 (1996), 352–5.
29 Letter, 22 June 1919, Swiss Federal Archives Berne (SFA), J2.55#1995–125#5. The Fund in Aid of Swiss Relief was co-founded with the British anthropologist and journalist Edith Durham, and included Joyce Tarring, Lady Clare Annesley, and T. R. Bridgwater.
30 O. Bosshardt, *Die Schweizer Hilfsaktion für die hungernde Stadt Wien* (Berne: A. Francke AG, 1921), p. 127.
31 Bosshardt, *Die Schweizer Hilfsaktion*, p. 132. In January 1920 the CISE was transformed into the Comité Suisse de Secours aux Enfants, also known under its German name as Schweizer Kinderhilfskomitee (SKK). It is referred to as CISE or 'Berne Committee' in this chapter.
32 Bosshardt, *Die Schweizer Hilfsaktion*, p. 81, p. 132.
33 Woltereck to Leipzig mayor, 22 November 1919, LCA, SchuA 892.
34 Woltereck to Komitee, 22 December 1919, LCA, SchuA 892.
35 Letter, 1 January 1919, SFA, J2.55#1995–125#5.
36 Emily Hobhouse to L. T. Hobhouse, 19 December 1919, BL, Box 15.
37 Minutes of meeting 13 July 1922, LCA, SchuA 898.
38 Committee members included Professor Kruse, Director of the University Institute of Hygiene; Dr Ackermann, Director of Education, who served as chairman of the committee; Professor Dr Thiemich, Director of the University Kinder-Krankenhaus; Dr Pötter, school doctor; Dr Schönfeld, the Director of the Deutsche Bank, Leipzig branch, serving as Treasurer; Professor Dr Woltereck, and Ida Mansfeld; see Hobhouse and Schwyzer, 'Report on Conditions Affecting Child Health in Leipzig', in *Congrès des oeuvres de Secours aux enfants des pays éprouvès par la guerre* (Geneva, 1920), p. 16.
39 Ackermann to the Union Internationale de Secours aux Enfants, 20 February 1920, LCA, SchuA 892.
40 The NEM system refers to the so-called Nährungs-Einheit in Milch scale introduced by Professor von Pirquet.
41 Report, 24 December 1919, LCA, SchuA 892.
42 Cox, *Hunger in War and Peace*, p. 108.
43 Report, 24 December 1919, LCA, SchuA 892.
44 A. E. Merke, 1 November 1920, Geneva State Archives (GSA), Collection UISE, T Ri/67–3 Archives Privées 92.10.4.

45 Leipzig City Council School Office to Chemnitz City Council, 30 April 1921, LCA, SchuA 892.
46 Minutes Komitee, 13 April 1920, LCA, SchuA 893; Degen to school directors, 21 December 1920, SchuA 895.
47 Hobhouse to Ackermann, 9 January 1920, LCA, SchuA 892.
48 Minutes Komitee, 13 January 1920, LCA, SchuA 892; Hobhouse to Ackermann, 26 January 1920, LCA, SchuA 892.
49 Minutes Komitee, 10 February 1920, LCA, SchuA 892, and Ackermann to Hobhouse, 18 February 1920, SchuA 892.
50 Report, Leipzig City Council, 5 July 1922, LCA, SchuA 898.
51 Hobhouse was involved in a Fats Guild to provide dairy foods to members of the German section of WILPF and supported Ruth Fry's project to feed German students by employing Leipzig University students to serve school meals in the holidays in return for a dinner: Emily Hobhouse, 'The State of German Children', *The Nation*, 14 August 1920.
52 'Eine Engländerin über die verheerende Wirkung der Hungerblockade auf die Kinder Leipzigs', *Leipziger Neue Nachrichten*, 11 November 1920.
53 See, for instance, 'Speißung von 7500 Schulkindern durch Deutsch-engländer', *Leipziger Tagblatt*, 16 April 1920; 'Kinderspeißungen', *Leipziger Volkszeitung*, 16 April 1920.
54 Hobhouse to Mrs Steyn, 27 December 1921, BL, Box 15.
55 Minutes Komitee, 13 July 1922, LCA, SchuA 898.
56 Hobhouse, final report, April 1922, LCA, SchuA 898 and Report no. 950, 7 December 1922, LCA, SchuA 899.
57 Ackermann to Hobhouse, 28 March 1923, LCA, SchuA 899.
58 J. Droux, 'A League of Its Own? The League of Nations' Child Welfare Committee (1919–1936) and International Monitoring of Child Welfare Policies', in M. Rodríguez, D. Rodogno, and L. Kozma (eds), *The League of Nations' Work on Social Issues: Visions, Endeavours and Experiments* (Geneva: United Nations Publications, 2016), p. 103.
59 SFA, J2.55#1995–125#6.
60 Letter, 20 July 1919, SFA, J2.55#1995–125#6.
61 Jebb to Bosshardt, 24 July 1919, SFA, J2.55#1995–125#6.
62 Letter, 6 September 1919, SFA, J2.55#1995–125#6.
63 Letter, 15 September 1919, SFA, J2.55#1995–125#6.
64 SFA, J2.55#1995–125#3.
65 Schwyzer to Hobhouse, 30 December 1919, BL, Box 15. Schwyzer referred to the prominent ICRC member Suzanne Ferrière (niece of ICRC vice president Frédéric Ferrière) and Clara Guthrie d'Arcis (founder of the World Union of Women for International Concord).
66 GSA, Collection UISE, T Ri/65–3 Archives Privée 92.3.2.
67 GSA, Collection UISE, T Ri/65–3 Archives Privée 92.3.4.
68 Buxton to Brailsford, 28 October 1921, Jebb papers, BLPES, Box 7/EJ/B/02/06.
69 Report, 24 November 1919, SFA, J2.55#1995–125#3.

70 GSA, Collection UISE, T Ri/65-3 Archives Privée 92.3.4. A first meeting was held on 17 December 1919 with Jebb, d'Arcis, Ferrière, Cramer, Werner, and Monroe (member of the Internationale Spital Hilfsaktion in Vienna).
71 Letter, 2 December 1919, GSA, Collection UISE J2.55#1995–125#3; also letter, 22 December 1919, T Ri/65-3 Archives Privée 92.3.4
72 GSA, Collection UISE, T Ri 65/3 92.1.1.
73 Both were members of the honorary committee: see Brochure, Union Internationale de Secours Aux Enfants, Genève 1920, SFA, J2.55#1995/125#1. On Cecil's and Smuts's imperial-internationalism see E. Baughan, 'The Imperial War Relief Fund and the All British Appeal: Commonwealth, Conflict and Conservatism within the British Humanitarian Movement, 1920-25', *The Journal of Imperial and Commonwealth History*, 40:5 (2012), 845–61.
74 K. Staub, 'Der vermessene menschliche Körper als Spiegel der Ernährungs- und Gesundheitsverhältnisse am Ende des Ersten Weltkrieges', in D. Krämer, C. Pfister, and D. M. Segesser (eds), *'Woche für Woche neue Preisaufschläge': Nahrungsmittel-, Energie- und Ressourcenkonflikte in der Schweiz des Ersten Weltkrieges* (Basel: Schwabe Verlag, 2016), p. 298.
75 Staub, 'Der vermessene menschliche Körper', p. 302.
76 Minutes meeting 24 November 1919, SFA, J2.55#1995–125#3.
77 SCF, Committee of Enquiry into needs of Germany, 9 July 1920, BLPES, EJ 242.
78 Hobhouse to Buxton, 7 February 1920, BLPES, 7EJB/B/02/03.
79 Minutes of meeting 24 November 1919, SFA, J2.55#1995–125#3.
80 Letter, Hobhouse, 4 March 1920, SFA, J2.55#1995–125#69.
81 Hobhouse to Buxton, 7 February 1920, and 1 February 1920, BLPES, 7EJB/B/02/03.
82 Jebb to Buxton, 9 September 1920, BLPES, 7EJB/B/02/01.
83 Jebb to Etienne Clouzot (Secretary General SCIU), 3 February 1921, Archives of the ICRC, UISE Collection, ACICR O UISE 001.
84 MS of Hobhouse speech at Leipzig Rathaus, 25 November 1920, BL, Box 15.
85 Hobhouse to R. I. (Mrs) Steyn, 19 December 1920, BL, Box 15.
86 L. Stanley and H. Dampier, 'Cultural Entrepreneurs, Proto-Nationalism and Women's Testimony Writings: From the South African War to 1940', *Journal of South African Studies*, 33:3 (2007), 501–19.
87 Memo concernant l'UISE, 1930, 9–10, quoted in Marshall, 'Construction of Children', 136–7.
88 Letter to editor, *Manchester Guardian*, 6 July 1923.
89 K. Watenpaugh, *Bread from Stones: The Middle East and the Making of Modern Humanitarianism* (Berkeley: University of California Press, 2015); M. Tusan, '"Crimes against Humanity": Human Rights, the British Empire, and the Origins of the Response to the Armenian Genocide', *American Historical Review*, 119:1 (2014), 47–77.
90 On the Declaration of the Rights of the Child as enshrining a social contract rather than individuated rights see R. Gill and D. Leeworthy, 'Moral Minefields: Save the Children Fund and the Moral Economies of Nursery Schooling in the South Wales Coalfield in the 1930s', *Journal of Global Ethics*, 11:2 (2015), 222–3.

91 E. Baughan, *Saving the Children: Humanitarianism, Internationalism, and Empire* (Berkeley: University of California Press, 2022), pp. 76–7.
92 J. Droux, 'Life during Wartime: The Save the Children International Union and the Dilemmas of Warfare Relief, 1919–1947', in J. Paulmann (ed.), *Dilemmas of Humanitarian Aid in the Twentieth Century* (Oxford: Oxford University Press, 2016), p. 190.
93 See Rooke and Schnell, '"Uncramping Child Life"', p. 185.
94 By this point German, Czech, Soviet, and Austrian national committees had withdrawn from the SCIU: Droux, 'Life during Wartime', p. 191.
95 C. Sambells, '"Children Are to Be Regarded as Propaganda": Contradictions of German Occupation Policies in the Child Evacuations to Switzerland, 1941–1942', *European History Quarterly*, 51:1 (2021), 76–97.
96 Droux, 'Life during Wartime', p. 197. Likewise the British government allowed the neutral ICRC, Swiss and Swedish Red Cross to bypass the British blockade to provide food relief during the famine in German-occupied Greece to avoid a repeat of the embarrassment caused by direct Allied and British relief missions in the First World War: see D. Palmieri and I. Herrmann, 'Two Crosses for the Same Aim? Swiss and Swedish Charitable Activities in Greece during the Second World War', in J. Paulmann (ed.), *Dilemmas of Humanitarian Aid in the Twentieth Century* (Oxford: Oxford University Press, 2016), p. 175.
97 The SCIU provided clandestine aid to Jewish children in France: Droux, 'Life during Wartime', p. 388.
98 Droux, 'Life during Wartime', p. 186. On postwar 'hunger politics' as a factor in the rise of theories of racial hygiene among German welfare eugenicists see Weindling, *Health, Race and German Politics*, p. 306. For instance, Hobhouse's supporter in Leipzig, Professor Abderhalden, came to advocate euthanasia: see M. Kaasch and J. Kaasch, 'Emil Abderhalden: Ethik und Moral in Werk und Wirken eines Naturforschers', in A. Frewer and J. Neumann (eds), *Medizingeschichte und Medizinethik: Kontroversen und Begründungsansätze 1900–1950* (Frankfurt am Main: Campus Verlag, 2001), pp. 204–45.

11

'The most deplorable victims'? The language of humanitarianism and relief to intellectuals in the era of the Great War

Tomás Irish

In 1922 a British organisation called the Committee for the Relief of Russian Intellectuals issued a public appeal for support to alleviate the suffering caused by the Russian famine. The organisation focused specifically on the provision of aid for the brain-workers, or intellectuals, of Russia, whose salvation was deemed 'absolutely necessary for the regeneration of Russian economics'. The appeal made a seemingly unusual comparison of different categories of sufferers; it asked contributors to purchase ten-dollar American Relief Administration (ARA) packages to be sent to named intellectuals in Russia. The cost price of the ARA parcels was $7.50, with 25 per cent of the money being put towards the feeding of 'the starving peasants of the Volga'. The appeal pointed out that anyone giving money via the ARA to an individual intellectual 'will have the satisfaction of knowing that by so doing he not only gives food to an intellectual and his family for a month or two, but that at the same time some child or adult peasant of the Volga will also be fed for a similar period'.[1]

The juxtaposition of the suffering of an 'intellectual and his family' with a peasant suffering in the Volga famine may seem, at the outset, striking. Much scholarship on the historical origins of modern humanitarianism in the aftermath of the First World War has emphasised how universal suffering was an increasingly important means of determining who should receive aid.[2] However, the Greater War served to further practices that were premised upon aid being distributed based on the social status of groups, rather than their suffering, meaning that humanitarianism remained differentiated. Intellectual relief is perhaps the most striking example of this.

This chapter will explore the emergence of intellectual relief as a distinct component of humanitarianism during and immediately after the First World War. Intellectual relief is defined here as aid that was given to institutions and individuals involved in cultural and intellectual pursuits. This form of humanitarianism manifested itself in two main ways. First, it was an extension of general humanitarian relief, ensuring that those deemed to be intellectuals were able to eat, clothe themselves, and maintain good health. In other words it constituted the provision of general relief to people engaged in intellectual pursuits. Second, intellectual relief can also be defined as the provision of specialist equipment and up-to-date books books and periodicals to people involved in intellectual activities; in other words bespoke aid was provided for people who had specific needs. All of this was necessitated following the violence of the First World War and the conflicts that followed it, where millions of people were displaced, property was destroyed, and hunger and disease were rife.

Intellectual relief was a significant endeavour. While precise numbers are difficult to ascertain, tens of thousands of people across Central and Eastern Europe were provided with aid because they were categorised as 'intellectuals' or were involved in intellectual pursuits of different types. Many of the well-known humanitarian organisations of the period, such as the American Relief Administration, the Society of Friends' Emergency War Victims' Relief Committee, the Imperial War Relief Fund and the Young Men's Christian Association, devoted significant energy and funds to intellectual relief alongside the provision of other forms of relief. The work of these larger organisations sat alongside smaller, amateur organisations that were formed to aid 'intellectuals' alone. Intellectual relief should not be seen as a niche or peripheral practice in this period; it was a widespread part of the general pursuit of humanitarianism, from large-scale operations to smaller ones.

Intellectual relief tells us much about the emergence of modern humanitarianism in the era of the Great War. Historians such as Keith D. Watenpaugh, Bruno Cabanes, and Michael Barnett have pointed to the transformation of humanitarianism – as both a practice and an ideology – in this period.[3] While these historians disagree on certain details, there is a broad consensus that the First World War led to the emergence of humanitarianism which was professional, increasingly secular, transnational, and characterised by permanent institutions that focused on human suffering irrespective of identity.[4] As Barnett notes, 'need, not identity' increasingly became the benchmark to determine who received aid.[5] However, the emergence of modern humanitarianism was a process which was neither smooth nor linear.[6] The period following the First World War saw the persistence of older forms of humanitarianism, which were hierarchical, often elitist, and privileged the identity of recipients. This chapter will focus on the emergence of intellectual relief in the period of the Greater War to demonstrate that humanitarian activities in this period were frequently highly elitist, selective, and informed by issues of class, education, and connections to power, as much as they were by genuine need. Understood as an organised practice, intellectual relief was new; however, it embodied many assumptions that were at odds with more 'modern' forms of humanitarianism that emerged in the period. As will be shown in this chapter, the practitioners and recipients of intellectual relief appropriated the language of modern humanitarianism – with its frequent emphasis on famine, starvation, and death – in order to justify their endeavours in the new context. The phenomenon of intellectual relief poses uncomfortable and seemingly counterintuitive questions about the development and characteristics of modern humanitarianism and two of its fundamental questions: whom do we help – and why?

Why intellectual relief?

The meanings of intellectual relief as a humanitarian practice are difficult to identify; few humanitarian agencies explicitly outlined their rationale for a focus on intellectuals and its importance was often assumed, rather than explained. The general humanitarian problems facing Europe after the First World War, including the mass displacement of people (especially from Russia) and famine conditions in parts of Central and Eastern Europe, were compounded by issues that were specific to intellectuals. The exchange and purchase of publications was rendered difficult owing to wartime antipathies and postwar inflation, while, in some cases, libraries and laboratories had been destroyed during the conflict. For intellectuals the process of postwar reconstruction was premised not only on the restoration and maintenance of their physical health but also on them having the tools in order to do intellectual work. But why was it deemed important?

Like so much post-First World War humanitarianism, there was a distinct anti-Bolshevik component to intellectual relief. Aid to intellectuals was most common in territories that had formerly come under the control of the German, Habsburg, or Ottoman Empires, many of which had been reconstituted as democratic 'successor states'. These were seen as potentially susceptible to Bolshevism by the victorious allies following the war and during the conflicts that came after 1918. In March 1919 Bela Kun briefly installed a Bolshevik regime in Hungary.[7] At the Paris Peace Conference the American Secretary of State, Robert Lansing, famously claimed that 'full stomachs mean no Bolsheviks'; in a general sense humanitarianism sought to preserve and promote the post-war democratic and capitalist order.[8]

The period immediately following the First World War was also accompanied by prognostications of civilisational decline, made most famous by Oswald Spengler and Paul Valéry.[9] While the writings of Valéry and Spengler largely referred to an imagined, intangible crisis of civilisation, intellectuals, suffering the effects of war, displacement, famine, and epidemic, were tangible manifestations of this phenomenon. In a general sense their upkeep might be seen as a means of consolidating the 'stability and status associated with pre-war Europe' which the historian Charles Maier has called the 'recasting' of bourgeois Europe.[10] In this way the preservation of intellectuals and intellectual practices was important not necessarily for the specialist knowledge that these people had or could produce but for their wider social standing in their respective communities. In 1921 James Bryce wrote that 'in times when class strife is threatened there is a special need for thinkers and speakers able to rise above class interests and class prejudices'.[11]

Some individuals connected to wider humanitarian efforts made a strong connection between intellectuals and the problem of building new, democratic states. An unnamed director of the American Relief Administration wrote in late 1920 that the futures of Poland, Czechoslovakia, Austria, and Hungary depended upon 'the brains of this intellectual class'.[12] In late 1921 a pamphlet published by European Student Relief claimed that the new states of Central and Eastern Europe were suffering from a dearth of 'professional men to meet the rapidly developing demands of the new order'.[13] This emphasis on the role to be played by educated individuals in the building of new states was especially prominent in schemes that specifically assisted students, although they are not the primary focus of this chapter.[14]

This chapter will use the term 'intellectual' in a broad sense to identify the figures who were active in cultural fields and were the recipients of humanitarian assistance in this period. This decision reflects the widespread usage of the term 'intellectual' – both as a noun and as an adjective – in contemporary sources to describe those in need of aid and to justify its importance. The term 'intellectual' came into usage before the First World War and took on different meanings and emphases in different nations, usually relating to the political and social function of a learned individual in their respective society.[15] As will be shown in this chapter, the postwar humanitarian crisis led to the emergence of a new transnational discourse around intellectuals which emphasised the common suffering of the group across Europe.

The term 'intellectual' appears in a wide range of humanitarian sources from the postwar period. A large appropriation from the Commonwealth Fund to the American Relief Administration in 1920 was logged as 'food drafts for intellectuals'.[16] Michael Hainisch, the president of Austria, wrote of his thanks to the ARA for its help in providing aid to 'intellectuals' in 1921.[17] In 1922 the entomologist and evolutionary biologist Vernon Kellogg wrote (on behalf of the American National Research Council) of the need for relief of 'intellectuals' in Austria, Poland, and Russia.[18] The term 'intellectual' (or 'intellectuel' in French) was the most frequently used by those involved in the provision of aid and those with whom they dealt, but it proved to be an imprecise term in identifying a specific group of people.

It was often taken to encompass scholars, writers, journalists, lawyers, and artists and sometimes included schoolteachers, doctors, clergy, ex-officers, or other middle-class professionals. It also sometimes specifically included university students – whose relief was also part of a widespread postwar initiative – although this was not always the case.

The politics of relief

Intellectual relief was often an explicitly political project and not all countries were treated equally. Germany was widely condemned in Allied countries for its culpability in starting the First World War – enshrined in article 231 of the Treaty of Versailles – and for the way that it fought that conflict, especially during the invasion of Belgium in August 1914. German intellectuals issued strident defences of their country's conduct in this period, with the 'Appeal to the Civilized World' – which denied that Germany had violated Belgian neutrality or committed atrocities in Belgium – being the most infamous example.[19] Having been the pre-eminent intellectual nation before the war, with its scholars receiving more Nobel prizes than any other nation and its universities seen as pioneering in research, Germany and its intellectual life were stigmatised during and after the war, recast in the allied imagination as key drivers of German militarism. As the intellectual world had become increasingly interconnected in the decades at the end of the nineteenth century, Germany's wartime and postwar isolation caused significant disruption to the movement of people, publications, and ideas.[20]

The wartime cleavage in the intellectual world informed how intellectual relief emerged in its aftermath. Many organisations, such as the League of Nations and the American Relief Administration, refused to provide intellectual aid for still-stigmatised Germany. Others, such as the Society of Friends and European Student Relief, had fewer qualms about dealing with the former enemy. Certain ex-enemy states, such as Austria, were less closely associated with atrocities in the minds of allied and neutral publics, meaning that there were fewer issues when it came to providing aid. This was important to how aid was articulated; in 1920 the ethnologist Franz Boas established the Emergency Society for German and Austrian Science and Art. In 1923 Stephen Duggan, director of the Institute of International Education, wrote to Boas to suggest changing the formal title of the body to the 'Emergency Society for Austrian and German Science and Art', placing greater emphasis on a different ex-enemy state with whom most allies had fewer issues.[21]

Political considerations shaped where many organisations chose to focus their activities, but also how recipient states interacted with these efforts. Vanquished states in the recent war appropriated the language of intellectual relief to make the case for the revision of postwar treaties. In Germany Reinhold Schairer wrote a report for the World Student Christian Federation which described the 'collapse of intellectual life' in Germany. Schairer argued that the greatest form of intellectual relief would be revision of the Treaty of Versailles but, in the meantime, he suggested practical means of assisting German intellectual life.[22] Hungary, another vanquished state, also mobilised the language of intellectual relief to make the case for revision of the Treaty of Trianon of 1920. Hungary lost two-thirds of its territory under the terms of the Trianon which, as vocal advocates of treaty revision frequently pointed out, amounted to the loss of significant intellectual capital: two universities, 745 libraries (containing over four million volumes), and a number of museums. Revisionists like Oliver Eöttevényi argued that this cultural loss undermined the 'respect for national ideas' in the new Hungarian state.[23]

Feeding bodies

One of the key components of intellectual relief in the period of the Greater War was saving lives of those deemed intellectuals. Intellectual relief was, by definition, premised upon the identity of the recipients and was highly selective; in this way it deviates from the work of many large humanitarian organisations of this period who emphasised need and suffering in the distribution of aid, and who devised elaborate means to 'objectively' measure and verify that need.[24] One of the key means of providing aid to intellectuals in the early 1920s came through feeding programmes which were introduced to address severe food shortages. Intellectuals were provided with bespoke food and medical aid, separate from the wider populations in which they lived, in order to keep them alive.

Following the end of the First World War, humanitarian organisations, philanthropists, and scholars began to receive reports detailing the physical needs of intellectuals in places like Austria and Poland and, later, in Russia. These reports tended to focus on accounts of individual experiences in order to make the case for intellectual relief. Pitirim Sorokin, an anti-Bolshevik scholar who lectured at Petrograd University until he was forced to leave Russia in 1922, described faculty meetings there as being like 'some kind of undertaker's bureau', with each session beginning with an announcement of all the recent deaths of colleagues owing to starvation or malnourishment.[25] One Viennese scholar wrote that 'owing to permanent underfeeding, I have suddenly lost all my teeth, and the consequent pressure of the jaw upon the bones of the ear has resulted in continual headache'.[26] An appeal

Figure 11.1 Students and professors being fed in Innsbruck, June 1921, with gift from the Commonwealth Fund

issued by the Committee for the Relief of Russian Intellectuals cited three representative examples of starvation:

> Professor A. and his wife have sold even their bed and bedstead for food. They sleep on the bare floor awaiting death from starvation. B. is in the same condition. C. has become thin and transparent like a ghost. He lives by selling his last home effects.[27]

In the case of Austria and Germany postwar inflation and its impact on exchange rates meant that many intellectuals and scholars were unable to afford to buy literature or print their own research findings. In Austria in 1920 many felt that the middle class was suffering disproportionately owing to the effects of inflation. In January 1921 the *Neue Freie Presse* in Vienna argued that 'not the manual labourers, but the brain workers in the defeated countries, especially Austria, were the most deplorable victims of the war'.[28]

Perhaps the most striking manifestation of this kind of aid was the intellectual kitchen (sometimes also referred to as the professors' mess or intelligentsia kitchen). These were feeding stations where intellectuals (and frequently *only* intellectuals) were fed daily while famine conditions often ravaged their wider communities. In December 1920 an intellectual kitchen was created at the University of Vienna for academic staff which was funded by a $5,000 gift from both the Rochester Fund and the Commonwealth Fund. At its peak, over two hundred academics attended daily, paying a token fee for subsidised meals.[29] By mid-1921 intellectual kitchens were established in Vienna, Graz, and Innsbruck in Austria and in Warsaw, Krakow, Lwów, and Wilna in Poland.[30] One student's account of the impact of American relief in Russia stated that the opening of ARA kitchens in Petrograd in 1922 was like 'a ray of light in bad weather. This kitchen, with its clean white table cloth and flowers, seemed like paradise to us.'[31] A female student in Petrograd reported that the American kitchens saved her 'from physical as well as moral death'.[32]

Intellectual kitchens served an important purpose not only because they fed intellectuals but in how they did it. The grouping of scholars together was intended to facilitate intellectual exchange and to spur the emergence of new ideas. The setting, where clean white tablecloths and attractive flowers were a regular feature, was suggestive of the prewar bourgeois standing of intellectuals, and contrasted with the poverty and famine which they frequently confronted in their private lives. A description of the scene at the University of Vienna's kitchen stated that 'one might be inclined to think oneself attending a banquet to celebrate some distinguished scientist or at some aristocratic club – and this, indeed, was the aim aspired to'.[33] Writing in 1924 the historian James Shotwell argued that the kitchen at the university of Vienna had been a success because it got intellectuals together to discuss problems collectively and avoid 'self-pity'.[34]

The poverty of intellectuals in the aftermath of the war in Central and Eastern Europe manifested itself not only in nutritional terms but also in their self-image. Archival records suggest that a consistent element of intellectual need in the early 1920s related to the personal appearance and circumstances of intellectuals. Many accounts reflected upon the old and often tattered clothes that intellectuals and their families wore. Shoes were especially prominent in these stories. One description of a Viennese professor in 1920 claimed that his wife and daughter were never seen together in public because they shared one pair of shoes.[35] It was frequently reported that intellectuals had sold items of clothing, furniture, and jewellery in order to get by.[36] It also led, rather naturally, to lifestyle changes which were frequently remarked upon in reports of conditions. One report written from Kyiv in 1923 described how 'buying a new book, going to a dentist, using the municipal baths, attending a concert or even a "movie" are luxuries too extravagant to be thought of'.[37] Cumulatively, the reports about intellectual need which described material deprivation strongly suggested that self-image was intrinsically linked to an intellectual's social standing and, by extension, to their ability to produce new research work.

The emphasis placed upon the physical appearance and lifestyle options of intellectuals in this period suggests that their perceived importance related not only to their ability to produce and disseminate knowledge but to their social standing as members of the middle classes. Another measure of this is clothes aid to intellectuals which emphasised their difference from their wider communities. In 1924 Elisabeth Bredin, working for the American Section of European Student Relief in Russia, noted that general ARA relief clothing could be seen on 'young and old, fat and thin'; the ubiquity of the 'relief costume' meant that it was decided to give intellectuals bespoke suits in different patterns and colours.[38] Another report quoted an intellectual in receipt of clothes aid as finding it 'a little distressing to have a good suit yourself when your wife and children are shivering with cold'.[39]

Emergency relief to intellectuals aimed to keep these individuals alive amidst famine and economic depression. This was a highly selective and elitist process which assumed that the salvation of these lives was of great importance to their wider communities. The emphasis placed on personal 'respectable' appearance, in addition to wellbeing, suggests that, beyond the rescue of the knowledge that these individuals held, the maintenance of a class identity was also an important consideration.

Displacement

Displacement was a key part of the postwar intellectual crisis. The First World War, and the conflicts which followed it, led to widespread dislocation of people across Europe. Hundreds of thousands of Russians were uprooted during the civil war, ending up in Turkey, the Balkans, and the eastern Mediterranean.[40] Mass deportations from Bolshevik Russia took place in 1922, exacerbating the issue.[41] People were displaced elsewhere in Europe, with the collapse of multiethnic empires and the drawing of new national boundaries between states meaning that tens of thousands of people were no longer in a state which they considered to be their own. Thousands of intellectuals were caught up in this wider mass dislocation of people and their plight, too, was a focus of postwar intellectual relief.

Unlike the feeding of intellectuals described in the previous section, aid to refugee intellectuals gained relative prominence during the First World War through initiatives to house displaced Belgian and Serbian scholars.[42] The discourse surrounding intellectual displacement during the war often spoke of the need to preserve national intellectual life in exile; in that way it was deemed important to keep key individuals alive as custodians of that national culture. The Swiss scholar Gonzague de Reynold, who was a key figure in the League of Nations' Committee on Intellectual Co-operation, wrote in 1923 that Russian refugee scholars in exile carried with them the 'sacred flame of civilisation' which had been temporarily extinguished in their homeland. It was incumbent upon European civilisation, de Reynold argued, to help them 'maintain that flame'.[43] The idea of temporarily holding intellectual life in trust aligned with wider declinist prognostications of the decline of civilization made famous by Spengler, Valéry, and others.

Hubs of displaced Russian intellectuals emerged across Europe, in Prague, Berlin, and Paris; in Czechoslovakia the president, Tomaš Masaryk, took a leading role in providing education to exiled Russians.[44] In the autumn of 1921 the Czechoslovak foreign ministry organised the transport of one thousand Russian citizens from Constantinople to Czechoslovakia to complete their studies. These students were chosen on the recommendation of a group of displaced Russian university professors; they verified the authenticity of the documents presented by the students and authenticated the story of their educational backgrounds. The students committed to go to Czechoslovakia only for educational purposes and not to pursue political activities.[45] Aid was also organised from within the affected communities; Zemgor, a Russian émigré organisation, was founded in 1921 to co-ordinate a wide range of activities including relief. Led by Prince George E. Lvov, it placed a strong emphasis on education and ran educational institutions across Europe for displaced Russians.[46]

Aiding refugees usually meant placing them in cities and institutions where they could live safely and healthily, and continue with their intellectual work. An illustrative example can be seen by an appeal published in the *Times* newspaper in May 1923. It was signed by a number of leading figures in the British legal world who sought to raise £1,000 from fellow lawyers to save twenty-five members of the Russian bar who were then stranded in Constantinople, among twenty thousand others. The appeal claimed that these men were all 'highly educated and gently brought up'.[47]

Relief to displaced people in this period was often highly selective, with people being aided because of their status or involvement in intellectual pursuits. Similarly to feeding initiatives, intellectual relief for displaced people suggested that some lives were more important than others, and the language used to do so could often be shocking. The American archaeologist Thomas Whittemore oversaw a scheme to place Russian refugee youth, primarily those in Constantinople, in elite schools and universities across Europe, called the Committee for the Education of Russian Youth in Exile (CERYE).[48] Whittemore's committee was explicitly elitist, with the main criteria for the granting of assistance being intellectual excellence. In 1923 he wrote that he did not seek to help everyone in need, but was instead 'trying to educate as many as possible of those who matter'.[49] Whittemore invoked the metaphor of ideas being held in trust on behalf of national learning. He described the Russian exiles whom he aided as 'seedlings for the scientific reforestation of Russia', by which he meant they were an intellectual elite who would receive an excellent education in Western Europe before returning home to Russia after the expected collapse of the Bolshevik regime.[50] On returning to Russia, these students would be 'useful as experts and specialists'.[51] By 1922 the CERYE had placed 227 students in universities and advanced schools in France, Belgium, Switzerland, Greece, Yugoslavia, Czechoslovakia, Turkey, Germany, Bulgaria, Italy, and also Syria.[52] The CERYE sought to support scholars working in certain areas which it deemed essential to reconstruction, but there was also a clear political dimension to its work; many of the young intellectuals who received assistance were the sons and daughters of white Russians and often belonged to noble or military families.

Feeding minds

Intellectual relief was frequently justified – by those seeking aid as well as those providing it – using the metaphor of starvation and famine to describe cultural or academic needs. The utilisation of this language suggests that a vocabulary had emerged by the end of the war which could be mobilised to underscore the imperative of assistance. However, the proliferation of the metaphor of humanitarian need suggests that intellectual suffering – in its own right – needed to be given a humanitarian accent in order to convince philanthropists, humanitarians, and publics of its wider importance.

The first evidence of the application of the metaphor of humanitarianism to intellectual deprivation can be found in the prisoner-of-war camps of the First World War. International appeals were launched to ensure that camps were stocked with scholarly and scientific literature to cater to their diverse populations. Alfred T. Davies, who oversaw the development of a Camp Education Department in Britain to supply camps with scholarly literature, stated in December 1916 that his scheme was 'absolutely essential to save the prisoners from mental starvation'.[53] This metaphor was not limited to the English language; in a copy of *l'Intermède*, the newspaper for Würzburg Camp which held French prisoners of war, the camp library was described as 'a wonderful intellectual dining room'.[54]

The metaphor of intellectual starvation became much more widespread in the aftermath of the war, and could be applied equally to individuals, institutions, or whole countries. The idea of intellectual starvation was the consequence of a number of interlinked circumstances that were themselves a result of the conflict. The international circulation of scholarly material was severely impeded during the First World War, meaning that many individuals and institutions, especially those in Central and Eastern European countries, found that they had gaps in their collections by the war's end. In many cases no new literature had been received since 1914, a gap which was seen as especially detrimental to researchers in the sciences. This situation was compounded in places like Austria and Germany by soaring international exchange rates and, from 1922, hyperinflation, which made the purchase of international scholarly literature prohibitively expensive.[55]

By the end of the war in Western Europe, this gap in scholarly literature was seen as a pressing component of post-conflict reconstruction. Many schemes emerged to provide books to institutions and individuals in Austria, Germany, Hungary, Russia, and elsewhere. Many of these spoke the language of humanitarianism in order to describe the imperative of supplying up-to-date literature to those in need of them. In 1920 the British author H. G. Wells published an account of his recent visit to Russia where he claimed that scientific men 'value[d] knowledge more than bread'.[56] In the same year Franz Boas's aforementioned society issued a public appeal which argued that 'Germany and Austria are starving not only physically, but intellectually'.[57] The language of humanitarianism was not restricted to those advocating for intellectual aid to a given country but was also utilised by intellectuals who needed access to scholarly material to continue their work. In 1926 a YMCA worker in Ukraine claimed that his local contacts felt that the emphasis on food aid being delivered to them was misplaced. He reported that 'the professors said, "although we hunger for food, our craving for books is even more acute".'[58]

The supply of books to libraries and institutions across Europe took place on a variety of scales. In November 1922 the International Committee on Intellectual Co-operation (ICIC) at the League of Nations issued an international appeal on behalf of the intellectual life of Austria. The appeal called on institutions across the world to send material to Austrian institutions, with the League offering to act as an intermediary in the exchanges. In September 1924 a similar appeal was issued by the ICIC on behalf of intellectual life in Hungary, although on this occasion contributors were asked to liaise directly with Hungarian institutions.[59] In 1924 the New York-based Laura Spelman Rockefeller Memorial agreed to assist German university and some state libraries in addressing the gaps in their social science collections. The Memorial dealt directly with the state libraries of Bavaria and Prussia, but gave the Emergency Association of German Science (Notgemeinschaft der Deutschen Wissenschaft) – an emergency organisation set up to represent the needs of German scholars – full authority to purchase books for university libraries using American funds.[60] Smaller, ad hoc committees also came into existence in this period, such as the British Committee for Aiding Men of Letters and Science, founded in 1920, and the Friends of Russian Scientists group, established by H. W. L Dana in Boston in 1922, or Boas's aforementioned Emergency Society for German and Austrian Science and Art.[61]

The mobilisation of the language of humanitarianism in order to highlight the imperative of replenishing the scholarly literature of Central and Eastern Europe is illustrative of a number of dynamics that informed the wider operation of humanitarianism in the period of the Greater War. First, it suggests that a humanitarian lexicon had become standardised as a means of explaining need, which was usually through the rubric of hunger and starvation. Second, it seems that intellectuals and those advocating for their aid were aware that their requests for assistance did not organically fit within the wider postwar humanitarian agenda on their own terms. Instead, the claims of scholars, institutions, and nations were packaged using the language of humanitarianism to underscore their importance.

The mobilisation of the language of humanitarianism in intellectual relief was not universal. Indeed, some humanitarian actors consciously pushed back against it. Writing around the time of the Russian famine in 1922, Thomas Whittemore explained his distaste for using 'higher colors in my descriptions' of the need of displaced Russian students to make it more alike the 'lurid painting of the Volga Relief'. He claimed that it was not possible to use 'heartrending scenes of starving children and pictures of cannibal feasts in Constantinople'; the importance of his work of settling displaced elite students in universities and schools across Europe should stand on its own terms and required no further elaboration.[62] For some involved in the organisation of intellectual relief, the language of humanitarianism had its limits.

Legacies

Intellectual relief was widespread and took on many forms in the era of the Great War. The tension between issues of general need versus the specific claims of an educated elite exemplify the slow and difficult process through which modern humanitarianism emerged from its nineteenth-century predecessor.[63] With some exceptions, the immediate crisis to European intellectual life caused by the Greater War had come to an end by 1925 and much of the humanitarian activity cited in this chapter ceased not long after. What were the legacies of this period of activity?

In 1933 Adolf Hitler began his assault on intellectual freedoms in Germany, leading to Jewish (and other) scholars from Nazi-controlled territories seeking refuge in Britain, North America, and elsewhere.[64] The post-1933 emigration of intellectuals has a vast historiography but, by comparison to that which preceded it in the early 1920s, it is rarely presented as a humanitarian issue of saving lives.[65] Those active in the placement of migrant intellectuals at the time were quite explicit that their work not be understood as humanitarian, narrowly defined, but instead should be viewed as providing employment opportunities for scholars who had lost their jobs in German universities. The Emergency Society of German Scientists and Scholars Abroad (Notgemeinschaft deutscher Wissenschaftler im Ausland) described itself as an 'employment agency' which placed scholars at suitable universities, on the basis of their expertise and the needs of the institution in question.[66] The British-based Academic Assistance Council did likewise, emphasising the disciplinary fit between displaced scholar and institution rather than the imperative of saving human life.[67] Much of the historiography of the post-1933 emigration emphasises individual biographies, the experience of exile (both literal and intellectual), and the transformational impact that the placement of eminent intellectuals had on recipient institutions and societies.[68] Intellectuals fled Nazi-controlled areas for a variety of reasons from 1933, making it qualitatively different from the forced and immediate displacement occasioned by the Russian Civil War, for example.[69] The League of Nations' International Committee on Intellectual Co-operation, which moved to act to save intellectual life in Austria and Hungary in the early 1920s, did not act to help German Jewish scholars who were being forced out of their positions by the Nazi government, deeming it a national political issue which was beyond their remit. Germany had, in any case, ceased to be a member of the League of Nations and the ICIC by 1933.

Yet there are important connections between the early 1920s and what followed after 1933. Key individuals had experience of intellectual relief after the First World War and applied this again after 1933; Walter Kotschnig was 'saved from starvation' by American aid while a student in Austria following the war and later became the general secretary of the International Student Service.[70] In the 1930s he formed an important link between important groups working to help scholars who were forced to flee Nazi Germany, including the Emergency Society of German Scientists and Scholars Abroad and the Emergency Committee in Aid of Displaced German Scholars in the United States.[71] In Britain Sir William Beveridge was briefly the head of the Universities Committee set up by the Imperial War Relief Fund in 1920 and then founded the Academic Assistance Council in 1933.[72] Moreover, key agencies looked back to their actions and experiences following the First World War when attempting to navigate the challenges of the Second World War; the Rockefeller Foundation, for example, reflected on the events of the 1910s and 1920s to set out an agenda in 1939 in order to 'keep alive in Europe the spark of intellectual and cultural life'. Unlike much post-First World War relief, this agenda was tightly focused on five well-defined areas.[73]

The period since the Second World War has seen intellectual relief remain prominent in dealing with the aftermath of conflicts and natural disasters. John Krige has argued that America funded and shaped the reconstruction of European science after the Second World War as a manifestation of American hegemony.[74] A university for displaced people was established in Munich in 1945 by the United Nations Relief and Rehabilitation Administration (UNRRA) which resembled some initiatives from the First World War and interwar period.[75] Guillaume Tronchet's work has shown how most crises of displacement in the twentieth and twenty-first centuries have in many cases also been university crises, where students have frequently been the victims of conflict but also recipients of bespoke aid as a consequence. For example, UNESCO created scholarships for Palestinian refugee students in Gaza and Jordan from 1953 on.[76] Intellectual relief has not been restricted to large organisations like the United Nations. Individual philanthropists have also intervened to aid intellectual life in different contexts, often using similar language to that of the 1920s. In the early 1990s the philanthropist George Soros founded the International Science Foundation to support scientists in Russia following the fall in the value of the ruble. This provided grants for specific research programmes and emergency grants to Russian scientists, and enabled Russian scientists to purchase up-to-date scientific journals.[77]

The issues that animated intellectual relief during and after the First World War have been, in certain cases, formalised in international law and the structure of international organisations. This can be seen in the example of legislation concerning prisoners of war. Whereas the 1906 Geneva Convention made no explicit mention of the importance of the intellectual wellbeing of prisoners of war, the 1929 Convention relative to the Treatment of Prisoners of War had articles dealing with intellectual relief for prisoners. Article 17 established the principle that 'belligerents shall encourage as much as possible the organisation of intellectual and sporting pursuits by the prisoners of war'.[78] The 1949 Geneva Convention gave further substance to the rights of prisoners to receive intellectual relief.[79] These clauses made possible the production of seminal works such as Fernand Braudel's *The Mediterranean and the Mediterranean World in the Age of Philip II*, written in confinement during the Second World War.[80]

Human rights discourses have identified an important place for education, especially that of children. Article 26 of the United Nations' universal declaration of Human Rights (1948) states that education is a human right, and the 1989 UN Convention on the Rights of Children added that not only was education a right but that children must have equal opportunity in accessing education.[81] Meanwhile, the end of the Second World War saw the establishment of UNESCO, which was built on the precedent set by the League's intellectual co-operation bodies in the interwar period, which were themselves a product of intellectual crisis and the processes of relief.[82]

Conclusion

Post-First World War intellectual relief was influential in birthing practices, organisations, and legislation that would be utilised later in the century to deal with a variety of crises, from war to natural disaster. That said, it is notable that later examples articulated their importance in a different manner from those of the Greater War; the metaphor of saving lives was less apparent, with the emphasis instead placed on the expertise of individual scholars in exile or the human right to education. Indeed, intellectual relief in the era of the Great War seems unusual in the fact that it was a major transnational problem that traversed multiple countries and impacted tens, and possibly hundreds, of thousands of people. It was simultaneously understood as an issue of humanitarian, intellectual, and political importance, and that informed not only how initiatives were undertaken but how they were portrayed.

The language that accompanied post-First World War intellectual relief spoke of the death of intellectual life of whole nations. In that way it mirrored – and was reinforced by – wider discourses about the demise of civilisation. The contrast to the language of post-1933 intellectual relief is notable here. The difference, of course, is that intellectual relief of the early 1920s failed. It was cited as a means of reinforcing the new democratic and capitalist order in the face of Bolshevism and the threat of future wars. By the mid-1930s this order had broken down, and, by extension, so had the project of intellectual relief as it had been understood in the early 1920s. One important consequence of 1920s intellectual relief was the emergence of a transnational conversation about the societal standing of intellectuals, which was initially led by humanitarian organisations and later taken up by the League of Nations' Committee on Intellectual Co-operation and International Labour Organization.

Intellectual relief demonstrates how Greater War humanitarianism was in transition from older, hierarchical, and elitist forms to its modern iteration which prioritised need. This chapter has shown how this process was far from linear or smooth, and was often paradoxical. Intellectual relief privileged helping older, traditional elites but did so using the language of need in order to fit into the new humanitarian context.

Notes

1 'Committee for the Relief of Russian Intellectuals', Parliamentary Archives (PA), Stow-Hill papers, STH/DS/2/1/u, p. 3.
2 M. Barnett, *Empire of Humanity: A History of Humanitarianism* (Ithaca: Cornell University Press, 2011), p. 82.
3 B. Cabanes, *The Great War and the Origins of Humanitarianism, 1918–1924* (Cambridge: Cambridge University Press, 2014); K. Watenpaugh, *Bread from Stones: The Middle East and the Making of Modern Humanitarianism* (Oakland: University of California Press, 2015); Barnett, *Empire of Humanity*.
4 Watenpaugh, *Bread from Stones*, pp. 2–9; Cabanes, *Great War*, pp. 4–7; Barnett, *Empire of Humanity*, pp. 82–3.
5 Barnett, *Empire of Humanity*, p. 82.
6 Watenpaugh, *Bread from Stones*, p. 5; pp. 22–3.
7 R. Gerwarth, *The Vanquished: Why the First World War Failed to End* (London: Allen Lane, 2016), pp. 118–52.
8 J. M. Thompson, *Russia, Bolshevism and the Versailles Peace* (Princeton: Princeton University Press, 1966), p. 222.
9 J. Ifversen, 'The Crisis of European Civilisation after 1918', in M. Spiering and M. Wintle (eds), *Ideas of Europe since 1914: The Legacy of the First World War* (Basingstoke: Palgrave Macmillan, 2002), pp. 14–31.
10 C. S. Maier, *Recasting Bourgeois Europe: Stabilization in France, Germany, and Italy in the Decade after World War I* (Princeton: Princeton University Press, 1975), p. 6.
11 J. Bryce, *Modern Democracies*, vol. 1 (London: Macmillan, 1921), p. 87.
12 Director of the American Relief Administration, 'The Situation of the Intellectual Class in Central Europe', *ARA Bulletin*, 2:3 (1920), 36.
13 'Why Do They Go On Studying?', Library of the Society of Friends (SOF), London, YM/MfS/FEWVRC/MISSIONS/10/5/2/3.
14 B. L. Hartley, 'Saving Students: European Student Relief in the Aftermath of World War I', *International Bulletin of Mission Research*, 42:1 (2018), 295–315; D. Laqua, 'Activism in the "Students' League of Nations": International Student Politics and the Confédération Internationale des Étudiants, 1919–1939', *English Historical Review*, 132:556 (2017), 605–37.
15 S. Sand, *La fin de l'intellectuel français? De Zola à Houllebecq* (Paris: la Découverte, 2016); S. Collini, *Absent Minds: Intellectuals in Britain* (Oxford: Oxford University Press, 2006); J. Habermas, 'Heinrich Heine and the Role of the Intellectual in Germany', in J. Habermas (ed.), *The New Conservatism: Cultural Criticism and the Historians' Debate* (Cambridge: Polity, 1989), pp. 71–99; C. Lasch, *The New Radicalism in America 1889–1963: The Intellectual as a Social Type* (New York: Alfred A. Knopf, 1966); R. Pipes (ed.), *The Russian*

Intelligentsia (New York: Columbia University Press, 1961); D. Bering, *Die Intellektuellen: Geschichte eines Schimpfwortes* (Frankfurt: Klett-Cotta, 1982).
16 Commonwealth Fund Files, Rockefeller Archive Center (RAC), New York, Grants, SG 1, Series 18, Subseries 1 (FA290), Box 12, Folder 119.
17 'Official Statements on Relief Benefits: President Hainisch of Austria', *ARA Bulletin*, 2:14 (1921), 13.
18 Vernon Kellogg, 'Foreign University Conditions', *Bulletin of the American Association of University Professors (1915–1955)*, 8:2 (1922), 5.
19 M.-E. Chagnon, 'American Scientists and the Process of Reconciliation in the International Scientific Community, 1917–1925', in T. Irish and M.-E. Chagnon (eds), *The Academic World in the Era of the Great War* (London: Palgrave Macmillan, 2018), pp. 213–17; M.-E. Chagnon, 'Le Manifeste des 93: La mobilisation des académies françaises et allemandes au déclenchement de la Première Guerre mondiale (1914–1915)', *French Historical Studies*, 35:1 (2012), 123–47.
20 T. Irish, *The University at War, 1914–25: Britain, France and the United States* (Basingstoke: Palgrave Macmillan, 2015), pp. 6–11, pp. 24–38.
21 Duggan to Boas, 11 January 1923, American Philosophical Society Archives (APSA), Philadelphia, MSS B.B61.
22 Reinhold Schairer, *The Collapse of Intellectual Life in Germany*, undated report c. 1923, World Student Christian Federation Records, Yale University Divinity Library Special Collections (YUDLSC), RG46, Series 31. D (c) Germany, Box 132, Folder 1010.
23 O. Eöttevényi, 'Cultural Effects of the Treaty of Trianon', in A. Apponyi (ed.), *Justice for Hungary: Review and Criticism of the Effect of the Treaty of Trianon* (London: Longmans, Green and Co. Ltd, 1928), p. 249.
24 Barnett, *Empire of Humanity*, p. 82.
25 Sorokin, 'Academic Life in Soviet Russia', RAC, Laura Spelman Rockefeller Memorial (FA061), Series 3: Appropriations Subseries, 3_03, Emergency Relief, Box 9, Folder 105, p. 4.
26 'Account of a "savant" in Vienna', SOF/YM/MfS/FEWVRC/4/3/7/3.
27 'Committee for the Relief of Russian Intellectuals', 1, PA/STH/DS/2/1/u.
28 'Relief Work for the Brain-Workers of Austria', 15 January 1921, SOF/YM/MfS/FEWVRC/MISSIONS/4/3/8/5.
29 'Ivan', 'The Professors' Mess', RAC, Rockefeller Foundation (RF) Records, SG. 1.1, Series 100, Box 77, Folder 728. The gift amounted to approximately $75,000 in today's currency.
30 'Extension of Assistance to the Intellectual Classes', *ARA Bulletin*, 2:12 (1921), 29.
31 Report of A. Mordovskaya, European reports – Russia, letter no. 21, YUDLSC, RG 46, Series 23.D Europe, Box 297, Folder 2717.
32 Report of Anna Alexandrova, European reports – Russia, letter no. 28, YUDLSC, RG 46, Series 23.D Europe, Box 297, Folder 2717.
33 'Ivan', 'The Professors' Mess', RAC, RF, SG. 1.1, Series 100, Box 77, Folder 728.

34 Shotwell to Fosdick, 17 January 1924, RAC, LSRM (FA061), Series 3, Subseries 3_06, Appropriations – Social Studies, Box 52, Folder 558.
35 'Unhappy Vienna', c. December 1920, SOF/YM/MfS/FEWVRC/4/3/7/2.
36 'Committee for the Relief of Russian Intellectuals', PA/STH/DS/2/1/u, 2.
37 K.A. Macpherson, Report on Intelligentsia in Kiev, 26 January 1923 RAC, LSRM (FA061), Series 3: Appropriations Subseries, 3_03, Emergency Relief, Box 9, Folder 105, pp. 3–4.
38 Elisabeth Bredin, 'Distribution of New Clothing to Russian Professors, 1924', RAC, LSRM (FA061), series 3: Appropriations, subseries 3_03, Emergency Relief, Box 10, Folder 112.
39 Harold Gibson, 'The Position of University Professors and Teachers in Russia Today', League of Nations Archives (LNA), Geneva, 13C, R1049, 23815–24805x, p. 1.
40 M. Housden, 'White Russians Crossing the Black Sea: Fridtjof Nansen, Constantinople and the First Modern Repatriation of Refugees Displaced by Civil Conflict, 1922–23', *The Slavonic and East European Review*, 88:3 (2010), 497–8.
41 S. Fitzpatrick, *The Cultural Front: Power and Culture in Revolutionary Russia* (Ithaca: Cornell University Press, 1992), pp. 37–51; S. Finkel, *On the Ideological Front: The Russian Intelligentsia and the Making of the Soviet Public Sphere* (New Haven: Yale University Press, 2006), pp. 13–38.
42 Grace Osler to George Dock, 17 November 1914, Osler Library, Montreal, Grace Revere Osler (GRO) papers 326/1.5; Edwin B. Frost, Letter to *Science, New Series*, 40:1032 (1914), 522; Émile Cammaerts and Henri Davignon (eds), *A Book of Belgium's Gratitude* (London: John Lane, 1916); M. Paunovic, M. Igrutinovic, D. Zec, and F. Baljkas, *Exile in the Classroom: Serbian Students and Pupils in Great Britain during the First World War* (Belgrade: Centre for Sports Heritage – South East Europe, 2016), pp. 59–133.
43 Gonzague de Reynold, *La vie intellectuelle dans les divers pays: Russie. Rapport sur la situation et l'organisation des intellectuels Russes hors de Russie* (Geneva: League of Nations, c. 1923), p. 24.
44 R. C. Williams, *Culture in Exile: Russian Emigrés in Germany, 1881–1941* (Ithaca: Cornell University Press, 1972), pp. 111–38; M. Raeff, *Russia Abroad: A Cultural History of the Russian Emigration, 1919–1939* (Oxford: Oxford University Press, 1990), pp. 47–64.
45 'Speech of Eduard Beneš, 30 May 1922', *Recueil de Documents Étrangers: Supplément aux bulletins de presse étrangère*, 109 (1922), p. 135.
46 C. Gousseff, *L'exil russe: La fabrique du réfugié apatride (1920–1939)* (Paris: CNRS, 2008), pp. 271–3.
47 'Russian Refugee Barristers', *The Times*, 3 May 1923, p. 5.
48 T. Irish, 'Educating Those Who Matter: Thomas Whittemore, Russian Refugees and the Transnational Organisation of Elite Humanitarianism after the First World War', *European Review of History: Revue européenne d'histoire*, 28 (2021), 441–62.
49 Whittemore to Elisabeth Cram, 23 November 1923, Bakhmeteff Archive of Russian and Eastern European Culture (BAR), Columbia University Rare Book

and Manuscript Library (CURBML), New York, Committee for the Education of Russian Youth in Exile Records, 1914–1939 (CERYE), Subseries IX.1,Box 94, Folder 35.
50 Whittemore report, 20 September 1923, 13 October 1922, RAC, Office of the Messrs Rockefeller (OMR), Series Q, Box 42, Folder 369.
51 Unsigned report, c. 1922, The Committee for the Rescue and Education of Russian Youth in Exile, RAC, LSRM (FA061), Series 3: Appropriations Subseries, 3_03, Emergency Relief, Box 8, folder 94, p. 5.
52 'Mr Thomas Whittemore', in Pratt to Rockefeller, 13 October 1922, RAC, OMR, Series Q, Box 42, Folder 369. Account of Whittemore work, YUDLSC, Series 24.D (aa) Russia; Series 25.D (ab), Box 298, Folder 2723.
53 Alfred T. Davies, 'Books for Prisoners', *The Times*, 29 December 1916, p. 11.
54 'Camp de Würzburg', *L'Intermède*, 14 January 1917, p. 47.
55 T. Irish, 'The "Moral Basis" of Reconstruction? Humanitarianism, Intellectual Relief, and the League of Nations, 1918–1925', *Modern Intellectual History*, 17:3 (2020), 769–800.
56 H. G. Wells, *Russia in the Shadows* (London: Hodder and Stoughton, 1920), p. 41.
57 APA, MSS B.B61, Boas, Draft of circular letter, December 1920.
58 MacNaughten to Ruml, 30 September 1926, RAC, LSRM (FA061), series 3: Appropriations, subseries 3_03, Emergency Relief, Box 10, Folder 113.
59 Irish, 'Moral Basis', 789–94.
60 Beardsley Ruml to Friedrich Schmidt-Ott, 12 January 1925, Schmidt-Ott to Ruml, 27 October 1924, RAC, LSRM (FA061), Series 3: Appropriations, Subseries 3_06, Appropriations: Social studies, Box 61, Folder 658; see E. Piller, '"Can the Science of the World Allow This?": German Academic Distress, Foreign Aid and the Cultural Demobilisation of the Academic World, 1919–1925', in T. Irish and M.-E. Chagnon (eds), *The Academic World in the Era of the Great War* (London: Palgrave Macmillan, 2018), pp. 189–212.
61 'British Committee for Aiding Men of Letters and Science in Russia', *The Athenaeum*, 7 January 1921, p. 25; Isidore Levitt, 'Relief for Russian Scientific Men', *Science*, 56:1449 (1922), p. 389.
62 Unsigned report, c. 1922, The Committee for the Rescue and Education of Russian Youth in Exile, RAC, LSRM (FA061), Series 3: Appropriations Subseries, 3_03, Emergency Relief, Box 8, Folder 94, 3.
63 R. Jinks, '"Marks Hard to Erase": The Troubled Reclamation of "Absorbed" Armenian Women, 1919–1927', *American Historical Review*, 123:1 (2018), 92.
64 J.-M. Palmier, *Weimar in Exile: The Antifascist Emigration in Europe and America* (London: Verso, 2006).
65 S. Lässig, 'Strategies and Mechanisms of Scholar Rescue: The Intellectual Migration of the 1930s Reconsidered', *Social Research*, 84:4 (2017), 782; E. J. Levine, *Allies and Rivals: German-American Exchange and the Rise of the Modern Research University* (Chicago: University of Chicago Press, 2021), p. 223.

66 Fritz Demuth to Alan Gregg, 8 April 1936, RAC, RF, Projects, SG 1.1., Series 717: Germany, Box 2, Folder 12.
67 S. Crawford, K. Ulmschneider, and J. Elsner, 'Oxford's Ark: Second World War Refugees in the Arts and Humanities', in S. Crawford, K. Ulmschneider, and J. Elsner (eds), *Ark of Civilization: Refugee Scholars and Oxford University, 1930–1945* (Oxford: Oxford University Press, 2017), p. 4.
68 A. Fair-Schulz and M. Kessler (eds), *German Scholars in Exile: New Studies in Intellectual History* (Lanham: Lexington Books, 2011); A. Grenville, *Jewish Refugees from Germany and Austria in Britain 1933–1970: Their Image in AJR Information* (London: Valentine Mitchell, 2010); E. Schwarz, 'Mass Emigration and Intellectual Exile from National Socialism: the Austrian Case', *Austrian History Yearbook*, 27 (1996), 1–20; D. Kettler, *The Liquidation of Exile Studies in the Intellectual Emigration of the 1930s* (London: Anthem Press, 2011).
69 Palmier, *Weimar in Exile*, p. 12.
70 'Walter Kotschnig to Give Lecture', *The Pomona Progress Bulletin*, 18 March 1931. 5.
71 Joseph Malherek, 'Walter Kotschnig and the German Refugee Scholar Crisis, 1933–36', Botstiber Institute for Austrian-American Studies, accessed 11 November 2022, https://botstiberbiaas.org/walter-kotschnig-and-the-scholar-crisis/.
72 G. Brewis, *A Social History of Student Volunteering: Britain and Beyond, 1880–1980* (New York: Palgrave Macmillan, 2014), p. 52.
73 'A War Time Program for the Foundation in Europe', RAC, RF, RG3, SG 3.1 and SG 3.2 (FA112), SubGroup 1: Administration Program and Policy: Relief, Series 900, Box 26, Folder 216.
74 J. Krige, *American Hegemony and the Postwar Reconstruction of Science in Europe* (Cambridge, MA: MIT Press, 2006), p. 2.
75 A. Holian, 'Displacement and the Post-War Reconstruction of Education: Displaced Persons at the UNRRA University of Munich, 1945–1948', *Contemporary European History*, 17:2 (2008), 167–95.
76 G. Tronchet, 'L'accueil des étudiants réfugiés au xxe siècle: un chantier d'histoire globale', *Monde(s)*, 15 (2019), 107–8.
77 P. Gwynne, 'George Soros Reduces Scope of His International Science Foundation', *The Scientist*, 8 January 1996, www.the-scientist.com/news/george-soros-reduces-scope-of-his-international-science-foundation-58210; G. Soros, *Soros on Soros: Staying Ahead of the Curve* (New York: John Wiley and Sons, 1995), p. 130.
78 Article 39 stipulated that '[r]epresentatives of the protecting Powers and of duly recognized and authorized relief societies may send works and collections of books to the libraries of prisoners, camps'. 'Convention relative to the Treatment of Prisoners of War. Geneva, 27 July 1929: Part III Captivity Section IV Relations of Prisoners of War with the Exterior – Art. 39, accessed 11 November 2022, https://ihl-databases.icrc.org/en/ihl-treaties/gc-pow-1929/article-17.
79 *Proceedings of the Meeting for the Study of Treaty Stipulations Relative to the Spiritual and Intellectual Needs of Prisoners of War and Civilian Internees*

(Geneva: March 1947), https://library.icrc.org/library/docs/CI/CI_1948_B3_04_ENG.pdf.
80 H. Caygill, 'Braudel's Prison Notebooks', *History Workshop Journal*, 57 (2004), 151–60.
81 UN General Assembly, Resolution 44/25, *Convention on the Rights of the Child* (20 November 1989), accessed 10 November 2022, www.unicef.org.uk/what-we-do/un-convention-child-rights/.
82 J.-J. Renoliet, *L'UNESCO oubliée: la Société des nations et la coopération intellectuelle, 1919–1946* (Paris, 1999); Irish, 'Moral Basis'.

12

The imperial 'guardians' of slavery: international humanitarianism, colonial labour policies, and the crisis of imperial governance under the League of Nations, 1919–26

Christian Müller

Introduction

'The part which Africa has played in the Great War may easily mean the greatest revolution in negro and white relationships since the commencement of the Christian era.'[1] The end of the Great War in November 1918 triggered a global wave of great expectations as to the future of the postwar international order.[2] This global momentum of new openness, based on the far-reaching claims to self-determination in Woodrow Wilson's Fourteen Points, placed into a new perspective the legitimacy of colonial governance and the labour regimes in the colonies. John H. Harris, Secretary of the Anti-Slavery and Abolitionist Society in London (ASS) was among the many non-governmental protagonists in early 1919 to expect that, in Africa and elsewhere, European civilisation and humanitarianism as claims to global moral leadership and trusteeship would be seriously tested.[3] The European empires needed to prove that they were able to integrate the humanitarian demands of a global public forum into a lasting social justice and co-operation under the nascent League of Nations. The impact of the Great War thus triggered tensions of how to align colonial policies of trusteeship to the rising demands of humanitarian activists in the public arena of post-1918 international politics. These new policies of humanitarianism had to show the potential of 'breath[ing] into the continent [of Africa and others] the breath of a new life'.[4]

This chapter shows that the topic of anti-slavery functioned as a crucial bridge to connect late nineteenth- and early twentieth-century activism in influencing statist humanitarian policies between the aspirations of European metropoles and their colonial empires after 1918. Anti-slavery activism as a moral claim for European trusteeship to spread civilisation was the driving force of nineteenth-century humanitarianism.[5] However, research has mostly consoled itself with the fact that by 1886 slavery was abolished on a global scale.[6] We know relatively little about what happened to the course of emancipation after abolition. Yet this development is vital for evaluating the legacies of this classic humanitarian cause as an element of inter-imperial competitions about civilisational missions and imperial legitimacies. In the last decades before the First World War the anti-slavery issue gained new momentum after the formal abolition of the legal status of slavery around the world in the 1880s. Private ownership over humans gave way to multiple ways of bondage and coercion that did not match the ownership of one person over another, but established a dual system of hegemonic economic command over the labour capital of individuals and social control over the physical mobilities of labourers. Slaveries after abolition persisted even if hegemonic private ownership over individuals ceased to exist.[7] Increasingly internationalised debates on the moral problem of slavery tied into the political and ideological claims of a 'new imperialism' towards Africa and Asia that promoted a civilisational lead of the European empires.[8] Research has highlighted the continuous problem of social conditions of slavery, the enforcement of civilisational hierarchies as part of the discursive fabric of anti-slavery, and the externalisation of violence.[9] The combination of moral trusteeship and civilisational responsibilities promoted paternalistic welfare of the colonies and triggered processes of competition and imitation between the European imperial powers and non-governmental Christian and philanthropic associations since the late 1880s.[10] These relations between imperial governments and civil society actors were mutually formative and depended upon each other through vivid networks of border-crossing activities that used international co-operation in different forms.[11]

In placing humanitarianism in the context of European imperialism and the challenges of a postwar order, this chapter uses the context of the League of Nations and imperial competition to understand the paradoxical notions of altruist internationalism and imperial nationalism.[12] In the last two decades research has re-evaluated the role of the League in the interwar period and explored hitherto overlooked or underestimated areas beyond the older evaluation of the League's political 'failure' in preventing a new war.[13] The social realm in particular and the contributions of the League's mission for technical and expert co-operation have triggered more balanced views on the connected relations between imperialism, internationalism, and social policies.[14] The claims to social peace as a prerequisite for a lasting international peace were prominently included as the 'third League' in the League's Covenant so that both the International Labour Organization (ILO) and the Permanent Mandates Commission (PMC) used humanitarian credentials to claim protecting the less 'advanced nations' and territories of the world from precarious labour conditions, exploitation, and slavery.[15] The rise of different international 'vulnerable' subjects protected by the League – the slave, the labourer, but also the displaced person and the child – placed imperial humanitarianism between governments and non-state advocacy lobbying under the League's agenda to set universal, imperial social standards as normative rights.

The chapter explores the relations between the Imperial Powers to 'amplify the Congo Basin Treaties' from the 1880s and 1890s under the League of Nations Covenant. It depicts humanitarian internationalism as a polycentric public movement to press for the extension of the League's social rights regime in the realm of labour and 'native welfare'.[16] A critical transnational approach towards anti-slavery in the interwar years will help identify the role of unofficial and official norm entrepreneurs in Geneva in inter-imperial and cross-border knowledge transfer and political rhetoric.[17] The mutually formative relationship between organised lobbying of anti-slavery activists, technical experts, and imperial interests brought about a social definition of slavery in 1926 while at the same time installing the old imperial powers as the humanitarian 'Guardians' of slavery.[18] Humanitarianism as seen through the prism of anti-slavery offers a laboratory of early League policy-making that negotiated the means to reconfigure the fragile imperial status of legitimate governance that the Great War unveiled as the moral and material deficit of the victorious colonial empires.[19] The challenges of the postwar world endowed the cause of anti-slavery with a new meaning as all countries participating in the League were trying to re-establish and relegitimise their claims for imperial governance under moral and humanitarian terms.

The First World War and the overstretched peace: anti-slavery humanitarianism and the crisis of empires 1914–18/19

The decades prior to the First World War saw an increasing competition between imperial anti-slavery societies that promoted their own moral claims to civilisation to challenge other empires in their achievements to humanitarian efforts in their own colonies. Humanitarianism in the form of anti-slavery movements found a moral stance to implement sensibility to suffering of others into the moral fabric of imperial governance. The British Anti-Slavery Society in particular established strong links with the Geneva-based International Bureau against Slavery to blame competing colonial powers, among them Portugal. Prewar conflicts between British Quaker claims for moral superiority and Swiss Calvinist claims for international administrative and moral leadership remained unsolved.

The First World War put a temporary hold on the inter-imperial rivalries among the Allied powers. The war profoundly affected the activities of concerted anti-slavery activism in Europe. The Allied powers drew extensively on compulsory labour and military drafts in Africa with the promise of a reorganisation of the colonial order and elements of self-government.[20] By 1917 the British ASS as the most active association focused its anti-slavery rhetoric of future imperial trusteeship on accusing Germany's colonial mismanagement. In their publications the moral claims against the German authorities likened the atrocities and the treatment of the civilian population in Belgium and northern France to the German colonial rule in Africa. Claiming that the German conduct in the occupied territories showed a neglect of the very same civilian rules signed for Africa in the General Act of Brussels in 1890, the British ASS fuelled the war propaganda of the Allied governments to accuse the German government of being unfit for legitimate colonial governance.[21]

With the entry of the United States into the war in April 1917, the possibilities for future pathways towards moral governance multiplied. Woodrow Wilson's Fourteen Points pointed towards a global recalibration of order and the abolition of traditional hierarchies. In the expectations of many African and Asian societies, the promises seemed to include a chance to overcome and order anew the prewar relations of imperial governance.[22] This included a new take on forced labour and social conditions of slavery in Africa in particular, but also in other parts of the world where the Europeans made imperial claims to imperial trusteeship.[23] At the end of the war the critique of colonial governance did not amount to expecting the end of empires but focused instead on how the great efforts of the colonies would take effect in the negotiations for an increased status of colonial regimes and their role within the empires.[24] John Harris in England started to lobby for a new colonial order under the idea of moral trusteeship in promoting his scheme of 'Native Races and Peace Terms' in January 1917 to Arthur Balfour, the British Foreign Secretary.[25] Harris and the ASS asked for a voice of the Africans in the peace negotiations mediated by the British anti-slavery movement and an international mechanism that would render practical the lofty mechanics of the Berlin and Brussels Acts of 1885 and 1892 respectively.[26] Harris's main claim was that European control of the land to end slavery and the slave trade had not worked. Therefore the British government and the new colonial order after a peace treaty had to revert to African land ownership in order to secure free and independent labour beyond unfree fake contract labour.[27]

The question of free labour directly translated into the moral claims and high expectations for a new global order of labour towards the end of the war. In early 1918 Stephan Bauer, the head of the old International Labour

Bureau in Berne, hoped for a profound translation of humanitarian into social labour rights when he claimed that the 'protection of labourers [is] an internal question of peace of primary order which will give international peace its full human and economic weight'.[28] Harris insisted that, in order to address slavery as a common malpractice and thorn in the flesh of a new global order of empires and intra-imperial labour conditions, 'civilization must therefore take heed [...] if Africa is to be saved from a future disaster. [...] Public Opinion is beginning to realize that oppression and fraud practice upon the child races of the world is an unerring boomerang.'[29] Harris with his hegemonic view joined the messianic outlook towards Woodrow Wilson as the heightened saviour to deliver the new peace settlement with a leading role of the European powers towards leading the colonies in their road to self-government. He claimed Christian duty, honour of the white races, and preservation and increase of labour supplies for the tropics as guiding issues for humanitarian imperial politics after 1919.[30] The arrival of Woodrow Wilson in France on 13 December 1918 further fuelled the hopes that finally the world would be ordered in just, equal, and peaceful terms.[31] Thus, the expectations placed in humanitarianism as a principal of new political order were almost too high to meet in reconcilable and realistic solutions.

The international anti-slavery movement had taken a serious blow from the war and by early 1919 consisted only of the British and Foreign Anti-Slavery Society and the International Bureau in Geneva. The pan-African movement added to the scattered picture and hoped to achieve its own goals under a possible new international order.[32] The leader of the National Association for the Advancement of Colored People (NAACP) and the pan-African movement, William Du Bois, and the ASS leader Harris agreed on the 'momentous event in the history of Africa' and hoped to address the question of slavery as part of the wider negotiations around the Paris Peace Conference. Yet the aims and scopes to promote international co-operation and security for Africa were a tortuous debate in Paris.[33] The main problem in colonial affairs was to legitimise the principle of trusteeship – the concept that British overseas rule and administration could claim legitimate authority and responsible government 'towards subject people'.[34] Among the high hopes for the Wilsonian ideals of equality and self-determination, transnational movements from all over the world were eagerly launching campaigns and petitioned the national delegations in Paris and Versailles. The First Pan-African Congress aligned with the British ASS and the Geneva International Bureau on the mandates question and on the demands for future African development to gain more influence on African labour conditions.[35] However, Du Bois rather championed France as the natural leader of humanity since the Enlightenment and recalled the French fight for the 'ideas of 1789' since the beginning of the war against Germany in 1914.[36]

In Paris the imperial governments shortly turned towards blaming the continuous problem of slavery in Africa on the defeated Germans and their alleged colonial malpractices. Yet, with the influx of humanitarian lobbying, the prewar inter-imperial rivalry among the victorious empires soon resurfaced. Clemenceau and other French delegates happily embraced Du Bois's argument in February 1919 to support the French victory with claims for moral leadership and humanitarianism in the colonies. Further, this argument could legitimise French punishment of the 'barbarian' Germans in the coming Peace Conference who 'acted [in their colonies] against humanity'.[37] The pan-African rhetoric was also a welcome antidote against the British allegations towards the 'badly governed colonies of France and Portugal', as Lord Robert Cecil put it.[38] Pan-African backdoor lobbying during the Paris Peace conference also implicitly criticised the US American and British colonial practices and contributed to competition between the different anti-slavery movements.[39]

Anti-slavery activism, humanitarianism, and the imperial reactions 1920–23

On 25 April 1919 the Allied Powers agreed on the mandates to form 'a sacred trust to civilization' by providing for the vast majority of the former German and Ottoman colonies 'tutelary administration'.[40] The high expectations among philanthropist networks and associations towards an international accountability of colonial governance also revived the question of slavery and abolitionism. In the Convention of Saint-Germain-en-Laye of 10 September 1919, signed next to the Peace Treaty with Austria, the Allied governments simply confirmed the Berlin and Brussels Colonial Acts without any mechanism for a future solution of slavery and the slave trade in Africa.[41] The future Director of the Mandates section, the Swiss-American internationalist William Rappard, saw the League's main challenge to 'bring the Colonial Powers, and particularly the Mandatory Powers, to live up to the pledges which they gave in accepting the Covenant'.[42] The new League in its infant phase offered a mechanism for international co-operation where 'humanitarian entrepreneurialism', enacted by single-issue movements or individuals, could influence the future work of the League.[43]

The anti-slavery issue was an essential topic in the development of the Mandates Commission from its initial stages in early 1920 to its constitutive meeting in February 1921. John Harris in particular lobbied Rappard to promote its expertise on labour and indigenous questions in Africa and parts of Asia.[44] Rappard was impressed with this entrepreneurialism of norms and lobbying of issues, signalling to Harris that the co-operation of the ASS was 'absolutely essential for the League of Nations'.[45] Both Harris and Rappard agreed that the League and non-governmental organisations should closely co-operate to implement humanitarianism through means of the new global public sphere and publicity.[46] 'The Council should have the feeling that the eyes of the world are upon it, and that it would be held to account by public opinions and by the Assembly.'[47] The ASS promoted its anti-slavery cause with an evangelical agenda on the League's secular platform, implying that a universal Protestant agenda would also help boost Britain's 'lofty moral traditions' as the leading humanitarian actor.[48] Equally the Geneva-based International Bureau aspired to become the clearing house and international secretariat of all anti-slavery associations.[49] While Harris supported Claparède and Junod, he was rather critical of a potential clash of interests when lobbying the League for a specific anti-slavery course in the preparation of the Second Pan-African Congress.[50]

When the Permanent Mandates Commission (PMC) constituted itself in early 1921, it appeared to the public as a 'spa for retired African governors'.[51] Although it was a club of former colonial officials, the integration of many members in their governments' foreign and colonial policies made the PMC harder to control and more independent than expected.[52] The anti-slavery activists tried to keep back doors open to their lobbying influence.[53] This relative openness and the constant pressure to impress the slavery issue on the League's members suggested a co-ordinated approach of the ASS, the International Bureau, and the NAACP on their anti-slavery lobbying in Geneva.[54] In 1921 Rappard even entertained the idea that a Geneva-based association should become part of the PMC, yet this position received no formal approval in the Council.[55]

The Mandates system was both a tool to legitimate the Paris territorial settlement and 'a mechanism for spreading common norms about trusteeship'.[56] The Allies were aware that through the PMC the promises made about self-determination before 1918 were put aside in favour of civilizsational tutelage, yet the different anti-slavery initiatives seemed to agree on the principle of trusteeship.[57] Internationally, the promotion of anti-slavery issues as a major topic for the League initially concentrated on the former German colonies-turned-mandates. Based on the assumption that the slavery issue in the League would focus on the reorganisation of African labour and the redistribution of former German territories, the Second Pan-African Congress in 1921 and its demands became a 'test of [the League's] sincerity in promulgating the Mandates scheme' to tackle the question of slavery.[58]

However, the different anti-slavery movements could not agree on a joint course. Their interests all fell short of complete self-government, but opposed each other in promoting specific empires in the lead of anti-slavery politics in Africa.⁵⁹ The Pan-African congresses in London, Brussels, and Paris in summer 1921 thus failed to exercise co-ordinated international pressure towards the League and specific empires.⁶⁰ Harris was careful not to involve the ASS in any far-reaching scheme that would tie the independent political ambitions within the British Empire to a general cause. He was dubious of supporting any claim for self-determination of African territories even in the careful formulation of 'local self government for backward groups [...] to complete self government under the limitations of a self governed world'.⁶¹ The NAACP claimed that in order to achieve this, 'a man of Negro descent [...] be appointed a member of the PMC as soon as a vacancy occurs'.⁶² While Drummond's secretary Baker urged to consider 'this Dubois [sic], about whom everybody is talking', Harris had severe reservations because Du Bois privileged France over Britain in the claims for humanitarian lead.⁶³

As in 1919, Du Bois and the International Bureau promoted in summer 1921 the French lead for a 'sacred trust' of the anti-slavery mission as part of the mandates, discussion by highlighting no longer German, but now British malpractices in colonial governance. 'England [...] fostered ignorance among the natives, has enslaved them and is still enslaving some of them', similarly to Portugal, Belgium, and Spain. 'France alone of the great powers has sought to place her cultured black citizens on a plane of absolute legal and social equality.'⁶⁴ Harris accused Du Bois that he 'had complicated things badly' because he and the Geneva International Bureau were 'blind to all the defects of the French government'.⁶⁵ The national and imperial competition was key to the controversy over lobbying the League among the different anti-slavery movements. This offered an opportunity to put domestic pressure on the governments to trigger action in Geneva, especially in the Assembly and the PMC.⁶⁶ In Britain the ASS took sides with the allegations of the missionary couple Haslewood that accused the British government in 1920 of tolerating slavery in Hong Kong as an 'evil perpetuated under its flag'.⁶⁷ The domestic agitation of the ASS pushed the British government to realign its anti-slavery position in the League to promote colonial governance with humanitarian characteristics.⁶⁸

From late 1922 the anti-slavery cause became a key issue for the PMC. Lobbied by the British ASS and Sir Frederick Lugard, Sir Arthur Steel-Maitland, Conservative MP and representative of New Zealand in the League, convinced the League Assembly in September 1922 that its member states had to report on slavery in their own territories for the next Assembly in August 1923.⁶⁹ The newly selected British delegate to the PMC, Lugard was quick to lead the League's anti-slavery machinery.⁷⁰ Lugard, since summer 1922 the British replacement for Ormsby-Gore in the PMC and former governor-general of Nigeria and Hong Kong, was more than 'glad to assist the League in its investigation of this subject'.[71] In his report on 'Slavery in Abyssinia' from 22 November 1922 Lugard promoted anti-slavery as a humanitarian ideal in the garments of economic interests.[72] He was well aware that Abyssinia was lying at the crossroads of commercial interests between France, Britain, and Italy in Africa. Consequently, Drummond stopped circulating the slavery memorandum after complaints from the French and Italian governments.[73] The Abyssinian case should stimulate a broader discussion that would include both slavery in all its forms and the 'allied questions of compulsory labour, paid and unpaid'.[74] The ASS followed with a petition in March 1923 to raise the 'obligations of the League with regard to the abolition of slavery'.[75]

The Abyssinia question raised again the inter-imperial competition in the League over the claims to humanitarian politics. Rappard already indicated the problem in December 1922 that governments would be 'naturally very sensitive and would resist any reflection which a broader interpretation of the term of slavery might cast on their administration'.[76] The British Foreign Office, which faced new domestic contestation over the slavery issue in the Empire in both Africa and Asia, became more reluctant in 1923.[77] Most governments, like the British, did not want to expose their own labour practices and possible problems of slavery and forced labour in the colonies. Drummond lamented in April 1923 that the replies to the Council's slavery questionnaire 'contain either no information or too meagre information to serve as a basis' for a Council report.[78]

The reluctance to adopt an open policy on the slavery issue found another expression in the tightened access of non-governmental organisations to the League's institutions. Although Rappard and Drummond expected the anti-slavery discussions would have 'great public influence [...] that some definite steps shall be taken to stop the abuse', they became increasingly reluctant to countenance non-governmental influence on issues involving imperial sovereignty.[79] The demands from the International Bureau and the ASS certainly claimed to extend the competence and responsibility of a future commission or organisation.[80] In July 1923 the Council restricted free access of non-governmental organisations to provide evidence and stir campaigns within the League except through their own national governments.[81] This marked a turning point in the social and humanitarian work of the League as it narrowed the fluid influence of non-governmental organisations to official government channels and promoted the official position of the PMC as the authoritative voice of imperial sovereignty.[82] The active norm entrepreneurs of the international associations needed to find new ways of influencing policy-making after July 1923. The structural manifestation of channels of influence ended the League's open phase of dialogue between non-governmental organisations and governmental representatives and led to a more formalised procedure of information channel and lobbying opportunities into the League.

The Temporary Slavery Commission and the road to the Convention 1924–26

The stricter formalisation of access to the League indicated that governments were careful to control channels of information and influence on humanitarian matters. The shift represented the quest of the empires to retain the established civilisational hierarchies. It was an attempt to formalise and guard the relatively open and improvised League as a permanent *Hotel de Genève* with its informal meetings in hotel rooms and lobbies. In July 1923 Flora Shaw, Lord Lugard's wife, noted that dinner conversations in Geneva focused on the question of 'how to defend the best results of western civilization from the attacks likely enough to be made by degenerate Europeans and inferior races'.[83] The members of the PMC, among them Lord Lugard, believed 'in their civilizing mission and in their right to rule'.[84] Lugard's doctrine of the 'dual mandate', although authoritarian and paternalistic, promised progressive development of the colonies and mandates to legitimise imperial governance at its severe contestation.[85]

The governments were reluctant to release any details on slavery and labour conditions in their own territories to keep the power of information. In an influential article in *The New Statesman* in August 1923 Harris ventilated his frustration with 'certain Powers' – mostly Portugal and Britain – to place before the League 'material known to be in the pigeonholes of Foreign Offices'.[86] Triggered by the discussions about Abyssinia and the continuous pressure from the non-governmental organisations, the Assembly decided to establish a temporary commission that would prepare a slavery report for September 1924.[87] The nature and composition of this commission would determine the outcome of slavery question under the League. Harris had proposed in January 1923 'an organisation composed chiefly of the Mandates Section, ILO, and the Anti-Slavery Bureau, but with the addition of one or two representatives from unofficial bodies'.[88] Rappard likewise wanted an independent expert body under his PMC, fearing that 'the commission would be paralysed in its work' if delegates purely represented their own governments.[89] Independence and technical expertise should overcome inter-imperial competition of prestige.

The slavery question as a matter of labour regimes touched upon the International Labour Office. Harold Grimshaw, chief of the ILO diplomatic section, asked to assign the task of a slavery inquiry to the ILO as the League's organisation to deal with labour conditions.[90] With its motto to establish world peace through social justice, the ILO had worked since 1920 towards the standardisation of labour regimes with a European bias.[91] Grimshaw was keen to transfer the slavery question to the ILO in order to expand its expertise in non-European labour issues.[92] The League, however, did not follow this suggestion and established the Temporary Slavery Commission (TSC) under the PMC for two years.

The TSC was supposed to mirror the character of the PMC as an 'independent body of experts' that critically assessed evidence on slavery.[93] It comprised representatives from Britain, France, Italy, Portugal, Belgium, and the Netherlands, mostly former colonial officers and some also members of the PMC.[94] This overlap made their position on slavery complicated because the Foreign and Colonial Offices of their own countries tried to influence the slavery discussions through them.[95] Next to Grimshaw for the ILO, Rappard aimed at including two more independent members, Dantès Bellegarde from Haiti and Henri Junod as head of the International Bureau. 'As most of the members [...] will doubtless more or less directly represent governments, the co-operation of two purely disinterested friends of the natives would, I believe, greatly strengthen the commission.'[96] Drummond was sceptical about Junod: 'I am not sure that it is a wise plan to put representatives of organisations on Committees of this kind.'[97] The Council, following Drummond's advice, nominated Dantès Bellegarde 'for political reasons', but failed to select Junod.[98]

The TSC considered themselves experts in the field of slavery, but they needed independent information from unofficial channels.[99] The Committee was anxious not to subvert the principles of state sovereignty through information-gathering from non-governmental organisations and private associations. Some governments like Switzerland and Britain only reluctantly acknowledged the reliable character of some organisations because they would assume 'full responsibility' for the replies of people the Foreign Offices considered 'thundering nuisances'.[100] Because of these problems the TSC oscillated between independent expertise and national competition for prestige. Especially Lugard and his Portuguese counterpart envisaged the groundwork for a 'charter defining what the Commission considered as just and humane towards the natives'.[101] Although Rappard reminded the TSC about the purely international character of the Covenant, the delegates agreed that article 22 offered an entry point into internal politics. 'The question of slavery was a humanitarian question of international interest, which would be made the object of a general treaty to which the Council [...] could ask all states to adhere.'[102] Lugard wanted to include compulsory labour so that his concept of free wage labour for Africa was emanating from the discussion. The Commission should not 'show hesitation' and should inquire into the question of slavery from every point of view without taking too much notice of the 'susceptibilities of the governments'.[103]

The discussions about the nature of information from competent and trustworthy organisation revived the inter-imperial competition of status in 1924 and 1925.[104] Both in the TSC and in the Mandates Commission on African labour and free labour, the humanitarian competition of empires included anti-slavery agitation from non-governmental sources. While some members feared the allegations and propaganda of national associations against other nations, Bellegarde pointed out that it 'was not altogether reasonable to rely entirely on the governments in order to obtain the complete truth in respect to the facts. [...] Certain governments, careful of their reputation, might perhaps refuse to reply.'[105] The quest for independent expertise involved an aspect of imperial competition, because some members acted 'as national representatives rather than as "independent" international experts' to stage this inter-imperial competition over the moral lead of the League.[106] The main protagonists were Lugard for Britain, Freire de Andrade for Portugal, and Delafosse for France. Lugard impressed Rappard by his rigorous approach and remained in close liaison with Harris and the ASS, and he paraded his understanding of anti-slavery humanitarianism in the context of his book *Dual Mandate*.[107] Writing in 1922 as an application for his position in the PMC, Lugard promoted a paternalistic approach to educating Africans towards free labour and gradual self-government by placing the moral and material wellbeing of Africans above the utility for the European empires.[108] Both in the PMC and the TSC Lugard attempted to challenge and isolate Portugal over its practices in Angola and Mozambique.[109]

The controversy between Lugard and Freire de Andrade, and to a lesser extent Maurice Delafosse, reached its peak in 1925. Lugard supported the ASS memorandum on slavery to the League in May 1925 and drafted the Anti-Slavery Convention based on the ASS report.[110] Discussions arose from the inclusion of forced labour as a malpractice amounting to modern slavery. Portugal and France strictly opposed the inclusion of state-forced development programmes under the slavery definition, especially because Freire de Andrade argued that Africans were naturally lazy and should be 'forced to work' for their development of civilisation.[111] The work by the US American E. A. Ross published in 1925, criticising Portuguese practices, further fuelled the controversy.[112] Although Lugard himself remained an independent expert, his position fitted neatly with the ASS's and the Foreign Office's attempt to display Britain's moral leadership, and to leave Portugal, France, and Belgium exposed to defend their colonial practices, especially forced labour.[113] The draft for a Slavery Convention listed various forms of ownership, coercive labour, and forced labour yet seemed too challenging for the diplomats. Lord Robert Cecil, one of the architects of the League, presented a weaker draft to the Sixth Commission of the Assembly in autumn 1925, leaving out in his speech Lugard's emphasis on forced and free labour.[114] In response the Assembly nominated a draft Convention committee and tasked the British, French, Italian, Portuguese, and Dutch delegates to review the British proposal. Albrecht Gohr wrote to Lugard that they could only 'hope for a general minimum convention as fruit of their commission', but tried to defend the main ideas behind the scenes with the subcommittee on the draft convention.[115]

The Slavery Convention in 1926 provided the League of Nations with a wide definition of slavery and the tools to interpret its meaning.[116] The Convention added slaves to the increasing list of international vulnerable subjects officially worth of humanitarian action and legal protection on an international scale. Slavery was defined as a social 'status or condition of a person over whom any or all of the powers attaching to the right of ownership are exercised'. The legal definition did not enumerate or identify specific forms of slavery or slave-like conditions and remained open to many interpretations of the actual status of labour and labourers. Another success of the European empires was the exclusion of forced labour that was referred to the ILO for a special Forced Labour Convention (signed in 1930).[117] The Convention was a commitment to progressive abolition without specific periods and thus placed the empires in charge of its implementation. The principle of the Berlin and Brussels Acts to respect national and imperial sovereignty prevailed. The Convention did not address the question of how to identify and exchange information on slavery and neglected claims of an international bureau. Yet the convention highlighted the commitment to implement the third 'League' on social and humanitarian issues while in turn empowering the European empires to exercise imperial trusteeship with their own yardsticks of social peace and justice. The League's key powers reinstalled themselves as the imperial guardians of slavery through a monopolisation of the humanitarian framework under their respective sovereignties.

Conclusion: the imperial guardians of slavery. The International Slavery Convention, humanitarianism, and the legitimacy of empires

In 1918–19 the victorious empires Britain, France, Portugal, Italy, and to a lesser extent Belgium and the Netherlands, renewed their claim to rule legitimately over vast parts of the world on moral and humanitarian grounds. During the early 1920s the classic humanitarian cause of emancipation developed into a tool to readjust moral politics of imperial governance. Using Imperial Germany as a scapegoat for failed imperial practices, the remaining empires renewed the classic civilisational rhetoric of imperialism stemming from the 1880s and 1890s to strengthen the claim to imperial trusteeship in 1919. Humanitarian internationalist associations shaped this humanitarian momentum to promote continuous legitimacy of imperial governance with religious and moral overtones.

The chances of humanitarianism after 1919 consisted in experimenting with the new Geneva system in which the volatile outset of a League as a permanent *Hotel de Genève* fostered lobbying and informal negotiating until the mid-1920s. Yet this open situation for humanitarian lobbying did not result in a more open situation of pushing a humanitarian solution against slavery. Anti-slavery humanitarianism embedded in the competition of imperial identifications and imaginations was in itself inherently pro-colonial and pro-establishment. The non-governmental humanitarian organisations assisted in rejuvenating this imperial rule of trust and moral and material development by reviving the pre-war imperial competitions over moral leadership from within the European metropoles. The shift from international collaboration to national prestige and imperial competition highlighted broader political tendencies of nationalism and ideological tensions in the mid-1920s and revived trends underlying late nineteenth-century and pre-war international humanitarianism. The anti-slavery issue helped to strengthen moral claims of good governance in a humanitarian inter-imperial competition. In particular the British Empire, with Lugard as its main international figure in Geneva, lectured the Portuguese and French on their role in the civilisational development of the rest of the world.

The 1926 Slavery Convention contributed to the tensions between humanitarian universalism and interested benevolent imperialism. The diplomats in the League established themselves as the 'guardians' of slavery under the League by defining slavery in terms that would not harm the European claims to imperial trusteeship or scrutinise their colonial labour practices. Anti-slavery as part of the League's social and labour regimes did not result in an increase in international and inter-imperial co-operation or a rise of altruistic humanitarianism. On the contrary, after 1919 imperial humanitarianism as a facet of non-governmental internationalism re-enforced imperial claims to national superiority on moral grounds that aligned with governmental strategies to strengthen imperial governance. Anti-slavery humanitarianism as imperial vehicle left a legacy of civilisational hierarchies with moral and religious overtones that lasted into the post-Second World War period of decolonisation and influenced with its humanitarian rhetoric the underlying inequalities in the politics of development.

Notes

1 J. H. Harris, 'African Reconstruction after the War', *The Missionary Review of the World*, 32:2 (1919), 103.
2 J. Leonhard, *Der überforderte Friede:. Versailles und die Welt, 1918–1923* (Munich: Beck, 2018).
3 Harris, 'African Reconstruction', 104.
4 J. H. Harris, *Africa: Slave or Free?* 2nd ed. (New York: Dutton, 1920), p. 244; see A. Ribi [Forclaz], '"The Breath of a New Life"? British Anti-Slavery Activism and the League of Nations', in D. Laqua (ed.), *Internationalism Reconfigured: Transnational Ideas and Movements between the World Wars* (London: Tauris, 2011), pp. 93–113; A. Ribi Forclaz, *Humanitarian Imperialism: The Politics of Anti-Slavery Activism, 1880–1940* (Oxford: Oxford University Press, 2015).
5 S. Salvatici, *A History of Humanitarianism, 1755–1989*, trans. P. Sanders (Manchester: Manchester University Press, 2019), pp. 6–7, pp. 25–31.
6 J. Osterhammel, *The Transformation of the World: A Global History of the Nineteenth Century*, trans. P. Camiller (Princeton and Oxford: Princeton University Press, 2014), p. 101, pp. 185–7, pp. 212–19, pp. 1057–82.
7 M. Zeuske, *Handbuch Geschichte der Sklaverei*, 2nd ed. (Berlin: de Gruyter, 2019), vol. I, p. 499, vol. II, pp. 970–1; S. Miers, *Slavery in the Twentieth Century* (Walnut Creek: AltaMira Press, 2003), p. 33; S. Dresher, *Abolition: A History of Slavery and Antislavery* (Cambridge: Cambridge University Press, 2009), pp. 371–411; F. Cooper, 'Conditions Analogous to Slavery: Imperialism and Free Labor Ideology in Africa', in F. Cooper, T. C. Holt, and R. J. Scott (eds), *Beyond Slavery: Explorations of Race, Labor, and Citizenship* (Chapel Hill: University of North Carolina Press, 2000), pp. 107–50; F. Cooper, 'From Free Labor to Family Allowances: Labor and African Society in Colonial Discourse', *American Ethnologist*, 16:4 (1989), 745–65.
8 D. Laqua, 'The Tensions of Internationalism: Transnational Anti-Slavery in the 1880s and 1890s', *International History Review*, 33:4 (2011), 705–26.
9 Osterhammel, *Transformation*, p. 837; S. Miers and R. L. Roberts, 'Introduction', in S. Miers and R. L. Roberts (eds), *The End of Slavery in Africa* (Madison: University of Wisconsin Press, 1988), pp. 1–15; J.-G. Deutsch, *Emancipation without Abolition in German East Africa, c. 1884–1914* (Oxford: Oxford University Press, 2006), pp. 7–8; Cooper, 'Conditions Analogous to Slavery', 108; S. Miers, 'Slavery and the Slave Trade as International Issues 1890–1939', *Slavery & Abolition*, 19:2 (1998), 16–37.
10 M. Jerónimo and J. Monteiro, 'Internationalism and the Labours of the Portuguese Colonial Empire (1945–1974)', *Portuguese Studies*, 29:2 (2013), 144; Ribi, *Imperialism*, p. 1.
11 Drescher, *Abolition*, p. 407; Ribi, *Imperialism*, p. 3.
12 M. Barnett, *Empire of Humanity: A History of Humanitarianism* (Ithaca: Cornell University Press, 2011), p. 7; R. Skinner and A. Lester, 'Humanitarianism and Empire: New Research Agendas', *The Journal of Imperial and Commonwealth*

History, 40:5 (2012), 738–9; S. Miers, 'Humanitarianism at Berlin: Myth or Reality', in S. Förster, W. J. Mommsen, and R. Robinson (eds), *Bismarck, Europe and Africa: The Berlin Africa Conference 1884–1885 and the Onset of Partition* (Oxford: Oxford University Press, 1988), pp. 333–45; Ribi, *Imperialism*, pp. 6–7; Ribi, 'Breath', p. 94.

13 S. Pedersen, 'Back to the League of Nations?', *American Historical Review*, 112:4 (2007), 1091–117; P. Clavin, 'Europe and the League of Nations', in R. Gerwarth (ed.), *Twisted Paths: Europe, 1914–1945* (Oxford: Oxford University Press, 2007), pp. 325–54; K. Dykmann and K. Naumann, 'Changes from the "Margins:" Non-European Actors, Ideas and Strategies in International Organisations', *Comparativ*, 23:4/5 (2013), 12.

14 J. Van Daele, 'The International Labour organisation (ILO) in Past and Present Research', *International Review of Social History*, 53:3 (2008), 485–511; Pedersen, 'Back to the League', 1111–13; S. Pedersen, *The Guardians: The League of Nations and the Crisis of Empire* (Oxford: Oxford University Press, 2015), pp. 9–12.

15 W. Rappard, *International Relations as Viewed from Geneva* (New Haven: Yale University Press, 1925), pp. 17–20. See Miers, 'Slavery', 16–37; Ribi, *Imperialism*, pp. 6–8; Pedersen, *Guardians*, pp. 8–9; D. Maul, *The International Labour Organisation: 100 Years of Global Social Policy* (Berlin: de Gruyter, 2019), p. 3.

16 Memorandum Frederick Lugard to the British Government, n.d., Bodleian Library, Oxford [hereafter BOD], Mss Lugard, L 98/1. K. Grant, 'Christian Critics of Empire: Missionaries, Lantern Lectures, and the Congo Reform Campaign in Britain', *Journal of Imperial and Commonwealth History*, 29:2 (2001), 52.

17 P. Clavin, 'Time, Manner, Place: Writing Modern European History in Global, Transnational and International Context', *European History Quarterly*, 40:4 (2010), 626; D. Gorman, *The Emergence of International Society in the 1920s* (Cambridge: Cambridge University Press, 2012), p. 18.

18 W. Rappard, *The Geneva Experiment* (Oxford: Oxford University Press, 1931), p. 58.

19 Leonhard, Der *überforderte Friede*, pp. 522–38, pp. 708–15.

20 Z. Steiner, *The Lights that Failed: European International History 1919–1933* (Oxford: Oxford University Press, 2007), pp. 1–11; H. Jones, 'International or Transnational? Humanitarian Action during the First World War', *European Review of History*, 16:5 (2009), 697–713.

21 British Anti-Slavery Society, *Slavery in Europe: A Letter to Neutral Governments from the Anti-Slavery Society* (London: Anti-Slavery Society, 1917).

22 J. Leonhard, *Die Büchse der Pandora: Geschichte des Ersten Weltkriegs* (Munich: Beck, 2014), pp. 1005–6.

23 W. E. B. Du Bois to US War Department, 27 November 1918, W. E. B. Du Bois Papers (MS 312), Special Collections and University Archives, University of Massachusetts Amherst Libraries [quoted as Du Bois Papers (MS 312)]. Leonhard, *Der überforderte Friede*, p. 523, p. 526.

24 R. Aldrich and C. Hilliard, 'The French and British Empires', in J. Horne (ed.), *A Companion to World War I* (Oxford: Oxford University Press, 2010), pp. 531–4.
25 *Anti-Slavery Reporter and Aborigines' Friend* [*ASRAF*], V 6:2 (July 1916), 34–46; [John H. Harris], *Native Races and Peace Terms* (London: Anti-Slavery Society, 1917).
26 [Harris], *Native Races*, pp. 3–4; *ASFAR* V 9:1 (April 1919), 2–9; Foreign Office Correspondence with Harris, November 1918 to February 1919, BOD, Anti-Slavery Papers [ASP], Mss Brit. Emp. S 18 C 166, fols 181–7.
27 *ASRAF* V 7:3 (October 1917), 50–9; [Harris], *Native Races*, pp. 4–5.
28 S. Bauer, *Arbeiterschutz und Völkergemeinschaft* (Zurich: Orell Füssli, 1918), p. 3. For the German hopes to utilise the 'humanitarian' issue of labour with Bauer's influence through the International Labour Office to ameliorate their position at the Paris Peace Conference see the correspondence in December 1918 between the German Embassy in Berne and the Foreign Office: Politisches Archiv des Auswärtigen Amtes Berlin (PAAA), Gesandtschaft Bern, RAV 26-1-1354.
29 Harris, 'African Reconstruction', 104, 108.
30 Harris, 'African Reconstruction'.
31 Leonhard, *Büchse der Pandora*, p. 977; Leonhard, *Der überforderte Friede*, pp. 522–3, pp. 1172–5; Sluga, *Internationalism*, p. 47.
32 W. E. B. Du Bois, Memoranda on the future of Africa, c. January 1919. Du Bois Papers (MS 312); C. G. Contee, 'Du Bois, the NAACP, and the Pan-African Congress of 1919', *The Journal of Negro History*, 57:1 (1972), 13–28; E. Manela, *The Wilsonian Moment: Self-Determination and the International Origins of Anticolonial Nationalism* (Oxford: Oxford University Press, 2007), p. 12, p. 123.
33 W. E. B. Du Bois, 'Opinion – My Mission', *The Crisis*, 18:1 (May 1919), 8; *ASRAF* V 12:4 (October 1918), 63–9; Sluga, *Internationalism*, pp. 47–9; Ribi, *Imperialism*, p. 46.
34 J. Darwin, 'Imperialism in Decline? Tendencies in British Imperial Policy between the Wars', *Historical Journal*, 23:3 (1980), 657–8; Ribi, *Imperialism*, p. 47.
35 Harris, *Africa: Slave or Free*, pp. 246–53; Du Bois, Memorandum to Blaise Diagne and Resolutions of the Pan-African Congress, 21 February 1919, and Claparède to Du Bois, 16 February 1919, Du Bois Papers (MS 312).
36 Du Bois, Memorandum Confidentiel pour MM. Diagne et Candace, January 1919, Du Bois Papers (MS 312).
37 Diagne, Speech at the First Pan-African Congress, Paris 1919, Du Bois Papers (MS 312). See the staunch rebuttal against German slavery on the basis of Wilson's fourteen points, no. 5: Africanus [Ludwig Scholz], *The Adjustment of the German Colonial Claims: Dedicated to the American and British Delegates of the Peace Conference* (Berne: n.p., 1918), p. 5, pp. 7–9.
38 Pedersen, *Guardians*, p. 28.
39 S. Dunstan, 'Conflicts of Interest: The 1919 Pan-African Congress and the Wilsonian Moment', *Callaloo*, 39:1 (2016), 136–7, 139.

40 K. Grant, *A Civilised Savagery: Britain and the New Slaveries in Africa, 1884–1926* (New York and London: Routledge, 2005), pp. 135–66; M. Mazower, *No Enchanted Palace: The End of Empire and the Ideological Origins of the United Nations* (Princeton: Princeton University Press, 2001), pp. 28–56; Gorman, *Emergence*, pp. 21–51.
41 'Convention [... of] Saint-Germain-en-Laye, September 10, 1919', in *League of Nations Treaty Series*, VIII (1922), 27–38 (art. 11; 35–7), https://treaties.un.org/doc/Publication/UNTS/LON/Volume%208/v8.pdf.
42 Rappard to Harris, 24 December 1920, League of Nations Archives Geneva [LoN], S 265.
43 Steiner, *Lights*, p. 349; Ribi, *Imperialism*, pp. 48–9; Pedersen, 'Back to the League', 1111; Pedersen, *Guardians*, p. 46.
44 Harris to Rappard, 21 December 1920, LoN, S 265; Ribi, *Imperialism*, pp. 50–3; Ribi, 'Breath', 98–9.
45 Rappard to Harris, 2 and 11 January 1921, LoN, S 265.
46 Rappard to Harris, 11 November 1921, LoN, S 265; Ribi, *Imperialism*, p. 54.
47 Rappard to Harris, 31 January 1921, LoN, S 265.
48 *ASFAR* V 11:3 (October 1921), 74.
49 R. Claparède and E. Mercier-Glardon, *Un bureau international pour la défense des indigènes* (Geneva: n.p., 1917), p. 6; *ASFAR* V 9:1 (April 1919), 9; Claparède to Du Bois, 3 May 1921, DuBois Papers (MS 312).
50 Ribi, *Imperialism*, pp. 55–7.
51 Pedersen, *Guardians*, p. 62.
52 Rappard to Harris, 17 October 1921, LoN, S 265; Pedersen, *Guardians*, pp. 62–3.
53 Harris to Rappard, 20 December 1920, LoN, S 265; Claparède to Du Bois, 8 March 1921, DuBois Papers (MS 312); *ASFAR* V 11:1 (April 1921), 3–6.
54 Harris to Rappard, 6 January 1921, LoN, S 265.
55 Harris to Claparède, 20 September 1920, BOD, ASP, Mss Brit. Emp. S 22, G 471; Rappard to Mercier-Glardon, 25 January 1921, LoN, R 6.
56 Pedersen, *Guardians*, p. 77.
57 Ibid.; Ribi, *Imperialism*, pp. 56–7.
58 Claparède to DuBois, Geneva 8 March 1921, Du Bois Papers (MS 312); *ASFAR* V 11:3 (October 1921), 104.
59 Ribi, *Imperialism*, pp. 57–8, argues that the main conflict was about self-determination. Yet the conflict arose in championing specific nations.
60 Du Bois to Harris, 26 May 1921 and Harris to Du Bois, 16 July 1921, BOD, ASP, Mss Brit. Emp. S 22 G 432.
61 *The Crisis*, 23:1 (November 1921), 8; Johnston to Buxton, 21 January 1922, BOD, ASP, Mss Brit. Emp. S 22, G 444.
62 *The Crisis*, 23:1 (November 1921), 8, 18.
63 Pedersen, *Guardians*, p. 61.
64 'Manifesto to the League of Nations', *The Crisis*, 23:1 (1921), 7–8, 18.
65 Harris to Junod, 29 July 1921, and Harris to Lord Mayo, 17 October 1921, BOD, ASP, Mss Brit. Emp. S 22, G 432.

66 Rappard to Harris, 17 October 1921, LoN, S 265.
67 S. Pedersen, 'The Maternalist Moment in British Colonial Policy: The Controversy over "Child Slavery" in Hong Kong, 1817–1941', *Past & Present*, 171:1 (2001), 162, 165, 170.
68 *ASRAF* V 12:1 (April 1922), 7; Pedersen, 'Maternalist Moment', 162, 168, 172.
69 Ribi, *Imperialism*, p. 63.
70 'Lugard and Abyssinia', in *Westminster Gazette*, 5 May 1922; Drummond to Rappard, 2 December 1922, LoN, S 1669, 5; Harris to Lugard, 29 January 1923, BOD, ASP, Mss Brit. Emp. S22, G 444; J. H. Harris, *Freeing the Slaves* (London: Anti-Slavery Society, 1925), p. 1; Lady Lugard to E. J. Lugard, 22 July 1923, BOD, Mss Lugard, L 119/4, fols 9–10.
71 Lugard to Drummond, 10 November 1922, LoN, R 61.
72 Lugard to Drummond, 6 and 10 November 1922, enclosed 'Memorandum on Slavery in Abyssinia', LoN, R 61; H. Darley and N. A. Dyce-Sharp, *Slave Trading and Slave Owning in Abyssinia* (London: n.p., 1922), p. 9.
73 Drummond to Lugard, 22 November 1922, LoN, R 61; Rappard to Drummond, 6 December 1922, LoN, S 1669, 5.
74 Lugard to Drummond, 22 December 1922, LoN, R 61.
75 Harris to Rappard, 16 January 1923, LoN, R 62; Anti-Slavery and Aborigines Protection Society, *Slavery and the Obligations of the League of Nations* (London: Anti-Slavery Society, 1923), enclosed in Harris to Rappard, 26 March 1923, LoN, R 62; *ASRAF* V 13:3 (October 1923), 99–104.
76 Rappard to Drummond, 30 December 1922, LoN, R61.
77 Drummond to Lugard, 22 November 1922, LoN, R 61; Rappard to Drummond, 30 December 1922, LoN, S 1669, 5; Ronald McNeill, HC Deb 19 July 1923 vol. 166 c2503; BOD, Mss Lugard, L 105/1.
78 Drummond Aide-Memoire for Council, 16 April 1923, LoN, R 62. Miers, *Slavery*, 101–2.
79 Rappard to Drummond, 4 December 1922, LoN, R 61.
80 Harris to Rappard, 16 January 1923, LoN, R 62; Memorandum International Bureau to Drummond, 3 August 1923, LoN, R 64.
81 Rappard to Harris, 18 August 1923, LoN, S 1669, 3; League of Nations, *Official Journal (Council)*, 4:8 (1923), 938; *ASRAF* V 13:3 (October 1923), 99.
82 League of Nations, *Official Journal (Council)*, 5:7 (1924), 909.
83 Flora Shaw, Lady Lugard to Major E. J. Lugard, 29 July 1923, BOD, Mss Lugard, L 119/4.
84 Pedersen, *Guardians*, p. 107.
85 Rappard to Lugard, 12 February 1923, LoN, R 6, 1/10005/248, jacket 1; F. Lugard, *The Dual Mandate in British Tropical Africa* (Edinburgh and London: Blackwood, 1922), pp. 48–58, p. 197, p. 217, p. 229; Pedersen, *Guardians*, p. 108.
86 J. H. H[arris], 'Slavery and the Foreign Office', *The New Statesman*, 4 August 1923, 49–50; BOD, ASP, Brit. Emp. S 22, G 447. Rappard had already

circulated the information before the print; see Rappard to Harris, 31 May 1923, LoN, S 265.
87 *ASFAR* V 13:4 (January 1924), 147.
88 Harris to Rappard, 16 January 1923, LoN, R 62.
89 Rappard to Drummond, 14 March 1924, LoN, R 70 (on the Belgian nomination). The letters of Flora Shaw, Lady Lugard, however present a critical view of informed expertise even from within the PMC: Lady Lugard to E. J. Lugard, 29 July 1923, BOD, Mss Lugard, L 119/4, fols 15f.
90 Grimshaw to Harris, 4 February 1924, BOD, ASP, Mss Brit. Emp. S 22, G 446.
91 J. P. Daughton, 'ILO Expertise and Colonial Violence in the Interwar Years', in S. Kott and, J. Droux (eds), *Globalizing Social Rights: The ILO and Beyond* (Basingstoke: Palgrave, 2013), pp. 85–97.
92 D. Maul, *Human Rights, Development and Decolonization: The International Labour organisation 1940–1970* (Basingstoke: Palgrave, 2012), pp. 17–27.
93 Ribi, *Imperialism*, p. 71.
94 Miers, *Slavery*, pp. 102–6.
95 Ribi, *Imperialism*, p. 71; for a different assessment of the PMC see Pedersen, *Guardians*, pp. 61–5.
96 Claparède to Rappard, 13 May 1924, and Rappard to Drummond, 15 May 1924, LoN, R 64.
97 Drummond to Rappard, 15 May 1924, LoN, R 64.
98 Drummond to Rappard, 15 May 1924, LoN, R 64.
99 Minutes of the First Session of the Temporary Slavery Commission, First meeting, Geneva, 9 July 1924, LoN A.18.1924.VI [quoted as *TSCM*], 6–7.
100 Rappard to Drummond, 11 January 1924, LoN, R 62; Harris to Darley, 4 May 1925, BOD, ASP, Mss Brit. Emp., S 22, G 447.
101 *TSCM* 1, 10.
102 *TSCM* 1, 10–11.
103 *TSCM* 1, 19–20, 25.
104 *TSCM* 1, 17–19; *TSCM* 2, 18–21.
105 *TSCM* 1, 18.
106 Grimshaw to Harris, 9 and 12 February 1925, BOD, ASP, Mss Brit. Emp., S 22, G 446.
107 Harris to Grimshaw, 1 June 1923, and Rappard to Secretary General Drummond, 26 April 1924, LoN, R 70.
108 Lugard, *Dual Mandate*, p. 5, pp. 57–8, p. 217. Rappard referred to the book in 1923 as 'the bible' of the PMC. Flora Shaw to E. J. Lugard, 22 July 1923, BOD, Mss Lugard, L 119/4, fol. 10.
109 *Minutes of the Permanent Mandates Commission* [PMCM] Session 5, 27–8; PMCM 6, 47–50; PMCM 7, 194–205; LoN, R 74; *TSCM* 2, 18–19, 84.
110 Anti-Slavery and Aborigines Protection Society, *The Abolition of Slavery: Appeal to the League of Nations* (London: Anti-Slavery Society, 1925), p. 4; Ribi, *Imperialism*, p. 73.
111 *TSCM* 2, 84; *PMCM* 7, 194–205.

112 E. A. Ross, *Report on Employment of Native Labor in Portuguese Africa* (New York: Abbot, 1925), pp. 58–60; Gilchrist to Harris, 22 March 1926, LoN, R 62. See M. Jerónimo, *The 'Civilising Mission' of Portuguese Colonialism, 1870–1930* (London: Palgrave, 2015), pp. 134–94.
113 Pedersen, *Guardians*, p. 238.
114 Lugard, 'Origins of the Slavery Committee', n.d., BOD, Mss Lugard, L 98/2, 6, 8; J. Allain, *The Slavery Conventions* (Leiden: Brill, 2008), pp. 31–166; Miers, *Slavery*, pp. 121–33; Miers, 'Slavery', 28.
115 Gohr to Lugard, 30 September 1925, BOD, Mss Lugard, L 101/1.
116 'Slavery Convention': adopted 25 September 1926 (accessed 19 August 2022), www.ohchr.org/en/professionalinterest/pages/slaveryconvention.aspx.
117 Miers, *Slavery*, pp. 134–52.

Afterword

Branden Little

Since the centenary of the First World War and the strategically timed publication of a special issue of *First World War Studies* in 2014, historians have intensified greatly their investigations into humanitarianism. As the chapters in *Humanitarianism and the Greater War* reveal, a decade of scholarly conversations has produced tremendous insights into the historical contours of saving lives and rebuilding war-torn societies. But even as historians uncover new facets of the past, there remains sharp differences of interpretative emphasis and even difficulties in obtaining agreement about basic definitions.

Historians disagree about whether and to what extent the actions of aid givers should be praised. Celebratory narratives emphasise that the delivery of aid was exceedingly improbable because bitter rivalries divided the warring coalitions. Any relief materials delivered whatsoever, according to this interpretation, constituted a moral victory. Lives were spared because of humanitarian intervention. Such histories ask how much more horrific the war would have been had it not been for campaigns against famine, disease, imprisonment, and homelessness. These preponderantly positive accounts have become less prominent than they once were, submerged by a rising tide of treatments by Davide Rodogno, Keith Watenpaugh, Silvia Salvatici, and Agnieszka Sobocinska, among other luminaries, that suggest that the best intentions of individuals or aid agencies often went awry.[1] Yet some of the complexity narratives, if we elect to label them as such, also adhere to an alt-celebratory fixation. They focus on horror rather than heroics, on starvation blockades, genocide, pandemic diseases, malnutrition-induced deformity, and mass displacement of peoples from their homes. In these stark interpretations humanitarian action achieved little in a world consumed by violence and hate. Humanitarians themselves were not saints but flawed people, frequently racist, and incessantly self-serving.

Historians also struggle to define the terms 'humanitarian' and 'humanitarianism' in a way that is concise and satisfying. If defining these terms distracts or detracts from research, perhaps we should develop surrogates to describe the ideologies, methods, and implications of intervention. Previously I have proposed concepts that characterised certain humanitarian sensibilities. Americans delighted in rescuing others from the flames of war as self-appointed 'firemen of the world'. They relished transforming other nations through acts perceived as 'redemptive interventionism'. And they adapted administrative techniques used by societies engaged in industrialised killing as 'analogues of war' that became effective 'humanitarian countermeasures'. Whether these phrases have any merit at all is less important than the need to continue to probe the contours of what we mean by the use of such loaded terms as 'humanitarian' and 'humanitarianism'.[2]

The inability to define these terms has pernicious consequences. Historians disagree about whether or not humanitarianism in the era of the First World War advanced human-rights advocacy.[3] This lack of consensus appears to amplify the bitter divide over aid work and its legitimacy today. Convinced nations singularly pursue strategic interests and insincerely frame their policies as humanitarian; many practitioners and ethicists view all aid as suspect. Historians have appropriated much of that critical awareness.[4] Even our sources can mislead, as Elisabeth Piller warns in her chapter on Polish hunger, if we fail to consider the narrative biases that often emanate from the curated archival collections of a few extraordinary aid organisations.

Fortunately, neither these debates nor methodological challenges have stifled research. A compellingly complex portrait of humanitarianism in the era of the First World War has emerged thanks to scholars from around the world.

A global reaction to a greater war

In recent years histories of humanitarianism have successfully enlarged the classic 1914–18 narrative to encompass war and its aftermath. The argument that the war did not simply end because vast suffering continued has gained such widespread acceptance that talk of a greater or longer war lasting a decade or more is now routine. Historians featured in this volume including Christian Müller, Christoph Jahr, and Kimberly Lowe emphasise the ways in which humanitarian activity continued after the armistices of 1918. With few exceptions, however, historians have done little to connect humanitarian exertions in the First World War to agencies, individuals, and imperatives to undertake life-saving work in the Second World War and afterwards. This undoubtedly reflects a lack of consensus about the extent to which the war was a catalyst for humanitarianism even though the war is perceived as transformative politically and culturally. Development, 'modernisation', and refugee-focused scholars perceive such long-term connections. Just as they should consider prewar humanitarianism, historians of the greater war would be wise to trace arcs of humanitarian endeavour beyond the 1920s.[5]

Until recently most scholarship on humanitarian activity in the First World War focused on the North Atlantic world with occasional excursions into the eastern Mediterranean. Now, thanks partly to this volume, the portrait of international responses to the war is greatly enhanced. In examinations of Argentina's participation and Portugal's African colonies, María Inés Tato and Ana Paula Pires reveal a much wider expanse of humanitarian engagement with what is still considered a predominantly European war. Similarly, Hanne Deleu connects Japan's humanitarian awakening to Allied politics and compassion for war victims. Kimberly Lowe, Paul Nathan Jahr, Christian Müller, and Elisabeth Piller push the geography of relief exertions further eastward into Europe and Russia and into imperial peripheries than they have been described in Atlanticist narratives.

Perhaps what is most striking about these explorations into new regions is the commonality of experience among humanitarians worldwide. Active participation by innumerable associations in practically every war-affected country reveals the extent of mobilisation by imperial networks. Diasporic communities also stretched across the world and maintained intimate ties to the theatres of violence – such that wherever Portuguese residents dwelled – in Brazil, the United States, and Macau – they raised funds for Portugal's prisoners of war. And once formed, humanitarian organisations frequently felt morally obligated to continue service even though they often lacked the means to do so for any length of time. One wonders how the history of emotions might inform our understanding of aid officials' feelings, including those who laboured for years and those whose incipient organisations imploded, or of the feelings of recipients of aid. The tyranny of aid work and its moral dynamics – damned if you do or don't do it well enough – are undoubtedly underemphasised in many histories, celebratory or otherwise, because they stress the novelty or irrelevance of the work involved rather than the burdens of doing it.

We still know little about the fervour of participation in humanitarian campaigns. If they applied Christopher Capozolla's notion of 'coercive voluntarism' to humanitarian service, historians might be surprised to discover how grudgingly donations were made to various *causes célèbres*.[6] Thanks to the work of Pierre Purseigle and Peter Gatrell, we already know this grudging humanitarianism to be true of hosts of refugees who soon soured on their guests. Likewise, Sophie De Schaepdrijver has shown that saving

Belgium eventually slipped from its paramount place as an Allied symbolic priority because the intensifying scale of suffering made comparisons of tragedies meaningless.[7] Notions of donor fatigue, prevalent as they are in modern philanthropic conversations, could be applied to great effect by historians of the greater war. How might we assess any differences between donations? Did the same inspiration that compelled a wealthy industrialist to give vast sums of money motivate a schoolteacher's donation of a few cents? Did donating to one cause preclude donating to another? One compelling taxonomy of giving written for institutions seeking to cultivate donors, *The Seven Faces of Philanthropy* (1994), offers insights into the different reasons people contribute to charitable causes.[8] Historians should borrow from whatever scholarly insights that might help them to better understand the past.

Just as a genuinely global civil society demonstrated concern for war sufferers in tangible ways, it shared similar means of fundraising by the use of films, music performances, auctions, bazaars, and sporting events, to raise awareness and money. Gifts of aid also took remarkably similar forms – care packages for soldiers and displaced peoples frequently contained the same types of items irrespective of nationality; basic needs governed their composition. As demonstrated by the universality of such aid, the fabric of the global community that had been forged during the *fin de siècle* was not fully rent by two warring coalitions. Historians could profitably survey these lines of continuity among humanitarian activities and the extent to which they were expressions of modernity.[9]

Faith also transcended national borders and connected peoples worldwide. Despite the proliferation of secular aid agencies in the war, faith-oriented communities engaged in far-reaching humanitarian activities. Thanks to continuing research, we know much more about Jewish, Catholic, and Quaker aid organisations than a decade ago.[10] Still more research remains to be done to appraise the contributions of Muslims, Methodists, Mennonites, and Mormons.

Historians of gender and childhood have also demonstrated how similar were many war experiences of men, women, and children across the warring world. War injuries and suffering powerfully affected masculinity and its discourses.[11] Although male leadership predominated in relief agencies, vast humanitarian needs encouraged energetic female participation by such groups as the Portuguese Women's Crusade, the Japanese Ladies' Solidarity organisation for Belgium, and the Canadian Six Nations Women's Patriotic League. Children were also effectively conscripted as junior humanitarians.[12] Expectations that relief service would enhance civic prestige constituted a unifying thread that connected these exertions.

Multifaceted humanitarian motivations

We have now developed a deeper awareness that multiple motivations impelled humanitarian action. Admittedly, much of this knowledge is based on studies of leaders of prominent humanitarian organisations, their staff, and their evangelists. These studies nevertheless provide a valuable foundation for further study.

There is much to be gleaned from transnational investigations such as Hanne Deleu's chapter which identifies Japanese aid to Belgium as being enmeshed with a 'transnational solidarity' of compassion. And it was also a reflection of Japan's geopolitical ambition. Deleu reminds us that humanitarian activity drew upon complementary inspirations even though critics of aid doubt its efficacy if it is tainted by anything but the purest of motivations, impartiality, and neutrality. Many humanitarians did not share such concerns, Bertrand M. Patenaude argued in his authoritative excavation of the American Relief Administration's efforts to end famine in Soviet Russia in the 1920s.[13] As did the Japanese who sought to mitigate suffering among the Belgians while improving the image of Japan abroad, Americans believed that they could combat hunger while strengthening democracy because doing so was, in their estimation, humanitarian.

Humanitarianism wherever it was entangled with statecraft or strategic posturing is viewed as suspect if not illegitimate. But almost all humanitarian action in the *greater war* was undertaken with some partisan motive – such as to preserve intellectual life (Tomás Irish's chapter), or children's minds and bodies (Tatjana Eichert and Rebecca Gill'schapter) in the hopes that they would be safeguarded from destruction and would perform vital service to the postwar world. Humanitarian exertions were necessarily selective. Few universal campaigns to aid all war victims were conceived during the war (although a global child-feeding advocacy emerged after the war (Eichert and Gill)). Focused aid campaigns were crafted along national, demographic, professional, and confessional lines. In his chapter Tomás Irish poignantly asks who constituted 'the most deplorable victims of the war'.[14] Populations threatened with starvation or death by injury or disease aroused considerable sympathy. Through myriad campaigns humanitarians revealed preferences and prejudices, such as caring for European soldiers in Mozambique and Angola (Ana Paula Pires), Jewish communities in Central and Eastern Europe (Christoph Jahr), Polish civilians threatened by starvation and disease (Elisabeth Piller), and at-risk children in Germany (Eichert and Gill) or intellectuals in Vienna (Tomás Irish).

Even if they harboured visions of grand geopolitical benefits or narrow attachments to a small group of war victims, many donors and aid workers sincerely believed that they were helping others by participating in campaigns to amass medical supplies, procure food, manufacture clothing, or donate cigarettes, sundries, and books. One could lament the partiality associated with any exclusive campaigns. But such criticism would discount the fervent commitment to alleviate the distress of certain communities. Surely, dedication to an aid campaign was better than apathy about the totality of distress.

Many aid programmes were initially projections of anticipated needs visualised by the donor public rather than responses to specific appeals by soldiers or civilians who were harmed by war. Calibrating donations with actual need remained a daunting, controversial, and ever-changing task. Prominent aid officials including Herbert C. Hoover eventually discouraged small donations of foodstuffs because they were inefficient to ship to war victims. Soliciting gifts of cash became the hallmark of the largest aid organisations which sought to leverage economies-of-scale efficiencies through bulk purchases. Some aid societies were thankful to receive any donations even as they sometimes resented their competitors.

More than money, food parcels and medicines comprised the materials delivered by humanitarian agencies. Aid included medical books and laboratory equipment to train doctors at European universities. Housing, railroad, telegraph, and seaport construction assistance proliferated in response to shortages of shelter in war-devastated communities and to speed the distribution of supplies. Seeds to revitalise agriculture, shoes, and suits of clothes were regularly donated items, too. The diversity of aid undoubtedly was the source of its universal appeal – just about anyone could contribute something. Arguably, we take for granted the formation of a vast constellation of aid societies ministering to practically every conceivable need such as the Belgian Soldiers' Tobacco Fund. There is likely much to be gleaned from detailed explorations of these varied and often ephemeral, chronically underfunded and sometimes failed organisations that were dwarfed by larger-scale administrations. By studying minor and even failed organisations as Elisabeth Piller suggests, we could discover how individuals worldwide personalised the war, undertook to organise constituencies, and laboured in an unforgivingly combative field of charitable exertion.

A much more comprehensive portrait of infighting among self-identified humanitarians has emerged. In his chapter Cédric Cotter reveals that the Vatican bristled at what it considered to be an unholy alliance of Protestant evangelicals and many humanitarian agencies. Religious criticisms such as the Vatican's arose because the Protestant-infused social gospel approach to alms-giving had been divorced from a sacred context. Protestants also slighted Catholics and many confessional aid societies as anachronisms incapable of efficient action unlike ostensibly secular 'modern' aid programmes that were nevertheless directed by Protestants or Jews.

Despite the drift of war humanitarianism toward predominantly Protestant and Jewish interpretations, Pope Benedict XV wielded authority in matters of morality and humanitarianism that no other religions, denominations, sects, or individuals could. The Vatican's ecclesiastical domain and its political neutrality transcended militarised borders that rent the warring coalitions. To a similar extent Cardinal Désiré-Joseph Mercier's stature in German-occupied Belgium infused his symbolic leadership with an eternal dimension. Even in the United States where Catholicism was routinely subjected to blistering attacks by a preponderantly Protestant society, entities like the Commission for Relief in Belgium and the US Food Administration did not flinch from issuing appeals by the Pope or Mercier whose moral authority seemed unquestionable.

Evidence of recipients' gratitude enhanced an organisation's reputation among its supporters even though many recipients could not easily determine who was helping them, nor did they think it mattered greatly. Early in the war Belgians wrote thousands of letters thanking the US president even though he was not personally responsible for the efforts to feed the country. Elsewhere, Cotter notes, '[p]risoners of war frequently failed to distinguish between visiting International Committee of the Red Cross (ICRC) delegates and representatives of the Mission Catholique Suisse: they were, after all, all Swiss citizens inspecting prisoners of war camps'. A soldier's appreciation of such distinctions was immaterial compared to the grotesque circumstances that led to his captivity. Interaction with armed forces chaplains of various denominations had probably further blurred in soldiers' minds customary ecclesiastical lines and associations with intercessory aid.

Divergent expectations and differing needs of aid givers and recipients created enduring frictions. Humanitarian agencies attempted to differentiate among themselves to lay claim to donations and popular support. Numerous entities vied for donations for various Belgian causes; Quakers split along British and American lines; and disputes emerged between the differing visions of the Save the Children International Union and the British Save the Children Fund. But the tensions between the ICRC and various national Red Cross societies also facilitated the postwar establishment of the League of Red Cross Societies – independent of Geneva and linked together in an associational framework.

Uncomfortable ethics and state power

Histories of humanitarian relief in the *greater war* often overemphasise the activist role of non-governmental agencies that acted in opposition to states or in a manner that endeavoured to coerce compliance with their life-sustaining agendas. Neville Wylie and Cédric Cotter demonstrate that neutral governments performed vitally important humanitarian duties. Even the most ostensibly private relief organisations such as the Commission for Relief in Belgium relied on neutral patronage and the financial support of belligerent countries. The state was not just a foil to relief workers' ambitions but a necessary concomitant. Piller's investigation into the stillborn Commission for Relief in Poland and Jahr's study of the Berlin-based Hilfsverein reveal how intertwined the negotiations of humanitarian actors and governments were. Behind-the-scenes humanitarian diplomacy that secured such agreements as at Berne for repatriating soldiers (1918) and at Riga for arranging famine relief (1921) relied on governmental sanction but remains much less visible than the public face of aid officials or campaigns.[15]

As much as the state is viewed with suspicion by many scholars for being engaged in humanitarian arenas, historians could consider voluntary contributions of bandages, clothing, and food to soldiers and civilians as augmenting state power rather than diminishing it. Historians have not dwelt much upon the meaning of state inadequacy to provide fully for soldiers' needs even though such provisions are now considered normal 'kit' and obligatory from a human-rights perspective. It was the inability of government to meet these basic needs that gave rise to a partnership with civil society, something Wylie aptly calls 'the new humanitarianism'. The internationally articulated demand for dependants' allowances and disability pensions expressed confidence in expansive governmental action. Millions of letters sent to the missing soldiers tracing bureaux in Copenhagen and Geneva by family members seeking information suggested both a demand for information and an admission that only certain organisations possessed the authority to accumulate such records in partnership with governments. Likewise, Eichert and Gill persuasively contend that the postwar international movement spearheaded by Save the Children relied on governments to serve 'as guardians of children as productive citizens of the future'. Much like the multi-causal motivations of humanitarian actors, private and public sectors were inexorably fused in humanitarian service.

Many aid initiatives were conceived as humane alternatives to war's destructivity. Humanitarians exalted the idea of life-saving activity combating the malign forces that were responsible for the war. In his chapter Phillip Dehne asserts that humanitarians and their scribes crafted a triumphal narrative that celebrated their partial victories over warring governments. 'Among righteous humanitarians, blockaders made for easy scapegoats for the deep difficulties facing Europeans.' Historians are no less susceptible to lionising and lambasting figures from the past than others less trained to interrogate evidence. Although the British minister of blockade,

Robert Cecil, is often vilified, deep diving into archival sources reveals that he secretly conspired with Herbert Hoover to contest forcible deportations of civilians and quietly disregarded Germany's obstructionism to relief measures in Belgium and northern France from the humane perspective of wishing to feed civilians. Might we consider Cecil a closeted humanitarian?

Humanitarianism was inseparable from the violence of the First World War, not its antithesis. Synergies existed between military and relief personnel, strategic planning, combat, transportation, and medicine. As Dehne reminds us, systems of the Allied naval blockade relied upon maritime preponderance, administrative talents, and logistical expertise that were applied to the distribution of emergency relief supplies. State decisions to subsidise aid or otherwise facilitate its distribution reflected strategic calculations and often humanitarian imperatives, too. Delivering aid to postwar Russia aroused more sympathy among Allied officials as an anti-communist measure than as a singularly humane act, Kimberly Lowe demonstrates. But saving Russians from needless deaths by starvation undeniably inspired aid workers' voluntarism and donations. Ana Paula Pires establishes that Portugal wished to curry Britain's favour. Lisbon's qualified and ephemeral neutrality, which ended in 1916, and its dispatch of a military expedition to Africa not only preserved its relationship with London but also obligated the dispatch of Red Cross medical personnel to Africa to aid Allied forces and prisoners of war captured by German troops. As humane as medical aid, national Red Cross societies frequently repaired wounded soldiers who returned to duty. Engineers, quartermasters, and many ordinary sailors and soldiers also performed humanitarian services, but much less is known of their experiences than of traditional battlefield duty.

Moral quandaries exist. As were the belligerents' national Red Cross societies, many self-described humanitarians in the First World War were abjectly partisan and understood their exertions as a means of accelerating victory by defeating their foes. To what extent was the Red Cross acting in a humanitarian capacity? If blockade functioned as an Allied tool of economic warfare which promised to accelerate the Central Powers' surrender and thereby end the war sooner than it might have otherwise been achieved, could that tool be considered a humanitarian instrument?

Several nations in the *greater war* fashioned humanitarian identities. Just as wartime sacrifices are understood to have given a great impetus to nation-forming narratives in Australia and Canada, the strand of another national identity emerged in the United States, in Switzerland, and in Nordic countries; their societies believed they were defined by their humanitarian activity.[16] Cotter indicates that 'few other neutral countries [besides Switzerland] had established credible "humanitarian" credentials before 1914. For most the Great War provided their first significant opportunity to expand into this area.' As with American, Argentinian, and other peoples, the war provided innumerable opportunities to claim that their participation was essentially humanitarian.

Historians have not much contemplated the ethics of aid even as they have described conditions in which ethical dilemmas existed. Philosophers have also struggled to define humanitarianism because there is no simple distinction between 'pure' forms of aid work and aid as surrogate for war. Historians often express the hope that there is or should be. Maybe the search for such distinctions is an aspiration, or, at worst, a distortion of genuinely conflicted hearts and minds engaged in bitter struggles.

Much of the tension we confront with the apparent hypocrisy of 'humanitarian wars' is their selectivity (choosing to 'help' one cause or people and not another), integration (distributing arms and aid), and fusion (aid as an extension of strategy). But part of the conundrum confronting would-be humanitarians wishing to eschew politics and remain neutral is that the Good Samaritan ideal of helping one's neighbour was a sufficiently elastic concept as to be stretched to accommodate practically any type of argument or action. Borrowing from the Prussian theorist of warfare, Carl von Clausewitz, aid in the *greater war* became an instrument of policy by other means and a mechanism for peoples to use for various purposes.

Perhaps as an alternative construct to pure or malign aid, we could propose a *Pax Humanica*, adapting concepts advanced by Immanuel Kant's *Perpetual Peace* (1795), of a conditional peace comprised of a prevailing power. A prevailing spirit of unquestionably humanitarian values such as that advanced during the war by Hoover's organisations, the ICRC, and Save the Children – impartiality, neutrality, efficiency – could be considered normative rather than an absolute condition in which the entire world accepted or submitted to such ideals. And even if misanthropes delivered aid, it might be considered better than if no aid were given because, were it not for the willing participation of millions worldwide with earnest hopes to alleviate suffering, far more civilians and soldiers would have succumbed to the dehumanising and lethal forces war unleashed.

The challenge of recovering past stories remains an archival chore and a creative task in which analysis, conceptualisation, and other professional duties endure. There is still an uncharted sea of possibilities for historians of humanitarianism to explore. We have repeatedly challenged ourselves to uncover the experiences of recipients of aid and have hardly touched the surface of this important subject. Relief dynamics in Africa, the Balkans, and much of the modern Middle East remain obscured. Despite great strides in political and social history, we have done little to develop detailed demographic analyses with the exception of Mary E. Cox's superlative study *Hunger in War and Peace: Women and Children in Germany, 1914–1924*

(2019). Despite their great promise to reveal evolving global processes, few transnational studies of humanitarian action exist as we tend to craft narratives along national lines. And although the First World War has inspired innumerable cultural histories of commemoration, monuments, and memory, histories of humanitarianism have as yet done little to consider the enduring heritage of these titanic undertakings. Perhaps we will have shed light on these shadowy areas by the war's 125th anniversary.

Notes

1 D. Rodogno, *Night on Earth: A History of International Humanitarianism in the Near East, 1918–1930* (Cambridge: Cambridge University Press, 2022); K. D. Watenpaugh, *Bread from Stones: The Middle East and the Making of Modern Humanitarianism* (Berkeley: University of California Press, 2015); S. Salvatici, *A History of Humanitarianism, 1755–1989: In the Name of Others* (Manchester: Manchester University Press, 2019); A. Sobocinska, *Saving the World? Western Volunteers and the Rise of the Humanitarian-Development Complex* (Cambridge: Cambridge University Press, 2021).
2 B. Little, 'An Explosion of New Endeavours: Global Humanitarian Responses to Industrialized Warfare in the First World War Era', *First World War Studies*, 5:1 (2014), 1–16; B. Little, 'Humanitarian Relief in Europe and the Analogue of War, 1914–1918', in J. Keene and M. Neiberg (eds), *Finding Common Ground: New Directions in First World War Studies* (Leiden: Brill, 2010), pp. 139–58.
3 M. N. Barnett, 'Conclusion: Practices of Humanity', in M. N. Barnett (ed.), *Humanitarianism and Human Rights: A World of Differences?* (Cambridge: Cambridge University Press, 2020), pp. 235–51; I. Hermann, 'Humanitaire et paix: une équation impossible?', in V. Lathion, R. Durand, F. Bugnion, F. Dubosson, I. Herrmann, and D. Palmieri (eds), *Action humanitaire et quête de la paix: Le prix Nobel de la paix décerné au CICR pendant la Grande Guerre* (Geneva: Fondation Gustave Ador, Georg Editeur, 2019), pp. 29–45.
4 M. Walzer, 'On Humanitarianism: Is Helping Others Charity, or Duty, or Both?', *Foreign Affairs*, 90:4 (July/August 2011), 69–80; R. Brauman, *Humanitarian Wars? Lies and Brainwashing* (London: Hurst & Co., 2019).
5 D. Ekbladh, *The Great American Mission: Modernization and the Construction of an American World Order* (Princeton: Princeton University Press, 2010); S. R. Porter, *Benevolent Empire: U.S. Power, Humanitarianism, and the World's Dispossessed* (Philadelphia: University of Pennsylvania Press, 2017).
6 C. Capozzola, *Uncle Sam Wants You: World War I and the Making of the Modern American Citizen* (New York: Oxford University Press, 2008), p. 8.
7 P. Purseigle, 'The Reception of Belgian Refugees in Europe: A Litmus Test of Wartime Social Mobilisation', in J. Crawford and I. McGibbon (eds), *New Zealand's Great War: New Zealand, the Allies and the First World War* (Auckland: Exisle Publishing, 2007), pp. 69–84; P. Gatrell, *The Making of the Modern Refugee* (Oxford: Oxford University Press, 2013); S. De Schaepd rijver,

'Champion or Stillbirth? The Symbolic Uses of Belgium in the Great War', in B. Barnard, M. van Berlo, and G. van Istendeal (eds), *How Can One Not Be Interested in Belgian History? War, Language and Consensus in Belgium since 1830* (Dublin: Trinity College and Academia Press, 2005), pp. 55–81.

8 R. A. Prince and K. File, *The Seven Faces of Philanthropy* (San Francisco: Jossey-Bass, 1994).

9 D. Gorman, *The Emergence of International Society in the 1920s* (Cambridge: Cambridge University Press, 2012); D. Gorman, *International Cooperation in the Early Twentieth Century* (London: Bloomsbury Press, 2017).

10 J. Granick, *International Jewish humanitarianism in the Age of the Great War* (Cambridge: Cambridge University Press, 2021); C. Tessaris, 'The War Relief Work of the American Jewish Joint Distribution Committee in Poland and Lithuania, 1915–18', *East European Jewish Affairs*, 40:2 (2010), 127–44; T. M. Proctor, 'An American Enterprise? British Participation in US Food Relief Programmes (1914–1923)', *First World War Studies*, 5:1 (2014), 29–42; P. J. Houlihan, 'Renovating Christian Charity: Global Catholicism, the Save the Children Fund, and Humanitarianism during the First World War', *Past & Present*, 250:1 (2021), 203–41.

11 S. Levsen, 'Masculinities', in U. Daniel, P. Gatrell, O. Janz, H. Jones, J. Keene, A. Kramer, and B. Nasson (eds), *1914–1918-online. International Encyclopedia of the First World War*, 7 January 2015, DOI: 10.15463/ie1418.10531, https://encyclopedia.1914-1918-online.net/article/masculinities?version=1.0.

12 B. Little, 'A Child's Army of Millions: The American Junior Red Cross', in L. Paul, R. Johnson, and E. Short (eds), *Children's Literature and Culture of the First World War* (New York: Routledge, 2016), pp. 283–300.

13 B. M. Patenaude, *The Big Show in Bololand: The American Relief Expedition to Soviet Russia in the Famine of 1921* (Stanford: Stanford University Press, 2002).

14 Quoted in Irish.

15 C. Cotter, 'The 1918 Bern Agreements: Repatriating Prisoners in a Total War', *Humanitarian Law & Policy Blog* (April 2018), http://blogs.icrc.org/law-and-policy/2018/03/29/1918-bern-agreements-repatriating-prisoners-of-war/.

16 L. Sturfelt, 'Humanitarianism (Sweden)', in Daniel et al. (eds), *1914–1918 online. International Encyclopedia of the First World War*, January 2018, DOI: 10.15463/ie1418.11214, https://encyclopedia.1914-1918-online.net/article/humanitarianism_sweden; N. A. Sørensen, 'Humanitarianism (Denmark)', in Daniel et al. (eds), *1914–1918 online. International Encyclopedia of the First World War*, November 2018, DOI: 10.15463/ie1418.11309, https://encyclopedia.1914-1918-online.net/article/humanitarianism_denmark.

Index

activism 8, 34, 211–13, 220–2, 252, 255
Adachi, Mineichirō 62, 64
Ador, Gustave 106, 108–10, 219
Africa 17, 69, 70–4, 76, 79, 89, 252–3, 255–60, 262–3, 275, 281–2
Albania 196, 201
Albert I (King, of Belgium) 51, 58–9
Allied Powers 4, 6, 9, 11, 17, 34–6, 38, 40–6, 51, 53, 59, 61–3, 73, 76, 87, 147–54, 156–7, 159, 164, 169, 173, 177, 190, 197, 199, 215, 223, 232, 234, 255, 257–8, 281
Alliance Israélite Universelle 88–9
altruism 6, 70, 77, 81, 97
de Alvear, Marcelo T. 41, 45
American Friends Service Committee 5, 15
American Jewish Joint Distribution Committee 5, 16, 94–7
American Relief Administration 5, 12, 15–16, 96, 157, 165, 169, 170–1, 174–6, 178, 219, 230–1, 233–4, 237–8, 277
de Andrade, Gomes Freire 72, 263
Anglo-Jewish Association 88–90
Angola 70–7, 80, 82–3, 263, 277
anti-Bolshevism 12, 18, 147, 157, 164–6, 168–71, 175, 178, 202, 219, 232, 235, 245, 281
anti-imperialism 13, 221
antisemitism 87, 89, 93, 96

anti-slavery movement 11, 13, 18, 70, 252, 254–60, 263, 265
Argentina 3–4, 7, 9, 10, 17, 31–3, 35, 38–46, 116, 149, 155, 275, 282
aristocrats 2, 7, 16, 51, 58–9, 61–2, 111, 113, 137–8, 237
armistice 4, 5, 17, 82, 109, 147–8, 151–6, 159, 202, 212–13, 274
Asia 17, 59, 63, 253, 255, 257, 260
Australia 3, 4, 281
Austria(-Hungary) 3, 5, 7, 9, 69, 86–9, 93, 95, 107, 110–13, 124, 128–31, 134, 136–7, 139, 150, 157–8, 170, 192, 196, 199, 201, 213, 215–17, 220, 222, 232–7, 241, 243, 257, 277

Balfour, Arthur 213, 255
Balkans 3, 34, 38, 87, 89, 196, 201, 238, 282
Basten, Charles 54
Bauer, Stephan 255
Belgium 1, 4, 6, 10–11, 17–18, 20, 32–4, 41–5, 51–6, 58–9, 61–4, 80, 82–3, 111, 115, 130, 148, 152–4, 168–9, 173, 187–91, 194–5, 197–201, 223, 234, 238, 240, 255, 259, 262, 264, 276–9, 281
Bellegarde, Dantès 263
Benedict XV (Pope) 107, 109, 115, 279
beneficiaries 8–9, 19–20, 40, 43, 75, 87, 89, 115, 201
Blancas, Alberto 33, 43, 45

blockade 11, 17, 34, 36, 42, 95, 147–59, 164, 188–91, 197, 199, 212–13, 217, 220–1, 273, 280–1
Boas, Franz 234, 241
Bodenheimer, Max 91–2
Brändström, Elsa 7, 16, 19, 111
Brazil 10, 40, 43, 71, 74, 80–1, 275
Bryan, William J. 127, 131
Bulgaria 90, 111, 240
bureaucracy 6, 18, 20, 157, 188
Buxton, Dorothy 211–12, 215, 219, 220–1

calories 14–15, 214–17
Canada 4, 41, 281
Canadian Six Nations Women's Patriotic League 56, 276
Cape Verde 79, 82
Catholicism 44, 57, 71, 73, 106–7, 276, 279
Cecil, (Lord) Robert 153–4, 157, 174, 220, 257, 264, 281
Central Commission for Relief of the Starving (Pomgol) 172, 175, 177
Central Europe 147, 151, 154, 156, 163, 214–15, 220, 222, 231–3, 237, 241–2, 277
Central Jewish Committee for the Relief of Sufferers of War (Evrejskij komitet pomošči žertvam vojny) 96
Central Powers 36, 44–6, 87, 91, 96, 136, 139, 149, 157, 188, 192, 196–7, 199, 281
Chicherin, Georgy 96, 167, 171–3
children 1, 4, 9, 14–16, 18, 42–3, 53–7, 77, 80, 88, 106, 109, 149–50, 155–6, 163, 165, 168, 210–17, 217, 222–3, 230, 239, 244, 254, 276, 277, 280
  girls 52–4, 56–7, 63–4, 149
  nutrition 12, 149–50, 155–6, 163, 210, 216–17, 219, 221–3, 277
  orphans 1, 4, 8, 43, 55, 77, 80, 88
  rights 15, 210–11, 222, 244–5
  school feeding 211, 213–18, 220, 223
  welfare 210, 213, 218–21, 223
China 13, 43, 111, 136
civilisation 43, 45, 52, 59, 60–2, 74, 76, 88, 126, 164, 167, 239, 245, 252–4, 257–8, 261, 263, 265
Clemenceau, Georges 152, 257
Clémentel, Étienne 154
colonialism 11, 17, 31, 40, 69–77, 79, 82, 126, 218, 252, 255–9, 261–2
Comité international de secours aux enfants 215–16, 218–21
Comité National de Secours et d'Alimentation 20, 42
Comité Suisse de Secours aux Enfants see Schweizer Kinderhilfskomitee
competition 11, 38, 77, 105–6, 108, 110, 112–18, 210, 218, 253–4, 257, 259–63, 265
Commission for Relief in Belgium 4, 6, 7, 33, 42, 148, 188–92, 199, 200–2, 279–80
Commission for Relief in Poland 187–9, 195, 196–202, 280
Committee for the liberation of Russian Jews see Komitee für die Befreiung der russischen Juden
concentration camps 212, 222
Czechoslovakia 169, 172, 174, 233, 239, 240

Dávila, Adolfo 32, 42
Dearing, Frederic 135, 137–9
debts 165, 172–4
Delafosse, Maurice 263
de la Plaza, Victorino 32
della Faille, Georges 58
Denmark 7, 11, 90, 110–17, 136–7, 139, 173
deportations 42, 129, 238, 281
Devine, Edward 137

diaspora communities 17, 35, 71, 80–2, 87, 114–15, 149, 198, 275
disability 36, 42, 82, 280
displacement 1, 3, 5, 14–15, 106–7, 231–9, 243–4, 254, 273, 276
donors 4, 20, 32, 41, 55, 58, 62–4, 87, 95, 174, 219, 276–8
Drummond, Eric 168, 259–60
Du Bois, William E.B. 256, 259

Eastern Europe 17, 86, 89–91, 95–6, 163, 167, 171–2, 177, 231–3, 237, 241–2, 277
Eastern front 91–2, 95, 110–13, 117, 163, 166, 189, 200–1
Economic Association for the Sick and Wounded Soldiers of the Allied Nations 61
economic warfare/war economies 3, 34, 147, 149–6, 158, 223, 281
emotions 4–5, 7–8, 10–11, 16–17, 21, 40, 42, 44, 51–6, 59–61, 63–4, 70–1, 80–1, 115–17, 127, 157–8, 191, 194, 198–200, 211, 220–2, 275, 277, 281
empire 3–4, 13, 19, 36, 45, 59, 60, 64, 69–72, 74, 79–80, 82, 93, 117, 149–50, 165–6, 220–1, 238, 252–7, 259–61, 263–5, 275
Entente 79–80, 87, 115, 129, 188, 199
epidemics/disease 3, 13–14, 56, 60, 106–8, 112, 133, 136–7, 163–4, 167, 169, 172, 194, 197, 217, 231–2, 273, 277
Estonia 111, 155, 169

Female Aid Commission for Portuguese Soldiers 74, 77, 82
Feminine Commission for the Motherland (Comissão Pró-Pátria) 76, 82
Ferdinand, Franz 69, 72
Fight the Famine Council 211, 215

food
food scarcity 3–5, 13–14, 17, 33, 42–3, 53, 132, 134, 147–9, 151–3, 156, 158, 163–4, 166–9, 171–3, 177–8, 190–1, 194–5, 197–200, 210–11, 214, 220, 223, 230–2, 235–8, 240–2, 273, 277, 280–1
food aid 4, 6, 8–9, 12, 15, 17, 42, 92, 109, 111, 137, 148, 153–5, 157, 163–6, 169–75, 177–8, 187–90, 192, 195–7, 199–200, 210, 212–14, 216, 218, 221, 233, 235, 237–9, 241, 278, 280–1
forced labour 94, 132, 134, 139, 255, 260, 263–4
France 5, 7, 10–11, 31–2, 38, 40–2, 44–5, 60, 70, 76, 80, 88, 90, 108, 110–11, 114–5, 126, 128, 133, 147–57, 168, 170, 173–4, 188, 196–7, 219, 223, 239–40, 255–7, 259–60, 262–5, 281
Francis, David R. 129–31, 134–5
Frick, Edouard 171–2
fundraising 8, 10, 39–40, 42, 44, 46, 55–6, 58, 61, 75, 77, 80, 93, 136, 276

gender norms 8–9, 16, 20, 35, 52, 56–7, 59, 63–4, 212
Geneva Conventions 11, 13, 16, 38, 75, 105–6, 124, 126, 141, 244
genocide 1, 3, 10, 13, 273
George, David Lloyd 152, 168, 173–4
Gerard, James W. 130, 132–4, 136, 138–9, 195
Germany 4, 6–7, 9–11, 31, 34, 36, 39, 41–3, 45, 53–4, 57–8, 61, 69, 73, 75–6, 79, 81–2, 86, 88, 90–7, 108, 110–15, 124–7, 130–40, 147–58, 169, 172–4, 187–92, 194–201, 210–19, 221–2, 232, 234–6, 239–41, 243, 255, 257–9, 265, 277, 279, 281
Gohr, Albrecht 264
Gorvin, John 168, 171, 178

gratitude 11, 20, 33, 56, 58–9, 108–9, 115, 133, 217–18, 279
Great Britain 4–6, 10–11, 31, 33–5, 38–9, 42–4, 60, 63, 70, 72–3, 76, 79, 80, 88–90, 93, 95, 111–12, 129–31, 133–5, 141, 147–54, 164, 166, 168–70, 172–4, 177–8, 188–92, 191–2, 195–201, 210–12, 214–23, 230, 239, 242–3, 252, 254–65, 279–81
Greece 13, 90, 240
Grew, Joseph 136
Grimshaw, Harold 261–2

Hague conventions 11, 13–14, 72, 126
handicrafts 52, 56–7, 63
Harding, Warren 170–1
Harris, John H. 255–9, 261, 263
Hilfsverein der deutschen Juden 86, 88–97, 280
von Hindenburg, Paul 92, 196
Hobhouse, Emily 12, 210–22
Hodgson, Robert MacLeod 168–9
Hoffmann, Arthur 108–9
home front 3, 8, 17, 70, 82, 116, 213
Hoover, Herbert 15–16, 19, 20, 42, 96, 148, 152–7, 165–6, 169–71, 174–6, 178, 188, 190–1, 195–6, 202–3, 219, 221, 278, 281–2
Hoover Institution Archives 20, 202

immigrants/migration 10, 31, 34–5, 38–9, 60, 63, 71, 74, 88–90, 94, 242–3
imperial governance 13, 18, 253–5, 257, 261, 265
independence 10, 12–13, 40–1, 82, 116, 188, 194, 200, 203
India 4, 13, 166, 169
inflation 5, 217–18, 232, 236, 241
intellectuals 11, 18, 40, 44, 77, 61–2, 64, 167, 214, 230–40, 242–5, 277
International Commission on Russian Relief 173

International Committee of the Red Cross 1, 7, 12, 16, 20, 32, 38–9, 74, 106–17, 125, 129, 133, 140–1, 169, 171, 211, 218, 222–3, 279, 282
International Agency for Prisoners of War 107, 114
International Committee for Russian Relief 165–6, 169–71, 174–8
International Labour Organization 253, 261–2, 264
internment 3, 4, 11, 15, 39, 90, 105–12, 114, 117, 124–6
Israelitische Allianz zu Wien 88–9
Italy 3, 13, 32, 38, 43–4, 107, 116, 155, 168, 170, 172–3, 240, 260, 262, 264

Jackon, John Brinckerhoff 134–6
Japan 4, 10–11, 17, 51–63, 89, 125, 127, 131, 168, 173, 275, 277
Japanese Ladies' Solidarity Organisation for Belgium 56, 276
Jebb, Eglantyne 153, 156, 202, 212, 215, 218–22
Jewish Aid-Committee for Poland and Lithuania 92, 95
Jewish humanitarianism 5, 7, 16–17, 86–97, 276, 278–80
Junod, Henri 258, 262

Kahn, Bernhard 90, 94, 97
Karl (Prince of Sweden) 113
Kellogg, Vernon 195, 233
Keynes, John Maynard 156
Kinsky, (Countess) Nora 16, 138

Larreta, Enrique Rodríguez 40, 42, 45
League of Nations 5, 12, 14–15, 17–18, 60, 63, 147–8, 153, 155, 157–9, 163, 168–9, 171, 173, 218, 222–3, 234, 238, 241, 243, 245, 252–4, 257–62, 264
  Permanent Mandates Commission 253, 258

League of Red Cross Societies 5, 56, 60, 63, 117, 125, 140, 169, 173, 279
Lenin, Vladimir 164, 167, 172
Lithuania 92, 94–5, 164
Ludendorff, Erich 92, 94, 196
Lugard, (Sir) Frederick 259–63, 265
Lusitania 134, 188, 195, 197

Machado, Bernardino 72, 74
Marye, George 130
media/press 2, 12–13, 19, 33–5, 38, 42, 44–5, 51–60, 62–4, 70–1, 74–5, 77, 88–9, 109, 115, 150, 152, 199, 201–2, 211, 217, 231–2, 236, 239, 261, 276
Middle East 1, 88–9, 188, 282
Miss Hobhouse Hilfe 213, 215, 218
missionaries 13–14, 16, 259
mobilisation 8, 10, 17, 21, 31, 35, 38, 41, 44, 54, 56–7, 59, 63, 70–1, 74–7, 79–82, 114, 116, 242, 275
Mozambique 7, 70–7, 82–3, 263, 277

Nansen, Fridtjof 165–6, 169–78
Nathan, Paul 86, 88–9, 92–4, 96–7
National Association for the Advancement of Colored People 256, 258–9
natural disasters 13, 244–5
Near East Relief 1, 5, 14, 16, 222
the Netherlands 4, 44, 90, 96, 111–12, 114, 116–17, 129, 155, 189, 191–2, 198, 262, 264
neutrals/neutrality 3, 5–8, 11–12, 14, 17–18, 31–2, 34–5, 38–9, 41–3, 45–6, 72–3, 91, 94, 105–10, 114–17, 124–7, 129–30, 132, 134, 136–8, 140, 148–50, 157, 190–2, 195, 198–200, 215, 219, 234, 277, 279–82
non-governmental organisations 2, 5, 14, 20, 124, 127, 244, 252–3, 258, 260–3, 265, 279

norm entrepreneurs 125, 254, 260
North America 59, 88, 163, 166, 169, 171, 175, 178, 187, 189, 242
Norway 4, 112–13, 116, 174
nurses 7–8, 31, 35, 40, 55–7, 60, 63, 74–5, 82, 111, 138

occupation 3–4, 15, 17, 42, 93–4, 148, 169, 187, 189–90, 192, 194, 196–7, 199–201, 223, 255
Œuvre Internationale de Louvain 61
Œuvre Universitaire Suisse 111
Odier, Edouard 113
Ohnesorg, (Dr.) Karl 135
Ottoman Empire 4, 13, 87, 89, 91, 111–12, 128–9, 149, 232, 257

Page, Walter Hines 131–4, 138, 196
pacifism 18, 44, 222
Palestine 87–9, 244
pan-African movement 256–9
Paris Peace Conference 11, 147–8, 151–4, 156–8, 232, 256–8
patriotism 8–9, 35, 38, 52, 54–9, 61, 63–4, 66, 74, 79, 81, 93–4, 125, 137, 141, 276
Payró, Roberto J. 42
Penfield, Frederic 128, 130, 133
Philip, Hoffman 133
pogrom 88, 96
Poland 1, 7, 10, 18, 32, 87, 91–5, 155, 157, 164, 177, 187–9, 192, 194–203, 233, 235, 237, 274, 277, 280
Portugal 7, 10, 17, 69–77, 79–83, 85, 254, 257, 259, 261–5, 275, 281
Portuguese Women's Crusade 77, 81–2, 276
prisoners of war 1, 3, 4, 6–7, 11, 15–16, 60, 76, 81, 106–14, 117, 124–6, 129–41, 163, 169, 171–2, 175, 217, 240, 244, 275, 279, 281
propaganda 11, 33, 38, 41–3, 54, 72, 169, 171, 178, 188, 212–13, 223, 255, 263

protecting power 6–8, 17, 33, 111, 117, 124–31, 136–7, 139–40

Quakers 5, 15, 96, 168, 170, 177, 212, 216, 218, 254, 276, 279

racial inequality 9, 59–69, 75, 90, 273
rape 14, 88
Rappard, William 257–8, 260–3
rationing 42, 194
Red Cross societies/movement 5–6, 8–9, 13–14, 32, 35, 38–9, 45–6, 60, 74–7, 80, 82–3, 106–13, 115, 117, 130, 135, 137, 139–40, 170, 173–4, 216, 220, 223, 279, 281
refugees 1, 3–5, 10, 14–15, 32, 42, 44, 53–4, 92, 117, 163, 168, 171, 194, 222–3, 238–9, 242, 244, 275
relief parcels 4, 57, 107, 111, 276
Relief Credits (International Committee for Relief Credits) 168, 172–3
Relief Organisation of German Jews *see* Hilfsverein der deutschen Juden
religious groups 2, 7, 14, 16, 44, 57, 86–97, 106–7, 126, 129, 167, 172, 194, 223, 242–3, 252–4, 256, 258, 265, 276–9
reparations 10, 81, 152, 156, 168, 212, 216, 258
repatriation 90–1, 107–9, 112–13, 126, 128, 136, 169, 171–2, 175, 280
Rockefeller Foundation 20, 187, 194–9, 243
Romania 16, 87, 111–12, 195, 201
Roosevelt, Theodore 127
Rumbold, (Sir) Horace 135
Russia 1, 4, 7, 9–10, 18, 51, 54, 60, 87–91, 93–4, 96–7, 110–15, 124, 127, 129–40, 136, 157, 163–4, 166–78, 192, 194–5, 199, 201, 230, 232, 235, 237–44, 275, 281
Russian Revolution 12, 96, 163, 175
Russo-Japanese War 52, 55, 57, 89, 125, 127, 131

sanitation 4, 41, 74, 75, 132, 136
Satsuma, Jirōhachi 61–2
Save the Children 1, 5, 12, 15–16, 18, 20, 153, 210–12, 215–16, 218–23, 279–80, 282
Scandinavia 17, 106, 110, 112–13, 136–7, 139, 281
Schiff, Jacob H. 94–5
Schweizer Kinderhilfskomitee 219–20
Second World War 14, 19, 31, 63–4, 82, 188, 201, 223, 242–5, 265, 274
Serbia 32, 110–11, 188, 196, 201, 238
Shaw, Flora 261
Shibusawa, Eiichi 61–2
Siberia 3, 7, 111, 130, 133, 136, 170–1
Simon, James 86, 94, 96–7
slavery 70, 252–65
social work 8, 14, 15, 20
South Africa 4, 125, 212–13, 215, 218, 221–2
South America 17, 31, 33, 35, 40, 88, 116, 163
Soviet Union 164–5, 169–75, 177, 277
Spain 4, 7, 31, 33, 43–4, 115–17, 124, 132, 137, 139, 140, 189, 191–2, 198, 259
Stalin, Joseph 96, 167
Steyn, (Mrs.) R.I. 221
Supreme Allied Council 165, 168–9, 173, 178
Sweden 7, 11, 110, 112–14, 116, 130, 134, 136–7, 139, 174, 195
Switzerland 4, 7, 11, 17, 32, 81, 105–12, 114–17, 126, 140–1, 198, 210, 213–16, 218–21, 223, 240, 254, 256, 262, 279, 280–1

tracing 107, 112, 114, 280
Treaty of Versailles 148, 151–2, 155–8, 213, 234–5, 256
troops 58, 73–7, 80, 281
trusteeship/moral trust 252–3, 255–6, 258, 264–5

Tsuda, Umeko 56
Turkey 10, 129, 133, 238, 240

Ukraine 89, 96, 164, 167, 241
Union of Jewish organisations for the Protection of the Rights of the Jews in the East *see* Vereinigung jüdischer Organisationen Deutschlands zur Wahrung der Rechte der Juden des Ostens
United Nations 157–8, 244–5
  United Nations Relief and Rehabilitation Administration (UNRRA) 158, 244
United States 2–7, 10–11, 17, 31–3, 35, 41–3, 56, 71, 80, 86, 91, 94–7, 109, 114, 116–17, 124–41, 147–50, 152–7, 165–71, 173, 175, 178, 187–8, 190–2, 194–203, 213–16, 222, 232, 237, 241–4, 255, 257, 274–5, 279, 281–2
urban (populations) 8, 192, 194, 213

Vatican 11, 17, 44, 88, 105–10, 112–13, 115, 117, 125, 278, 279
Vereinigung jüdischer Organisationen Deutschlands zur Wahrung der Rechte der Juden des Ostens 92
Villanueva, Benito 32, 42
Volga Region 163, 165–7, 178, 230, 242

volunteers 7, 31, 34, 38, 40–1, 45, 74–7, 80, 82, 110, 153, 189

war crimes 41, 190
Warfield, William 135, 139
welfare 15, 55, 60, 63, 194, 210–11, 213–14, 217–18, 220–1, 253–4
Western front 3, 52, 73, 117, 201
Wilson, Charles 131
Wilson, Woodrow 152, 170, 194, 196, 198, 252, 255–6
Woltereck, Richard 214
Women's International League for Peace and Freedom 212
women 8, 16, 35, 40, 42–3, 52–3, 55–7, 63–4, 76–7, 80–2, 111, 114, 136–8, 211–13, 215–17, 219, 220–1, 276
  rights 18, 63, 77, 82
  women's organisations 44, 51, 55–7, 63, 74, 76–7, 81–2, 137–9, 210–12, 221, 276

Yamawaki, Fusako 56
Young Men's Christian Association 111, 125, 130, 139–40, 231, 241
Yrigoyen, Hipólito 32
Yugoslavia 173, 240

Zionism 91–2, 95, 97

EU authorised representative for GPSR:
Easy Access System Europe, Mustamäe tee 50,
10621 Tallinn, Estonia
gpsr.requests@easproject.com

www.ingramcontent.com/pod-product-compliance
Lightning Source LLC
Chambersburg PA
CBHW051602230426
43668CB00013B/1946